The Wines of Germany

The Wines of Germany

Stephen Brook

MITCHELL BEAZLEY

The Wines of Germany
by Stephen Brook

First published in Great Britain in 2003 by Mitchell Beazley, an
imprint of Octopus Publishing Group Limited, 2–4 Heron Quays, London E14 4JP

ISBN: 1 84000 791 5

The author and publishers will be grateful for any information
which will assist them in keeping future editions up-to-date.
Although all reasonable care has been taken in the preparation
of this book, neither the publishers nor the author can accept any
liability for any consequences arising from the use thereof, or the
information contained therein.

Phototypeset in Berkeley Book by Intype Libra Ltd

Printed and bound in the UK

Contents

List of maps

Acknowledgments

I must begin by saluting the original commissioners of this book for having the courage to do so in the first place. A new book on German wine is long overdue. I would like to thank Julian Jeffs, general editor of the Faber wine book series now Mitchell Beazley's Classic Wine Library, and Toby Faber for their vision in commissioning this book.

My task was made far easier by the help given to me by the German Wine Institute in Mainz. Ulrike Bahm organized most of my travels with breathtaking efficiency. In Baden I was in the very capable hands of Barbara Wanner, who organized several visits to the region over the years. I just hope I never have to follow her mega-BMW down the Autobahn again in my modest Peugeot.

My first wine-related visits to Germany were in the mid-1980s and I was astonished by the eagerness with which I was received. Bernhard Breuer has been the most stimulating of producers with whom to discuss the more vexatious issues relating to the German wine industry. The late Graf Matuschka-Greiffenclau, at that time president of the VDP, organized my first wine tour of Germany, and continued to be helpful and generous whenever I visited the Rheingau. Over almost twenty years I have enjoyed good talks, and good lunches, with Dr Franz-Werner Michel of Hochheim and with Wolfgang Schleicher at Schloss Johannisberg. It was a great honour to participate in celebrations commemorating 900 years of winemaking at Schloss Johannisberg, where more TBA passed my lips in two hours than I ever expect to drink again. My thanks too to the Spreitzer family of Oestrich-Winkel and to Dieter Greiner of the state domaine in the Rheingau.

In the Mosel I have learned a great deal from Dr Manfred Prüm, Ernst Loosen, and Dr Carl von Schubert, among others. Annegret Reh-Gartner and her husband Gerhard have been wonderful hosts at their home in Oberemmel, and I have enjoyed additional hospitality from Egon Müller, Nik Weis, Dr Peter Pauly, Dr Heinz Wagner, and The Jüngling family of Paulinshof. Christian Ebert displayed wonderful motoring skills when my car was stuck in the ice outside his house, making it possible for me to arrive at my next appointment on time. In the Nahe I wish to thank Stefan Rumpf, Erich Maurer, Dr Martin Tesch and the Salm family. In the Pfalz I was received with great kindness by Stefanie Weegmüller and Bruno Schimpf. In Franken I enjoyed hospitality of the estates of Horst Sauer, Johann Ruck, Fürst Löwenstein, and Juliusspital. My thanks in Württemberg go to Erbgraf zu Neipperg, Michael Graf Adelmann, and the Wöhrwag family. Jan Kux gave me an excellent introduction to the wine industry in Sachsen.

Stuart Pigott knows more about German wine than I ever will, and over the past two decades has been only too happy to share bottles, knowledge, and enthusiasms with me.

Julian Jeffs read my manuscript with care and rigour and made numerous useful suggestions.

Introduction

The heart of this book, and the sections that I expect will be of greatest interest to the reader, are those dealing with the various wine regions and their leading producers. Readers are welcome to skip the introductory chapters and head straight for the gazetteer if they wish. However, in these chapters I address the strange and complex question of why German wines, as rich in history and renown as any in the world, are looked down upon by a substantial proportion of the wine-loving public.

German wines present a special case. Many erudite and experienced wine writers, including Hugh Johnson and Jancis Robinson, have argued that Riesling is the greatest white wine variety. I am inclined to agree, though there is little point in setting up a false confrontation between Riesling and its obvious, and preferred, rival, Chardonnay. It is easy to document the fact that about a century ago, German wines fetched considerably higher prices than their French counterparts. Even today the rarest wines of Germany, its precious Eiswein and Trockenbeerenauslesen from top estates, fetch astronomic prices at auction.

What is striking is that the quality of top German wine is widely recognized and applauded, while at the same time it is hard to think of any established wine country that is held in lower popular esteem than Germany. My local wine merchant is a fan of great German wine, but he tells me: "If a customer comes in and asks me what I recommend to accompany a certain dish or meal, and I say, 'German wine', they'll usually walk straight out of the shop."

The reason for this gulf between expert and popular opinion can be explained, and some of the chapters that follow will attempt to do so. The story is surely an object lesson to any emerging wine region in how *not* to promote its wines and in how *not* to create a legislative framework to monitor them. The story is a depressing one, but there are signs that the errors of the past are gradually being corrected. If the British and other European consumers continue to scorn German wines, there is ample evidence that their virtues are increasingly appreciated in countries such as the United States and Japan. The top wines will never lack for a market, but that only accentuates the gulf between the best and the worst of Germany.

Germany remains a country dominated by white wine production, and white grapes account for around three-quarters of the 105,000 ha (259,455 acres) of vineyards. Germany is rightly associated with Riesling, but there are large wine-producing areas where Riesling is either absent or a minor player. Local traditions remain strong in Germany, and are not necessarily related to quality. Pinot Noir has long been grown in one of the most northerly regions, the Ahr, and the quality can be outstanding. Silvaner can be excellent in Franken, but it's harder to make a case for Württemberg's Trollinger or southern Baden's Gutedel. In Franken and other parts of southern Germany, there's a tradition of blending red and white grapes to produce a rosé known either as *Rotling* or *Schillerwein*. Rosé made from Pinot Noir and known as *Weissherbst* remains extremely popular throughout Germany. Because such wines are mostly consumed locally and almost never exported, they are little known, but they are discussed in this book.

Although every wine region of Germany is covered, it has been impossible to include more than a selection of the country's 14,000 wine producers. Most properties are quite small – only a handful encompass more than eighty ha (198 acres) – and there are thousands, perhaps tens of thousands of growers. Not all of them bottle and sell their own wines, and in regions such as Baden and Württemberg the cooperative movement remains strong. In others, such as the Rheingau and Mosel, there are many more individual estates selling their own wine. To visit them all and taste all their wines would not only take years but be of limited service to the reader outside Germany, because only a handful of the wines are available outside the region of production. Nonetheless, I believe that all the major producers are included, as well as a selection of less well-known properties that are making excellent or interesting wine.

Rather than write an entire chapter on the history of German viticulture and wine production, which could make for heavy reading, I have included brief historical sections in each regional chapter and provided a general outline here. Organized viticulture, as opposed to the harvesting of wild vines, can certainly be traced back to Roman times, and vestiges of their press-houses remain along the banks of the Mosel. The Emperor Charlemagne encouraged the planting of vines in the regions known today as the Rheingau and Pfalz. In medieval times it was the church that acquired and expanded large wine estates, and some of these survive to this day. The church was aided by tax exemptions, which allowed it to make major investments in viticulture. This ecclesiastical economic power was not universal; strong in the Mosel and Rheingau, it was far less marked in what is today the Pfalz and Nahe. Many of the church domaines continue to exist, although mostly secularized, and the same is true of the secular charitable foundations such as the Bürgerspital in Franken. It is estimated that by the end of the fifteenth century the area under vine was four times that planted today.

Some German wine was exported in medieval times, though one can't help wondering how stable these white and light red wines would have been. There are records of shipments in the early thirteenth century to the court of King John of England, and three centuries later to the court of Henry VIII.[1]

The expansion of vineyards throughout the Middle Ages could not continue indefinitely. By the mid-sixteenth century there was a wine glut, certain harvests were too abundant for the casks available, and prices plummeted. No doubt expansion, then as now, often took place in sites not ideally suited for viticulture, so quality at the lower end of the scale may well have been dismal, especially in an inclement vintage. Before the outbreak of the Thirty Years' War in 1618 it's estimated there were 350,000 ha (864,850 acres) under vine, a colossal area. The decades of war dealt a major blow to some wine regions. Some vineyards became the sites of battlefields and were destroyed or uprooted forever; those that survived suffered from a lack of manpower. Elsewhere, shortage of food prompted peasants to plant corn and other crops where vines had once flourished. Public enthusiasm in Britain for German wines, or Rhenish wines as they were usually known, was unabated, so merchants cooked up fraudulent blends which they passed off as German, which did their

[1] Julian Jeffs, *Wines of Europe*, p. 308.

reputation little good. Nonetheless, they were dispatched to the court of Charles II in 1673 and were commended for their positive diuretic and other qualities by physicians of the time.[2]

It was not until well into the eighteenth century that there were signs of recovery and widespread new plantings. The concept of *Naturrein*, unsugared wine, was introduced around 1750, and Riesling became the variety of choice for quality wine production. After 1800 and the Napoleonic wars, many estates were secularized. At the same time, growing prosperity led to the creation of private wine estates in many parts of Germany. The development of efficient transport networks inevitably aided those regions close to ports and railway termini. The unification of Germany in 1871 helped the industry by removing customs and duty barriers; earlier in the century there had been more than thirty toll stations along the River Main. By the end of the nineteenth century the German wine industry was well into the modern era.

Just as the industry should have been prospering, however, disease, notably in the form of phylloxera, dealt it a hammer-blow. First observed in 1874 in northern Germany, it soon spread, although some of the steep slate slopes of the Mosel were unscathed. No sooner had that problem been solved by the planting of American rootstocks, than a further blow awaited German wine producers with the outbreak of war in 1914. Instead of enjoying a new era of prosperity, the vineyard areas were in crisis. From 350,000 ha (864,850 acres) around 1600, the area under vine had dropped by one third by 1914, and by the end of World War II to a mere 123,000 ha (303,933 acres). The Third Reich had ostensibly come to the aid of the wine industry by centralizing its structure and placing all aspects of the business under essentially political control. Whatever its intention, this was not a formula for higher quality. The persecution of the Jews led to the closure of many merchant houses and a loss of commercial expertise. After the war there was a gradual recovery, but German viticulture remained a shadow of its Renaissance self, with no more than 100,000 ha (247,100 acres) under vine.

It is not easy to provide accurate information on such matters as vineyard size. Official statistics and previous books may cite a figure, but that may refer to the recognized area bearing that vineyard name or the

---

[2] Ibid, p. 311.

plantable area; it does not necessarily mean that all the surface has been planted. Many printed sources are clearly unreliable: this becomes apparent when one adds up the vineyard area of all single sites only to find they far exceed the surface reported for the entire village. Except in the case of the most celebrated sites such as Forster Kirchenstück, it is probably safe to assume that the area under vine is slightly, or even considerably, less than the figure given.

Attentive readers will also note that there is little consistency in the use of names and their synonyms. Pinot Noir in Germany is usually referred to as Spätburgunder, but some growers use the French name on the label. Rather than impose uniformity on such usage throughout the book, I have tried to use the name appropriate within the context. Similar problems arise with Pinot Blanc (Weissburgunder or Weisser Burgunder), Pinot Gris (Grauburgunder, Grauer Burgunder, Ruländer), and Müller-Thurgau (Rivaner).

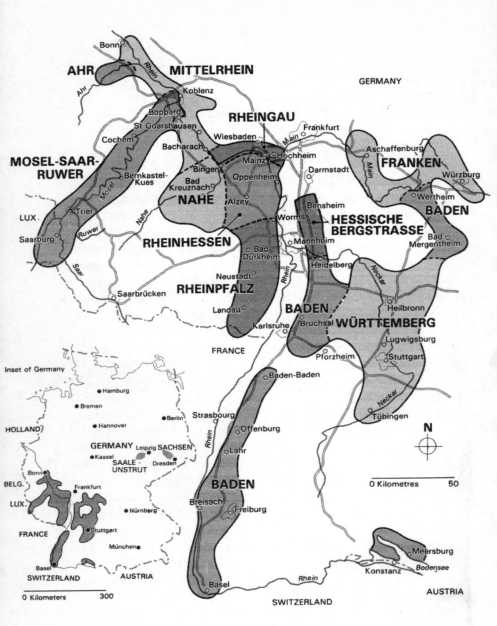

The Wine Regions of Germany

1

The Wine Law of Germany

During the nineteenth century, the various wine regions regulated themselves. It could hardly be otherwise, because Germany was divided into numerous kingdoms and principalities until 1871. Within each region growers' associations were established, but not until 1874 did a national association come into being. The industry was developed by large estates, some of them established as state domaines. By the end of the nineteenth century small growers, finding it difficult to compete with the large estates, formed cooperatives. The legal framework was provided by a law of 1867, and the following year the first wine cooperative was founded at Mayschoss in the Ahr. The trend to form cooperatives was repeated at ensuing periods of economic crisis throughout the first half of the twentieth century. And there were plenty to choose from: phylloxera, two world wars, and the economic miseries of the late 1920s and early 1930s. It wasn't until 1892 that a national Wine Law came into effect; its major defect was that it allowed chaptalization but made it impossible for the consumer to distinguish between chaptalized and unsugared wine. This Law was revised in 1909 by restricting the amount of chaptalization that could take place. These restrictions meant that, especially in poor vintages, much wine was made from unripe grapes without recourse to the sack of sugar, and such wines usually were sold off to the sparkling-wine houses.

In 1930 a new Wine Law was passed. It outlawed hybrid grape varieties, banned the blending of red and white wine and the blending of German and imported wines, and defined *Naturrein* as a wine made without chaptalization.

A decisive turning point in the fortunes of the German wine industry occurred in 1971, when a new Wine Law was introduced. Work had begun on it in 1951 but it was only in 1969 that draft regulations were published. They soon had to be redrafted to take into account the new regulations of the EEC.[1] The proposals that became the 1971 Wine Law were more than a modification of previous laws. They were, in fact, revolutionary in their underlying assumptions. One would imagine that the purpose of such regulations is, first, to encourage the production of wines of high quality, and, second, to provide guidance and protection for the consumer. However, the 1971 Law met neither of these expectations.

Almost every European country has laws that govern its wine industry. In France, such laws are designed to promote the notion of *terroir* and thus to protect the diversity and typicity of each region. It is argued that without the *appellation contrôlée* system, grape varieties that are problematic – being either difficult to grow or low-yielding – might otherwise disappear from commercial production. In regions such as Burgundy an intricate hierarchy of vineyard classification maintains the nuances between sites that provides one of the fascinations of this region and its wines.

In Italy the DOC system works in much the same way, but goes much further in specifying how certain wines should be made, especially in such matters as the composition of blends or the length of oak-ageing. In Spain, too, a category such as *reserva* indicates how the wine has been aged, and posits an arguable link between vinification and quality, on the assumption that producers will only set aside their best wines for lengthy cask-ageing.

On top of these national sets of regulations is the tier of European Union legislation, much of which lays down where vineyards may, or may not, be planted, and addresses such vexed issues as labelling and bottle size.

In non-European countries regulation is minimal. Rules considered commonplace in France and Italy, such as limits on yields and lists of accepted grape varieties, are simply non-existent in, for example, California or New Zealand. In most New World wine regions there are instead fledgling attempts to define geographic origin without implying any link between region of origin and quality.

[1] Ian Jamieson, *German Wines*, p. 46.

The German system differs, however, from all others. Whereas the French laws seek to identify the best *terroirs*, and the Italian laws take a view (however erroneous) on the best grape varieties and vinification methods for specific wines from specific zones, the German Law pays no attention to them. Instead the 1971 Law sets up a hierarchy of quality levels. Quality is not defined by the origin of the wine, nor by the grape variety or varieties used to produce it, but solely by the ripeness levels of the grapes.

At first glance there seems to be a certain logic to this. In theory, the riper the grapes, the better the wine is likely to be. The error lay in using ripeness levels as the sole criterion for establishing quality, ignoring other factors, including site, that inevitably come into play.

At this point let me set out what the 1971 Law states. The lowliest quality level for German wine is *Deutscher Tafelwein* (German table wine), which can be just about anything, although hardly any wine bears this appellation in practice. The minimum alcohol level is 8.5 per cent. Marginally higher is *Landwein* (country wine), a category introduced in 1982; it establishes a very broad geographical identity for a wine. It has to have half a degree more alcohol than Tafelwein, and may have no more than 18 grams of residual sugar. The German concept of Landwein differs from the French *vin de pays* in that it can be produced from the same vineyards as higher quality wines. Few wines of discernible quality are bottled under such designations, with the exception of wines, such as Rieslings aged in new barriques, that "fail" tasting tests for lack of typicity. All wines have to be submitted to a tasting panel, and approved samples are issued with a unique AP (*Amtliche Prüfung*) number which is printed on the label.

There follow two kinds of quality bands. The first is *Qualitätswein bestimmter Anbaugebieter*, better known by its abbreviation of QbA. This means a quality wine from a specified region. The criteria for QbA are set very low, and the wines may be chaptalized. Some extremely fine wines appear under the QbA designation, along with wines of no obvious quality such as Liebfraumilch. Thus from the consumer's point of view, the letters QbA on the label give very little help when it comes to assessing the likely quality of the wine in the bottle.

(Liebfraumilch, incidentally, is legally defined as a QbA from the Rheinhessen, Pfalz, Nahe or Rheingau; it must contain at least seventy per cent Riesling, Kerner, Silvaner, or Müller-Thurgau, and must have at least 18 but not more than 40 grams of residual sugar. The original Liebfrauenmilch came from vineyards alongside the church at Worms, but even in the nineteenth century the name had been hijacked by other regions. The 1909 Wine Law allowed Liebfraumilch, as the wine was also called, to be produced outside the Rheinhessen, and from that point on the name had become a brand. When the then chancellor of Germany, the wine-loving Konrad Adenauer, visited London in the 1960s, he was fêted with a banquet at the Guildhall. He must have been delighted that his hosts selected Liebfraumilch as the wine to accompany the dinner.)

The second tier is more complex: *Qualitätswein mit Prädikat*, commonly abbreviated to QmP. These wines, unlike QbA, may not be chaptalized. The word Prädikat refers vaguely to added characteristics that lift the wine into a supposedly higher quality level. Thus QmP can be broadly translated as a "quality wine with distinction." There are various categories of ripeness within the broad band of QmP. In ascending order, they are: Kabinett, Spätlese (late-harvest), Auslese (selective harvest), Beerenauslese (selected harvest of individual grapes or bunches), and Trockenbeerenauslese (selected harvest of individual grapes or berries that have dried or raisined on the vine through the action of botrytis). In addition there is Eiswein (ice wine, made from grapes naturally frozen on the vine and pressed while still frozen, see pp. 45–47). Eiswein used to be a style indicator and was attached to other Prädikat categories such as Auslese or Beerenauslese; since 1982, it has constituted a category on its own. Any wine labelled Eiswein has to have a must weight no lower than that required for a Beerenauslese.

Some of these terms are of recent origin. Spätlese only came into use shortly before World War I, although late harvesting was not a novel practice. The term was only applied to grapes that were picked after the main harvest was completed. Auslese, as generally understood before the 1971 Wine Law, was either a selection of bunches picked after the Spätlese harvest, or a selection of the sweetest bunches from the already picked Spätlese harvest. Terms such as Beerenauslese and Trocken-beerenauslese were in use throughout the twentieth century but were not legally defined, and their use was at the discretion of the individual producer.

The ripeness levels are specified for each QmP category, but they can vary from region to region. Ripeness is measured according to the Oechsle scale. This system of measurement, devised by Ferdinand Oechsle (1774–1852), is based on the principle that the presence of sugar entails that must is heavier than water. Oechsle is a measurement of the density of the must in relation to water; this figure will indicate the amount of sugar in the must. An example of such a reading would be 1.079, which, in the Oechsle system, is shorn of its first two figures to give a reading of 79. As a rule of thumb, divide the Oechsle figure by eight to obtain the approximate potential alcohol.

In cooler areas such as the Mosel, Riesling must qualifies for Kabinett level at a lower Oechsle reading than in a warm region such as the Pfalz. A Riesling grape can attain 100 Oechsle with relative ease in a good site in the Pfalz, whereas such a level would be considered exceptional in the Mosel. This makes sense, although it becomes virtually impossible for consumers to memorize the different regulations that apply to QmP wines in all the different wine regions of Germany.

Those regions are also delimited by law. Very roughly from north to south, they are: Ahr, Mittelrhein, Mosel-Saar-Ruwer, Rheingau, Rheinhessen, Nahe, Hessische Bergstrasse, Franken, Pfalz, Württemberg, and Baden. In 1990 two wine regions within the former East Germany were added: Saale-Unstrut and Sachsen.

The style of the wine is also specified on the label and strictly defined. Thus a wine labelled as Trocken (dry) must have no more than 8 grams per litre of residual sugar. A wine labelled as Halbtrocken (half-dry) must have a residual sugar level of between 9 and 18 grams. If, for example, a winemaker has a batch of must that can be defined as Spätlese, it now becomes a stylistic and commercial question as to how that must will be vinified. Producers such as Kerpen in the Mosel and Johannishof in the Rheingau, disliking the term Halbtrocken, have replaced it with the term *Feinherb* ("delicately dry"), which hardly seems much of an improvement.

Although the words Trocken and Halbtrocken are intended to guide the consumer, the taste of a wine is not solely determined by residual sugar. How a wine tastes has much to do with acidity levels. In a wine with low acidity, residual sugar will be more apparent than in a wine with high acidity. Thus a Mosel Riesling with 10 grams of acidity can tolerate a residual sugar level of 20 grams without that sugar being easily discernible on the palate. The identical sugar level in a broader and less acid

Riesling from Württemberg will be far more apparent. Nonetheless, the words Trocken and Halbtrocken do provide minimal guidance.

There were two important matters that the 1971 Law failed to address. The first is that of yields. It can be argued that legislation is not required to set maximum yields, and that New World wine regions get by quite happily without such rules. In Australia or California the market will determine whether the quality of the wine is balanced by its price. A seriously overcropped vineyard will usually produce dilute wines that can, or should, only be sold at a relatively low price.

Most European wine regions are yield-regulated, however. In France there is a device known as the PLC (*plafond limite de classement*) which offers flexibility to regulators in vintages when the crop is exceptionally large and healthy; if application for PLC is granted (and it usually is) the normal maximum yield can be increased by up to twenty per cent. The system is widely abused, but the absence of any such system at all in Germany has led to more serious abuses. For some varieties such as Müller-Thurgau yields of 200 hl/ha (eighty-one hl/acre) – almost four times the maximum yield permitted for white burgundy, for example – are easily attained, and any deficiencies in the matter of ripeness can be rectified by generous chaptalization. The average yield across Germany has ranged in recent years from eighty-three hl/ha (33.6 hl/acre) in 1997 to 121 hl/ha (fifty hl/acre) in 1999. In 1999, even a supposedly top-quality region such as the Rheingau managed to produce an average of 106 hl/ha (forty-three hl/acre); given that the top estates will probably have kept yields down to sixty or seventy hl/ha (24.3–28.3 hl/acre), one can imagine how high the yields were at less conscientious estates. This situation was, however, an improvement on 1982, when the average yield across Germany was 173 hl/ha (seventy hl/acre). Under pressure from the European Union, the wine regions within Rheinland-Pfalz agreed in 1999 to limit yields, but maximum levels were set at very generous levels – eighty-eight hl/ha (35.6 hl/acre), with provisions for carrying over excess production for succeeding vintages – that most conscientious growers would still consider too high. The same is true of Baden, Württemberg, and other regions that followed suit in 1990.

It's true that prestigious regions such as Napa Valley are not yield-regulated, yet few would claim that the wines have suffered as a consequence. Growers interested in the quality of their grapes will prune and, if necessary, green harvest to ensure the grapes ripen fully at good sugar levels. In other words, there is no need to stipulate yields because conscientious grape farmers will limit them without being forced to do so. In Germany too, the best producers are self-regulating. If much of Rheinhessen and Baden is given over to industrial-scale grape farming and winemaking, much the same is true of heavily irrigated areas in Australia or Chile.

Far more serious than the failure to regulate yields is the rejection implicit in the 1971 Law of any notion of *terroir*. The concept of *terroir* is often used as a form of claptrap to mask deficiencies in viticulture or winemaking. What some French winemakers airily call *goût de terroir* is often nothing more than bacterial contamination. But even the most sceptical critic of the abuses of *terroir* would concede that some vineyards are better than others.

But this is what the German Wine Law adamantly refuses to do. It is of course common knowledge in all the wine regions of Germany that some sites are superior, in some cases vastly superior, to others. This is especially true within northern regions, where ripening can often be problematic. Exposure to sun and wind, and drainage, are matters of crucial importance in determining the quality of the wine produced on any site. Many of the prestigious regions have been cultivated since Roman times, and it became perfectly obvious which sites were superior. In the Rheingau, the vineyards close to the river tend to be inferior to those on the mid-slope. But Erbacher Marcobrunn, which is situated nearer the river, is an exception. The point, however, is that based on the experience of generations of growers and winemakers it has been found to produce consistently great wine.

The Wine Law makes not the slightest distinction between one site and another. Bernhard Breuer, a Rheingau producer who fought doggedly for a vineyard classification in his region, provides a somewhat speculative explanation: "Both the elimination of distinctions between vineyards and the devilish hierarchy of sweetness were a result of the prevailing philosophy at the time. The student riots of 1968 were still fresh in people's minds, and, for the first time, Germany was governed by a socialist/liberal coalition. There was a widely held belief in the virtues of egalitarianism, so elitism and competition were frowned upon. When translated into viticultural terms, this meant that there was a belief that any grape and any vineyard could produce top quality wines."

Such egalitarianism, however misguided, had clear political benefits for those who espoused it. With no distinction possible (other than price) between Erbacher Marcobrunn and the most wretched Rheinhessen potato field now planted with grapes, smallholders could feel they had cocked a snook at the great estates with their prestigious sites. Their self-satisfaction would, of course, soon fade once the free-for-all of the 1971 Law led to plummeting prices. In France the *Syndicats* of every wine region proudly assert that their main role is the "protection of the appellation." In Germany, after 1971, it seemed that the wine industry was hell-bent on destroying rather than protecting its long-term interests.

On the other hand, the Wine Law did perform one service by greatly reducing the number of named sites. Before 1971 there were some 30,000 sites, each with its own name. The wine law reduced this to around 2,600. This in itself was laudable, but the results were often unsatisfactory. Many renowned vineyards were expanded, absorbing lesser-quality sites which thereafter disappeared from the map. As a consequence, the expanded vineyards often contained many parcels of lesser quality within their borders. The knowledgeable consumer who always relished the wines from a particular site may not have realized that after 1971 the vineyard would have lost much of its integrity. Stand today with any grower in the Mosel or Rheingau and he will be able to point to a famous vineyard and tell you where the original portion lies, and which sectors were tacked on in 1971.

Some sites, such as the legendary Bernkasteler Doktor, have a very specific *terroir* and are limited to a mere five or ten ha (12.3 or 24.7 acres). Other vineyards, however, can be as large as 200 ha (494 acres) – or more. Only the most knowledgeable consumer would be able to distinguish between a truly individual site, and a vast tract of vineyard that just happens to bear an impressive name.

But there was, and there remains, an even worse abuse within the Wine Law. There are three tiers of vineyard groupings within each region. A large region such as Rheinhessen is divided into *Bereiche*. These in turn are divided into *Grosslagen*, which are composed of individual vineyards or *Einzellagen*. There were logical grounds for doing this. If a grower had very small parcels of vines in a number of vineyards, it would be impractical to bottle each vineyard designation separately, giving 200 cases from vineyard X, and eighty-five from vineyard Y – a marketing nightmare. Instead, he could use a Grosslage name and blend the wines from various sites within the same district. The system was of even greater benefit to a wholesaler (*Kellerei*) or cooperative (*Winzergenossen-schaft*), because large volumes of wine from a district contained within a Grosslage could be bottled under the Grosslage name, and even more so under a Bereich name.

What was, and is, villainous about the system was that the Grosslagen names were hard to distinguish from the names of Einzellagen. How many consumers would know that Piesporter Goldtröpfchen was the name of one of the finest sites on the Mosel, while Piesporter Michelsberg was a Grosslage name that incorporated a vast area of utterly mediocre vineyards on overfertile flat land at some distance from the river? Another well-known example is that of Niersteiner Pettenthal (a distinguished Einzellage) and Niersteiner Gutes Domtal, a Grosslage every bit as mediocre as Piesporter Michelsberg. A bottle of Gutes Domtal may be devoid of a single drop of wine from Nierstein and still be entitled to the label. The upshot of the adoption of famous names to identify a large characterless region was not only to confuse, and no doubt con, the consumer, but to wreck the reputation of both Piesport and Nierstein. One taste of Gutes Domtal, and no discerning drinker will see any reason to buy another bottle with the name Nierstein on the label. In its promotional material, the merchant house of Schmitt Söhne declares of its Gutes Domtal range: "These wines are from the village of Nierstein . . ." Well, perhaps, but I suspect the term "village" is expanded beyond the boundaries of Nierstein itself.

The same is true of many Bereiche. Ian Jamieson cites the example of the vast Bereich Bernkastel within the Mosel. Its 12,760 ha (31,530 acres) cover about seventy-five per cent of the entire region. It is obvious that a wine labelled with the name of this Bereich need not contain a drop of wine from Bernkastel itself. Even worse, the law allows for twenty-five per cent of such a wine to consists of wine or *Süssreserve* produced outside the Bereich.

A similar terminological rape was perpetrated by the quality hierarchy. Kabinett had once been a name reserved for exceptional wines from aristocratic Rheingau estates such as Kloster Eberbach and Schloss

Johannisberg, which stored such wines in locked cabinets within their cellars; in 1971, it became a lowly band within the hierarchy of sweetness, and the traditional spelling, Cabinet, was altered. The word Auslese means selective harvesting, but there was nothing in the 1971 Law to require a wine bearing that name to have been picked selectively; all that mattered was the Oechsle level of the grapes.

The bands of sweetness were an open invitation to dodgy practice. Some of it was done with good intentions. In exceptional years, such as 2001, grapes from top estates easily reach Kabinett or Spätlese level. But there will always be a market for simpler, less costly wines even from top estates. If the vineyard does not yield any QbA in a certain vintage, then the grower will probably declassify a good deal of his Kabinett into QbA. Similarly, if he has far too much Spätlese and far too little Kabinett in his cellar, then much of the former will be downgraded into the latter. No harm in that, but it does show up the inanity of the system. So does the fact that, almost without exception, the top estates of Germany have set their own boundaries between the Prädikat bands at much higher levels than the law requires. Time and again, a grower will tell you, "I'd far rather offer a splendid Spätlese than a modest Auslese."

Far worse is the practice of blending in a tank of Auslese to "lift" a batch of Kabinett to Spätlese level. This has been common practice at many wholesalers and cooperatives, because there is nothing in the law to prohibit it. What compounds the offence is that it is legal to blend a cask of Ortega or Optima or some other high-sugar wine into a vat of Riesling in order to boost its sweetness level into a higher category, and still label the resulting wine as Riesling. (Of course, Germany is not alone is allowing apparently varietal wines to contain a proportion of wines made from other varieties than the one specified on the label.)

For Roman Niewodniczanski at Van Volxem in the Saar, there is a more subtle drawback to wine laws that focus primarily on ripeness levels. "The system means that harvesting practices are dictated by the wine laws, and this in turn means that growers don't really focus on what is special and specific about their vineyards. They worry about must weights and acidity in order to ensure that they have enough official 'Kabinett' or 'Auslese' for their markets." The Studert brothers in Wehlen admit that before each harvest they have to estimate in advance what styles they need to produce to satisfy their consumers, and then vinify accordingly, which they find ludicrous.

Johannes Selbach from the Mosel adds: "The problem with our wine laws is that there is no flavour profile attached to each level of quality. There are now vastly different residual-sugar levels in Kabinetts."

Another consequence of the officially sanctioned worship of sugar levels above all else is that it tempted growers to abandon traditional varieties, which may have been tricky to cultivate but at least gave good quality wine, in favour of high-yielding, early ripening crossings that routinely attained high must weights, even in mediocre years. Because the Wine Law implied, at least to the consumer, that an Auslese was "better" than a Spätlese, and a Spätlese superior to a Kabinett, then producers logically charged more for the higher-ranking category. It was thus in the interests of cooperatives and other large producers to generate as much Spätlese and Auslese as possible, because those wines fetched the highest prices. The fact that many of these wines were made from flabby nondescript new varieties and were by any standards inferior to the classic varieties was played down.

Given the northerly and often inclement climate of German wine regions, their wine institutes have since the late nineteenth century worked hard to produce new varieties free from the admitted deficiencies of the classic varieties such as Riesling, Silvaner, and Pinot Noir. It was understandable that growers would welcome new varieties that budded late (thus minimizing the risk of spring frosts), ripened early (before the autumn rains and their attendant grey rot), and gave abundant yields. In the 1960s and 1970s the research institutes released numerous new crossings, which were adopted by growers more interested in volume than quality. The presence of so much mediocre plant material in the vineyards of Germany is a blight to this day. The Weinsberg Institute in Württemberg is still busily producing red crossings, and released six of them in 1999. (It should not be assumed that all crossings are mediocre. As will become clear in the chapter on grape varieties, crossings such as Rieslaner and Scheurebe can produce excellent wine.)

Although it is easy, and necessary, to criticize the 1971 Law, it has to be remembered that the situation before 1971 was also fairly chaotic. Qualitative terms were used in an impressionistic way. If a producer found himself with a particularly superb Auslese in his cellar, he might well have bottled it apart from his regular Auslese from that vineyard and would have labelled it as *Feinste* (finest) or *Edelste* (most noble) Auslese to distinguish the two. The system had to be based on trust. If you were in the habit of buying each year from the same growers, as was often the case, then you would have no reason to doubt that the "finer" and costlier Auslese was what it purported to be.

Such terms are now illegal, because they are too subjective to be capable of definition. But growers are still confronted with the same problem of how to distinguish between different wines within the same category. Some traditional estates still cling to the practice of bottling individual casks separately. Thus at Maximin Grünhaus in the Ruwer, there might be four or five different *Fuders* of Auslese, each of which will have been bottled separately. Many other estates, especially in the Mosel-Saar-Ruwer, use a capsule system. In a year such as 1989 when Auslesen were abundant, an estate might have bottled, for example, a Graacher Himmelreich Riesling Auslese, and from the same site, an even better quality as Auslese Goldkapsel (gold capsule), and a third, yet more wonderful wine as Auslese Lange Goldkapsel (long gold capsule). Other estates, such as Selbach-Oster, distinguish between different qualities by using a star rating on the label. Such systems are "in-house" classifications, so they vary from estate to estate. One produce may define his Auslese ** by minimum must weight at harvest, another by a cask selection. The principle, though, is simple: the more stars on the label, the better and more costly the wine. Many other estates will make no clear distinction on the label, trusting that the price differences between various bottlings will imply that the wines are not of the same quality.

This all adds up to more confusion for the poor consumer. The only sure way to find a path through this jungle of nomenclature and capsules is to pay attention to the AP number. These letters stand for *Amtliche Prüfung*. Before being bottled a wine must be presented to a tasting board for approval. The tasting test can't be very rigorous, any more than the French *label* that gives the nod to AC status, because it is very rare for a wine to be rejected, unless it has obvious faults: out of a maximum score of five points, a total of 1.5 constitutes a pass.[2] Each successful wine is

[2] Robert Joseph, *Wine* magazine, February 1990.

given an AP number, which must be printed on the label. Thus, if an estate has three different Auslesen from the same vineyard, each bottling will bear a different AP number. When tasting wines of Auslese quality and above, I invariably jot down and record the AP number, so that I can be certain which wine I have actually tasted.

One stipulation for obtaining an AP number is that the wine should be clear. In the case of white wines, which tended to be bottled early, this presents little or no problem. But in the case of red wines, samples must be presented to the panel when they may well still be cloudy, and in such cases they may be denied an AP number, even though the wine may be of exceptional quality and will be limpid when eventually bottled.

The 1971 Law did put an end to some practices that were hardly conducive to quality. For instance, under the Wine Law of 1930 it used to be legal not only to chaptalize must but to add sugar (pure or dissolved) to finished wines, the sole restriction being that the added matter could not consist of more than one fourth of the quantity of the liquid! It was also legal to add water to wine in order to reduce acidity, and to doctor red wines by adding up to twenty-five per cent of foreign wine![3]

It didn't take long for everyone in the wine business to recognize that the principal beneficiaries of the 1971 Wine Law were the largest producers, who could exploit such new entities as Grosslagen to foist mediocre wine on an unsuspecting public. In France, AC wines, whatever the faults of the system, only account for twenty-eight per cent of production; in Germany, almost the entire crop is bottled as Qualitätswein.[4] Given the abysmal quality of much wine sold as QbA, it is not surprising that the general public, especially in export markets, responded by thinking that if this was what was meant by quality, then they could give German wine a miss in future.

The German wine industry has never faced up to the consequences of a system that apparently exalted "quality" but made it available at ludicrously low prices. The tanker-loads of soupy Spätlesen and Auslesen churned out by Rheinhessen cooperatives and other offenders ended up on the shelves of supermarkets priced at a few pounds. This inevitably robbed such terms of any value they may once have had. Such a strategy

[3] Fritz Hallgarten, pp. 11, 85.

[4] Robert Joseph, *Wine* magazine, February 1990.

may have meant short-term gain for the large producers, but it has meant long-term disaster for the industry as a whole. Growers in regions such as the Rheinhessen and Pfalz were encouraged to produce as much as possible, aided by unrestricted yields from new crossings. Inevitably prices tumbled and many growers were forced out of business.

From time to time attempts are made to reform the system. The difficulty is that the bodies that propose laws and amendments tend to be dominated by those very producers who have done most to destroy the German wine industry. And the politicians required to vote the laws onto the statute books are more likely to be put under pressure by wholesalers and cooperatives than by associations of quality-oriented producers. In France, for example, the wine industry is regulated by bodies such as INAO, which are not part of the government of the day. In Germany, the Wine Law is indeed part of the laws of the land, which makes it very difficult to alter or reform. "All changes to the Wine Law," observes Bernhard Breuer, "must be subjected to parliamentary debate, often by people who know nothing about the wine business or who are representing various vested interests."

In the early 1990s, ideas were circulated for imposing maximum yields on the various regions. Not surprisingly, those yields were generous in the extreme, and tended to be well in excess of what most conscientious growers were already obtaining from their vines. The subtlety, though, lay in the detail. Among the provisions was one that allowed growers to "carry over" surplus production for a limited time. So you could continue to produce as much as you like, and any crop that exceeded the maximum could be stored and used up in future vintages when the yield was low. Meanwhile the production within legal limits could remain overcropped and no doubt as dismal in quality as it would have been before the new rules came into force.

In 1992 amendments were proposed that would have led to the elimination of the controversial Grosslagen, although the even larger units known as Bereich would remain in place. In the end nothing came of this proposal, although the VDP, Germany's leading growers' association, has outlawed the use of Bereich names since 1995 and Grosslage names by its members since 1997. In 2000 there was a further attempt to break the link between Grosslage names and sites of historical importance, but in cooperative-dominated regions such as Württemberg, where Grosslage names were almost equivalent to brands, there was strong opposition to any change.

The defenders of the Grosslage system point out that whereas Grosslagen such as Piesporter Michelsberg may cover a vast area, many others are quite small and offer useful opportunities to merchants and cooperatives with relatively large volumes to sell. Although the cited examples of Piesport and Nierstein are certainly unfortunate, most Grosslage names are no more confusing to consumers than Einzellage names. There is also support for the Grosslage concept from some restaurateurs, though not for especially noble reasons. According to a leading estate in Johannisberg, "restaurants like Grosslage wines because they can buy them cheaply but then present them to customers as though they were single vineyard wines."

Initiatives for reform have come from the top end of the industry, mostly from the VDP association to which almost all the most prestigious estates belong. Progress has been slow, and the industry remains deeply divided between a quality-conscious sector and the large-scale producers. It seems unlikely that serious reform will be forthcoming, and the problems of the industry, and the low image of German wine as a whole, are set to continue.

2

Vineyard Classification: The Right Way Forward?

This chapter takes a look at the protracted but partially successful attempts of recent years to undo one of the worst features of the 1971 Wine Law: the fiction that all vineyards are equal. It is a long and complex story, but an important one, because many of the top winemakers in Germany argue, quite persuasively, that re-establishing a vineyard classification is the only way to restore the renown of German wines.

In Bordeaux the best growths were identified by local brokers and merchants, who knew from long experience which wines had the best track record and which fetched the highest prices. By and large, the 1855 classification in Bordeaux has stood the test of time. In Germany there was a long-standing vineyard classification, usually based on the tax assessments for the various vineyards of a region. This classification was codified in maps that were published at various times. These maps have recently been republished by British wine experts Hugh Johnson and Stuart Pigott and they have been used as the basis for the current classification.

Those who favour a new classification system for German vineyards argue that by achieving a consensus on which vineyards are the finest in the land and labelling them as such on wine bottles, it will be possible for producers and consumers alike to focus on the best sites, while lesser sites can continue to be bottled as single-vineyard wines or, better, be allowed to fade away, with their production used for blended wines such as *Gutsriesling* (Estate Riesling) or *Ortsriesling* (Village Riesling). This would reduce the number of vineyard names from 3,000 to a far more manageable number. If unanimity could be achieved in identifying the first growths of a region, and if there were strict standards pertaining to the farming and vinification of such sites, then it would be acceptable to charge high prices for the wines, which in turn would validate their quality.

The precursor to the movement toward classification was the founding in 1983 of the Charta Association of growers in the Rheingau. What was interesting about Charta was not only that it insisted on far higher standards of viticulture and winemaking than the Wine Law required, but that it sought to define the "authentic" style of Rheingau Riesling.

I shall look first at this stylistic issue, because it soon became intertwined with the arguments for classification. I well recall that when in the mid-1980s I was researching *Liquid Gold*, my book on sweet wines, I had an appointment to see Bernhard Breuer in Rüdesheim. He generously pulled out some fine old botrytized wines from his cellars, but also insisted that I taste some other Rieslings, which were anything but sweet.

It was, and remains, Breuer's contention that the great wines of the Rheingau in the past were essentially dry. Not bone dry, because of Riesling's naturally high acidity, which, set against a small amount of residual sugar, left the wine tasting dry. It was, he argued, customary to chaptalize the must and ferment it to dryness, giving wines with between 11 and 12 degrees of alcohol. It was clear from the historical records of great estates from the late eighteenth century onward that there was also a production of intensely sweet wines. These, Breuer argued, were very much the exception: the reward of nature in years when noble rot descended on the vineyards, concentrating the sugars and glycerol level of the grapes. Such wines were, as they are today, highly labour-intensive and inevitably costly.

It was the agenda of the Charta Association not merely to improve the tarnished image of Rheingau Riesling but to encourage a style of wine that was technically Halbtrocken, with residual sugar levels of between 9 and 18 grams per litre, but balanced by high natural acidity. The idea was to return to a style of wine broadly comparable in its structure to a fine Chablis. To promote this style, Charta devised a new bottle to give the wines an identity, and mounted a series of banquets, both in the Rheingau and in various cities of the world, at which these Rieslings were served with a wide range of foods, including, with surprising success, roast partridge.

Not everyone, though, was persuaded by Breuer's premise. Stuart Pigott has written: "Although the Charta association's assertion that dry wines are *the* traditional style of the region has much truth in it, I think that things were always a little more complex than this statement would lead one to believe. In lesser and average vintages the great majority of the region's wines certainly fermented through to dryness. However, those producers with deep cold cellars, where the fermentation was slower and less energetic, must have had many barrels of wine with a slight sweetness almost every year. This continues to happen today. In the top vintages I'm sure that the majority of the region's Riesling wines were not bone dry."[1]

Whatever the exact truth of the matter, there is no doubt that a major stylistic shift took place after World War II. Dr Dirk Richter recalls the 1947 vintage in the Mosel. "The river overflowed its banks and flooded the cellars, and the cold water caused the fermentation to stick. When the wines were first tasted, their sweetness came as quite a shock. But the vintage proved very popular and successful with the public." In the postwar years sugar was often in short supply, so the natural sweetness of a white wine could be both appealing and appreciated as a form of nutrition.

Technical advances soon made it easy to produce sweet wines on a regular basis. To retain natural sweetness in a wine, the fermentation, except when it halted of its own accord, had to be arrested. This could be done by the addition of sulphur dioxide or by chilling, but the resulting wine was not always stable. The invention of sterile filtration made it possible to arrest fermentation and ensure that the residual sweetness in the wine did not reactivate any dormant yeasts remaining.

Another technique was developed in the 1950s: that of allowing the wine to ferment to complete dryness and then "balancing" the wine to its required sweetness level by the addition of *Süssreserve*. This is nothing other than unfermented grape juice. Its production and use were quite strictly regulated; roughly speaking, it had to have the same origin as the wine to which it was being added. (On the other hand, a respected producer in the Saar says it would be legal to use a *Süssreserve* from a different village or even a different variety.) A wine may legally contain up to twenty-five per cent of *Süssreserve*.

[1] Stuart Pigott, *Riesling*, pp. 119–20.

For large-volume producers, such techniques were a godsend. Nothing masks the deficiencies of a wine more than sugar. In a dry wine, dilution and traces of rot are easily detectable on the palate; gloss a wine with a fair amount of sugar in the form of grape juice, and such faults are harder to detect. This encouraged the production of poor quality wines made superficially attractive by their sweetness; wines, moreover, that could be sold at a low price that would guarantee a large market share in countries to which it was exported. The long-term consequence of this cynical strategy was, as we have seen earlier, disastrous.

Although it remains legal to add *Süssreserve* to a German wine, many leading producers frown on the method, being convinced that such a wine is never as well balanced as one that acquires its sweetness through arrested fermentation. The technical explanation for this is as follows: "The sugar in a ripe grape is composed of roughly equal amounts of glucose and fructose. The glucose ferments before the fructose, so if you stop the fermentation the residual sweetness is fructose – and fructose tastes more fruity and refreshing than glucose. If you ferment the wine to dryness and then add *Süssreserve*, you don't gain that extra dimension."[2]

The founders of Charta were well aware that fairly abominable wines were being produced in the flagship region of the Rheingau, of all places, and they feared that the diminished reputation of the region would besmirch the wines of conscientious producers as well unless a counter-action was initiated. Other than Breuer, the founders were Dr Helmut Becker, the renowned researcher at the wine college at Geisenheim; Dr Hans Ambrosi, an elder statesman of the region who was then the director of the State Domaine at Eltville and co-author with Breuer of a number of books on German wine regions; and Graf Erwein von Matuschka-Greiffenclau, the owner of Schloss Vollrads.

Although all of these gentlemen were formidable personalities, Graf Matuschka was to become, with Breuer, the public face of the Charta Association. Almost stereotypically tall, dark, and handsome, with a penchant for very fast cars, Matuschka was passionate about matching German wine with food. As well as owning one of the most impressive of the Rheingau's medieval estates, he was also a restaurateur and the driving force behind the banquets for which Charta soon became known.

[2] Oz Clarke and Margaret Rand, *Grapes and Wine*, p. 195.

Charta events became a major success with that small sector of the wine press that was well disposed toward German wine in the first place. In Britain a handful of wine merchants such as Alex Findlater took up the cause with enthusiasm and stocked a range of Charta wines. Everyone had a marvellous time at the Charta tastings and feasts, but I am not aware that it had the slightest impact on the British market.

"I can't dispute," admits Breuer, "that Charta flopped in Britain, but at least the press began to understand that there was a quality-conscious movement in the Rheingau. The great botrytis wines of years such as 1959 and 1976 were a fine talking point among connoisseurs, but they only represented a tiny proportion of our production, and no estate could survive commercially by producing only botrytis wines. Our aim in markets such as Britain was to place top German wines onto the wine lists of the country's leading restaurants. We didn't succeed, though this battle was eventually won within Germany. In retrospect, I think we did help to combat the negative image of Riesling outside Germany, though I have to admit that the high quality of wines from Austria and Australia also helped."

Charta did establish quality levels that set standards for most top producers. The wines were pure Riesling, of course, and had to be estate grown. Oechsle levels were set higher than the wine law required. The wines were tasted blind by a panel before being accepted as worthy of the Charta bottle and label. The wines had to be bottle-aged for eighteen months before being released. Charta members were encouraged to taste each other's wines with a critical palate, and this in turn stimulated a healthy competitiveness between estates. Improvements in vinification were discussed and introduced.

As for the style of the wines, Breuer established a rule of thumb, suggesting that the best balance in a Charta wine would be a residual sugar level derived by adding the figure three to the acidity level. A typical acidity level would be eight grams per litre, which, it was recommended, would be balanced by a residual sugar level of eleven grams per litre.

Although such ratios were mere suggestions and not requirements, there were legitimate criticisms of certain Charta wines, especially those from the 1980s, as overacidic. Dieter Greiner of Kloster Eberbach says: "Breuer and Matuschka were right to assert that traditional Rheingau Riesling was fairly dry, but their misconception was in thinking that the wines needed to have high acidity, and to stipulate minimum acidity levels. Some of the wines turned out to be too high in acidity and tasted sour rather than fresh."

Breuer made no secret of the fact that he had a broader programme riding on the back of the Charta Association. He had no wish to see Charta perceived as an exotic element within the Rheingau; he wanted the wines to establish a profile for the region. He hoped to discourage the continuing production of sweeter styles, notably Spätlese, and was unhappy about estates such as Schönborn and Langwerth von Simmern (neither of them Charta members) that produced basically dry wines for the domestic market, but also churned out quite large quantities of sweet wines for export. Breuer conceded that this may have been a workable commercial formula, but he thought it disastrous in terms of creating a regional profile for the Rheingau. "What does Marcobrunn mean," he said to me in the mid-1990s, "if some of the vineyard's wines are sweet and others are dry? As far as I am concerned, the long-term goal of Charta is a stylistic definition of the region which will help our best growers to survive. That means dry wines in the Charta style, and botrytis wines in exceptional years."

Once the Charta style was broadly established within the region, Breuer pressed on with the next phase of his programme by proposing a classification of the vineyards. If classification was going to work, then the Rheingau, with its relatively homogeneous band of vineyards and only two grape varieties of any significance, was an ideal place to start. Because many of the most famous vineyards of the region had been expanded in 1971 – Marcobrunn being one of the few exceptions – it was acknowledged that it would be unusual for entire vineyards to be classified as a first growth. A draft classification, largely modelled on the old maps published by Johnson and Pigott, was formulated in 1992. It was envisaged that up to one-quarter of the Rheingau's vineyards would gain first-growth status. Although any resulting classification would be an internal matter for Charta members, Breuer nourished hopes that eventually the entire region would follow the association's lead and accept the as yet unborn classification.

But it soon became apparent that Breuer and his supporters were walking into a minefield. It was hard to dispute that a classification would probably end up favouring the large and famous estates with substantial holdings in the best sites. Good and conscientious producers not blessed with outstanding vineyards, but nonetheless capable of making excellent wine, might find themselves at a commercial disadvantage, especially if Charta took the system to its logical conclusion and sought to eliminate the use of "lesser" sites on wine labels.

Talking to Graf Matuschka in the mid-1990s, I soon realized that there were already some tensions between himself and Breuer, and that he felt his colleague was trying to move too fast and was insufficiently sensitive to the concerns of growers whose good but not exceptional vineyards might end up being excluded from any classification. When we last talked, the proposed classification was still being drafted, but he estimated that about forty-five per cent of his own estate at Vollrads would not be classified and its production would have to be bottled as Gutsriesling. "I am prepared to accept this, but I can understand that growers with smaller properties may well resist such proposals."

Both Matuschka and Breuer were not only leaders of Charta, but influential members of the Rheingau VDP (*Verband Deutscher Prädikats- und Qualitätsweingüter*), the prestigious growers' association which had members in every wine region of Germany. The VDP was founded in 1910 and its members owned 3.7 per cent of German's vineyards. It insists upon far higher viticultural standards than the wine law requires. In the course of the 1990s it entered controversial areas, pressing for vineyard classification, which of course was contrary to the official Wine Law's premise that all vineyards are equal. This was a period of crisis for the VDP, and more than one-quarter of its members resigned or were required to leave because they were not prepared to meet the ever more stringent criteria being laid down. The silver lining was that ninety new members were admitted, many of them from a younger generation, estates such as Heger, Kühn, and Christmann, that were keen to promote the ideas of the VDP. As has been mentioned earlier, the terms "Bereich" and "Grosslage" were banned from VDP members' labels. It took some courage for the VDP's president during this period, Prinz Michael zu Salm-Salm, to press ahead with the drive toward classification against the opposition of many of his own members and the unwillingness of the government to modify the 1971 Wine Law. "In 1994," he recalled, "we stopped attacking the German wine laws, because it soon became obvious we were never going to be able to change them. So we made changes from within, hoping that the standards we adopted would gradually be adopted by all quality-conscious producers in Germany."

To return to the situation in the Rheingau: by the late 1990s, Charta and the VDP had joined forces, because there was no point in duplicating their efforts. By this time Graf Matuschka was also the president of the Rheingau winegrowers' association, and as such the spokesman for all the growers. Because he was still a powerful figure within Charta, there was, in the eyes of many, a conflict of interest in his dual role, especially because he was seeking to impede or delay the Charta-inspired classification. Charta retaliated by pointing out that eighty per cent of all Rheingau growers had at least some vines in the proposed first-growth vineyards, so it was not true to state that only the large and aristocratic estates would benefit from classification.

Matuschka's delaying tactic was to propose in 1997 that any proposed classification should be subjected to "scientific" analysis. Breuer and his allies were deeply suspicious. A scientific analysis, by definition, had to focus on measurable factors such as climate, sun exposure, and so forth. The upshot, it was feared, would benefit lower locations, while ignoring other factors such as higher humidity and the greater risk of rot.

Dr Franz Werner Michel, the proprietor of the Domdechant Werner estate in Hochheim and until a few years ago the powerful head of the German Wine Institute, broadly supported Matuschka's ideas. "The Hugh Johnson maps," he told me, "were based on speculation and opinion. They had no scientific basis, and it would have been a mistake to base a classification on these documents. So I supported the idea of a scientific study. It was to be conducted at Geisenheim, entirely independently of the growers' association headed by Graf Matuschka. So nobody knew what the results would be until they were published. The Geisenheim team were asked to examine such factors as temperature, water retention, and susceptibility to frost. The analysis was extremely rigorous, because vineyards were subdivided into plots of twenty-five square metres (thirty square yards) for the purpose of analysis.

"But there was also a political element. There had to be an Oechsle threshold. We had to decide what the minimum Oechsle level had to be for a first-growth wine, and that meant that vineyards that didn't attain that degree of ripeness on average would be excluded. Evidently, the higher the threshold, the fewer vineyards would qualify."

This was a crucial issue. Growers who wanted a strict and rigorous definition of "first growth" would favour a high threshold; those who wanted to be reasonably certain that a proportion of their own vineyard holdings would be included among the first growths would opt for a lower level. And of course average Oechsle is only a measure of sugar ripeness, leaving out the other factors that were supposed to determine first-growth status.

The number chosen was 83 Oechsle, which everybody admits was generously low. Dr Michel was keen to set the threshold considerably higher, but as the representative of the Hochheim growers he was obliged to respect their wishes for a lower figure. "Although I favoured a higher threshold, I had no problem accepting what we recognize was a compromise. At a higher figure, perhaps only ten or fifteen per cent of vineyards would have qualified, and there would have been many unhappy growers with no first-growth vineyards at all."

In the event the figure of 83 Oechsle was fed into the Geisenheim computers, and the scientists duly announced that 1,120 ha (2,768 acres) of Rheingau vineyards were "first growth": about thirty-five per cent of the total. The Hochheim growers were among those who rejoiced, because sixty per cent of their vineyards had qualified. Dr Michel was particularly pleased to learn that ninety per cent of his estate was first-growth. "But this," he insisted, "was the luck of the draw. I had no say in the processes at Geisenheim."

So the new definition of first growth, or *Erstes Gewächs*, as such wines would be labelled, was as follows: the grapes would have to come from a classified vineyard, and be hand-picked at a minimum must weight of 83 Oechsle. Because the wines would be bottled as QbA, there were no restrictions on chaptalization or even the use of *Süssreserve*. There is no stylistic definition of the wine. Wines must be presented to a tasting panel, which will determine whether the wine conforms to the ideal image of an Erstes Gewächs: a wine that is full-bodied, fruity, dense, with good acidity and extract, and no excessive sweetness if it is supposed to be dry. Successful wines would carry a special label denoting that it was Erstes Gewächs. Some forty wines were submitted to the panel from the 1999 vintage, but only fifteen were accepted, a pass rate of thirty per cent, which does suggest that strict standards are being adhered to. The system is open to all, and not restricted to members of Charta or the VDP.

Hochheim was happy, but elsewhere there was dismay, scorn, and derision. Wolfgang Schleicher, the director of Schloss Johannisberg, told me he had favoured a threshold of 85 Oechsle, because anyone harvesting at 83 Oechsle would need to chaptalize. Others pointed out that it was ridiculous to classify more than one-third of an entire region as first growth. In Alsace, the proportion of Grand Cru vineyards is 11.5 per cent, and in Burgundy the proportion of Premiers Crus was eleven per cent, and of Grands Crus a mere three per cent.

Ernst Loosen, the outspoken Mosel producer, thought the whole basis for determining first growth status was ludicrous: "It was crazy to base it on sugar levels. Even Montrachet can be chaptalized. Each vineyard is either great or not great. In the Rheingau they wanted to create something new but fell back on the Prädikat system. It makes no sense."[3]

Stuart Pigott pointed out that some sites long regarded as among the region's finest had been excluded, while some flat vineyards close to the Rhein that had never produced superior wines were admitted.[4] The fiercest criticism came from Bernhard Breuer. "The results of the Geisenheim classification were bizarre. Some parts of Rüdesheimer Berg Schlossberg weren't classified, none of Berg Roseneck was classified. On the other hand, I found that certain parcels I own were classified, even though I would never dream of using them for my top wines but only use them for my generic Rieslings. Hardly any of Rauenthaler Baiken is classified, and the same is true of Steinberg." Other growers in the region suggested that Breuer's angry reaction had to do with the fact that one of his top vineyards, Rauenthaler Nonnenberg, had been excluded, but Breuer strenuously denies this.

"The detail about which vineyards are included or not included is not the most important thing. What I find unacceptable is that it is still legal to chaptalize, and that there is no requirement for the wine to be in a dry style. It's possible to release a Spätlese as a first growth." The inclusion of Spätlese, despite the opposition of many growers to this style, was presumably at the behest of large estates such as Schönborn that still export large quantities of Spätlesen.

Breuer's response to the classification was to leave the VDP in June

[3] *Harper's* "German Wine Supplement," April 2001.
[4] *Fine Wine Folio*, Vol 12, No 11.

2000. Although there are some great German estates, such as Maximin Grünhaus, that have never joined the VDP, while amply qualified to do so, it is true to say that the vast majority of leading properties are members. To resign from the VDP is a strong statement of dissent. Breuer clearly felt that although the Rheingau growers' association was defending the interests of the region as a whole, it was the duty of the VDP to maintain high standards that would ensure high quality:

"I left the VDP without fanfare. I had fought to restrict yields, which at present is seventy-five hl/ha [30.3 hl/acre] with twenty per cent PLC [*plafond limite de classement*] – but only for wines with the VDP symbol. That's too high. I also said that although concentration was allowed by the EU, it shouldn't be allowed for Erstes Gewächs because it could be misused to beef up wines from lesser sites. I also wanted to outlaw the use of oak chips for VDP members. On all these issues I was completely overruled, so I resigned. The history of German wine production is full of diluted concepts such as Hochgewächs in the Mosel and the destruction of the idea of Cabinet by changing a single letter. My decision to resign was a personal one and I made no effort to persuade others to join me, even though I know there are other producers who agree with me. I still respect the VDP greatly for its commitment to quality and I certainly have no wish to set up a rival organization. At any rate the whole debate means that quality will remain a major issue."

As for the low pass rate of wines submitted to the tasting panel, Breuer was sceptical. "I recall that when I was on the panel that assessed Charta wines, a grower would often present three wines, hoping the panel would identify the best, which would then be commercialized as a Charta wine. In other words, growers were using the panel as a kind of market research. I suspect something similar may be going on with the Erstes Gewächs panel. I don't dispute that wines likely to come onto the market as Erstes Gewächs will be of good quality, but I wanted to ensure that the rules precluded the possibility of mediocre wines getting through, and the rules don't do that."

If the first vintage of Erstes Gewächs is anything to go by, it will represent a tiny segment of production, even if one-third of the vineyards qualify. In 2000 no more than one per cent were offered as Erstes Gewächs, and nobody thinks the proportion will rise above five per cent. Most growers with classified vineyards, Breuer included, have decided to work with the new system, but a handful will have nothing to do with it.

Gunter Künstler in Hochheim, many of whose vineyards are classified, won't be using the term on his labels. "The best marketing strategy is to win the trust of your customers. And anyway, it's nonsense to have a minimum Oechsle level of 83. It should have been set at 93 or 95. Nor do I like the fact that is acceptable to use concentrators. We have enough rain and sunshine here to make great wines without such aids. It's the equivalent of doping in the Olympics. It is ridiculous that practices forbidden for Kabinett wines, such as chaptalization, are permitted for an Erstes Gewächs."

So after fifteen years of argument, classification has got off to a rocky start in the Rheingau. The risk is that if it isn't evident that a high-priced Erstes Gewächs is the finest wine in any producer's range, then the label will lose its cachet. Many growers admit it is now essentially a marketing ploy, because top estates have had no difficulty selling their wines without it. Because the addition of the Erstes Gewächs category is another example of labels becoming more rather than less complicated, the concept of first growth in the Rheingau needs to catch on fast and establish itself. In practice growers such as Robert Weil are featuring just the vineyard name on the front label, consigning all other information to the back label. This should reinforce the notion of Erstes Gewächs as the highlighting of an outstanding site, even though the honour has been too casually bestowed.

Meanwhile, the other regions have been looking on with fascination while the relatively homogeneous Rheingau has stumbled toward its faulty and compromised system. For the growers of the Pfalz the situation was more complicated. The core of the region was the Mittelhaardt, a band of villages between Neustadt and Bad Dürkheim that contained the Pfalz's most celebrated sites, many of them obvious candidates for first-growth status. But the rest of the Pfalz was very different. Riesling was not dominant in other parts of the region, and many of the vineyards were given over to industrialized production. Yet here and there were growers of the highest quality. Everyone had heard of Forster Jesuitengarten, but how could one decide on the claim of a hitherto unknown site to equivalent status?

In the Pfalz the basis for classification was, as elsewhere, the ancient tax maps. In the early nineteenth century the Pfalz was part of Bavaria, so it was the Bavarian authorities who had drawn up a taxation map in the late 1820s. Every village was mapped and assessed for tax purposes, including the villages of the less prestigious southern Pfalz. The Mittelhaardt maps are quite instructive: in Wachenheim, only Gerümpel is rated as a top site, and in Forst only the lower part of Ungeheuer is rated. But these maps are only a basis for discussion, though there is general acceptance that assessments of quality and consistency made two centuries ago are still by and large valid today.

It was the VDP that took the initiative in the Pfalz, with the following estates especially keen: Biffar, Bürklin-Wolf, Koehler-Ruprecht, and Christmann. They drew up the following criteria for *Grosses Gewächs* ("great growths") wines: maximum yields of forty-eight hl/ha (19.4 hl/acre) – slightly lower than the Rheingau, a minimum must weight of 90 Oechsle for Riesling and of 95 for Pinot Noir, hand-harvesting only, dry wines only, no chaptalization of white wines, and obligatory oak-ageing (though not necessarily barrique-ageing) for Pinot Noir. Three varieties are permitted: Riesling, Pinot Blanc, and Pinot Noir. The wines are bottled as QbA, and blind-tastings by a panel both before and after bottling will monitor quality.

As for vineyards with no ancient renown, growers who wish to see them granted Grosses Gewächs status are required to submit at least six vintages from the site, which would then be tasted blind against other Grosses Gewächs. A commission would also be dispatched to the vineyard before the harvest to see whether the vines were capable of producing wine of the required quality. The system is open to all, not just to VDP members, although at present only VDP estates are participating.

The tasting panel is rigorous, and in the difficult 2000 vintage, two-thirds of the wines were rejected. Just about every well-known estate in the region has agreed to participate, with the significant exception of Müller-Catoir; by 2001 there were twenty participating wineries. The Pfalz classification does not have the official status of the Rheingau model, which is now enshrined in the laws of the state of Hessen. Steffen Christmann, who has been closely involved in the classification, is not troubled by this: "Once a classification is made official and part of the law it becomes very difficult to modify. We're still feeling our way, and can easily make changes if we want to."

Gregor Messmer in Burrweiler in the southern Pfalz has some worries about the new system. "I have four ha [9.9 acres] in the Schäwer vineyard, which can produce great Riesling – but not all of it. If I set aside the best parcel for Grosses Gewächs, what do I do with the production from the rest of Schäwer? Grosses Gewächs wines are supposed to be high-priced, but if I list mine at €20 [£13.10], while my regular Riesling Spätlese Trocken from Schäwer is priced at €10 [£6.54], will the difference in quality justify the huge difference?" Despite such reservations, Messmer thinks it probable that most estates with outstanding sites will go along with the classification.

The situation is similar in the Nahe, where in 1997 the VDP set the ball rolling. Here the classification is based on a map from 1901. The rules are almost identical to those in the Pfalz, except that chaptalization is permitted. Not everyone was happy with the idea of classification, and one estate, Plettenberg, left the VDP in protest. Until 2000, only VDP estates were eligible to participate, but since then it has been open to all. At present these wines are known as Selektion, which is bound to cause confusion now that the German Wine Institute's Classic and Selection have been introduced (see page 52).

There is similar confusion in Rheinhessen, where a category called Rheinhessen Selektion has been in place since 1992. Wines are made to strict criteria and enjoy a good reputation. A few estates, such as Michel-Pfannebecker, still produce them. The Rheinhessen Grosses Gewächs system is closely modelled on that of the Pfalz. The only permitted varieties are Riesling and Pinot Noir, although Silvaner may be added in the future. Only six growers are participating at present. There were seven, until Gunderloch withdrew in 2001. When I asked why, given that their flagship wines from Nackenheimer Rothenberg are indisputable first-growth wines, Fritz Hasselbach replied that he was unhappy about the inclusion of Pinot Noir, for which there is no strong tradition in the Rheinhessen. He was also sceptical about the potential of the Rhein-hessen interior, in particular Grosslage Wonnegau, to produce outstand-ing wines. This is rather odd, because anyone who has tasted recent vintages from participating wineries such as Wittmann and Keller in the southern Rheinhessen can hardly dispute that their quality is brilliant. Despite the reservations of Gunderloch, it seems likely that the move-ment toward Grosses Gewächs in the Rheinhessen will continue.

In June 2002 the various regional associations of the VDP at least managed to agree on the same classification model to be used by them all. The Mosel-Saar-Ruwer and Ahr were not quite ready to sign up, but it was stated that it was only a matter of time before they would be. In the spring of 2003 the Mosel-Saar-Ruwer VDP estates laid out their proposals for a system of classification. As well as similar standards and tests, the regions would all use a special bottle with a Grosses Gewächs logo stamped on it. There would in future be two categories: Grosses Gewächs, and a lesser category of *klassifizierte lagenwein*, i.e. wine from a classified site. The idea is to create a pyramid, with Gutswein, or estate blends, as the base, and then the two categories above. This system will come into force in 2004. In the long term it is hoped that the system will be open to estates that are not members of the VDP.

The individual regions were given a great deal of freedom, and the ruling committee of the VDP was anxious not to dictate rules and regulations from above. Thus each region was free to determine which sites (or in many cases, which sections of Einzellagen) were to be classified. Moreover, the list was not to be set in concrete, and if a Grosses Gewächs failed to deliver the expected quality in the future, it could be declassified. It's estimated that in any region, the proportion of vineyards that will be classified as Grosses Gewächs will be no more than one to three per cent.

The following are the grape varieties permitted for Grosses Gewächs for each region.

Baden: Riesling, Pinot Blanc, Pinot Gris, Pinot Noir.

Franken: Riesling, Silvaner, Pinot Blanc, Pinot Noir.

Mittelrhein: Riesling.

Mosel-Saar-Ruwer: Riesling.

Nahe: Riesling.

Pfalz: Riesling, Pinot Blanc, Pinot Noir

Rheinhessen: Riesling, Pinot Noir

Saale-Unstrut: Riesling, Pinot Blanc

Württemberg: Riesling.

Grosses Gewächs sites are listed within each regional chapter that follows.

It is far too early to predict whether these slow, conscientious, somewhat laborious moves towards a return to vineyard classification will have much long-term effect on the reputation of German wines. One would like to think so, but the whole system is entrenched in a new bureaucratic system of rules and regulations, tasting panels, and packaging. For some the Grosses Gewächs logo will prove little more than a marketing ploy and a justification for higher prices. For other estates, it may bring their wines to the attention of a wider public and clientele. At present, first-growth wines represent a tiny proportion of the market. Whether its lustre will spread out and illuminate the more benighted sectors of the German wine industry is more doubtful.

Prinz Salm is the first to acknowledge that explaining the system to the general public will be a major problem, especially since the very term Grosses Gewächs is not allowed to be printed on the label. As late as autumn 2002 the VDP was still discussing packaging and labels, and other ways to convey to the wine-drinking public why they could expect the wine in the bottle to be of superior quality.

"Nationwide we have had some problems gaining acceptance of our ideas as the only way forward for German wine as a whole. The VDP is perceived," said the Prince, "as an aristocratic elite with different aims from the 60,000 grape growers of Germany. But the growers are coming to realize that they are fighting a losing battle. Production costs are high in Germany, and we are never going to be able to compete with countries such as Chile. The only solution, the only way to survive, is to pursue quality above all else."

3

German Wine Styles

To a large extent the styles of German wine are dictated by the wine laws, which have codified specifically German styles such as Beerenauslese or Halbtrocken wines. But the need to fashion wines to the supposed demands of the market means that the German wine industry is more technological than most. A wine such as "Liebfraumilch" may be cheap, but it requires a well-equipped winery to produce it. Most aspects of German viticulture and winemaking do not differ greatly from other wine regions across the world, but this chapter will single out those features that are special to Germany.

VITICULTURE

Germany is so varied in its climatic conditions and range of grape varieties that generalizations about grape-farming are difficult to make and unreliable. It seems that just about everything has been tried, but many methods have also been abandoned. The wide-spaced, high-trained Lenz Moser method of planting vines, which originated in Austria, was popular for a while and it offered the prospect of generous crops of healthy grapes. But certainly in prestigious regions such as the Rheingau, it was apparent that it failed to deliver grapes of the desired quality, and estates that flirted with the method, such as Schloss Vollrads, have grubbed up the vines.

The Mosel remains distinctive, because vines are trained on wooden stakes thrust into the stony slaty soil. This is effective both because of the extremely steep slopes along the Mosel and its tributaries, and because it maximizes exposure to sunlight. On flatter sites other methods of training the vines are employed.

Vine density varies from 3,500–5,000 vines/ha (1,400–2,000 vines/acre) in the Rheingau to 8,000 vines/ha (3,238 vines/acre) in the Mosel. In recent years there has been a trend toward higher density as a means of controlling yields. Knipser in the Pfalz are replanting at 6,000 vines/ha (2,500 vines/acre), but are unable to contemplate even greater density patterns because that would require them to spend a fortune by replacing all their tractors. Other producers are opting for much higher densities. Egon Müller at Scharzhof in the Saar says that the old vines on the estate were planted at 10,000 vines/ha (4,000 vines/acre). When he replants, he tries to maintain a high density, although the drawback is that he can't mechanize the vineyards. So it's a costly choice.

Some German winemakers, such as Jan Kux of Schloss Wackerbarth in Sachsen, are troubled by the lack of choice when it comes to rootstocks. Grape farmers in Germany have access to about ten rootstocks, whereas far more are available to their French counterparts. A wider choice of rootstocks would allow a more precise matching of vines to soil and climatic conditions.

An enormous amount of research has been conducted into clones and crossings, and this matter is dealt with in chapter 5. The first viticultural research institutes were founded in the 1860s and 1870s at Weinsberg in Württemberg and at Geisenheim in the Rheingau, and both colleges flourish to this day. They have a dual role as training colleges. Weinsberg is the leading research institute dedicated to the development of new red crossings, and its counterpart at Geilweilerhof in the Pfalz is moving into the highly controversial area of genetically modified plants.

The uncertain German climate means that organic or biodynamic viticulture has been slow to develop, although in some regions such as the Rheingau there has been a marked reduction in the use of herbicides and fertilizers. There is also a movement toward minimal vineyard treatments, something akin to the French *lutte raisonnée* and known in German as *Kontrollierte Umweltschonend* (KUV). The major hazards of German viticulture include spring frosts and diseases such as oidium and mite infestations, as well as black or grey rot, so one can understand why most growers are unwilling to give up the possibility of treating against them when necessary. Nonetheless there are quite a few organic estates, and some are included in the directory of producers.

The question of yields has already been discussed. However, it is important to distinguish between quality wine production, where the need to reduce yields is widely accepted, and industrial wine production, where the goal is quantity rather than quality – or has been until very recently. It's interesting to look at statistics from the past for German wine production. In the 1920s the average yield was 25.5 hl/ha (10.3 hl/acre). By the 1940s it had risen slightly to thirty-five hl/ha (14.2 hl/acre), and then more steeply in the 1950s to fifty-two hl/ha (twenty-one hl/acre). By 1959 the average yield was seventy-two hl/ha (twenty-nine hl/acre), and the following year it soared to 116 hl/ha (46.9 hl/acre). There are numerous explanations for this steep rise. One was the growing use of chemical fertilizers; another was the feverish planting of high-yielding crossings in place of traditional varieties. Both these trends have been in retreat in the 1990s, but there are still parts of Germany, such as the Rheinhessen and parts of the Pfalz and Mosel, where yields can be extremely high.

An important change took place in German viticulture with the launch of *Flurbereinigung*. By the 1960s a growing number of vineyards were becoming uneconomical, either because they were virtually inaccessible or excessively steep and dangerous. *Flurbereinigung* was a joint venture between the growers and the government, which involved a radical restructuring of the vineyards. As a project, it originated in the nineteenth century, but took off in the 1960s and 1970s. It can only be undertaken if a majority of owners within the vineyard being considered vote in favour. Some growers are uncomfortable with the idea because uprooting vines could lead to the disappearance of rare ungrafted vines or other old parcels, and because replanting would mean a hiatus in production of around four years. If the drawback was a certain homogenization of sites, the positive aspects of the programme were that it provided access roads and improved drainage systems and thus prevented soil erosion, and imposed a more rational organization on what in some areas was a baffling hodge-podge of tiny vineyards. There is no doubt that without *Flurbereinigung* many more German vineyards would have fallen into disuse.

Even so, economic issues remain important. In the Mosel and Mittelrhein, where there are many very steep sites that cannot be mechanized, high labour costs are not always compensated for by the price obtained for the wine. Recent legislation places restrictions on the number of hours that can be worked by vineyard labourers before they become liable to pay tax on their earnings, which they are understandably reluctant to do. Yet there is no reservoir of additional workers that can be hired to supplement the present labour force. Many workers come over from Eastern Europe to work in the vineyards, but they are not allowed to work more than fifty days. Unfortunately such restrictions, which may have a sound basis in economics and good labour practices, make life increasingly difficult not for the large mechanized estates, but for quality-conscious domaines that rely on a large labour force to carry out important but labour-intensive tasks such as green harvesting.

VINIFICATION

German wine producers have been swift to adopt new technology, and any visit to a large *Kellerei* in the 1970s and 1980s was a progress through batteries of steel tanks, filters and centrifuges. The 1990s have seen a retreat from hi-tech winemaking, certainly at the artisanal level. Riesling in particular is all about purity of flavour, and allowing the typicity of the *terroir* to come shining through. So it is rare for winemakers to do anything that would detract from that purity. There have, for example, been experiments in barrel-fermentation for Riesling, but they are exceedingly rare.

If there is near unanimity in the rejection of ageing Riesling in new oak, there is much more debate about the "authentic" style of German Riesling. In the previous chapter I presented the views of Bernhard Breuer and others who argue that Riesling was always vinified dry, except in years when botrytis was abundant and great nobly sweet wines could be made.

Whether they are right or not will remain up for discussion, but what is clear is that a few generations ago there was not a great deal that a winemaker could do, in a pre-technological age, to influence the style of the wine. What could be controlled, to some degree, was the date of harvesting which determined the ripeness and sanitary condition of the grapes. Then they were fermented, invariably in wooden casks of various sizes, and thereafter the wine was very much in the lap of the gods. Documents in the possession of Schloss Johannisberg show that in the early nineteenth century Rheingau wine remained on the lees for at least six months before being racked, and at Schloss Johannisberg the practice was to leave the wine alone for up to twelve months.[1] Alfred Langenbach, writing in the early 1960s, asserts that the better wines from the Rheingau often spent three to four years in cask, in order to develop the bouquet.[2] The same was true in the Mosel, where most wines would have spent three years in cask, and ageing periods of up to ten years were not unheard of.[3]

Dieter Greiner of Kloster Eberbach confirms that this was probably the case. Most Auslesen a century ago were dry wines with up to thirteen per cent alcohol, probably balanced with six to fifteen grams per litre of residual sugar, and rich in sugar-free extract; such top wines would have spent three years in cask. Interestingly, Morton Shand, writing in the 1920s, remarks that Rheingau wines were "usually not quite as sweet as other Rhine wines." Of course this begs the question, but it does suggest that it was not only the botrytis wines that tasted sweet. Beerenauslesen and TBAs would, of course, have been sweet, but probably less sweet than modern examples, because the fermentation might have continued for many months or even years, giving rather more alcohol and rather less sweetness. But there would have been no firm rules, because all depended on the quality and richness of the must and the temperature at which fermentation was taking place.

It was only with the advent of sterile filtration in the 1960s that it became possible to produce sweet wines with residual sugar levels of between fifteen and forty-five grams, balanced according to the wishes of the winemaker – and the market he was supplying. Before then, one way of stabilizing wines destined for export was to add a small amount of pure alcohol, but this practice was forbidden after 1971. In the Mosel, with its notoriously frigid cellars, fermentations often terminated while there was still unfermented sugar in the wine, and these were stabilized by huge doses of sulphur dioxide. Alternatively, the wine would be left in cask for up to three years to ensure the fermentation really was complete by the time the wine went into bottle. Sterile filtration was to prove a far more effective method of stabilization.

[1] Staab, Seeliger, and Schleicher, *Schloss Johannisberg*, p. 43.

[2] Langenbach, *German Wines and Vines*, p. 21.

[3] Loeb and Prittie, *Moselle*, p. 161.

There is some evidence that until the mid-eighteenth century grapes were often trodden in order to crush them. Oxidation would have been quite common in those days, because it seems only that in the twentieth century was the need to press the grapes rapidly acknowledged. In the late twentieth century there was another revision of ideas when it came to pressing the grapes. Geisenheim, and indeed many other research institutes worldwide, began to favour whole-cluster pressing. The drawback was that the volume of grapes that could be pressed at any one time was considerably reduced, because whole-cluster pressing by definition required the retention of stalks and stems. The solution was either to stagger the harvesting to ensure your presses could cope with the crop, or to buy additional presses, which was a costly option.

Not everyone favours whole-cluster pressing, despite the fact that it gives clean must that ferments easily. Winemakers such as Werner Knipser in the Pfalz believe that the presence of solids in the must is beneficial, and that excessively clean musts lead to short-lived wines. This theory is hard to prove or disprove, but there are certainly a number of respected winemakers who are very wary of whole-cluster pressing.

A few decades ago, "cleaning up" the must and the wine after fermentation was seen as a priority. Winemakers, especially at larger wineries that could afford hi-tech equipment, would clean the must after pressing, and then add selected yeasts to ensure the tanks fermented through to dryness. There were of course vintages in this northern wine zone when a lesser or greater proportion of the crop would be affected by rot, so some attempt to clean up the must, either by racking or filtration or centrifuging, was unavoidable. Sweetness levels could then be adjusted by the addition of *Süssreserve*. The centrifuge enjoyed considerable popularity in the 1970s and 1980s and has certainly not been abandoned. Used either on must or wine, it mechanically extracts and expels anything that has a specific gravity greater than the must, leaving the must or wine cleaned of impurities. This technique has often been criticized for being too brutal, thus stripping the wines of aroma and character. Not only is this denied by enthusiasts for the technology, but they also point out that it allows winemakers greatly to reduce the amount of sulphur dioxide employed during vinification, because centrifuging is a reductive technique.

The centrifuge may have declined in popularity, but a new method of must clarification has been adopted, known as "flotation." The must is pumped into a tall tank and covered with a neutral gas; the latter binds with any solids making them lighter so that they float to the top, from where they can be skimmed off. Alternatively, gelatin can be added, in which case the combined solids sink to the bottom of the tank.

Of course, there are many winemakers for whom swift and unproblematic fermentation is not the supreme goal. If a winery has to process a large number of lots, and get them into bottle early, then the use of cultivated yeasts and centrifuges or filters simplifies the task. Bernhard Breuer is one of those who deliberately doesn't want a rapid fermentation. He prefers to let the must ferment slowly with the indigenous yeasts. Although most wineries will have bottled simpler white wines by the spring, if not earlier, he doesn't even want to rack the wine before May. He admits that swifter fermentations and early bottling can result in vigorous wines with zesty primary aromas, but that is not the style that he personally wishes to make. Nor is he greatly bothered if small amounts of residual sugar are left in his wines, because he uses a large number of small tanks and can then blend different lots to assure a consistent style. Virtually nobody in the northern German vineyards of the Rheingau or Mosel bottle, completely dry wines, so occasional stuck fermentations are not a major headache. Before bottling the wines will usually be fined and filtered.

Dr Uwe Matheus, general manager of the Hans Wirsching estate in Franken, points out that in the more northerly wine zones it's feasible to vinify with indigenous yeasts, because the high natural acidity of the wine will protect it. But elsewhere, he argues, there is a microbiological risk, especially in southern Germany, where pH levels can be as high as 3.5. In his experience wines from southern Germany fermented with indigenous yeasts can be less pure and clean in flavour.

Winemakers such as Breuer clearly favour extended lees contact before racking. It's a stylistic choice, one that I happen to like, though there are countless delicious Rieslings that are vinified in a more hi-tech manner. Werner Knipser cautions that if you seek extended lees contact, then it's important to use wooden casks rather than stainless steel tanks, otherwise you risk reductive aromas and hydrogen sulphide in the wine.

Traditional estates use the small oval casks typical of their region: the 500-litre *Halbfuder* or 1,000-litre *Fuder* of the Mosel; and the 610-litre *Halbstück* or 1,200-litre *Stück* of the Rhineland. There are excellent winemakers who are passionate about retaining such casks for ageing the wine; there are, equally, many of the same calibre that prefer to work entirely with stainless steel tanks. It is possible to argue that the use of wood, even neutral wood, will give more complex and subtle wines, but so much depends on the choices and skills of the individual winemaker. There is therefore little point being dogmatic about either method.

Fritz Hallgarten's *Rhineland Wineland*, a study of German wines published in 1951, candidly mentioned the various techniques then employed during vinification, and thus reveals that manipulations of wine and must are not recent inventions. Calcium carbonate was often added to the wine as a form of deacidification; it works by combining with tartaric acid to form calcium tartrate, which crystallizes and sinks to the bottom of the tank, from where it can be removed. Carbon dioxide could be added *ad libitum* to freshen up a wine. (Many wineries today are perfectly happy to retain at bottling the natural carbon dioxide formed in the wine during fermentation. That is why Rieslings from J.J. Prüm, among others, have a distinct spritz for a year or two after bottling.) Hallgarten also noted that it was permitted to add up to 10 grams of tannin per 100 litres of wine "to make it more durable." Purified charcoal could also be added "to remove certain defects, counteract some diseases, and also to improve the wine's appearance." He also mentioned that high-grade spirit could be added to barrels destined for export, the limit being one per cent of the volume.[4]

One problem that confronts winemakers in northerly regions such as the Mosel is high acidity. It can be tolerated as a vintage characteristic, but tart green acidity can be unpleasant. Deacidification is legal and widely practiced, although the most scrupulous producers, such as Dr Carl von Schubert of Maximin Grünhaus, try to avoid it. "I haven't deacidified since 1987," he tells me, "and I avoid it by leaving bunches on the vine for as long as possible in order to bring acidity levels down."

The issue is complicated by the presence of two kinds of acidity in the grapes: malic and tartaric. Tartaric is the riper of the two, and malic

---

[4] Ibid, pp. 16–21.

can have a tart green-apple flavour that signals unripeness. Early in its ripening process, a grape will have a good deal of malic acidity and very little tartaric; as ripening continues, the proportion of tartaric increases. This is the kind of ripe toothsome acidity that all growers aspire to, but the only way to ensure its presence is to keep the grapes on the vine for as long as possible – what the Americans call long hang-time – but sometimes climatic conditions make that impossible.

Another method of reducing acidity in the wine is to allow it to go through malolactic fermentation, which converts the malic acid into lactic acid. Most Chardonnay will go through the malolactic, although producers who favour a leaner, more austere style block the fermentation deliberately, because they do not want the rich buttery tones that it imparts. Riesling almost never goes through the malolactic, because there is a risk that it will give the wine a flabbiness that will cancel out the typicity of the variety. Nonetheless there are some well regarded producers, such as Lingenfelder in the Pfalz and the Stadt Bensheim winery in the Hessische Bergstrasse, that use malo or partial malo for some of their wines. I have to say I do not think malolactic fermentation does varieties such as Riesling or Scheurebe any favours. Bernd Philippi of Koehler-Ruprecht in the Pfalz represents my view succinctly: "If you don't want acidity in your wine, produce Pinot Blanc instead of Riesling."

Günter Braun of the Biffar estate in the Pfalz observes: "Malolactic fermentation can give Riesling a buttery yogurt tone, depending on when the malo takes place. I did once allow the malolactic to occur when I was making the wines at Christmann, and I have to say that nobody could spot the wine in a line-up alongside non-malo Rieslings. Still, I think with Riesling you almost certainly lose aroma, although I see no problem with malolactic for varieties such as Pinot Blanc or Chardonnay."

Yet it seems probable that more and more Rieslings will be going through malolactic fermentation. There is a vogue for full-bodied wines, even from regions such as the Saar that are not renowned for the style, and one of the easiest methods of attaining more weight and power in the wine is to reduce the acidic structure. It's clear that malolactic fermentation is widely used by large companies. Johannes Selbach admits that his négociant wines are produced with partial malolactic fermentation, and Gerhard Grans of the Mosel, who believes that the best way to reduce excessive acidity is to harvest late, assures me that the technique is increasingly popular with very large producers.

As for red wines, there has been a radical improvement in technique and quality. Until the 1980s most red wines in Baden and Württemberg and elsewhere were made by the method known as *Maischeerhitzung*, which means that the must was heated to extract colour and flavour as rapidly as possible. Not surprisingly, the resulting wines lacked structure and longevity, but that didn't usually matter, because the producers using this method were invariably making red wines for immediate consumption. Heating the must had the other advantage of speed: tanks could be liberated after a few days in time for the arrival of the next batch from the vineyards.

All serious red wine producers today will use maceration rather than heating the must. This technique ties up the tanks for anything from five to thirty-five days, but gives far more complex wines. This is the same method used in almost all wine regions of the world, from Bordeaux to Coonawarra.

The Wine Law applies, of course, to red wines as well as to white, and this has led to some absurdities. It seems ridiculous to release whole ranges of red wines at different Prädikat levels. No Burgundian producer would dream of deliberately releasing a band of wines from not very ripe fruit, and then other tiers from richer musts. But that is still the German approach, because the assumption has become deeply embedded that ripeness levels are of primary importance. All red wine grapes should be ripe at harvest – that should go without saying – but it is false to assume that a parcel picked at a higher must weight than its neighbour will necessarily produce a superior wine. This emphasis on must weight rather than location and soil and, for that matter, flavour, is misguided.

When winemakers talk about their wines, they tend to regale the listener or taster with statistics: specifically, alcohol level, acidity level, and sugar-free extract. The last of these is hard to define because it refers to non-volatile substances in the wine, such as tannin, glycerol, and minerals. It translates into a density of flavour, a mineral intensity in the wine. It's often assumed that the higher the sugar-free extract, the greater the wine, and it's no accident that many TBAs have extremely high sugar-free extract levels. But Steffen Christmann from the Pfalz cautions against too great a reliance on such statistics: "Many of my colleagues are pointing out that in the very difficult vintage of 2000 they had higher extract levels than in the excellent 1999 vintage. That may be true, but we analysed our rotten grapes from Ruppertsberg, and we found they had much high sugar-free extract than our healthy grapes. So you can have high extract and lousy wine!"

The use of the recent technology of must concentration is as controversial in Germany as in France. Its legal status was fuzzy until recently, the only firm rule being that it could be used legally only for Tafelwein. Elsewhere it was permitted only on an experimental basis. At Von Buhl in the Pfalz I was told that concentration is permitted but that the wine has to be bottled as QbA. The technique is widely used in Baden, both at cooperatives and at some of the better private estates such as Johner. It is also employed in Württemberg. Adelmann is quite pleased with the results he obtained when he used it on a batch of Lemberger, and the Neipperg estate also has a must concentrator. In the summer of 2002 the situation was clarified, and must concentration was finally authorized in Germany, although the VDP instructed its members not to use the technique for more than five per cent of a wine. It is essentially a method of removing excess water from the must, which is useful when a potentially fine vintage is marred by rainfall. As it concentrates all elements in the wine, if there is rot or any imbalance in the must, that too will be heightened by using the technology. As in France, there are some wine estates adamantly opposed to the technique. The Fürst von Löwenstein estate, with properties in the Rheingau and Franken, is one of; Reinhard Löwenstein (no relation) of the Mosel is scornful about concentration: "It means you can pick your grapes at a potential alcohol of eleven per cent and concentrate to thirteen per cent. What that means is that you can make alcoholic wine from insufficiently ripe grapes, which is a disastrous formula."

Annegret Reh-Gartner of the Kesselstatt estate in the Mosel-Saar-Ruwer thinks concentration will not prove effective with Riesling, but can see its uses with the Pinot varieties and other grapes cultivated in southern Germany. "One aspect of concentration is that it makes complete nonsense of our wine law, which is based on ripeness levels at harvest. If you can alter them, upward, by concentration, then QmP levels become meaningless." Jürgen Hofmann, the winemaker at the giant company Reh-Kendermann, has his doubts about the practice, fearing that the focus of winemaking will be on power and body rather than elegance.

Although it is probable that German winemakers will remain fairly reliant on technology, there is also a growing recognition that manipulation and intervention can do little to make up for any failure to grow grapes of the highest quality. More attention is being paid to the vineyard, less to the bags of tricks in the winery and cellar. One of Germany's most respected and influential winemakers, Hans-Günther Schwarz of Müller-Catoir, provides a perfect metaphor: "You can take a jacket to the cleaners, and it will indeed come back cleaner. But it won't come back any more beautiful than the original jacket."

ROSÉ

There is an appreciative market for rosé wines in southern Germany. The best of them are made from Pinot Noir, a style of wine known as *Weissherbst*. It has become a handy way of using up grapes, especially bunches tainted by rot, that are not good enough for red wine. It originated in Baden, which wanted to copyright the name, if not the process. But the attempt failed, and Weissherbst is now encountered wherever red grapes are grown. It can be delicious, a light refreshing wine with a gentle aroma and flavour of red fruits. Occasionally very sweet wines are made from Spät-burgunder Weissherbst. Botrytis destroys pigment in grape skins, among other effects, so a botrytis-affected bunch can be vinified but will have a colour closer to rosé than red. In the Rheingau, the state domaine at Assmannshausen sometimes produces a costly Eiswein from Spätburgunder Weissherbst.

Württemberg has a pink wine of its own, known as *Schillerwein*, which is made by vinifying red and white grapes together.

SPARKLING WINES

The first company in Germany dedicated to the production of sparkling wines was called Kessler and was founded in Württemberg in 1826. In Germany low-quality sparkling wines are usually known as Schaumwein, whereas better quality sparkling wines are often known as Sekt. Although German Sekt does not have a high reputation internationally, it used to be both popular and expensive, because it was made by the traditional method, known in German as *Flaschengärung*. Its heyday was in the mid to late nineteenth century. Regions such as the Saar were better known for their Sekt production than for their table wines. Large quantities of sweetish "Sparkling Moselle" made their way to England and other export markets. Shortly before World War I, Kaiser Wilhelm imposed a tax on Sekt as a fund-raising measure, and I believe the tax still remains in force.

There was strong demand for sparkling wine in the late nineteenth and early twentieth centuries, but that is not to say it was always of good quality. Thomas Mann gives a splendid fictional account of such a wine in *The Confessions of Felix Krull*[5]: "My poor father owned the firm of Engelbert Krull, makers of the now discontinued brand of champagne *Loreley extra cuvée* . . . The compressed corks were secured with silver wire and gilt cords fastened with purplish-red wax; there was, moreover, an impressive round seal – such as one sees on ecclesiastical bulls and old state documents – suspended from a gold cord; the necks of the bottles were liberally wrapped in gleaming silver foil, and their swelling bellies bore a flaring label with gold flourishes round the edges. This label had been designed for the firm by my godfather Schimmelpreester, and bore a number of coats of arms and stars, my father's monogram, the brand, Loreley extra cuvée, all in gold letters, and a female figure, arrayed only in bangles and necklaces, sitting with legs crossed on top of a rock, her arms raised in the act of combing her flowing hair. Unfortunately it appears that the quality of the wine was not entirely commensurate with the splendour of its coiffure. 'Krull,' I have heard my godfather Schimmelpreester say to my father, 'with all due respect to you, your champagne ought to be forbidden by law . . . What sort of vinegar goes into that brew? And do you use petroleum or fusel oil to doctor it with? The stuff's simply poison.' "

German Sekt has a French-based terminology to denote dosage levels: 1 to 15 grams of residual sugar for Brut, 12–20 for Extra Dry, 17–35 for Dry, and 33–50 for Half-Dry. It will be noticed that these bands are overlapping, and this allows for varying taste perceptions, and enables winemakers to match the labelling, to some extent, to the wine's flavour profile and structure.

[5] I am indebted to Julian Jeffs for drawing my attention to this passage.

There is a great deal of poor quality sparkling wine produced in Germany, most of it from raw material imported from other countries. Look out for the words "Deutscher Sekt" on the label, which at least guarantees that the produce is made from German grapes. The term was introduced in 1986. Almost all Sekt today is produced by the tank method or "transfer" system, and *Flaschengärung* wines are produced either in limited quantities by the large producers or as a sideline by good estates throughout Germany. Demand has never been stronger, and twice as much sparkling wine is produced in Germany as in the Champagne region.

However, there are some exceptional examples as well, though they are expensive, because they tend to be aged on the lees for many years. Very few of these wines leave Germany, but I have tried to indicate some of the more interesting sparkling wines in the directory that follows.

SWEET WINES

The regulations covering the production of sweet wines have been outlined in the chapter on the wine laws. This is a very important sector of German wine production because of the unique styles of these wines and, from top producers, their superlative quality. Although some first-rate sweet wines are made from varieties such as Silvaner, Rieslaner, and Pinot Gris, it is Riesling that is behind the most typical and rarest of German sweet wines. That's because of its acidity, the crucial balancing factor that can cut through the richest texture.

Late-harvesting has been established in Germany since the late eighteenth century, if not earlier, because it seems probable that some of the legendary wines that survive in the Bremen Ratskeller and in rare bottles from Würzburger Stein were very sweet at the outset. The great estates of the Rheingau produced magnificent wines (TBAs, though they might not have been labelled as such at the time), followed from 1921 onward by the Mosel.

Eiswein is perhaps the most bizarre of the sweet wine styles, deriving from grapes frozen on the vine. Such wines emerged by accident from time to time. The Staatliche Hofkeller in Würzburg claims to have made one in 1835, and there are reports of Eiswein from Traben-Trarbach in the Mosel in 1842 and again in 1846. J.J. Prüm made an Eiswein in

Wehlen in 1949. It was in 1961 that numerous estates produced Eiswein in the Mosel, and the fashion was under way. But these were regarded as freak occurrences, rather than winemaking triumphs – it was only from the 1970s that growers, discovering the appeal such wines had to rich consumers with a sweet tooth, deliberately planned for their production, introducing, for example, netting or plastic sheeting to protect the vines from birds and other predators, and from heavy rain. When plastic sheeting is used, as at Maximin Grünhaus, there are micro-pores in the plastic to allow ventilation to get through to the vines.

Until 1982, any quality level could be labelled as Eiswein, provided that the grapes were sufficiently frozen at harvesting. It soon became apparent in the 1970s that a Spätlese Eiswein, for example, was insufficiently ripe to sustain the high acidity of an Eiswein; the regulations were changed to require the must to be of at least Beerenauslese quality.

Varietal character is less important for Eiswein, although Riesling still reigns supreme in this style too. But there are good Eisweine from Silvaner and other varieties, and, surprisingly, from Pinot Noir. This is partly because the bunches cling to the vine throughout the winter, whereas other varieties, including Riesling, have a greater tendency to drop off. It is even possible to pick Eiswein grapes by machine, as Rheinhessen producer Guntrum has shown.

To some extent the popularity of Eiswein may have been encouraged by producers, because such wines are easier to produce than BA or TBA, which need to be picked so selectively. Eiswein, however, involves drama: will the prolonged freeze arrive before the grapes rot? And tales of family and friends arriving at an estate on a frosty night at four in the morning to pick grapes make for excellent copy in newsletters. On the other hand, there is a strong element of risk: a devastating attack by birds or an outbreak of rot on vines carefully nurtured for Eiswein production can reduce the crop to zero.

A leading grower in the Pfalz showed me the rows of vines set aside for Eiswein. I was surprised to see that the vines were more charged with bunches than those destined for dry wines. It was explained to me that this was so that any bunches that attracted rot later in the growing season could be cut out, and there would still, with any luck, be some usable bunches left. This may be a sensible way to lessen the risk, but it seems to me that the must will lose in concentration if too many bunches are left on the vine. It is also easier to produce Eiswein on flatter sites, because they are more prone to frost. Germany's best vineyards, with a few exceptions, are on slopes. Whereas a great BA or TBA can only be made from an outstanding site, a good Eiswein can be made from a mediocre one. I doubt that Dirk Richter would claim that his Mülheimer Helenenkloster is an outstanding vineyard, but it produces excellent Eiswein almost every year.

Heinz Wagner in the Saar points out that sometimes, as in 2001, there are some light frosts – too light to harvest legally for Eiswein – that occur before the deep frost needed for Eiswein. That means the grapes freeze partially, then thaw. He believes that an attempt to make Eiswein should be abandoned at that point, because otherwise the grapes can develop a "frost tone" that lacks the limpidity expected from a great Eiswein. But most producers are less scrupulous, or do not accept Wagner's view.

In general the best Eisweine are made earlier rather than later. There is no virtue in picking grapes in January or February, although from time to time that is a consequence of the late arrival of frost. In November or early December there is a far higher chance that the grapes will be healthy. Whereas noble rot is essential for BA or TBA, it is undesirable for Eiswein, although some producers will tolerate a small amount and believe it can give some additional complexity to the wine.

BEERENAUSLESE AND TROCKENBEERENAUSLESE

These highly concentrated wines have traditionally been made from botrytis-affected grapes, but not necessarily. The 1971 Law required a minimum must weight of 150 Oechsle, from all regions. There have been vintages such as 1990 when grapes attained high must weights but were not heavily marked by noble rot. If many Auslesen and some BAs can be made from late-picked but essentially healthy grapes, it is virtually impossible to achieve the high must weights of TBA without botrytis. And noble rot also contributes its own panoply of flavours and textures.

The 1971 Wine Law did considerable damage to the image of the great German sweet wines. The proliferation of crossings that routinely attained high must weights led to the production of substantial quantities of very sweet wines from grapes such as Albalonga and Ortega. They certainly had high residual sugar levels, but they lacked the finesse and length of flavour that Riesling, in particular, confers. Despite the overproduction of mediocre sweet wines, the connoisseurs who adore, and can afford, the genuine article, have been spoiled for choice, and almost all high-quality producers aim, when vintage conditions permit, to make nobly sweet wines, even if in minute quantities.

As for TBA, its appeal is its extremity. The harvesting is painstaking, with individual shrivelled berries being picked; sometimes it is done at the same time as the "normal" harvest, with the botrytized grapes going into a separate and much smaller basket. This is likely to occur when botrytis arrives early in the ripening season. Alternatively, the harvesters can be dispatched at the appropriate moment with the sole aim of picking these precious berries. Whatever method is used, the process is extremely costly in terms of labour. Wolfgang Schleicher of Schloss Johannisberg recalls that in 1967 thirty pickers obtained a grand total of thirty litres of TBA after picking on a single day. That explains why in most vintages when TBA can be obtained at all, quantities are very low, rarely exceeding 200 litres for any vineyard. That in turn explains why prices are so high. The resulting wines are immortal: their ultra-high residual sugar (at must weights of 200 Oechsle or more it is scarcely possible for the juice to ferment), extract, and acidity will ensure that.

Depending on their region of origin, BA and TBA can vary enormously in style. Those from Baden or the Pfalz tend to be dark-coloured and unctuous, almost syrupy; in contrast, those from the Saar tend to be paler, more crystalline and intense, and require years to develop their extraordinary complexity. TBAs will always be connoisseurs' wines because of their scarcity and cost. Estates that make them do not expect to make a profit, despite their very high prices. They are produced to show what can be accomplished by taking winemaking to a remarkable extreme. To me, they are objects of wonder: how did simple grapes come to be transformed into a liquid with such an extraordinary aroma and flavour? We drink them with awe and gratitude.

4

Going to Market

With the new Wine Law in place in 1971, the German marketing authorities set about promoting and selling their wines. Yet it has to be said that the marketing of German wine has been a spectacular own goal. Perhaps it was hard to imagine it could have been otherwise, because the Law promulgated the manifestly absurd notion that all sites were potentially equal, that all grape varieties were equal, that sugar levels were the sole determinant of quality in wine, and that it was permissible to deceive the consumer by hijacking famous names in order to sell poor quality wines.

In some respects the marketing of German wines under their new classification could be seen as a triumph. In Britain, at any rate, impressive quantities were sold, and the gentle sweetness of many of the wines attracted a loyal following. The only problem was that the wines were being sold at rock-bottom prices, comparable to industrial Lambrusco. Those who rejoiced in the flavour and price of mass-market German wine were happy with what they were drinking, and were not remotely tempted to trade up. If Moselblümchen or the brand of their choice was a "quality wine," then why bother to spend more?

German wine remained closeted within a loyal but unbudging sector of the market. The large wholesalers and cooperatives who turned out the stuff were perfectly happy. But the consequences were appalling. First, the great estate Rieslings of Germany became niche wines, much admired by certain journalists and a small segment of discerning drinkers who understood their true quality and unique character. Second, the image of German wines as a whole took a nosedive. For good reason, they became regarded as "naff." Inevitably the fine wines of Germany were tarred with the same brush. To this day, I cannot recall being served a German wine at a private dinner party, except when the host was a wine merchant or journalist.

The German marketing authorities had made one crucial error, from which their campaigns have yet to recover: they led from the bottom. Crudely put, the French sell their wines by saying: "Here is Château Margaux, and here is Château d'Yquem, and here is Chambertin. These are the world's finest wines. But we understand that not everyone can afford to drink them. Perhaps you would enjoy instead a charming Chinon, a racy Sancerre, or a juicy Côte du Rhône?" In contrast, the German approach has been: "Looking for a bargain? Here's our Green Tower sugar-blend, and it's only £2 per bottle. It's a quality wine, so grab it while stocks last." And on the subject of great estate wines: silence.

If you market primarily on the grounds of cheapness and value for money, then you need to be able to point to the next step on the journey. When it comes to German wine exports, there is dirt cheap wine and there is expensive wine; there is nothing in between. Dr Dirk Richter, a successful grower and négociant from Mülheim in the Mosel, is well aware of this problem: "In Germany there is too great a gap between the great wines at the top and the poor wines at the bottom. With French wine, a Beaujolais fan may move on to enjoy fine burgundy or Rhône. With Liebfraumilch wines, the only wines they are likely to move onto are Chardonnays from Australia or South Africa, not to fine Mosel or Pfalz Rieslings."

The notorious complexity of the German wine label has also deterred consumers. A label of a good German wine will almost certainly have to state: the producer, the region, the vintage, the grape variety, the vineyard name, the quality band (such as Kabinett), and the style (such as Trocken). That's a lot of information for any consumer to decode.

Many top producers are well aware of this, and there are countless initiatives by individual estates to simplify their labelling. Many estates, including some of the finest, have eliminated lesser sites from the label, and blended their output into a wine sold as Estate Riesling (*Gutsriesling*) without any vineyard designation. This also has the advantage of creating a wine that can be produced in reasonable quantity. If an estate bottles the production of all its different vineyards separately, the consequence is a large number of small-volume wines that may be easy to sell to connoisseurs and loyal customers, but impossible to sell to multiple retailers or chains.

Annegret Reh-Gartner has been running the Kesselstatt estate in the Mosel-Saar-Ruwer for almost twenty years. In 1983, it consisted of one hundred ha (247 acres). Under her stewardship the number of wines has been reduced, and the estate itself has shrunk to forty-two ha (104 acres). Originally, the estate owned vines in thirty-five different vineyards, but sites that were not of outstanding quality, or that had no renown outside the village where they were located, were sold off or leased; in some cases they were retained to supply wine for the Estate Rieslings. Only top sites were identified on the label: Piesporter Goldtröpfchen, Bernkasteler Doktor, Kaseler Nies'chen, Scharzhofberger, Josephshöfer, and a handful of others.

This approach made sense from a number of points of view. It meant the consumer or retailer was no longer confronted each year with a hundred or more new wines from which to choose. From the estate's point of view, it was easier to market reasonable volumes of high-quality wines, as well as Estate Rieslings that were aimed either at the bargain-hunter or, in the case of the Palais Kesselstatt brand, at the restaurant market.

Some estates initiated their own hierarchy. Peter Kühn, an outstanding producer in the Rheingau, offers a selection of wines that begins, at the simplest level, with Rheingau Riesling. The next quality level is Oestricher Riesling, and his best wines are labelled under the single vineyards of origin, Doosberg and Lenchen. For vintages from 2000 on, he also availed himself of the new Erstes Gewächs classification in the Rheingau. This is all perfectly sensible and relatively simple. The inevitable problem is that different estates have initiated different "simplifications" and it is difficult for the consumer, even within a single region, to compare like with like.

Nonetheless the general impulse is to simplify, and estates that have adopted regional classifications often label their "first growth" wines simply with the name of the vineyard and the vintage, consigning all other information to a back label. This assumes a certain level of vineyard recognition on the part of the consumer, aided of course by the fact that these top bottlings usually come with a high price tag attached.

This kind of solution, based on a qualitative hierarchy founded on site rather than sugar levels, is certainly a step in the right direction. It is also inherently elitist, and as such poses a problem for the wine marketing authorities, who need to be inclusive, especially because most of their funding comes not from the small quality-conscious estates but from the large wholesalers and cooperatives.

With enormous fanfare, the German Wine Institute launched its latest initiative in 2001 at the major German wine fair called ProWein, held in Düsseldorf. It announced two new categories of wine beginning with the 2000 vintage: Classic and Selection. The rules and regulations for each are lengthy and complex, and need not be spelt out here in any great detail. Classic is essentially a good quality QbA and has to be a varietal wine made from a grape variety that has a proven track record in the region of origin, effectively eliminating dubious wines made from crossings. It is up to each region to select the eligible varieties. The maximum permitted residual sugar level is 15 grams per litre. The labels are intended to be a model of clarity, citing only grape variety, region and producer.

Selection is a higher-quality style, and the grapes must have a minimum potential alcohol of 12.2 per cent. The maximum yield for Selection vines is sixty hl/ha (24.3 hl/acre) and the grapes must be hand-picked from a single vineyard. The maximum residual sugar level is 12 grams per litre. Both wines are supposed to present a move away from the oversweet styles of the past, but many of the wines at the higher end of the residual sugar scale can taste distinctly sweet, depending, as always, on the strength of the acidity. However, the word Trocken does not appear on the label. All Classic and Selection wines are subject to approval by a tasting panel. By spring 2002 some 350 growers had signed up to the Classic programme.

Quite a few good estates have released wines under one or both of these new labels, such as Selbach-Oster in the Mosel, Diel and Kruger-Rumpf in the Nahe. Many of the wines that I have tasted are of sound or even excellent quality. But it is fair to ask whether this initiative is going to prove effective. Its goal, after all, is not to improve the quality of German wine, because estates such as those cited above have been making fine wine for decades, but to give a boost to the image of German wine and to encourage consumers to try them. Carl-Josef Loewen in the Mosel produced a Classic Riesling, but found that it was perceived as a mass-market rather than a good-quality wine; he was content with the quality, but as a marketing venture it was fairly disastrous.

I recall reading through the press pack after the Düsseldorf launch, and I also recall that half an hour later I couldn't remember a word of it. If a writer with a fair knowledge of the German wine scene can't keep the new criteria in his head, what chance has the regular consumer? Of course, no one needs to know by heart the rules for an appellation or style (try asking a grower in the Coteaux d'Aix-en-Provence which grape varieties are permitted in the appellation, and then watch him struggle to reply), but the new terms have to mean something to the would-be purchaser.

It is not immediately apparent that Selection is a higher category than Classic, although price and packaging may indicate the difference. Nor is it clear that a varietal wine without the word Classic on the label is going to prove harder to sell than one which has. Because everyone agrees that the average German wine label needs simplification, is the creation of two new categories a move in this direction, or the precise opposite? With top estates in some regions moving toward a First Growth classification, how will the consumer perceive the difference between a high-priced First Growth and a high-priced Selection?

It must also be remembered that many estates, including most cooperatives in Baden, have introduced their own internal quality bands, quite a few employing the words Classic or Selection. Under the new regulations, such producers are allowed to retain these words on their labels for a further ten years. This is, of course, asking for trouble, because a cooperative's Selection range may well be distinctly inferior in quality to a Selection as defined by the new rules.

Perhaps the sceptics, myself included, will be proved wrong, and if, at Classic level, it makes possible the marketing of good, attractively packaged wines at sensible prices, then that can only be of benefit to the German wine industry and its tarnished image.

It has to be said that when it comes to simplification, most German wine producers are their own worst enemy. Understanding the wines of Burgundy is far from easy, but the hierarchy of supposed quality is not that complicated. What's more, there are only two grape varieties to worry about, and everyone makes wines in roughly the same style: dry.

Germany's best growers share the Burgundian passion for *terroir*. A top

Mosel producer would not dream of blending his Graacher Domprobst with his Wehlener Sonnenuhr because he knows the sites yield wines of different nuances and structure. This is the exact equivalent of a Burgundian grower having separate bottlings for his Volnay Santenots and his Volnay Champans. All this can make life quite difficult for the consumer, but those who cannot be bothered with the intricacies of the system can always settle for a Village wine from Burgundy or an Estate or Village Riesling from Germany.

The complication I am referring to in Germany is stylistic. I have in front of me the price list from one of Baden's top cooperatives, Winzergenossenschaft Königschaffhausen. Looking only for Pinot Noir, I first alight on six rosé wines from the variety: a QbA, a Kabinett, a Kabinett Trocken, a Spätlese, a Spätlese Trocken, and an Auslese. This list is followed by two red Pinot Noirs: a QbA and a QbA Trocken. But there is more: a rosé Eiswein, and two more Pinots, one rosé, the other red, under the Selection category. In addition there is a barrique-aged Pinot, and four more Pinots, two red, two rose, in inexpensive litre bottles. That makes a total of sixteen different wines from Pinot. Nor is this in any way atypical of a Baden cooperative.

When I ask cooperative directors why they have so many wines on offer each year (there can easily be a total of 300), I am told that there is demand for each style, so they feel bound to supply each style. The production of simple rosés or red wines with a dab of residual sugar is a canny way to disguise poor-quality or overcropped fruit, but hardly inspires confidence. Were I a cooperative director, I would produce the traditional litre bottling as a kind of jug wine, a dry rosé, and from the best grapes I would produce a red oak-aged Pinot . Were I to do that, I would probably be fired after a visit from a delegation of local customers who want their sweet rosé back on the list.

I asked Matthias Müller from the Mittelrhein why he, and most of his neighbours, offered so many wines: "My customers want to be able to taste a wide range of wines when they come here, even if they end up buying the same wine they usually buy. I did once simplify my range, and all that happened was that customers who weren't able to find the style of wine they usually bought from me went elsewhere."

If cooperatives and growers are merely supplying a local market, then none of this would matter greatly. But many of them have their eye on

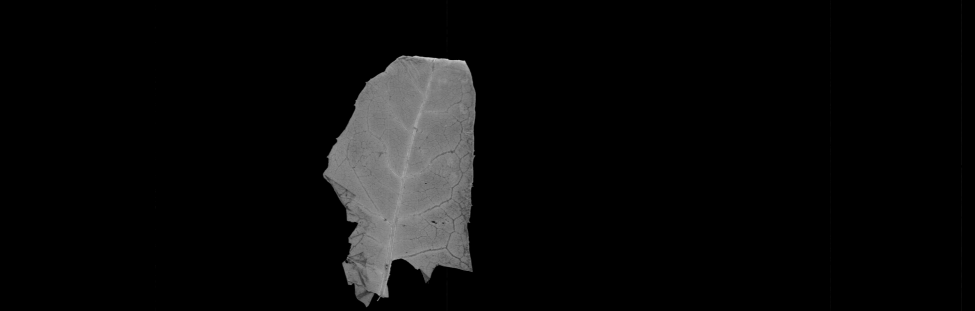

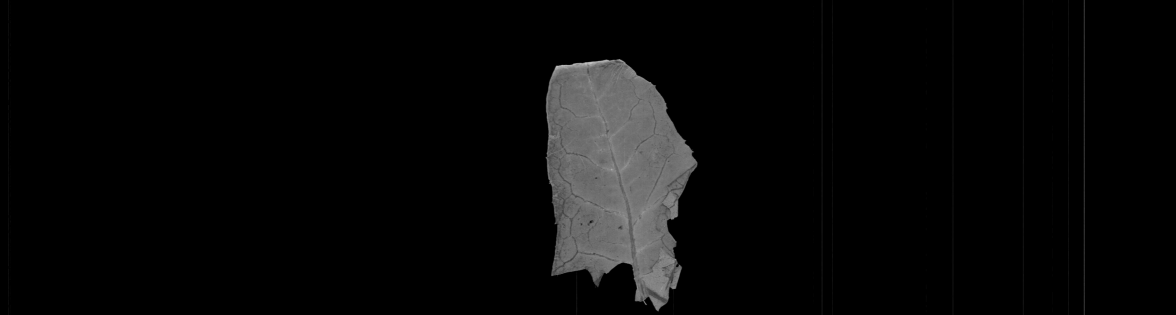

export markets. This is bound to be an uphill struggle, both because many of these wine styles have no appeal outside the region, and because the cake has been divided into so many segments that no single wine can be produced in sufficient volume to attract a serious importer.

Nor is the problem restricted to cooperatives and other large producers. The list from Deutzerhof, an outstanding estate in the Ahr, presents a similar picture. From the year 2000, and from nine ha (22.2 acres) which also contain at least three other grape varieties, there are two dry Pinots, both QbA, and two QbA rosés. There is also a Selection Caspar C, and a single vineyard bottling. At the Künstler estate in Hochheim, better known for its mighty Rieslings, there are no fewer than six Pinot Noirs on the list, four of them rosés. Presumably the owners of these estates have good reason for offering so many wines, and in cases where a particular *terroir* demands to be highlighted, such diversity can certainly be justified. But still I wonder: four rosés from one small estate?

Dieter Greiner is the director of the enormous Kloster Eberbach domaine in the Rheingau. Before he took on that job in 2000 he worked for the German Wine Institute. When I asked him about the excessive choice on wine lists, he replied: "The old traditional drinkers with their fondness for certain sites or styles are dying out." That may well be the case, though there is little evidence on the wine lists of southern German producers to back up this view. But where are the drinkers who are going to replace them? Greiner admits there's a problem: "At present younger drinkers don't drink German wines. They drink beer, and in northern Germany they always have. What is worrying is that even in parts of Germany where wine drinking is part of the culture, young people are more likely to drink an Italian Pinot Grigio than a good Riesling. That means it's crucial for wine producers to make wines and improve the packaging so as to appeal to a new generation, which certainly doesn't lack purchasing power."

Some years ago the leading Rheinhessen estate of Gunderloch leased a neighbouring estate, Anton Balbach. Fritz Hasselbach, the owner and winemaker at Gunderloch, wanted to differentiate the Balbach wines from the traditional Gunderloch ones. So he created wines such as a white Burgundian field blend and a Silvaner italianized on the label as Silvana; the labels are jazzy and clearly intended to appeal to younger drinkers seeking wines that are vigorous and tasty but not over-complex. The exercise does seem rather like a great operatic tenor recording an album of *The Best of Robbie Williams*. I have no idea whether Hasselbach has succeeded with this range, though I certainly wish him luck.

Focusing on packaging can be commendable; it can also be necessary. But it can sometimes compound the problem that consumers have little idea what to expect from a German wine. In an act of apparent desperation, certain négociant producers and their supermarket clients have gone out of their way to disguise the identity of the German wines they are trying to sell. This they do by adopting brand names such as Devil's Rock and others like it that are not remotely Germanic. Even worse, the wines are sold in Bordeaux bottles rather than the traditional German flutes. This is presumably because market research conducted by a British PR agency confirmed that a German wine poured from a Bordeaux bottle scored better among ordinary wine drinkers than the same wine poured from a flute. Yet Australian producers are enjoying something of a Riesling revival on export markets, even though the vast majority of the wines are bottled in flutes. It is all very confusing, but what it boils down to is that the great majority of British consumers, in particular, have a steadfastly negative image of German wines, despite all the efforts of the German Wine Institute and the expertise of the public relations companies.

There has been much discussion as to why this should be so. The Italian wine industry also dispatches some very mediocre wines to export markets, and its system of appellations and the multiplicity of its grape varieties are every bit as complicated as those of Germany, yet its image is positive. It is sometimes suggested that the British, in particular, have no affection for Germany and are not disposed to buy its products. But a look at the number of German cars on British roads soon dispels that view. More plausibly, it has been suggested that Italy, France, and Spain are popular holiday destinations, and tourists return with fond memories of the food and wine. Very few Britons spend their holidays in Germany. Similarly, there are virtually no German restaurants outside Germany, and thus no perfect context for the sale and consumption of German wines alongside good food.

German wine seems incapable of breaking out of this circle. Most wine is now bought in supermarkets, but the range of German wines available from British supermarkets and high-street chains, with very few exceptions, is dire. Liebfraumilch is still on the shelves, and large-volume wines such as Baden Dry or Fire Mountain Riesling are hardly of exceptional quality. New wines, such as St Ursula's "Almond Grove" are packaged in a Bordeaux bottle, with nothing to suggest from a distance that the wine is German. This strikes me as more a failure of nerve than a striking marketing initiative. The finest wines from Germany are certainly available in Britain, but only from a handful of specialist merchants such as Lay & Wheeler and Justerini & Brooks. The consequence is that there is very little opportunity for the average winelover to encounter fine German wine.

Another difficulty is that the great majority of German wine available in Britain is made in a lightly sweet style. Many of these wines, especially from the Mosel, are delicious, but they are not food-friendly. Yes, one can think of matches for a Scharzhofberger Spätlese, but it's not obvious. In 2001 a British wine merchant, with great enterprise, launched an excellent list of wines from top estates. When I asked him why there was scarcely a single dry wine on the list, he replied that there was a following for lightly sweet wines, even if not in great quantities, whereas top-quality dry wines were at least double the price and in competition with, for example, the wines of Alsace.

So, in the British market at any rate, German wines are stuck in a rut, and it's not easy to see how they will emerge from it. Advertising campaigns have been launched to persuade British consumers that German wines are drier than they were in the past, and, by implication, better. This may well be the case, but the dry wines on the supermarket shelves don't seem markedly superior in quality to the bad old blends.

In Britain, there is a hugely successful television programme called *Big Brother*, in which twelve nonentities volunteer to be incarcerated in a "house" where they are given inane tasks to perform. In a 2002 edition of the show, the inmates spent their drinks allowance on Black Tower. According to *Decanter* (October 2002), "their wine of choice, Black Tower, is now flying off the supermarket shelves. When deciding on Champagne, the foursome even opted for Laurent Perrier rather than Dom Pérignon so they could afford more Black Tower. 'We had a very positive response from consumers at a recent promotional tasting – they have seen it on *Big Brother*,' says brand manager Oliver Dickie."

From which it is reasonable to conclude that spending zillions on an advertising campaign to improve the image of German wines has got precisely nowhere.

Perhaps it doesn't matter. Most of the top German estates can get along quite nicely without help from the British. If they don't buy the wines, others will.

5

The Grape Varieties of Germany

Germany is indelibly associated with Riesling, and it remains true that this variety is responsible for its most sublime wines. But the vineyards of Germany are dispersed, and there are regions where Riesling is either not suited to the climate or has to play second fiddle to more reliable and successful varieties. Franken is the heartland of Silvaner, and the Burgundian varieties thrive all the way from the Pfalz down through Baden. Here and there other specialities crop up: Rieslaner in the Pfalz and Franken, Gutedel in the Markgräflerland. All these varieties will be discussed below.

What has complicated the German wine scene greatly is the profusion of crossings devised, tested, and propagated by research institutes. It was, and still is, a lengthy process: it can take twenty years or so for a new crossing to be tested, approved, and released. Some crossings are in decline, but new ones are being tested and planted all the time. Crossings are nothing new, and the earliest ones date from the 1870s. In marginal wine regions, growers have constantly searched for ways to improve the durability of their vines. Today clonal selection will help provide material with the best resistance to frost or disease or any other desired character-istic. (And in the future, if some German researchers have their way, genetic modification will perform the same job even more effectively.)

In the nineteenth and early twentieth centuries the best way to "improve" a variety and instil what a marketing man would today call "added value" was to cross it. The destructive onslaught of the phylloxera louse in the latter half of the nineteenth century showed just how susceptible the humble vine was to the even more humble bug. No wonder that growers would yearn for cuttings that, if not themselves immune to phylloxera, would at least stand up against other threats and, if possible, ensure higher yields as an insurance against the ravages of disease and nature.

The only problem was that most of these crossings performed every service except that of producing good wine. In the 1980s and 1990s it became increasingly evident that vast yields and immense crops did little more than ensure low prices that would in the long term drive grape farmers out of business. At Geisenheim, research into new crossings has been largely replaced, according to Professor Monika Christmann, the head of the oenology department, by research into clonal selection. But down in Württemberg, at Weinsberg, viticulturalists are releasing a string of new crossings, red rather than white, most of them intended to boost the colour and tannins of German red wines. Meanwhile in the Pfalz, at Siebeldingen, fungus-resistant crossings such as Regent have been created and propagated.

In terms of nationwide distribution Riesling remains the dominant variety in Germany, accounting for 21.4 per cent of plantings. It is closely followed by Müller-Thurgau, with 19.8 per cent. Pinot Noir is the most popular red, with 8.3 per cent, but the drab Portugieser still accounts for 4.7 per cent of German vineyards. Dornfelder occupies 3.6 per cent and is growing fast.

Until 1994 certain "international" varieties were prohibited in Germany. In that year, however, EU law took precedence in such matters over German law, and it became legal to plant such varieties as Sauvignon Blanc and Syrah, although surprisingly few growers have taken advantage of this.

White varieties

ALBALONGA
Created in Würzburg from Rieslaner x Silvaner, this crossing was mainly planted in Rheinhessen. Although late budding and fairly early ripening, it is also susceptible to botrytis. It can deliver a tasty wine when the grapes reach full ripeness, but these days it is encountered less and less.

AUXERROIS
This Alsatian variety, vaguely related to Pinot Blanc, is also found in the Kraichgau region of Baden, where some twenty ha (49.4 acres) are

planted; in Rheinhessen, Gutzler makes a varietal version. In all there are no more than eighty-three ha (205 acres).

BACCHUS
Created in 1959 by Dr Husfeld of Geilweilerhof from (Silvaner x Riesling) x Riesling, the aromatic Bacchus became very popular in the 1970s and 1980s, and by 1983 there were 3,500 ha (8,649 acres) planted, mostly in Rheinhessen but also in Franken, where to this day it accounts for twelve per cent of vineyards. Plantings have only declined very slightly and now stand at 3,200 ha (7,907 acres). Although it seems able to grow just about anywhere, Bacchus has many drawbacks, such as low acidity, and susceptibility to frosts and to rot. In poor years it doesn't always ripen properly, especially if cropped at more than eighty hl/ha (thirty-two hl/acre). It has proved successful in England, which is not necessarily a recommendation.

BLAUER SILVANER
A mutation from Franken. In 1964 the father of Martin Steinmann of Schloss Sommerhausen identified a single vine and recreated the variety and replanted it. The skin colour is unstable so it always produces a white wine.

CHARDONNAY
Authorized since the early 1990s, Chardonnay has not proved as popular as one might have expected; there were 400 ha (988 acres) throughout Germany in 1997, and by 2000 there were 600 ha (1,483 acres), mostly in the Pfalz and Baden. Many growers who toyed with Chardonnay have returned to Pinot Blanc, which gives higher yields and is simpler to vinify. Chardonnay also needs more hang-time, so there's a greater element of risk than with Pinot Blanc. The most serious Chardonnay growers such as Wittmann have sought out good French clones in preference to humdrum and overproductive clones supplied by Geisenheim, which have the additional flaw of excessive acidity levels. Some producers have remained loyal to Chardonnay on marketing grounds, because there is demand among German restaurants for drinkable native Chardonnays, which have more cachet than Weisser Burgunder.

CLEVNER

See Frühburgunder (p. 76) and Gewürztraminer.

EHRENFELSER

This crossing was developed at Geisenheim in 1929 from Riesling x Silvaner, and is found mostly in the Pfalz and Rheinhessen. It ripens slightly earlier than Riesling, and is a touch more generous in its yields. Like Riesling, it will survive long autumns and deliver decent quality late harvest wines. What it lacks is the vibrant acidity of good Riesling. Nonetheless, Ehrenfelser should be counted among the best of the Geisenheim crossings. It is in gradual decline, and there are no more than 230 ha (568 acres) in production.

ELBLING

This ancient variety may well have been brought to the upper reaches of Mosel Valley by the Romans in the fourth century. Its high acidity and lack of obvious flavour made it highly regarded in the past for sparkling wine. Although a very high-yielding and distinctly neutral variety, it has its uses in northern Germany because it will ripen in places where even Riesling can't reach ripeness. Thin skins make it susceptible to disease and rot. Plantings have remained steady for some years at 1,000 ha (2,471 acres).

FABER (FABERREBE)

Faber was created by Georg Scheu at Alzey in 1929 as a crossing of Pinot Blanc x Müller-Thurgau. By 1984 there were 2,300 ha (5,683 acres) planted, mostly in Rheinhessen, but also in the Nahe. Its main distinction lies in its acidity levels, which are higher than either Müller-Thurgau or Silvaner, although it ripens earlier and gives good yields. The wines can be quite good but lack personality, and Faber is falling from favour, with 1,500 ha (3,707 acres) in production.

FINDLING

This mutation of Müller-Thurgau is early ripening and attains good must weights, though it can't match the yields of Müller-Thurgau itself. But it has never really caught on, and by the 1990s, there were only forty-six ha (114 acres) planted, mainly in the Mosel. I have never tasted Findling, but its wine is said to be thoroughly neutral.

FREISAMER

An early crossing, Freisamer was created in Freiburg from Silvaner x Pinot Gris in 1916. It has been planted mostly in Baden. Although susceptible to spring frosts and oidium, it resists rot well and can be picked late at high sugar levels. Its principal booster, Bernhard Huber, says it won a reputation for unripe wines, because it was usually cropped at one hundred hl/ha (40.5 hl/acre); keep yields to forty to fifty hl/ha (sixteen to twenty hl/acre), as he does, and you can get fourteen per cent alcohol.

GELBER ORLEANS

In the nineteenth century this was a popular grape in the Rheingau and accounted for about one-quarter of all Rüdesheimer plantings in the 1870s and was also found at Johannisberg. It had very large berries and thick skins that resisted diseases; it also liked heat. Morton Shand wrote of it with enthusiasm: "This fine vine, which only ripens fully in the warmest and most chosen situations, lends to the wines of Rüdesheim its dark colour and most un-Riesling and grapey flavour." The variety was almost extinct, and the last known bottling was by the state domaine in Eltville in 1921. However, it has been revived in Rüdesheim by Bernhard Breuer, who planted it on the Schlossberg and made his first barrel of Orleans in 2000.

It has also been revived in the Pfalz by Knipser, who explains its decline by the fact that it ripens two weeks later than Riesling. He propagated some cuttings from Kloster Eberbach and now has 700 plants. The wines have high acidity, and an aroma of apples. Knipser's 1999 Spätlese Trocken was fresh, crisp, and charming, but his 1996 Gelber Orleans Eiswein was fiercely acidic.

GEWÜRZTRAMINER (TRAMINER)

The variety is mostly planted in Pfalz and Baden, where it gets the warmth it needs, and it thrives on the loess soils of the Kaiserstuhl. There are various clones at large, so its character can vary; that planted in Sachsen seems to give less pungent wine. In Baden it is most commonly encountered in Durbach, where it is known locally as Clevner.

The wine does not fetch high prices, so many growers are tempted to overcrop. Perhaps as a consequence, German Gewürztraminer never seems to attain the opulence and headiness of the best examples from Alsace. On the other hand it can have better acidity and a more discreet structure, making it better suited to food. By 2000, there were 850 ha (2,100 acres), of which almost half were planted in the Pfalz.

GOLDRIESLING
This nineteenth century crossing is a speciality of Sachsen. It has the advantage of ripening early, but gives unexceptional wine with a spicy nose.

GRAUER BURGUNDER (GRAUBURGUNDER)
See Pinot Gris.

GUTEDEL
This long-established variety, known elsewhere as Chasselas, is believed to have made its first appearance in Baden in 1780. It used to be widely planted in the Pfalz too, but today it is mostly found in Baden, Sachsen, and Saale-Unstrut, occupying 1,200 ha (2,965 acres). It is marketed as the speciality of the Markgräflerland in Baden, where it reaches its acme of dullness. It has thin skin and is prone to rot, so it seems scarcely worth the trouble of cultivating it, given its complete neutrality. As Werner Schön of Baden remarked: "If it smells of nothing and tastes of nothing, then you know it's Gutedel." A grower at Kirchhofen added, unconvincingly: "It tastes like water, but it grows on you."

HUXELREBE
Huxelrebe was developed by Georg Scheu at Alzey in 1927, a crossing of Gutedel x Courtillier Musqué. It proved popular, and by 1983, 1,700 ha (4,201 acres) had been planted in Rheinhessen and Pfalz. When pruned severely, it can give very high must weights, even when planted in unexceptional sites. Despite the wine's richness when late-picked, it can have good acidity. In the hands of a prudent grower and winemaker such as Bernd Philippi, it can give good results, but all too often it has been overcropped with dire results. It is in gradual decline, with 1,230 ha (3,039 acres) in production by 2000.

IRSAY OLIVER

This Muscat-style grape was developed as a table grape at Eger and is a crossing of Pozsony x Pearl of Csaba. I have only encountered it in Saale-Unstrut, presumably because of good connections between East Germany and Hungary. It can be aromatic but has low acidity.

KANZLER

Kanzler was created in 1927 at Alzey by crossing Müller-Thurgau x Silvaner. As an early-budding variety, it requires fairly warm sites. It ripens very early, gives good if not exceptional sugars, and is not as copious in its yields as many crossings. Planted in Rheinhessen and Pfalz, it is capable of giving decent wine, but is rarely vinified on its own these days.

KERNER

This crossing of Trollinger x Riesling was launched in 1969 and became enormously popular. By the 1980s it was the fourth most widely planted grape in Germany, primarily in Rheinhessen and Pfalz, but also in Mosel and Württemberg. It has good frost resistance because it buds late. If overcropped, as is often the case, the wine is lacklustre, but at reasonable yields of no more than eighty hl/ha (32.4 hl/acre), Kerner gives a wine that seems to borrow the best qualities of Silvaner and Riesling, without ever attaining the personality of either. It remains popular, and although in gradual decline, there are still 6,500 ha (16,062 acres) under vine.

KLINGELBERGER

Synonym for Riesling in the Ortenau in Baden.

MARIENSTEINER

This crossing of Silvaner x Riesling was developed in Würzburg in 1971. It never really caught on, but was planted here and there in the Pfalz, Rheinhessen and Franken. It gives reliable yields and high must weights, but can have excessive acidity in poor years.

MORIO-MUSKAT

Not a true Muscat, but a crossing of Silvaner x Pinot Blanc developed by Peter Morio. It became highly popular in Rheinhessen and Pfalz in the

1970s and 1980s, with 2,800 ha (6,919 acres) under vine by 1983, because it is not sensitive to site and can deliver enormous yields. Morio-Muskat has the grapey bouquet of Muscat but lacks finesse. And needless to say, when overcropped it produces fairly wretched and coarse wine. It is steadily declining in popularity, partly because of its susceptibility to rot and disease. Today there are about 1,000 ha (2,471 acres) in production.

MÜLLER-THURGAU

This most famous of crossings was created in 1882 by Dr Hermann Müller, who was Swiss-born from the canton of Thurgau but working at Geisenheim. Curiously, the parentage of the variety remained uncertain. Conflicting theories argued that it was either Riesling x Riesling or Riesling x Silvaner. Modern scientific research has established that Müller-Thurgau is Riesling x Chasselas de Courtillier.

For some decades the new crossing was ignored; planting in Germany did not begin until the 1920s and only took off in the late 1930s. By the early 1970s it had become more widely planted than Riesling. It must have come as a relief to national pride when a few years ago, Riesling was restored to its supremacy as the most widely planted grape variety in Germany, with Müller-Thurgau slipping into second place at around 20,000 ha (49,420 acres). It ripens earlier than Riesling but is less resistant to frost, and it is susceptible to disease such as downy mildew and black rot. Yields can be as high as 200 hl/ha (eighty-one hl/acre), though at such levels it can lack vigour. Nor does it have the tremendous acidic structure of Riesling, so Müller-Thurgau is invariably a wine for early drinking and thus plays a major part in the cheap blends (Liebfraumilch and worse) that have done so much damage to the image of German wine.

A few growers take Müller-Thurgau seriously, green harvesting to ensure low yields. Some low-cropped Müller-Thurgau is barrel-fermented, and up-market versions are often labelled as Rivaner to distance them from the very commercial and inexpensive Müller-Thurgaus.

MUSKATELLER

Muskateller on the label usually refers to Gelber Muskateller, which is better known internationally as Muscat à Petits Grains. It was an important variety in Württemberg in the nineteenth century, but has dwindled to next to nothing, and there are only about ninety ha (222 acres) planted in all of Germany. This is regrettable, because the wine can be delicious. Although it gives irregular yields, Helmut Darting in the Pfalz says it always has good acidity, and also stays healthy on the vine until late in the year, making it a good candidate for Eiswein. Bercher-Schmidt in Baden maintain that the wine can be elegant with fine aromas, but yields can be high and need to be controlled.

Another sub-variety of Muskateller is Roter Muskateller, which also has irregular yields and easily gets botrytis. A few vineyards remain in Baden.

NOBLESSA

This crossing was created in 1975 at Geilweilerhof from Madeleine Angevine x Silvaner. It proved moderately successful, and by 1983 there were 171 ha (423 acres) under vine, mostly in Baden. It is not especially site-sensitive, but is susceptible to spring frosts. Yields rarely exceed fifty hl/ha (20.2 hl/acre), and the variety gives high sugar levels. I have never tasted it.

NOBLING

The late-ripening Nobling is found mostly in Baden, where it was created in 1939 at Freiburg as a crossing of Silvaner x Gutedel. It reaches good ripeness levels even at yields of eighty to ninety hl/ha (32.4–36.4 hl/acre). It attracts botrytis easily. Nobling can sometimes have more character than Gutedel, but that is not saying a great deal. There are about one hundred ha (247 acres) under vine.

OPTIMA

Optima was created at Geilweilerhof in 1970 from (Silvaner x Riesling) x Müller-Thurgau. It was mostly planted in the Rheinhessen, but also in the Mosel; overall there are 200 ha (494 acres) under vine. Its selling point is that it usually ripens a week earlier than Müller-Thurgau but easily achieves very high sugar levels. The drawback is that it is low in acidity, rots easily, and the wine can be heavy. It was often made in a sweet style, but usually tasted flabby.

ORTEGA

This variety originated in Würzburg in 1948 as a crossing of Müller-Thurgau x Siegerrebe. It was very popular in the Mosel and Rheinhessen, and was also planted in Franken. Like Optima, it attains high ripeness levels with relative ease, even at high yields. Consequently it is a useful grape for relatively risk-free sweet wines, but low acidity levels mean that it often tasted cloying, despite an initial fruitiness on the palate. Plantings remain steady at around 1,000 ha (2,471 acres).

PERLE

A crossing from Gewürztraminer x Müller-Thurgau, developed at Alzey by Georg Scheu and Dr Breider. It was planted mostly in Rheinhessen and Franken. The grapes are a light pink in colour, but being tightly bunched they are susceptible to rot. The wine is aromatic. Vineyard area is diminishing and now stands at around one hundred ha (247 acres).

PINOT BLANC

Known usually as Weissburgunder or Weisser Burgunder, this is the same as the Alsatian variety and is very widely planted in Baden and the Pfalz, and indeed in most German wine regions, where its lively fruit and broader structure make it an attractive alternative to the more austere Riesling. It is also a wine that complements a wide range of dishes, which is not always the case with Riesling. There are 2,600 ha (6,425 acres) under vine. Many winemakers like to ferment or age the wine in barriques, and Pinot Blanc adapts better to this method than Pinot Gris usually does.

A vertical tasting at Bergdolt in the Pfalz, a specialist in the variety, confirmed for me that Pinot Blanc doesn't evolve aromatically in the way that Riesling does. It is rarely worth keeping more than a few years.

PINOT GRIS

Pinot Gris has become a very popular variety in southern Germany, especially in Baden. That is not surprising, because Baden is the eastern neighbour of Alsace, the French home of Pinot Gris. Although a white grape, its skins, when fully ripe, have a rust-red tinge, so the wine is often deep-coloured, depending on how long the winemaker allows the must to macerate with the skins.

It is also planted in the Pfalz, Rheinhessen, and as far east as Sachsen. In all, there are 2,800 ha (6,919 acres) under vine. The grape is usually known as Grauer Burgunder, but in areas where there was a tradition of producing sweet wine from this opulent variety it was known as Ruländer. There is a rule of thumb that Grauer Burgunder on a label signifies a dry or off-dry wine, and Ruländer a sweet wine. But it is not an infallible guide.

Although very few Alsatian producers let Pinot Gris anywhere near a barrique, many German producers like to vinify the variety in small oak barrels. It can work, but there are few wines less satisfactory than an overoaked Pinot Gris, which was commonly encountered some years ago, especially in Baden. In general, Grauer Burgunder has sufficient flavour and complexity not to require the oxidative vanilla tones often imparted by small oak barrels. It can have a rich texture and a distinct touch of spice on the palate.

Modern German Grauer Burgunder clones can be very high-yielding, according to Hans Ruck in Franken, and he and others have preferred to obtain low-cropping massal selections from old vineyards.

REICHENSTEINER

Reichensteiner was created in 1939 by Helmut Becker at Geisenheim, but it was not actually released for planting until 1978. It crosses Müller-Thurgau x (Madeleine Angevine x Early Calabrese). It resembles Müller-Thurgau but has the advantage of being less prone to rot. It was taken up by growers in Rheinhessen, Pfalz, and Mosel. It ripens well and has marginally better acidity than Müller-Thurgau, and 250 ha (618 acres) are planted. But as a wine it lacks character.

RIESLANER

Although this variety was developed at Würzburg as long ago as 1921 from Silvaner x Riesling, it was forgotten for decades and only revived and planted in the 1950s and 1960s.

Hans-Günther Schwartz, a fan of Rieslaner at Müller-Catoir in the Pfalz, describes it as follows. Its yields are lower than Riesling by one-third or one-half, and the bunches ripen very fast, so it's best picked at BA or TBA level. Under 100 Oechsle it's not much use. It is not only riper than Riesling but achieves higher acidity. But it is hard to cultivate and vinify, so it will never be a common variety and has yet to exceed seventy ha (173 acres). It can be tricky at flowering; the stems are weak and it's not uncommon for bunches to drop off; it's prone to disease and it ripens unevenly, so you have to pick selectively. It works best on light loamy sandy soils.

Because of its high ripeness levels and bracing acidity, Rieslaner is usually made as a sweet wine, but dry versions can be brilliant, as at Müller-Catoir. In 1998 and 1999 Schwarz preferred his Spätlese Trocken Rieslaners to his Rieslings, because the wines had more finesse, and were more exotic.

RIESLING

Riesling is the most spectacularly multifaceted grape variety of all, and its homeland is Germany, where more than 22,000 ha (54,362 acres) are planted. It can be enjoyed young and fresh, or, when made as a very sweet wine, kept for a century or more. Riesling is all about balance, the delicate interplay of sweetness, extract, acidity, and alcohol (or lack of it). Because it is invariably kept well away from new oak barrels, the *terroir* can come shining through, and Riesling responds sensitively to the nuances of soil and microclimate. Its hallmark, other than its wonderful fruitiness, is acidity, which can also be its downfall in cold years. In good vintages that acidity enlivens and refreshes and helps the wine to lead an interesting life in bottle for many years.

No one knows for sure when Riesling made its first appearance in Germany, but records of newly planted vineyards at Rüsselheim on the River Main near Frankfurt refer to *riesslingen* in 1435. There is another reference to the variety in documents relating to Worms from the 1450s. However, it seems probable that in those times Riesling was merely one grape planted alongside others. It was in the 1720s that the crucial decision was taken at Schloss Johannisberg to plant the entire site with Riesling as a monoculture. It took longer to dominate the Mosel, where it only became the major variety in the late nineteenth century.

It flowers and ripens late, but resists frosts well, and has been known to survive temperatures as low as −25°C. The greatest danger occurs when the sap rises fast after a warm winter and then a sudden frost occurs before the sap can retreat. This happened in 1984 in the Rheingau and many vines died. Depending on where it is grown, Riesling can deliver quite high yields – sixty to seventy hl/ha (twenty-four to twenty-eight hl/acre) – without apparent dilution. However, the top estates will often aim for significantly lower yields in order to make well structured wines of great longevity. And of course the yields for the great sweet wines are minute. On the other hand, Riesling can be cultivated to produce yields of 150 hl/ha (sixty-one hl/acre) or more, but at such levels it loses its distinction and character.

About fifty clones are listed, but no more than twenty of them are important. Those who have had the opportunity to make direct comparisons between old ungrafted vines and modern clones insist that yields today are much higher than they were in the past. Yet such is the resilience of Riesling that overall quality has been maintained. Qualitative factors include the size and density of the berries and clusters, which can vary from clone to clone. Bernd Philippi of Koehler-Ruprecht likes the Geisenheim clone for Riesling, because the clone associated with the Pfalz can be too aromatic. The high-yielding clones planted in the 1960s and 1970s are being replaced by far better material, so the overall quality of Riesling wine is set to improve even further.

RIVANER
See Müller-Thurgau.

RULÄNDER
See Pinot Gris.

SAUVIGNON BLANC
Because Germany has Riesling in abundance, growers probably never felt the need for another high-acidity variety. In the nineteenth century it was known in Germany as Muscat Sylvaner and quite widely planted in Württemberg, but little remains. Knipser and Mosbacher are among the few Pfalz estates to have Sauvignon vines. It is also planted at Durbach and Wolff Metternich in Baden.

SCHEUREBE
This highly regarded variety was named after its creator, Georg Scheu, who developed it at Alzey in 1916 from Silvaner x Riesling. What Scheu had in mind was a superior version of Silvaner, with more aroma and

better resistance to frost and disease. Yet its elegance and vigour are more reminiscent of Riesling than Silvaner. Yields are generous, but, as with any variety, it is important not to overcrop. There are around 3,000 ha (7,413 acres) in production.

It is tricky to vinify. It can be made as a dry wine, but if the grapes are not fully ripe, the wine can have a catty, grapefruity tone that is not entirely pleasant. It attains high sugar levels more easily than Riesling, so it often works better as a sweet wine of considerable raciness and complexity. It attracts botrytis easily and can deliver spectacular results at BA and TBA levels.

Most Scheurebe is planted in Rheinhessen, and the Pfalz has a great deal. It was first planted in Franken in 1953 by Hans Wirsching.

SCHÖNBURGER

This bizarre, pink-coloured crossing of Pinot Noir x (Chasselas Rosé x Muscat of Hamburg) was created in Geisenheim in 1979. It is resistant to most diseases and ripens early at high sugar levels. The Muscat in the parentage shows through, and the wine, which is white, can be blowsy. Although about sixty ha (148 acres) of Schönburger has been planted in the Pfalz and Rheinhessen, it has proved more popular in England than Germany.

SEPTIMER

Obscure crossing of Gewürztraminer x Müller-Thurgau, found mostly in the Rheinhessen. Dark pink grapes with low acidity. No more than twenty ha (forty-nine acres) are planted.

SIEGERREBE

A crossing created at Alzey: Madeleine Angevine x Gewürztraminer. Siegerrebe's main claim to fame is the almost preposterous ripeness levels it has occasionally attained, such as 326 Oechsle in 1971 at Nussdorf in the Pfalz. It often experiences poor fruit set at flowering, so yields tend to be very low, and they can be further reduced by susceptibility to spring frosts and thirsty wasps. It was mostly planted as a highly aromatic blending variety in Rheinhessen and the Pfalz. The wines, rarely if ever encountered as a pure varietal, are low in acidity. There are 160 ha (395 acres) under vine.

SILVANER

The historical origins of Silvaner are uncertain but it seems probable that it first inhabited Austria. It was planted in Franken in the mid-seventeenth century after the Thirty Years' War. By the early to mid-twentieth century, it was probably the most widely planted grape in Germany, but today it occupies around six per cent of the vineyards. Although Silvaner does not enjoy a high reputation, it can produce very good wine, with more body than Riesling. It has little aroma but is robust, even earthy, in flavour, and has little difficulty in ripening, its sugars usually balanced by good acidity. Much depends on where it is planted. Dr Michalsky of Weingut St Antony in Rheinhessen believes that, when it comes to Silvaner, limestone soils give racier wines, whereas loess soils give broader ones.

It performs best in the Rheinfront area of Rheinhessen, and in Franken, where it sometimes produces nobly sweet wines as well as the more customary dry ones. Unfortunately, many recent plantings, especially in the Pfalz and Baden, have been from high-yielding clones that do little to reveal the typicity of Silvaner. Joachim Heger of Baden describes the aroma of such clones as being that of jute. Despite the excellence of many Silvaners, the wines, like the Sylvaners of Alsace, are never likely to gain international popularity, but they do satisfy a knowledgeable local clientele.

Subsidies in Baden and elsewhere have encouraged growers to grub up old-vine Silvaner and replace it with other, more commercially attractive varieties, so the area under vine is likely to diminish in the future. Today it stands at 6,500 ha (16,061 acres).

Silvaner has also been known as Oesterreicher.

WEISSBURGUNDER (WEISSER BURGUNDER)
See Pinot Blanc.

WÜRZER
Würzer is a crossing of Gewürztraminer x Müller-Thurgau invented in 1932 by Georg Scheu. It was devised to deal with the irregular yields to which Gewürztraminer is prone. It delivers the goods in terms of yields, at around one hundred hl/ha (40.5 hl/acre), and the grapes ripen fully, releasing an aroma not unlike that of Gewürztraminer. It has mostly been

planted in Rheinhessen. There are more than one hundred ha (247 acres) in production.

The problem with Würzer, according to Rheinhessen grower Gerold Pfannebecker, is that when the vines are young they are too productive and you lose typicity, for which you need to wait twenty years. Michel-Pfannebecker still produces Würzer, but admits that currently available clones of Gewürztraminer are far more reliable in terms of crop levels than those with which Dr Scheu was confronted.

Red varieties

ACALON
A crossing of Dornfelder x Lemberger. Developed at Weinsberg, its properties are alleged to be good extract, early ripening, and good yields.

ANDRÉ
A Czech crossing of St Laurent x Blaufränkisch. It has the same parentage as Zweigelt but reversed. It was first grown and vinified in Saale-Unstrut at the Landesweingut Kloster Pforta and is also found at the Freyburg cooperative.

CABERNET CUBIN
A Weinsberg crossing, similar to Cabernet Mitos, but reversed, being Cabernet Sauvignon x Lemberger. When planted on good sites, it can give higher sugar-free extract levels than Cabernet Sauvignon. Helmut Darting has planted this crossing in the Pfalz.

CABERNET DORIO
A crossing from Weinsberg of Cabernet Sauvignon x Dornfelder. Capable of giving fruity, velvety wines with very high sugar levels, it has been taken up with some enthusiasm by growers in Württemberg.

CABERNET DORSA
A Weinsberg crossing of Dornfelder x Cabernet Sauvignon.

CABERNET FRANC

The only German example I know of is from Theo Minges in the Pfalz, but no doubt there are other plantings.

CABERNET MITOS

Yet another Weinsberg crossing, this being from Lemberger x Cabernet Sauvignon. It yields full-bodied and rather dense wines.

CABERNET SAUVIGNON

It never used to be possible to ripen Cabernet Sauvignon in Germany, but climatic changes through the 1990s have altered that. Nonetheless it is hard to point to good examples of the variety from Germany, despite the enthusiasm of growers such as Simon-Bürkle in the Hessische Bergstrasse, Heinrich Vollmer, Theo Minges and Lergenmüller in the Pfalz, Bercher, Männle and Blankenhorn in Baden and Aldinger and Wöhrwag in Württemberg. However, most of these producers blend the Cabernet with other varieties.

DOMINA

A crossing of Pinot Noir x Portugieser propagated at Geilweilerhof in the Pfalz. It has been adopted in the Ahr by Nelles, and in Franken by Fürst, the Bürgerspital, Ruck, and the Staatliche Hofkeller. The variety apparently exhibits different characters according to where it is grown. It is always deep-coloured, because the berries are small, but high yields require the conscientious grower to bunch-thin. It can attain high ripeness levels and has better acidity levels than Portugieser. Plantings are increasing but very slowly, and now stand at 210 ha (519 acres).

DORNFELDER

Dornfelder was bred at Weinsberg by August Herold in 1956 as a crossing of Helfensteiner (Frühburgunder x Trollinger) and Heroldrebe (Portugieser x Lemberger). Its original role was to add more colour to the pallid Trollinger, once the 1971 Wine Law forbad the addition of imported wines for that purpose. Large-berried, it yields abundant juice – up to 120 hl/ha (48.5 hl/acre) – and resists rot. It is easy to grow and attains higher ripeness levels than Portugieser or Trollinger. With so many virtues, including deep colour, it is not surprising that

Dornfelder has been a huge success. In 1996 there were 2,125 ha (5,251 acres) planted, but by 2001 there were at least 6,000 ha (14,826 acres) in the Pfalz, Rheinhessen, Württemberg, and even the Mosel. In the Pfalz in 2001 the price per kilogram was three times higher than for Riesling, and Helmut Darting's nursery reports strong demand for cuttings.

Its sappy juiciness has made Dornfelder extremely popular, and some growers have been tempted to take the variety more seriously, by reducing yields to around eighty hl/ha (32.4 hl/acre) and by ageing the wine in barriques. However, it has low natural acidity, and usually lacks length of flavour, even when oak-aged.

DUNKELFELDER

The origins of this crossing are unknown, according to Jancis Robinson. It is grown in the Pfalz by Egon Schmitt and others, and overall there are 300 ha (741 acres) planted. Schmitt discerns a thick chocolatey character but finds the wine lacks fruitiness, so he blends it with Cabernet Sauvignon.

FRÜHBURGUNDER

This ancient, small-berried mutation of Pinot Noir is mostly found in the Ahr, although there are parcels in Assmannshausen too, because it grows happily on slate soils and survives wet weather, as long as yields are kept to no more than thirty-five hl/ha (fourteen hl/acre). By 1985 it had degenerated and almost disappeared, but was revived with clonal selections. A small amount has also been planted in Sachsen by Proschwitz, in Franken by Fürst, and in the Pfalz by Knipser; there are also some twenty ha (forty-nine acres) in Württemberg, where Graf Adelmann believes the clone differs from that found in the Ahr and Rheingau. There are one hundred ha (247 acres) planted throughout Germany, of which about twenty-five ha (sixty-two acres) are in the Ahr. In some parts of Germany, Frühburgunder is confusingly known as Clevner.

As its name suggests, Frühburgunder ripens slightly earlier than Pinot Noir. It has lower acidity than Pinot Noir, giving it more softness and approachability.

HELFENSTEINER

This crossing was created at Weinsberg by August Herold from Frühburgunder x Trollinger. Its virtue is that it ripens a few weeks before Trollinger; on the other hand it is susceptible to problems during flowering, so yields are unreliable. It is rarely encountered, but around forty ha (ninety-nine acres) are planted in Württemberg.

HEROLDREBE

August Herold gave his name to this 1948 crossing of Portugieser x Lemberger. Almost all the existing 200 ha (500 acres) are planted around Stuttgart, where the vineyards are up to 400 metres (1,300 feet) high. Heroldrebe does well at these elevations; it has compact bunches that are prone to rot in poorly ventilated areas. It is late-ripening and gives large crops of unremarkable wine.

LEMBERGER

Lemberger (or Limberger) is the same variety as the Austrian Blaufränkisch and the Hungarian Kékfrankos. Within Germany, it is most often found in Württemberg. Graf von Neipperg says there's a legend that it was brought there from Austria by his forebears, because after the Thirty Years' War the Neippergs were based in Vienna rather than Germany. He thinks himself that immigrants after that war brought it to Germany. It does not enjoy the reputation it deserves, because the late-ripening Lemberger needs sunshine to get colour, and the age of the vines also makes a considerable difference to quality. In Württemberg the cooperatives favour high yields, which has resulted in dilute wines. In the hands of a conscientious producer, Lemberger can produce rich, complex wine with good acidic structure. Fortunately, plantings are increasing, though very gradually, and now stand at 1,200 ha (3,000 acres).

MERLOT

Not much Merlot is planted in Germany, though it can be found at Wehrheim in the Pfalz; at Aldinger, Schwegler, and Dautel in Württemberg; and, surprisingly, at Prinz von Hessen in the Rheingau.

MUSKAT-TROLLINGER

Muskat-Trollinger is a Württemberg rarity, a mutation of Trollinger known for its aromatic quality. Graf Adelmann believes it is a kind of Muscat. He produces it, as does Schlossgut Hohenbeilstein and Amalienhof.

PALAS

A recent crossing from the Weinsberg college in Württemberg: Trollinger x Rubin. It's a late ripening variety, yielding deeply coloured must, and is intended as a blending component.

PINOT MEUNIER

See Schwarzriesling.

PINOT NOIR

German red wine producers become somewhat annoyed when it's suggested to them that the Germans are newcomers when it comes to vinifying Pinot Noir (Spätburgunder). They point out that documents dating back to 1507 refer to the nuns of Assmannshausen in the Rheingau drinking red wines, and because their mother house was in Burgundy, it is quite possible that they were drinking Pinot Noir. Although Pinot Noir does not claim the same ancestry in the Ahr, it has been well established in that region for decades, and it is very common in Baden. Ernst Dautel recalls that Pinot Noir was bottled in Württemberg in the 1930s, but the quantities were small. It is easily the most important of Germany's red wine grapes, and grows on 9,250 ha (23,000 acres).

The fact that many German Spätburgunders were vinified with residual sugar – and in Baden some still are – hardly helped to consolidate Germany's reputation as a Pinot Noir producer. Even those that were vinified dry were often subjected to a brief fermentation at high temperatures to extract colour and flavour (not very effectively), because tank space was too valuable to permit a more extended maceration on the skins. Today, the best producers are thoroughly familiar with Burgundian techniques and are doing their best to apply them.

Clonal selection is a more vexed issue. Much German Pinot Noir is still produced from high-yielding German clones. Some growers, such as Gerold Pfannebecker in Rheinhessen, believe that German clones can give good-quality wine – but only when the vines are twenty years old. In contrast, French "Dijon" clones tend to deliver the goods even when the vines are young. A popular German clone is the Mariafeld clone, which gives large berries but widely spaced bunches. Some growers argue that this clone can be better in wet years because it has looser bunches. Knipser confirms that a French clone such as 777 gives excellent wine thanks to its tight small bunches, but it is also prone to rot, and in 2000 he lost his entire crop. Paul Fürst in Franken has begun releasing a bottling made from a single French clone that he has recently planted.

There is a strong German tradition of producing Spätburgunder Weissherbst – a long-winded term for rosé. Even more specific to Germany is the idea of producing botrytis wines from Pinot Noir. Botrytis destroys pigments, so most of the little colour that Pinot Noir has is eaten up by the botrytis spores, which explains why in Baden and elsewhere you can sometimes find Weissherbst BA or even TBA. And it can be delicious.

PORTUGIESER

This grape, also known as Blauer Portugieser, seems to be of Austrian origin. Almost five per cent of Germany's vineyards are planted with it: 5,000 ha (12,500 acres). Yields of 200 hl/ha (eighty-one hl/acre) are far from unusual, so it's hardly surprising that the wine lacks distinction and personality. Its popularity is somewhat puzzling, because the variety is susceptible to oïdium and to rot. As a wine, Portugieser is light in colour and has low acidity, and is not capable of ageing. It has been planted in most parts of Germany, especially in the Pfalz and Rheinhessen, and is sometimes vinified with a touch of residual sugar, which makes the wine even less palatable.

REGENT

Regent was developed at Siebeldingen as a red grape for use in the Pfalz and Rheinhessen. It is a crossing between (Silvaner x Müller-Thurgau) x Chambourcin. Ellwanger in Württemberg says it has a muddled history, having been developed as a disease-resistant variety that doesn't need to be sprayed. The Staatsweingut in the Ahr, however, finds that Regent tolerates but does not resist disease and you need to spray less. Its dark colour makes it useful for blending and it is proving to be one of the most successful new red varieties, because the wine can be of good quality. Plantings are increasing rapidly: in 1997 there were seventy ha (170 acres) under vine, but by 2000 there were 450 ha (1,100 acres).

REGNER

This crossing was developed at Alzey in 1929 from Luglienca Bianca (a table grape) x Gamay. It never really took off, and by the mid-1990s there were only 170 ha (420 acres) planted, mainly in Rheinhessen. Its main selling point is that it ripens very early, and can be planted just about anywhere. It's fairly reliable and attains good sugar levels, though acidity tends to be low.

ROTBERGER

Rotberger is a Geisenheim crossing of Trollinger x Riesling. It ripens earlier than Trollinger and is used for red and rosé and for sparkling wine. The Stadt Bensheim estate in the Hessische Bergstrasse has 2.5 ha (6.2 acres) of Rotberger, probably the largest planting in Germany. It has also been cultivated at various times in the Ahr, Baden, and Württemberg.

ROTER GUTEDEL

A red counterpart of Gutedel that I have never encountered.

ST LAURENT

This red variety, more usually associated with Austria, seems to have been present in German vineyards since the early nineteenth century, but gradually fell out of favour. It was revived, according to Messmer in the Pfalz, in the 1970s, when a grower in the Pfalz found unfamiliar vines among his Portugieser. Nobody knew what it was, but everyone liked the wine. It was subsequently identified as St Laurent and began to be replanted. Weingut Wehrheim planted it in 1974. There are now about 270 ha (670 acres) under vine and it has been growing in popularity.

It was long thought that St Laurent was a mutation of Pinot Noir, but ampelographers deny this and believe the variety probably originated in southern Alsace. It ripens earlier than Pinot Noir and its thick skins protect it from botrytis. Helmut Darting in the northern Pfalz says it's not easy to grow and doesn't give a large crop. Yet it gives an enjoyable wine, juicy and fresh, with few tannins.

SAMTROT

Samtrot is a mutation of Schwarzriesling (Pinot Meunier), and was first identified as such in the 1920s. It resembles Pinot Noir on the vine but gives lower yields and denser, softer wines. Because of its very small berries, the wine is concentrated and dark. Samtrot is not a productive variety, so it has never been popular as a cash crop, and is comparatively rare, except in Württemberg. There are about seventy ha (170 acres) planted.

SCHWARZRIESLING (MÜLLERREBE)

This is none other than Pinot Meunier, which has been taken up with some enthusiasm as a dry red wine in Baden and Württemberg, where it is also used to produce the pink wine known as Schillerwein. It's less aromatic than Pinot Noir but has higher acidity, and gives a simpler, fruitier wine than its noble cousin; it also has the advantage of ripening earlier. The wine is often enjoyable but never great. Nonetheless 2,400 ha (6,000 acres) are in production, and the area is slowly rising.

SPÄTBURGUNDER

See Pinot Noir.

SYRAH

Uncommon in Germany, but found here and there; Knipser grows it in the Pfalz.

TROLLINGER

Trollinger is the mainstay of Württemberg, especially of the area around Stuttgart, where this pale, dry wine is consumed with gusto. It occupies 2.5 per cent of German vineyards, and the area under vine has remained steady for some years at 2,600 ha (6,500 acres). It is the same variety (though perhaps not the identical strain) as the Tyrolean Vernatsch and the Schiava Grossa of Italy. Because it ripens late, it is often planted in excellent sites, which might be better suited for more worthy varieties. Trollinger produces in abundance and yields of 100–150 hl/ha (40.5–60.7 hl/acre) are not uncommon. But even at lower yields, it is not a wine that excites admiration from those living beyond the borders of Württemberg.

TROLLINGER MIT URBAN

Graf Adelmann of Württemberg claims his 0.16 ha (0.40 acres) is all that remains of this variety, which can be uninteresting or terrific, depending on the vintage.

ZWEIGELT

This Austrian crossing was created in 1922 by the eponymous Dr Zweigelt from St Laurent x Blaufränkisch. It grows easily, has good yields, and ripens early. In Austria it can produce juicy, delicious, deftly structured wine, and the little planted in Germany, mostly in Saale-Unstrut, seems to have similar qualities.

6

Rheingau

The Rheingau has about 3,200 ha (8,000 acres) of vines, grown by 1,500 owners. Riesling is the dominant variety, accounting for almost eighty per cent of plantation, and is known to have been cultivated here since at least 1435. A century ago there would also have been a considerable amount of Silvaner and Gelber Orleans, the latter recently revived in Rüdesheim by Bernhard Breuer and also in the Pfalz, although it remains a curiosity. Pinot Noir is important in Assmannshausen and a few other localities, and accounts for twelve per cent. The remaining vines are Müller-Thurgau (three per cent) and other varieties in small parcels. There is even a little Chardonnay. Schloss Reinhartshausen planted it some years ago on an approved experimental basis in cooperation with the wine college at Geisenheim, and today a handful of other growers, such as Lang, have planted it too. I'm not sure how significant the following statistics are, but I offer them for what they are worth. The average temperature is 9.9°C, and the hours of sunshine per annum range from 1,112 in a poor year such as 1984 to 1,362 in 1989 and to 1,656 in the legendary 1959 vintage.

The Rheingau is easily the most homogeneous of the German wine regions. At Mainz the Rhein has to make a westward turn, because it cannot penetrate the quartzite ranges to the north. So for some thirty kilometres (19 miles) it flows in a westerly direction, and the vineyards that rise up from the riverbank to the north enjoy a generally southerly exposure that makes them well suited to viticulture. A few kilometres inland the river influence diminishes and the slopes rise to heights at which grapes will not ripen, so the region is fringed to the north by woods and mountains that protect the vineyards from cold windy weather. But it's the river, making its long journey from Switzerland

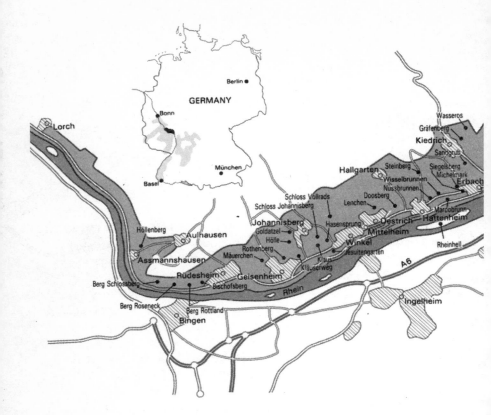

through Germany, that plays the crucial role here, as it does in other regions such as the Mittelrhein. Without its moderating influence, viticulture at such northern latitudes would be impossible.

Archaeological research suggests that viticulture was already practised here in Roman times. There is documentary evidence that there were vineyards in Walluf by 770, and at the same time Charlemagne was encouraging grape growing here, because he had a palace at Ingelheim on the southern bank of the Rhein. There's a legend that when he was gazing across the river toward the Rheingau he noted that on certain slopes the winter snows were the first to thaw. From this he assumed, not entirely correctly, that the microclimate had to be especially favourable for viticulture and he ordered the planting of vines on what is today the Rüdesheimer Berg. By 850 the Johannisberg hill was already being referred to as the Bischofsberg and was presumably planted with vines;

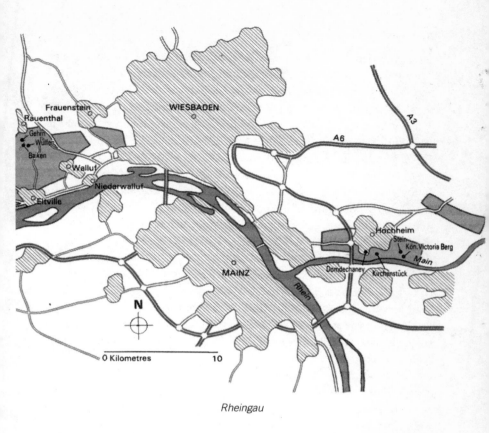

Rheingau

when in the eleventh century the Benedictines took over the existing priory in Winkel, they changed its name to Johannisberg, which it still bears today.

In 1155 Archbishop Adalbert I of Mainz granted the slope in Hattenheim known today as the Steinberg to the Cistercian order. Nearby the monks built a new monastery, Kloster Eberbach, today the headquarters of the state domaine and a popular location for special events such as wine auctions. The monastery soon developed vineyards and became a major economic force in the region. In 1803 it was secularized by Napoleon and became the property of the dukes of Nassau until 1866, when the dukes, who had backed the wrong side during the Austro-Prussian war, lost their properties and the monastic domaines came into the possession of the Prussian state.

By the eighteenth century many of the vineyards belonged to the aristocracy or the church or to farmers located in the villages of the Rheingau. Gradually some of them came into the hands of prosperous merchants from Frankfurt and Mainz. The best wines from the Rheingau were by this time very highly regarded. A recent history of Schloss Johannisberg records: "In 1830 the Rothschilds in Frankfurt bought a cask for 9,100 florins, in 1832 the king of Prussia one for 12,500 florins. In 1834 four butts even went to the Prussian court cellar in Berlin. They cost between 4,500 and 10,000 florins each. In the same year the most humble cask of Steinberger was sold at the Kloster Eberbach auction for 1,500 and the best for 5,010. For everyday table wines the price paid was 400–600 florins per butt . . . One litre of Johannisberg wine cost on average a good two florins. This corresponded at the time to the value of fifteen pounds of beef [6.8 kilograms]."[1] The Weil estate in Kiedrich priced its 1893 Auslese, presumably from its top site, the Gräfenberg, at three times the price at that time for Château Lafite. Nor, says Wilhelm Weil, was this the estate's top wine in that exceptional year.

No doubt it was in part the auctions at Kloster Eberbach that helped set the high prices for the region's top wines. The first auction was held in 1806. Whole barrels were offered to buyers, and then the wine was bottled by the monastery on behalf of the purchasers. These wines were always of high quality, and were none other than the celebrated Cabinet wines from the monastic vineyards. The auctions continue to this day, and the wines on offer tend to be a mixture of rare old bottles and special cuvées of wines in various styles and qualities.

There has been much argument about where the concept of Cabinet wines originated. Kloster Eberbach is the most renowned estate that selected its best wines for ageing in 1,200-litre casks and then stored them, after bottling, in a special locked cellar known as the Cabinet. However, Rowald Hepp, the winemaker at Schloss Vollrads, believes that this noble estate was setting aside Cabinet wines two years earlier, in 1728. When I challenged Dieter Greiner with Hepp's claim, he responded that Vollrads was the first estate to talk about Cabinet wines, but Eberbach was the first estate actually to lay down such wines. Fortunately, the issue is of minimal importance, other than to confirm that this is a long-established tradition in the Rheingau.

[1] Staab, Seeliger, and Schleicher, *Schloss Johannisberg*, p. 56.

Over the years there were major changes in the structure of the vine-yards. In the Middle Ages many of them were terraced, and some of those ancient terraces survive, but the rationalization scheme known as *Flurbereinigung* from the 1960s onward reorganized many of the vine-yards, constructing access roads and aiding mechanization. Morton Shand has left an interesting account of how the Steinberg was cultivated in the 1920s: "Every part of it can be reached by horse and cart. The drainage is of masonry, most elaborate in character, and is placed well below the further thrust of any vine root. Attached to the vineyard is a farm of . . . one hundred head of cattle, besides draught horses, main-tained solely for the purpose of supplying the vineyard with the 200 cart-loads of manure and the 1,200 trusses of straw which it absorbs annually. The vines are kept very low and planted a metre [3.28 feet] apart, the object being to ensure small-berried clusters. The vine-dressers, who have elaborate printed instructions issued to them, carry long needles with which to pick up those grapes – and these are the choicest of all! – that fall earliest from overripeness. The treading is done with special boots in large double pails fitted with perforated floors. The stalks are not separated."[2]

After 1971 many vineyard names disappeared forever. Morton Shand, writing in the 1920s refers to vineyards named Grauer Stein in Eltville, to Kesselring and Pfaffenberg in Rauenthal, and to Engerweg and Hinterhaus in Rüdesheim, none of which exists today. Or rather, they have been subsumed into larger vineyard entities.[3]

We tend to think of the past two centuries as a golden age for Riesling, although many other varieties were, as we have seen, cultivated here, especially in the nineteenth century. What is very striking, as one looks at older books about the region, is that by the mid-twentieth century Riesling's grip was clearly slipping. Fritz Hallgarten in the early 1950s was able to pen the following words: "Possibly the Rheingau will have to abandon its cultivation of the Riesling grape and adopt other kinds. A report from wine regions outside Germany encourages this opinion. In the Banat for example, new varieties of grapes, specially cultivated for a high sugar content, have been grafted on American vines, and the

[2] Shand, *A Book of Other Wines – than French*, pp. 46–7.
[3] Ibid, p. 43.

old kinds – Sylvaner, Kleinberger, Müller-Thurgau – completely abandoned."[4]

Despite the homogeneity of the Rheingau vineyards, there are nonetheless significant differences between the sites. The hills are undulating, so not all the vineyards enjoy a pure southern exposure; soil structure and drainage vary; there are considerable differences between the vineyards on relatively fertile soil close to the river, and those higher up in the hinterland.

From east to west, the Rheingau vineyards begin at Hochheim, across the river from Mainz. Hochheim is quite a charming village and some of the wine estates separate the main street of the old town from the vineyards that slope down to the railway line along the river shore. The specificity of the various Rheingau villages will be discussed in greater detail later in this chapter, but in general the microclimate at Hochheim delivers wines of considerable body and power. The next village to the west is Walluf, which may be underrated because it lacks a collection of well-known producers. The next village is Eltville, which is actually a small town, and inland from Eltville is the more rewarding village of Rauenthal, which has a number of outstanding sites.

Adjoining Eltville to the west is Erbach, where the Marcobrunn is the most distinguished vineyard, and unusual in that it lies close to the shore. Inland from Erbach is the lovely village of Kiedrich, and west of it is Hattenheim, where a number of celebrated estates such as Schönborn are located; some of its vineyards are situated on an island in the middle of the Rhein. The Steinberg is located inland from the village.

The next town to the west is Oestrich, which is conjoined with Mittelheim and Winkel. Winkel's best-known vineyard is at Schloss Vollrads on the slopes well beyond the sprawling village. Behind Oestrich is Hallgarten, where the only well known vineyard is Schönhell. After Winkel the next little town is Geisenheim, but along the slopes between the two is the hamlet of Johannisberg and its celebrated Schloss. Beyond Geisenheim the touristy town of Rüdesheim welcomes thousands of visitors from across the world. Its best vineyards lie to the west of the town, where the Rhein begins its swing northward. Once the river is moving steadily north toward Koblenz, it passes the village of

---

[4] Hallgarten, *Rhineland Wineland*, p. 42.

Assmannshausen, which is almost entirely planted with Pinot Noir, and then Lorch, the last of the Rheingau villages.

Riesling yields tend to be lower than in, for example, the Mosel. There is also a difference in vine density, with vines in the Rheingau planted at a maximum of 5,000 vines/ha (2,000 vines/acre) in some places only 3,500 vines/ha (1,500 vines/acre), whereas in the Mosel they tend to be planted at 8,000 vines/ha (3,200 vines/acre). When yield regulations were eventually imposed on the Rheingau, they were set at a maximum of eighty-eight hl/ha (35.6 hl/acre), with, however, the absurd provision that overproduction could be carried over to succeeding vintages. In 1989 yields of around 120 hl/ha (48.6 hl/acre) were widely reported, and the surplus was tacked onto the production of following years. Dr Franz Werner Michel, the former director of the German Wine Institute as well as a proprietor in Hochheim, thinks there is little point being too exercised about yields, citing years such as 1964, 1971, 1976 and 1983 when yields were abundant but quality remained high.

Although the "carry-over" provision encourages growers who routinely overcrop, they also have to bear the cost of storing the over-production until a short year occurs and it can be used up. So the practice is probably not as widespread as might be feared, and certainly the best estates keep their yields at well below the permitted maximum. Many of them are members of the VDP (see p. 22), which imposes a maximum yield of seventy-five hl/ha (30.4 hl/acre). Here too there is, perhaps not surprisingly, a loophole. What the VDP insists upon is that any production over and above seventy-five hl/ha (30.4 hl/acre) cannot be bottled with the VDP logo, but there is nothing to prevent the grower from using another label. However, if a grower is cropping ninety hl/ha (36.4 hl/acre), the proportion bottled as VDP wine will suffer from the same dilution as the overproduction. Reformers would like to see the Rheingau emulate other wine countries that require overproduction to be sent for distillation, which would discourage the routine overcroppers from such practices.

A more positive feature of Rheingau viticulture is that the use of insecticides and herbicides has diminished sharply, in large part because representatives of the Green Party in the regional government have encouraged greater environmental awareness among farmers of the state of Hessen.

Yet all is not well within the Rheingau, quite apart from the controversial Erstes Gewächs campaign (see p. 24). In the early 1990s Graf Matuschka told me he was concerned about the future of some domaines, because they operated on very slender margins, making them hard to sustain. Indeed, the 1990s saw the demise, for a variety of reasons, of a number of well-regarded estates: Aschrott in Hochheim, Schloss Groenesteyn in Kiedrich, and Richter-Boltendahl in Eltville. In addition, many small properties have given up wine production, and their vineyards have been absorbed by the larger estates. This is because it is impossible to operate profitably with fewer than three ha (7.4 acres) of vineyards. This trend, superficially regrettable, has been a godsend to other small family domaines, such as Leitz in Rüdesheim, which have been able to add excellent vineyards to their portfolio at reasonable cost.

One likely reason for the declining reputation of Rheingau wines is that the region is dominated by large aristocratic or ecclesiastical domaines, which are mostly run by administrators. Even when proprietors were actively involved in the estate and resident at its Schloss, they were not necessarily involved in the winemaking process. I once asked Graf Matuschka for the name of his cellarmaster; he could tell me the surname but not the first name, suggesting he was not on very close terms with the man who had been making his wines for decades. Administrators may be very competent at running things, but their primary job is to keep the estate profitable (or at least solvent); an obsession with quality is not part of the job description. These large estates – such as Schloss Schönborn, Johannisberg, Prinz von Hessen and Schloss Reinhartshausen – plus the state domaine at Eltville, control about one-quarter of the entire production of the Rheingau; thus they dominate the market from a commercial point of view, but do not necessarily make the best wines.

Ownership patterns have been changing. Some aristocratic estates remain: Fürst Löwenstein, Schönborn, Langwerth von Simmern, Knyphausen, and Prinz von Hessen. There are estates owned by banks and corporations: Johannisberg and Schloss Vollrads. And a major estate owned by a Japanese company: Robert Weil. There are two state domaines, and one small estate in Rüdesheim owned by a convent. But equally important are the many estates in the hands of local families, often for many generations: Allendorf, Breuer, Johannishof, Ress, Kühn, Künstler, and many others.

Dieter Greiner is convinced that the overall quality of wines from the Rheingau has improved radically since 1995. I think this is probably true. No longer is the region dominated, from a qualitative point of view, by the large noble domaines. Today, family domaines such as Leitz, Lang, Kuhn, Becker, Spreitzer, and many others are setting the highest standards and doing a great deal to rescue the somewhat tarnished reputation of the region. Despite the wrangling over the Erstes Gewächs the upshot is likely to be a lower tolerance for poorly made wines. Reformers remain unhappy about the refusal of many domaines to give up the production of non-botrytized sweet wines – in short, the Spätlese style – but in a sense the battle has been won. Greiner points out that in 1971 seventy per cent of Rheingau wines were sweet; today seventy per cent are dry.

The red wines remain an oddity, although there is a long tradition of red wine production from Assmannshausen. In the nineteenth century the wines were known as "red hocks" and recommended by London doctors to patients suffering from diabetes.[5] Although there was a tradition of harvesting the grapes as late as possible, non-German drinkers have often found the Pinot Noirs from Assmannshausen distinctly thin. There has been a revival in red wine production, especially from growers such as Kesseler and the Krone estate in Assmannshausen.

The vineyards

There is a single Bereich in the Rheingau: Johannisberg. There are ten Grosslagen and 123 Einzellagen. The Grosslagen are listed with the names of the principal villages each encompasses: Steil (Assmannshausen), Burgweg (Rüdesheim), Erntebringer (Johannisberg), Honigberg (Winkel, Erbach), Gottesthal (Oestrich), Deutelsberg (Hattenheim), Mehrhölzchen (Hallgarten), Heiligenstock (Kiedrich), Steinmächer (Rauenthal, Eltville), Daubhaus (Hochheim).

The following list cites the main villages of the region, and their principal vineyards. No attempt has been made here or in the other chapters to provide a complete list, because many sites, especially in southern

[5] Shand, p. 63.

Germany, either lack personality or are rarely or never cited on wine labels. But in the great wine-producing areas of Germany, the typicity of vineyards is as important, if as tricky to pin down, as in Burgundy or Piedmont.

From west to east the Grosslagen are: Assmannshäuser Steil, 139 ha (343 acres); Rüdesheimer Burgweg, 667 ha (1,648 acres); Johannisberger Erntebringer, 320 ha (790 acres); Winkeler Honigberg, 254 ha (628 acres); Erbacher Honigberg, 200 ha (494 acres); Oestricher Gottesthal, 321 ha (793 acres); Hattenheimer Deutelsberg, 253 ha (625 acres); Hallgartener Mehrhölzchen, 346 ha (855 acres); Kiedricher Heiligenstock, 171 ha (423 acres); Rauenthaler Steinmächer, 609 ha (1,505 acres); and Hochheimer Daubhaus, 356 ha (880 acres).

The Erstes Gewächs vineyards (often just part of the vineyard is classified) are:

Assmannshausen: Frankenthal, Höllenberg.

Eltville: Langenstück, Rheinberg, Sonnenberg, Taubenberg, Kalbspflicht.

Erbach: Hohenrain, Marcobrunn, Michelmark, Schlossberg, Siegelsberg, Steinmorgen.

Flörsheim: Herrnberg.

Geisenheim: Fuchsberg, Kläuserweg, Mäuerchen, Mönchspfad, Rothenberg.

Hallgarten: Jungfer, Schönhell.

Hattenheim: Engelmannsberg, Hassel, Mannberg, Nussbrunnen, Pfaffenberg, Schützenhaus, Wisselbrunnen.

Hochheim: Domdechaney, Hofmeister, Hölle, Königin Victoriaberg, Kirchenstück, Reichestal, Stein, Stielweg.

Johannisberg: Hölle, Klaus.

Kiedrich: Gräfenberg, Sandgrub, Wasseros.

Kostheim: Weiss Erd.

Lorch: Bodental-Steinberg, Kapellenberg, Krone, Pfaffenwies, Schlossberg.

Lorchhausen: Seligmacher.

Martinsthal: Langenberg, Rödchen, Wildsau.

Mittelheim: Edelmann, St Nikolaus.

Oestrich: Doosberg, Lenchen.

Rauenthal: Baiken, Gehrn, Rothenberg, Wülfen.

Rüdesheim: Berg Roseneck, Berg Rottland, Berg Schlossberg, Bischofsberg, Drachenstein, Klosterlay, Magdalenenkreuz.

Walluf: Berg-Bildstock, Vitusberg, Walkenberg.

Wicker: Mönchsgewann, Stein.

Winkel: Gutenberg, Hasensprung, Jesuitengarten, Schlossberg.

Plus Schloss Johannisberg, Steinberg, Schloss Vollrads, Schloss Reinhartshausen.

ASSMANNSHAUSEN

About 70 ha (173 acres) of Pinot Noir are cultivated here, and historical records trace this tradition back for five centuries or more. In the past the variety was known by different names such as Schwarzer Assmannshäuser. The village was known for its wine, as illustrated by documents in Mainz dated as early as 1107; in 1507 documents show that local nuns were drinking red wines, quite possibly Pinot Noir. The best sector in the vineyards is lower down around the cross in the Höllenberg, where the flowering takes place two weeks earlier than higher up, so there is a longer growing season.

Assmannshäuser Frankenthal. 45 ha (111 acres). Just south of Höllenberg. Contains Riesling as well as Pinot Noir.

Assmannshäuser Hinterkirch. 59 ha (146 acres).

Assmannshäuser Höllenberg. 55 ha (136 acres). Ninety per cent Pinot Noir. The slate soil warms up fast, which is an advantage in obtaining fully ripe grapes. But it drains rapidly, so water retention is a problem. Rainfall is usually very low. The owners include the state domaine, Kesseler, and Hotel Krone.

ELTVILLE

The village derives its name from Latin *alta villa*. With 740 ha (1,828 acres) of vineyards, this is largest commune in the Rheingau, producing wines that are usually full-bodied and spicy.

Eltviller Rheinberg. 30 ha (74 acres). Very close to the river.

Eltviller Sonnenberg. 68 ha (168 acres). Probably the best site in Eltville.

Eltviller Taubenberg. 80 ha (198 acres). Loess and loess-loam.

ERBACH

The vineyards stretch back some distance into the hills, and these inland sites give good but rarely great wine. The top site is the riverside Marcobrunn.

Erbacher Hohenrain. 18 ha (44.5 acres).

Erbacher Marcobrunn. 5.2 ha (12.8 acres). Rich in marl, this site consistently yields Rieslings that are rich, spicy, and full-flavoured; their richness and body mean that they can, however, lack some elegance. Schloss Schönborn is the principal owner with 2.7 ha (6.7 acres); others include Schloss Reinhartshausen, the state domaine, Langwerth von Simmern, and Knyphausen.

Erbacher Michelmark. 75 ha (185 acres).

Erbacher Rheinhell. 18 ha (44.5 acres). These vineyards are on the Mariannenau island in the Rhein just offshore from Erbach. An *Alleinbesitz* of Schloss Reinhartshausen, which has its Chardonnay planted here.

Erbacher Schlossberg. 5.6 ha (13.8 acres). Known for its elegant Rieslings.

Erbacher Siegelsberg. 16 ha (39.5 acres). Probably the second best site after Marcobrunn. Owners include Knyphausen, Langwerth von Simmern, Schloss Reinhartshausen, and Jakob Jung.

Erbacher Steinmorgen. South of the village along the river shore.

GEISENHEIM

The village is probably better known for its wine college than its vineyards, but there are some excellent sites here.

Geisenheimer Fuchsberg. 68 ha (168 acres). Its marl soil gives powerful wines.

Geisenheimer Kilzberg. 56 ha (138 acres).

Geisenheimer Kläuserweg. 57 ha (141 acres). Heavy soil, giving full and vigorous wines.

Geisenheimer Mäuerchen. 33 ha (81.5 acres). Loamy marl soil, producing racy Rieslings and some Pinot Noir.

Geisenheimer Mönchspfad. 160 ha (395 acres).

Geisenheimer Rothenberg. 36 ha (89 acres). The best site in the commune, distinguished by quartzite and ferrous soil with clay and slate. The wines are quite exotic, full-bodied and long-lived, and the owners include Deinhard and von Zwierlein.

Geisenheimer Schlossgarten. 18 ha (44.5 acres). Its loose sandy-loess soil results in light fresh wines. Schloss Schönborn is the largest proprietor.

HALLGARTEN

This village, inland from the river, is where the region's highest vineyards lie. The higher slopes used to be planted with Müller-Thurgau and Portugieser. Being relatively cool, Riesling can sometimes have difficulty in ripening. But in some years the wines have excellent body, complexity, and elegance.

Hallgartener Hendelberg. 53 ha (131 acres). The highest vineyard in the Rheingau, at 300 metres (984 feet).

Hallgartener Jungfer. 54 ha (133 acres). A site with deep loess-loam as well as tertiary clay and marl. Fairly spicy Rieslings.

Hallgartener Schönhell. 58 ha (143 acres). A fairly cool marl site with a long growing season. It lies west of the village on a slope. The wines can be powerful and long-lived, with a strong acidic structure. Erstes Gewächs for Löwenstein.

Hallgartener Würzgarten. 42 ha (104 acres). Marl soil, giving robust wines. Owners include Löwenstein and Prinz.

HATTENHEIM

Kloster Eberbach is located here, as well as its best-known vineyard, the Steinberg.

Hattenheimer Engelmannsberg. 20 ha (49.4 acres). Lively forward Rieslings.

Hattenheimer Hassel. 30 ha (74 acres). Deep loess and loess-loam.

Hattenheimer Heiligenberg. 36 ha (89 acres). Deep loess-loam.

Hattenheimer Mannberg. 11 ha (27 acres). An outstanding site located down by the river, alongside Marcobrunn. The principal owner is Langwerth von Simmern

Hattenheimer Nussbrunnen. 10 ha (24.7 acres). Another top site. The owners include Langwerth von Simmern, Schloss Schönborn, and Schloss Reinhartshausen.

Hattenheimer Pfaffenberg. 7 ha (17.3 acres). *Alleinbesitz* of Schloss Schönborn. The soil is loess-loam with sand, giving precocious wine that can be perfumed and fruity.

Hattenheimer Rheingarten. 40 ha (99 acres). Bordering the river and best for early-drinking wines. Langwerth von Simmern is the principal owner.

Hattenheimer Schützenhaus. 66 ha (163 acres). Deep loess and loess-loam.

Hattenheimer Wisselbrunnen. 18 ha (44.5 acres). Light tertiary marl and a high loam content that retains warmth. This is a precocious site, with flowering up to ten days earlier than in more inland sites. Often outstanding wines, a tad lighter than the Rieslings from Mannberg. The owners include Knyphausen, Schloss Schönborn, Ress, Langwerth von Simmern, Lang, and Schloss Reinhartshausen.

Steinberg. 32 ha (79 acres). This walled vineyard was first planted by the monks of Kloster Eberbach in 1131. After secularization, it belonged to the House of Nassau, then the Hohenzollerns, and is now an *Alleinbesitz* of the state domaine. It never attains the highest must weights, but the wines have a strong personality and a pronounced mineral character.

HOCHHEIM

280 ha (692 acres). The town was first mentioned in 775, and first documented as a wine village in 1239. Hochheim seems isolated but in Roman and medieval times the region's main town was Mainz; Wiesbaden, which today separates Hochheim from the rest of the Rheingau, did not really exist until the nineteenth century. The vineyards here enjoy a warmer microclimate than the rest of the region, being protected from the north wind, and flowering usually occurs a few days earlier than elsewhere in the Rheingau. This may be because of the proximity to the river, or because there are no forests behind the vineyards. Hochheim benefits further from the confluence of the Rhein and Main, gaining reflected warmth from both. The sedimentary soils, free of volcanic rock, may also contribute. These are heavy soils, with much loam and clay. The sugar levels are often the highest in the Rheingau by 5–10 degrees Oechsle, but the wines retain acidity. The vineyards can be susceptible to drought. The eastern sites have some chalk which can give the wine a mineral quality. The slopes with more sandy loam gives gentle and forward wines. The British term for Rhein Riesling, Hock, is derived from the town's name. Indeed, Hochheim seems to have been a Riesling-only village since the eighteenth century.

Hochheimer Berg. 35 ha (86.5 acres).

Hochheimer Domdechaney. 10 ha (24.7 acres). This top site below the church gives wines that are robust and masculine. It has very heavy soil, almost pure clay. The owners include Domdechant Werner, Schloss Schönborn, and the state domaine.

Hochheimer Herrnberg. 4 ha (9.9 acres).

Hochheimer Hofmeister. 34 ha (84 acres).

Hochheimer Hölle. 36 ha (89 acres). A chalky site along the river, and early ripening, giving balanced but less vigorous wine than the very best sites. The owners include Künstler, Domdechant Werner, and Schloss Schönborn.

Hochheimer Kirchenstück. 15 ha (37 acres). Dr Michel describes this as his top site along with Domdechaney, but its wines are more feminine. It lies west of Hölle and has light loam on the mid-slope. Gunter Künstler says that it's Hochheim's Lafite as compared to Stielweg, which is its Latour. The owners include Domdechant Werner, Künstler, Ress, and Schloss Schönborn.

Hochheimer Königin Victoriaberg. 5 ha (12.4 acres). This enclave, an *Alleinbesitz* of the Hupfeld estate, is situated low on the slope within Hölle. In 1850 Queen Victoria visited the vineyard, which produced one of her favourite wines. After her visit the Court was begged for permission to name the site after her and erect an (ugly) monument in her honour. Despite their cachet, the wines often have a pronounced earthiness.

Hochheimer Reichestal. 26 ha (64 acres). West of Stielweg. Owners include Domdechant Werner and Hupfeld.

Hochheimer Stein. 27 ha (67 acres). Less good than Hölle, because it has frost pockets.

Hochheimer Stielweg. 26 ha (64 acres). Between Domdechaney and the river, and another part lies west of Domdechaney. The wines are assertive and powerful.

JOHANNISBERG

90 ha (222 acres). The site was originally planted by Benedictines in 1106. The steepest vineyards are Schlossberg and Hölle, which have quartzite soils and are quite stony. As one moves toward Vollrads the soils become more sandy. Johannes Eser says the wines need time to develop

and often don't show well at new vintage tastings; but they can be very long lived.

Johannisberger Goldatzel. Between Hansenberg and the village, Goldatzel has deeper soil with good water retention. The wines are usually less mineral than those from many other sites.

Johannisberger Hansenberg. 3.8 ha (9.4 acres). Behind Hölle, and has some quartzite in the soil. Mostly owned by Mumm.

Johannisberger Hölle. 22 ha (54.4 acres). Can deliver racy but age-worthy Rieslings.

Johannisberger Klaus. 24 ha (59.3 acres). The lowest site, fairly flat, with heavy soil and some loess; part of the vineyard occupies the lower slopes beneath the Schloss. Owners include Prinz von Hessen, Schloss Johannisberg, Schloss Schönborn and Johannishof.

Johannisberger Mittelhöhle. 6.5 ha (16 acres).

Johannisberger Scharzenstein. 5.5 ha (13.6 acres). Above the village with deeper soils, Scharzenstein has quite good water retention, but the wines are less mineral. Owned largely by Mumm and Johannishof.

Johannisberger Schlossberg. 35 ha (86.5 acres). The steepest and stoniest vineyard descending from the Schloss terrace and the *Alleinbesitz* of Schloss Johannisberg.

Johannisberger Vogelsang. 14 ha (34.6 acres). This lies east of the village and spreads down past the Schloss. The soils are Johannisberg's lightest, having more gravel and sand, thus resembling the Winkel vineyards. They give fruitier, less complex wines.

KIEDRICH

Wilhelm Weil (see p. 123) says some compare this village to the Mosel because of its slate soils, which delay ripening. Consequently, growers can safely wait if necessary to get fully ripe grapes; they are also aided by frequent winds from the Taunus mountains that help keep rot at bay. The growing season can be 120–130 days. With grapes naturally healthy until late into the autumn, botrytis always comes late, often in November or December. By the river, the grapes develop botrytis more rapidly, but don't dessicate easily because of the humidity. Top estates can still be harvesting at Christmas. Kiedrich wines in general are noted for their balance, delicacy and spicy tones.

Kiedricher Gräfenberg. 11 ha (27 acres). Planted in the twelfth century by the monks from Kloster Eberbach. Southwest-facing, so not the hottest in the Rheingau but benefiting from the evening sunshine and giving elegant yet long-lived wines. Maturation is five to six days later than by the river.

Kiedricher Klosterberg. 66 ha (163 acres).

Kiedricher Sandgrub. 48 ha (119 acres). South of Wasseros, Sandgrub has, as its name suggests, more sandy soils, giving broader wines that nonetheless always have good acidity.

Kiedricher Wasseros. 36 ha (89 acres). Embraces Gräfenberg to the north and south. Similar wines to those from Gräfenberg and almost as good.

LORCH

Slate and quartzite soils dominate the most westerly commune of the Rheingau. The medium-bodied, racy Rieslings probably resemble those of the neighbouring Mittelrhein more than they do those of the Rheingau.

Lorcher Kapellenberg. 57 ha (141 acres). Known for very delicate Rieslings.

Lorcher Krone. 13 ha (32 acres).

Lorcher Pfaffenwies. 35 ha (86.5 acres).

Lorcher Schlossberg. 53 ha (131 acres).

MARTINSTHAL

The village lies inland between Rauenthal and Walluf at 180m. Its three sites are Langenberg, 19 ha (47 acres); Wildsau, 31 ha (76.6 acres); and Rödchen, 28 ha (69 acres). Relatively precocious wines.

MITTELHEIM

A narrow band of vineyards stretches northward from this village, which is squeezed between Oestrich and Winkel. The name is rarely seen on labels. The vineyards are Goldberg, 24 ha (59.3 acres); Edelmann, 93 ha (230 acres); and St Nikolaus, 50 ha (124 acres).

OESTRICH

The wines from Oestrich can be among the most opulent from the Rheingau, but sometimes lack finesse. Loess soils.

Oestricher Doosberg. 153 ha (378 acres). The original and best parcel lies on a ridge overlooking the river and descends toward the village; it faces both south and west, benefiting from daytime and evening sun. It also benefits from excellent ventilation. The grapes tend to stay healthy until late in the autumn. Doosberg can be better than Lenchen in dry years as it has better water retention. Schloss Schönborn is the largest proprietor.

Oestricher Klosterberg. 142 ha (351 acres).

Oestricher Lenchen. 145 ha (358 acres). A stream west of the vineyard gives autumn fogs which help provoke botrytis. There's more gravel in the soil than at Doosberg; this results in better drainage, which is beneficial in wet years.

Schloss Reichartshausen. 4 ha (9.9 acres). A small Riesling vineyard close to the river, and an *Alleinbesitz* of Balthasar Ress.

RAUENTHAL

For some reasons the wines from these slopes have lost some of their renown, but some decades ago these were among the costliest wines of the region, esteemed for their elegance and spiciness.

Rauenthaler Baiken. 15 ha (37.1 acres). Kloster Eberbach is the major owner of this famous site, together with Langwerth von Simmern and Schloss Schönborn. Magnificent and long-lived wines.

Rauenthaler Gehrn. 18 ha (44.5 acres).

Rauenthaler Langenstück. 26 ha (64 acres).

Rauenthaler Nonnenberg. 5 ha (12.4 acres). *Alleinbesitz* of Georg Breuer. The soil contains loam and gravel with schist below. The wines are exuberant and aromatic with a marked acidity.

Rauenthaler Rothenberg. 20 ha (49.4 acres). Gives Rieslings with pronounced acidity.

Rauenthaler Wülfen. 14 ha (34.6 acres).

RÜDESHEIM

380 ha (939 acres). These dramatically located vineyards lie beyond the little town and overlook the bend of the Rhein as it flows north toward Koblenz. Above the vineyards stands the enormous Germania monument. Until the mid-1970s many of the vineyards were terraced, but *Flurbereinigung* rationalized them. The wines derive their minerality from schist in the soil, as well as from a higher slate content as you move

westward and the slopes become steeper. The peculiarity of the Rüdesheim vineyards is that they tend to suffer from stress when there is insufficient rainfall. In hot summers such as 1997 it is not unusual for the vines to shut down until rainfall resumes. This means that Rüdesheim often performs better in rather wet years than in very hot and dry years. Johannes Leitz says Rüdesheim's tendency to deliver very healthy grapes means they are well suited for dry wines, and the village rarely produces Eiswein, BA or TBA. He adds that the village's warm soils mean that acidity can be relatively low.

Rüdesheimer Berg Roseneck. 29 ha (71.7 acres). Entirely planted with Riesling. A site west of the monument. The more westerly part is an amphitheatre opposite Bingen, and exceptionally steep. The soil is a crumbly red slate, which is quite unlike Mosel slate and much softer. There are elements of quartz and loess too. It gives intense fruit and crisp acidity and, in the eyes of many growers, is the most typical vineyard of the village.

Rüdesheimer Berg Rottland. 37 ha (91.4 acres). Entirely planted with Riesling on slate and quartz soils. Just above the village, and a site that rarely has drought problems. Owners include Leitz, Nägler, Martin Siegfried, Ress, and Geschwister Erhard.

Rüdesheimer Berg Schlossberg. 29 ha (71.7 acres). The most westerly vineyard around the ruined castle on the curve of the river and very steep. Very hot in summer, and thus very dry; strong wind keeps botrytis at bay. Capable of exceptional quality. Owners include Leitz, Breuer 2.6 ha (6.4 acres), Schloss Schönborn, Deinhard, Kesseler 1.3 ha (3.2 acres); Geschwister Erhard, and Nägler.

Rüdesheimer Bischofsberg. 34 ha (84 acres).

Rüdesheimer Drachenstein. 48 ha (119 acres). West of the convent vineyards. Stony with loess and not highly esteemed though there are some very good parcels. Stretches up to the forest.

Rüdesheimer Kirchenpfad. 20 ha (49.4 acres). Above the church.

Rüdesheimer Klosterberg. 39 ha (96.4 acres). Near the convent.

Rüdesheimer Klosterlay. 37 ha (91.4 acres). *Alleinbesitz* of the St Hildegard convent, where 80 nuns still live and produce their own wine.

Rüdesheimer Magdalenenkreuz. 48 ha (119 acres). To the east of the convent of St Hildegard. Deep loess-loam. Fairly flat on plateau land.

Rüdesheimer Rosengarten. 3.7 ha (9.1 acres). Loess soil.

WALLUF

This village east of Eltville is less well known than most others because it lacks a large or aristocratic domaine to lend it glamour. The production is mostly drunk locally, but can be of very good quality. The soils are sedimentary, with loam and gravel. Its vineyards, other than Walkenberg, are rarely seen on labels; they are Langenstück, 14 ha (34.6 acres); Vitusberg, 14 ha (34.6 acres); Oberberg, 13 ha (32 acres); Berg-Bildstock, 30 ha (74 acres); and Gottesacker, 17 ha (42 acres).

Wallufer Walkenberg. 29 ha (71.7 acres). Deep loess-loam characterizes the soil of Walluf's best site. Hans-Josef Becker's grandfather planted Pinot Noir here in 1905. At the time the dominant red variety was St Laurent, which disappeared in the 1950s. The grapes can attain high levels of ripeness. Becker owns 6.1 ha (15 acres), and the other important owner is Toni Jost.

WICKER

This little-known wine village lies east of Hochheim. Its sites are Mönchsgewann, 18 ha (44.5 acres); König-Wilhelmsberg, 2.3 ha (5.7 acres) and the *Alleinbesitz* of Hück in Hochheim; Nonnberg, 2 ha (4.9 acres); and Stein, 20 ha (49.4 acres).

WINKEL

Schloss Vollrads. 33 ha (81.5 acres). Although located within Winkel, the Schloss is entitled to use its name alone to identify its vineyards.

Winkeler Dachsberg. 52 ha (128 acres).

Winkeler Gutenberg. 51 ha (126 acres).

Winkeler Hasensprung. 104 ha (257 acres). Sandy soils. Winkel's best site after Vollrads and Jesuitengarten.

Winkeler Jesuitengarten. 26 ha (64.2 acres). A top site, with loess soil. Allendorf is a major owner.

Producers

WEINGUT FRITZ ALLENDORF

Kirchstr 69, 65375 Oestrich-Winkel. Tel: +49 (0) 6723 91850. Fax: 918540. www.allendorf.de. 58 ha (143 acres). 48,000 cases.

This large estate releases a wide range of wines, both still and sparkling, from vineyards in Winkel, Geisenheim, Rüdesheim, and Assmannhausen. The simpler wines can be assertive and rather fierce in their acidity, and that includes the Chardonnay. The Spätburgunder from Assmannshäuser Höllenberg is plump and rounded, but the acidity can be irksome. In 1999 there was delicious Beerenauslese from Winkeler Jesuitengarten.

FRIEDRICH ALTENKIRCH

Binger Weg 2, 65391 Lorch. Tel: +49 (0) 6726 8300. Fax: 2483. www.weingut-altenkirch.de. 17 ha (42 acres). 8,000 cases.

This estate was founded in 1826 and is today directed by Stefan Breuer. The vineyard holdings are in Lorch, Rüdesheim, Oestrich, and Mittelheim. The Lorch wines, both Riesling and Weissburgunder, are the most interesting, and there has been a steady increase in quality in recent vintages.

WEINGUT HANS BARTH

Bergweg 20, 65347 Hattenheim. Tel: +49 (0) 6723 2514. Fax: 4375. www.weingut-barth.de. 12 ha (29.7 acres). 7,500 cases.

Perhaps because he specializes in sparkling wines, Norbert Barth is an underrated producer, at least to judge by the range from the 1999 vintage that I sampled. His best Rieslings come from top Hattenheim vineyards, and are well balanced and concentrated. I would have expected the Wisselbrunnen Erstes Gewächs to be better than the Schützenhaus Spätlese Trocken, but I preferred the spiciness and length of the latter to the sumptuous but rather broad style of the former. The Hassel BA was exemplary, as was the pineappley Eiswein, with its splendid attack. Clearly an estate to watch.

J.B. BECKER

Rheinstr 5–6, 65396 Walluf. Tel: +49 (0) 6123 72523. Fax: 75335. 13 ha (32 acres). 6,000 cases.

In 1893 Jean-Baptist Becker founded this firm, and in 1905 he planted the first Pinot Noir in the Walkenberg. His son Josef expanded the domaine in the 1930s, and since 1971 the property has been run by Hans-Josef Becker and his sister Maria. With his flamboyant moustaches, Becker looks like a showman, but in fact he's a thoughtful and intelligent winemaker who has set high standards for the other growers of Walluf to follow.

He owns 6 ha (14.8 acres) in the Walkenberg, and leases 3.2 ha (7.9 acres) in Eltviller Rheinberg. Yields are low, around 55 hl/ha (22.3 hl/acre), and all grapes are hand-picked and fermented only in wooden casks, where the Rieslings are aged for six to nine months, Pinot Noir for twelve to twenty-four months. Becker can ripen grapes thoroughly in most years, and this allows him to focus on dry wines. He likes a truly dry style, with residual sugar levels at around 2 grams rather than 7. I prefer his Spätlese Trocken to his Auslese Trocken, because the latter can easily attain fourteen per cent, and is too burly and alcoholic for my taste, whereas the Spätlese is more elegant and better balanced. He has not yet adopted the concept of Erstes Gewächs.

For sweet wines too he likes a good dose of alcohol. His 1999 Riesling Auslese from Walkenberg had only 40 grams of sugar, but fourteen degrees of alcohol. His BAs can have even higher alcohol. "I don't worry about the balance of these wines, because their high acidity will keep them in balance. I want sweet wines with plenty of body, wines similar in style to Sauternes, wines you can drink with food."

Becker has had a long association with Mumm, producing a Riesling Sekt from Walkenberg grapes and left twenty-two months on the lees.

These are excellent wines and very reasonably priced for their quality. But they are quite austere.

GEORG BREUER

Grabenstr 8, 65385 Rüdesheim. Tel: +49 (0) 6722 1027. Fax: 4531. www.georg-breuer.com. 26 ha (64 acres). 11,000 cases.

The shrewd Bernhard Breuer, born here in 1946, has made a controversial reputation for himself as an ardent enthusiast both for dry-tasting Rieslings from the Rheingau and for the cause of vineyard classification (see chapter 2). With his high ideals, he needs to ensure that his own wines are of the highest quality. Fortunately they are among the finest Rieslings of the region, and he keeps yields down to 25–45 hl/ha (10.1–18.2 hl/acre) to ensure high levels of concentration.

The Georg Breuer estate was only created in 1980. Before that the family had been involved in a négociant business called Scholl & Hillebrand. Breuer used the new label for the family's estate wines, and over the years he gradually expanded that estate to its present size.

His finest vineyards are in Rüdesheimer Berg Schlossberg and Rauenthaler Nonnenberg, which he regards as first-growth sites, even if the classification that emerged from Geisenheim didn't agree. Since 1995 he has evolved his own hierarchical structure. The wines from Schlossberg and Nonnenberg are essentially dry; the next tier down is occupied by Riesling from Berg Rottland, which used to be released as Charta wines; next down are the village Rieslings from Rüdesheim and Rauenthal, the former the more elegant, the latter more fruity. Then there are two Rheingau Rieslings: Sauvage (Trocken) and Charm (Halb-trocken). The waters are slightly muddied by a wine called Montosa, which is a blended second wine from Rüdesheim and Rauenthal. When the climate obliges, Breuer produces BA and TBA. There is also a tiny production of high-quality vintage Sekt from Pinot Gris, Pinot Blanc, Riesling, and since 1988, Pinot Noir; in 2000 the current vintage was 1993.

This constitutes a tremendous range of wines. The top wines are expensive and the best values are to be found among the village Rieslings. The wines are vinified in a blend of wood and steel, and one unusual feature of the vinification is a six-hour skin contact when the grapes are fully healthy.

For all his devotion to the cause of Rheingau Riesling, Breuer has not been slow to experiment with other wines and other styles. He has 2.5 ha (6.2 acres) of Pinot Noir in top sites, and first produced a varietal Pinot Noir in 1994. These are not entirely successful, although the clones are Burgundian, yields are low, and the proportion of new barriques is kept to a sensible twenty-five per cent. The wine has lovely aromas, but lacks complexity on the palate. Breuer believes his Pinots will improve as the vines grow older.

Among his many ventures, I recall an oak-aged Rivaner (Müller-Thurgau) from Rüdesheim vines and a bizarre wine called Trius, a blend of Pinot Blanc from three growers in three regions, partly aged in barriques; production ceased in the late 1990s. Together with Bernd Philippi of Koehler-Ruprecht in the Pfalz, he is joint owner of an estate on the Douro, and is involved in a project with Stephan du Toit in Wellington, South Africa.

AUGUST ESER

Friedensplatz 19, 65375 Oestrich-Winkel. Tel: +49 (0) 6723 5032. Fax: 87406. www.eser-wein.de. 10 ha (24.7 acres). 7,000 cases.

Eser produced wines of rather patchy quality in the late 1990s, but seems to have bounced back with rich Erstes Gewächs wines from Winkeler Jesuitengarten and Erbacher Siegelsberg, both of which have the merest hint of sweetness to give them greater roundness.

JOACHIM FLICK

Strassenmühle, 65439 Flörsheim-Wicker. Tel: +49 (0) 6145 7686. Fax: 54393. 10 ha (24.7 acres). 6,500 cases.

It was only in the 1980s that Reiner and Kirsten Flick began to bottle their wines; in the mid-1990s they moved to the Strassenmühle, which gave them a permanent base from which to produce a wide range of wines. Other than Rieslings, they also make Dornfelder and a barrique-aged Weissburgunder. Flörsheim and Wicker are even further east than Hochheim, nudging the suburbs of Frankfurt. Their best sites are Wickerer Mönchsgewann and Hochheimer Hölle. These are relatively warm vineyards, so perhaps it is not surprising that the overall style of the wines is rich and rounded, with a relatively soft structure. Their Beerenauslese, from either Riesling or Weissburgunder, can be excellent. The Spätburgunder from Wickerer Stein in 1999 lacked complexity.

PRINZ VON HESSEN

Grund 1, 65366 Johannisberg. Tel: +49 (0) 6722 8172. Fax: 50588. www.prinz-von-hessen.com. 45 ha (111 acres). 25,000 cases.

This large estate was acquired by the Landgraf von Hessen in 1958. For many years its wines were far from remarkable, but under the direction of Markus Sieben there has been a great improvement in the late 1990s. Sites that are less than outstanding are used to produce the Gutsriesling, and vineyards are only designated on the label for the top sites such as Johannisberger Klaus and the Winkeler Jesuitengarten, which is the source of the estate's Erstes Gewächs. Overall, average yields are 60 hl/ha (24.3 hl/acre). The dry Rieslings as well as the concentrated botrytis wines from vintages such as 1999 are all excellent; the 2000s are a touch broader in their structure.

HESSISCHE STAATSWEINGÜTER DOMÄNE ASSMANNSHAUSEN

Höllenbergstr 10, 65385 Assmannshausen. Tel: +49 (0) 6722 2273.
Fax: 48121. 25 ha (61.8 acres). Production: 10,000 cases.

Although part of the vast Hessen state domaine (*Staatsweingüter*) since 1945, the Assmannshausen property and winery has long enjoyed a kind of autonomy, specializing as it does in red wine. Friedrich Dries has been here for more than thirty-five years, and was cellarmaster until 1992, when he was succeeded by his son Oliver. Dries studied at Weinsberg college in Württemberg and then worked in Baden, so he has been involved in red wine production throughout his life.

He is well aware that there is a constant battle between quality and economy. The Pinot Noir clones planted in the 1960s were overproductive, and they have been replaced by four clones from Geisenheim that have smaller berries and less compact bunches. They are planted on the very steep slopes of the village, in vineyards that are costly to maintain and prone to erosion. Moreover, over the past fifty years the estate staff has shrunk from fifty to six employees. Viticulture is close to organic, and yields range from 40–50 hl/ha (16.2–20.2 hl/acre).

Dries has had to fashion the domaine's output to match the fickle tastes of his customers. "In the 1960s many people were telling me we ought to replace Pinot Noir with Riesling, because the red wines were not selling well. But then I started to make the Pinot in a lightly sweet style, and suddenly they were in demand again. Then the fashion reverted to dry wines, and now there's new demand for sweeter ones." These have to be made with *Süssreserve*, and are popular with private domestic customers, though it's hard to imagine they would have any international appeal.

The wines are well made, but could be better. The Pinot is fermented in open-top tanks and in roto-fermenters, using selected yeasts, then aged in large casks. Dries is not looking for rich deeply coloured Pinots, but for lighter, aromatic, and pure red wines. At the same time he insists that the wines from top vintages can age fifty years. There is very little use of barriques, which, in a top year, seems like a missed opportunity.

Some of the grapes are used for a rather earthy sparkling wine, and the vintage Sekt includes a little Weissburgunder from Hattenheim. I was not impressed by most of the dry Pinots, but was charmed by a 1999 Höllenberg Frühburgunder Spätlese Trocken, with its strawberry aromas, silky texture, and good acidic structure. An intense 1999 Hollenberg Auslese Trocken was marred by a dash of residual sugar.

Weissherbst Eiswein from Höllenberg Pinot Noir is a house speciality, and has been made in almost every vintage since 1966. It may sound bizarre but the wine can be delicious. When conditions permit, Dries also makes a Spätburgunder TBA, as in 1989 (a splendid wine), 1992, 1995, and 1997.

Dries is set to retire in late 2002, and it will be interesting to see whether his successor in 2003, Ralf Bengel, will make changes at this very traditional estate.

HESSISCHE STAATSWEINGÜTER KLOSTER EBERBACH
Schwalbacher Str 52–62, 65343 Eltville. Tel: +49 (0) 6123 92300.
Fax: 923090. www.staatsweingueterhessen.de. 197 ha (487 acres). 90,000 cases.

By German standards this is a colossal estate, made manageable by its division into six domaines, including one in the Hessische Bergstrasse. The Rheingau estates consist of 130 ha (321 acres), including the property at Assmannshausen. Its twelfth-century origins were ecclesiastical, and the domaine still owns the ancient monastery of Kloster Eberbach. Here you can see a collection of old presses from 1668 onward, some of which remained in use until 1953. The best barrels from each vintage were stored in the famous Cabinet cellar. Some of the oldest wines were analysed in the late nineteenth century and it was discovered that none of them had a residual sugar level higher than 7 grams per litre.

For many years the domaine was directed by Dr Hans Ambrosi, who, among other achievements, was one of the pioneers of Eiswein production in the Rheingau. He also modernized the Eltville cellars. Tourists were shown the handsome old casks, but the wines were actually vinified in batteries of stainless steel tanks. "My job," he once told me, "is to deal with a bureaucracy that resists innovation, and at the same time to make a profit from wine production."

This is a problem that his successors, such as Rowald Hepp in the late 1980s (now at Schloss Vollrads) and since 2000 Dieter Greiner, have also had to grapple with. For the owner of the domaine, to which the director is answerable, is the state government of Hessen. It cannot be easy to run a flagship estate while keeping politicians happy. Fortunately in 1997 the structure of the domaine was altered so that it operates as a limited company, making it less susceptible to political interference.

Quality has always been variable. Many of the vineyards are picked by machine, and yields have been on the high side. Its reputation slumped in the 1980s, and later in the decade there was a switch of style, subsequently abandoned, toward wines with higher alcohol and less residual sugar. Greiner has ambitious plans: he would like to resume winemaking activities at Kloster Eberbach, because he believes the cellars are ideal for working with wooden casks. Cask fermentation was abandoned in the 1960s, but tastings of older vintages have confirmed that some stupendous wines were made in this way. Greiner worries that the methods used to produce the wonderful BAs and TBAs from vintages such as 1893 and 1921 are partly lost, but he's also sure they can be recovered; he is convinced that wood was an essential element in their grandeur.

The domaine has an unparalleled portfolio of outstanding sites (Rauenthaler Baiken, Rüdesheimer Berg Schlossberg, Erbacher Marcobrunn), including the renowned Steinberg. Yet the wines are hit and miss. In any tasting line-up there are excellent bottles interspersed with rather dull and routine wines. There is room for improvement, and Dieter Greiner seems quietly determined to see that it comes about.

HUPFELD

Rheingaustr 113, 65375 Oestrich-Winkel. Tel: +49 (0) 6723 999239. Fax: 996259. 12 ha (29.7 acres). 8,000 cases.

For decades the Hupfelds have dined out on the fact that they are the owners of the Königin Victoriaberg in Hochheim, but I never found the wines remarkable. The estate is unusual in that it is divided between vineyards in Hochheim and those in Oestrich-Winkel; Wolfram Hupfeld looks after the latter, his brother Henning after Hochheim. No doubt aided by the fine string of vintages of the late 1990s the quality of the Hochheim wines has improved considerably. Queen Victoria would have been delighted by them.

SCHLOSS JOHANNISBERG

65366 Geisenheim-Johannisberg. Tel: +49 (0) 6722 70090. Fax: 700933. www.schloss-johannisberg.de. 35 ha (86.5 acres). Production: 20,000 cases.

Who could fail to be impressed by Schloss Johannisberg? As you stroll up the drive you can see the Romanesque basilica on the left, partly hidden by the yellow Schloss, still inhabited by Princess Metternich. Both structures were rebuilt after the estate was largely destroyed by Allied bombers in August 1942. This had been a monastic estate since the twelfth century, but by the fifteenth century the property was run down and was eventually dissolved in 1563. It passed into private hands until 1716 when it was bought by the Prince Bishop of Fulda, who built the Schloss and cellars. The property was secularized in 1802, and five years later Napoleon presented it to the Alsatian Marshal Kellerman. In 1814 it was confiscated by the Allies, and Emperor Franz I of Austria presented it to Chancellor Metternich on condition that the Habsburgs received a share of every vintage. In the nineteenth century the cellarmaster devised a system of identifying quality levels by differently coloured wax seals, a tradition that continues to this day, somewhat to the confusion of consumers. The system was rationalized in 1971 in the following manner: yellow (QbA), red (Kabinett), green (Spätlese), rose-red (Auslese), rose red-gold (BA), gold (TBA), blue (Eiswein).

By the time of the death of Prince Paul Alfons von Metternich in 1992, the estate had passed into the ownership of the Henkell & Söhnlein wine company, although the prince's widow Tatiana was granted the right to inhabit the Schloss until her death.

Beneath the Schloss are the immense cellars lined with large (empty) wooden casks, candles flickering from sconces attached to them whenever visitors are invited to descend. And from the terrace is one of the most famous views in the German winelands: straight down the steep hill of the Schlossberg toward the Rhein. If you look closely you can see in the vineyards a marker for the fiftieth line of latitude, which passes straight through them. From the riverbank, the Schloss, with its vineyards spread out beneath like a vast hooped skirt, is also one of the celebrated sights of the Rheingau. Schloss Johannisberg was the first estate in Germany to adopt Riesling as its sole grape variety in the 1720s, so the Schlossberg can hardly have changed in nearly 250 years. It was here too that botrytized wine was supposed to have been made for the first time, thanks to the late arrival of a messenger from the Bishop of Fulda authorizing the harvest to begin. But such legends should not be taken too seriously, because botrytized wines had been produced at least a century earlier in Hungary and elsewhere. Nonetheless the 1775 vintage marked a turning point at the estate, which had never before produced wines of such lusciousness. It continued to produce them when conditions permitted, as in 1779, 1781, 1783, 1788, 1791, and 1794. The *Schatzkammer* (treasury cellar) of the Schloss contains vintages as far back as 1748.

Yet something is not quite right at Johannisberg. It has great vineyards, and a highly experienced team of winemakers and managers under the long-term directorship of the genial Wolfgang Schleicher. Yet all too often the wines have been disappointing. At a remarkable tasting in 2001 held to celebrate the estate's 900th birthday, an 1862 TBA was still fresh and subtle, a dazzling demonstration of what these vineyards are capable of. Most of the soil is composed of weathered quartz and loess at varying depths. The slope faces due south, fully exposed to the sun — when it's shining. About sixty per cent of the vineyard is classified as Erstes Gewächs, but Wolfgang Schleicher is understandably reluctant to divide the estate's production. The wines used to be made in large casks, but for some years they have been vinified in stainless steel tanks.

The wines are among the most expensive in the Rheingau, but I can think of a dozen estates that produce superior quality. At the very top level, wines such as the 1999 BA and TBA can still be fabulous. But the Kabinetts and Spätlesen all too often are dull — correct, clean, but dull. I can only assume that the winemakers have to operate under commercial constraints with the consequence that the wines are not as concentrated and glittering as they should be. There seemed to be a slight improvement in the 1999s.

The Mumm winery is part of the same enterprise, although its wines are vinified separately and the grapes are sourced from different parts of the region and are not all estate-grown. Both the Johannisberg and Mumm ranges are supervised by the same cellarmaster, Hans Kessler, who replaced the veteran Herr Heinrich in 1996. The Mumm wines are mostly dry or off-dry, whereas Schloss Johannisberg still offers a substantial proportion of its production in sweeter styles.

JOHANNISHOF

Grund 63, 65366 Johannisberg. Tel: +49 (0) 6722 8216. Fax: 6387. www.weingut-johannishof.de. 20 ha (49.4 acres). 10,000 cases.

The Eser family have been making wine here since 1685, and today the property is in the hands of Hans Hermann Eser and his engaging son Johannes. Their principal sites are Geisenheimer Kläuserweg, Johannisberger Hölle, and Winkeler Hasensprung. In 1996 they were able to acquire 6 ha (14.8 acres) in Rüdesheim from the Groenesteyn estate, which was selling up. The wines are fermented either in stainless steel or in wood, and often aged in a mixture of the two. No cultivated yeasts are used. The wines are bottled in the spring to retain freshness and acidity, and *Süssreserve* is only used in minimal quantities to fine-tune the balance if necessary. The wines are fresh and delicate, not especially powerful, but always well made and finely balanced. The Erstes Gewächs in 2001 from Rüdesheimer Berg Rottland is magnificent and in perfect balance.

WEINGUT GRAF VON KANITZ

Rheinstr 49, 65391 Lorch. Tel: +49 (0) 6726 346. Fax: 2178.
www.reinerwein.de. 14 ha (34.6 acres). 5,500 cases.

This noble estate, owned by the Kanitz family since 1926 and based in a striking Renaissance mansion, is one of the few wine properties in Lorch. Since 1994 it has been organic. The wines, as one would expect from this location, have lively and pungent acidity, but they are far from lacking in fruit and can age very well. Prices are reasonable for the quality.

AUGUST KESSELER

Lorcher Str 16, 65385 Assmannshausen. Tel: +49 (0) 6722 2513. Fax: 47477.
www.august-kesseler.de. 14 ha (34.6 acres). 8,500 cases.

This is one of the very few Rheingau estates where the dominant variety is not Riesling but Pinot Noir, which accounts for half the plantings in two fine sites: Assmannshäuser Höllenberg (some vines from 1939) and Rüdesheimer Berg Schlossberg. August Kesseler has been running the domaine since 1977 (now assisted by Max Himstedt) and made his mark with a Höllenberg Pinot Noir in 1988. The Pinots are aged either in large ovals or in barriques, depending on the vintage. In a top year such as 1999, barriques only were used, almost half of them new; in 2000, in contrast, hardly any barriques were used. The range of reds consists of a fairly simple QbA, and then a succession of Spätlese Trocken ranked with one to three stars. In some years, such as 1999, the top Pinot comes from the Schlossberg and is awarded three stars on the label. These are undoubtedly among the most convincing Pinots of the Rheingau, and sell out fast.

The cellars are located in a tunnel burrowed into the hill at Assmannshausen, so the Riesling fermentations are extremely slow, sometimes continuing as late as June. Kesseler likes a long cool fermentation to preserve the aromatic intensity of the wines, most of which are grown in the Rüdesheim sites. In 1999 he made two Erstes Gewächs wines, one from Berg Roseneck, the other, a splendid wine, from Berg Schlossberg. The range is completed with resplendent BAs and TBAs, released at astonishingly high prices.

BARON ZU KNYPHAUSEN

Draiser Hof, Erbacher Str 28, 65346 Erbach. Tel: +49 (0) 6123 62177.
Fax: 4315. www.knyphausen.de. 22 ha (54.4 acres). 10,000 cases.

I have a soft spot for this estate. The mild-mannered, charming Gerko zu Knyphausen was a generous and informative host on many occasions in the 1980s and the wines, if not among the greatest from the Rheingau, were always enjoyable. The family acquired the estate in 1818, and Baron Gerko is now the seventh generation to run it from the lovely manor house built in 1725. The vineyards are dispersed, with holdings in Erbach, Hattenheim, Kiedrich, Eltville, and Rauenthal. An extensive range of 1999s struck me as medium-bodied, forward, even plump, yet lacking a little grip and concentration. The 1999 Erstes Gewächs from Hattenheimer Wisselbrunnen seemed slightly below expectation, but its somewhat slack richness may also be a reflection of the precocity of this vineyard.

ROBERT KÖNIG

Landhaus Kenner, 65385 Assmannshausen. Tel: +49 (0) 6722 1064.
Fax: 48656. 8 ha (19.8 acres). 4,000 cases.

König has an excellent reputation for his red wines, Spätburgunder and Frühburgunder, from Assmannshäuser Höllenberg, but I have never had the opportunity to taste them.

WEINGUT KRONE

Rheinuferstr 10, 65385 Assmannshausen. Tel: +49 (0) 6722 4030. Fax: 48346.
3.8 ha (9.4 acres). Production: 1500 cases.

Tunnelled into the hills beneath the Frankenthal vineyard are the Krone cellars, and from deep within them you can see the blue slate soil that is unique to the village's vineyards. The luxurious Hotel Krone has owned vineyards here for many years: 2.2 ha (5.4 acres) within the prime Höllenberg site, the remainder in Frankenthal and in Rüdesheimer Berg Schlossberg. For many years there was little investment in the property, so the old vines, which date back forty-five years, were simply left alone and now provide an invaluable resource. The Hotel Krone has built up a cellar of 1,300 different wines, with a surprising proportion coming from its own vineyards. Since 1995 Peter Perabo has been the winemaker.

After destemming and crushing, the Pinot Noir grapes are fermented and left on the skins for up to three weeks without temperature control, but then the tunnelled cellars are cool at a steady 12°C and enjoy a high humidity level. The cap is punched down by hand. Depending on the vintage and fruit quality, the ageing process varies greatly. Most of the wines are aged in a variety of ovals and small barrels, mostly Allier, but also some German oak. Because of the high humidity, wines can be left in cask for lengthy periods without oxidation. Some wines have been aged for seven years, but this is atypical.

The wines are fairly consistent in quality and style, even in difficult years such as 2000, which turned out surprisingly well. These are dense Pinots, powerfully structured except for the simplest cuvées. In addition, Perabo makes a range of Weissherbst Auslesen and, since 2000, a dry barrel-fermented Weissherbst. The Auslesen are differentiated by a numbering system, and the dry red wines by a star system. Seventy per cent of the wines are sold through the hotel and through its sister establishment in Hattenheim, the Kronenschlösschen.

PETER JAKOB KÜHN

Mühlstr 70, 65375 Oestrich. Tel: +49 (0) 6723 2299. Fax: 87788.
www.weingutpjkuehn.de. 13 ha (32 acres). 8,500 cases.

The eleventh generation of his family to run this property, the shy Peter Kühn has transformed this property since 1980 into one of the best in the Rheingau. His main vineyards, cultivated without chemical fertilizers, are in Oestricher Lenchen, from which he makes wines in a sweetish style, and in Oestricher Doosberg, from which he makes dry ones. Eighty per cent of production is dry. Kühn is an inveterate experimenter, travelling to different wine regions to see whether any practices in the vineyard or cellar can be brought home to Oestrich and tried out there. In Lenchen he has devised a system whereby vines are trained along a single spur, giving better spacing than on an arched cane; the disadvantage is that you need to stoop to work with the vines and pick the bunches. But the tighter spacing encourages the roots to sink down into the ground and gives them better resistance to drought.

Kuhn has experimented with crop levels too. In 2000 his yields were on average 63 hl/ha (25.5 hl/acre); in 1995 they were as low as 34 hl/ha (13.8 hl/ha). But he wasn't convinced that the sharply lower yields in 1995 necessarily gave better wines.

All the Rieslings are vinified in stainless steel. His basic wine is a Rheingau Riesling, then a village blend called Oestricher Riesling, then single-vineyard wines from his two best sites. From 2000 onward he will also use the Erstes Gewächs classification. In addition he produces some sensational sweet wines, such as his 1998 and 1999 Beerenauslesen. He admits there's no profit in making these concentrated sweet wines, but it's good for the image of the estate and as a demonstration of what can be achieved if you take Riesling vines to an extreme without compromises.

One tenth of his vines are Pinot Noir, planted in 1983 and first vinified in 1993. The wines are aged in oak of different origins for twelve months, but they are far less interesting than his splendidly pure Rieslings.

WEINGUT FRANZ KÜNSTLER

Freiherr-von-Stein Ring 3, 65239 Hochheim. Tel: +49 (0) 6146 82570.
Fax: 5767. www.weingut-kuenstler.de. 26 ha (64.2 acres). 12,500 cases.

Spend five minutes with Gunter Künstler and it soon becomes apparent that he is very sure of himself, which is not to say he is complacent. He has been making the wines at the family domaine since 1987, and in 1996 he added to it by purchasing the Aschrott estate; this also enabled him to move the cellars into the more spacious Aschrott premises on Kirchstrasse. All the wines are now released under the Künstler label.

Although he makes very good sweet wines, Künstler's forte is dry

Rieslings from his fine portfolio of top sites within Hochheim. This makes sense because the warm microclimate of the village gives high ripeness levels to the grapes. He seeds grass between the rows, both to reduce vegetal growth and to provide natural fertilizer. He prunes to six to eight buds, so yields are low, and his Pinot Noir is even more drastically cropped, with yields of 35–40 hl/ha (14.2–16.2 hl/acre).

Once the Riesling grapes are picked, he allows the must to settle for two days and in most years this permits a natural clarification before fermentation. If that doesn't work, he will filter. He is not keen on whole-cluster pressing, saying that the technique gives initially fruity wines but insufficient extract. Using both large casks and steel tanks, he works toward a long cool fermentation, using indigenous yeasts if at all possible. He bottles quite early to retain the freshness of the wines, especially because the dry wines have quite high alcohol. The Auslesen are picked at Oechsle levels of between 100 and 106, so they have ample body and power.

Künstler is scornful about the Erstes Gewächs classification, even though most of his own vineyards have received the blessing of the scientists of Geisenheim. His first growths, he says, are the Auslesen Trocken from Hölle, Stielweg, and Kirchenstück. "Stielweg," he explains, "is all muscle and old-vine concentration, whereas Kirchenstück has attack, vigour and finesse."

Künstler has released a stunning collection of wines in the latter half of the 1990s. The 2000s were not on the same level, because the clay soils of lower Hochheim vineyards became waterlogged and rot was extensive.

When conditions permit, Kunstler makes delicious sweet wines, usually from Hölle, but I am less convinced by the Pinot Noirs. His sparkling wine, Cuvée "M", is unusually rich and almost voluptuous, yet finishes dry.

HANS LANG

Rheinallee 6, 65347 Hattenheim. Tel: +49 (0) 6723 2475. Fax: 7963. www.lang-wein.com. 18 ha (44.5 acres). 10,000 cases.

Hans Lang founded this estate in 1953 and after his death in 1972 his son Johann Maximilian (also known as Hans) took over. Most of his vineyards are in Hattenheim, and he has chosen Wisselbrunnen as his Erstes Gewächs. The Rieslings are very reliable, if a touch light, but Lang offers an unusually wide range of wines. The Silvaner is a pretty wine for summer drinking, and his barrel-fermented Weissburgunder and Grauburgunder are attractive. There are a few different cuvées of Pinot Noir; the basic quality is aged in large casks, the others in small oak from various sources. Lang claims to have been the first Rheingau producer to age Pinot Noir in small barrels. His best wine is called Johann Maximilian, though I find too extracted.

In January 1998 he picked an Eiswein but it had low acidity and lacked typicity despite its richness. So he fermented it in new oak, and did the same in 1999. The wine, which Lang calls Nobilis, is an acquired taste. For mine the new oak tone is somewhat raw, but may integrate with more time.

FREIHERR LANGWERTH VON SIMMERN

Kirchgasse 6, 65343 Eltville. Tel: +49 (0) 6123 92110. Fax: 921133. 26 ha (64.3 acres). 13,000 cases.

This renowned estate rejoices in labels as exotic as its name. They were designed in 1893, and although they win no prizes for legibility, they are unmistakable on the shelf. After many successful vintages in the early 1980s, the estate slipped in quality, despite a clutch of outstanding vineyards; Mannberg and Nussbrunnen in Hattenheim, Erbacher Marcobrunn, Rauenthaler Baiken, and Eltviller Sonnenberg.

However, a few years ago, the long-established estate director moved to the Friedrich Wilhelm Gymnasium in Trier, and a member of the Langwerth family returned to Eltville to take charge of the estate. In 2001 a new cellarmaster, Dirk Roth, formerly of Biffar in the Pfalz, was hired. Improvements in quality were already evident in 1999. There was an impressive Kabinett Trocken from Baiken, and a lush Beerenauslese from Mannberg.

The revival of this great estate's reputation is further testimony to the fact that there is no substitute for having a member of the family on hand to make the necessary investments in vineyards and cellar, and to crack the whip and ensure that standards are maintained.

JOSEF LEITZ

Theodor Heuss Str 5, 65385 Rüdesheim. Tel: +49 (0) 6722 48711. Fax: 47658. www.leitz-wein.de. 6 ha (14.8 acres). 3,000 cases.

In recent years this small producer has moved into the upper ranks of quality-conscious growers. When he started making the wines here in 1985 he followed the formula of the times – selected yeasts, swift fermentations, and early bottling – but he was unhappy with the results. Throughout the 1990s he has modified his cellar techniques, opting for natural yeasts, slower fermentations and ageing the wine on the fine lees. "Rapid fermentation," he declares, "gives wines that are fruity young but often collapse after a few years. With a slow fermentation my wines tend to stay closed for a year or so after bottling, and that means, sadly, that they don't always show well in the all-important tastings for the press six months after the vintage."

His vineyards in Rüdesheim include fifty-year-old vines in Berg Rottland. The vineyard often fares better in wet years than very dry ones, so his range of 2000s, of which about forty per cent were dry, were very successful. These are Rieslings of real substance and complexity.

FÜRST LÖWENSTEIN

Niederwaldstr 8, 65375 Hallgarten. Tel: +49 (0) 6723 999770. Fax: 999771. www.loewenstein.de. 22 ha (54.4 acres). 5,000 cases.

In 1979 the Löwensteins, who also own a wine estate in Franken, leased their Hallgarten property, which they acquired in 1875, to Graf Matuschka of Schloss Vollrads. In 1997, at Matuschka's own request, the Löwensteins took the property back into their own hands, and Robert Haller has been the expert manager of the two estates. With good sites in Hallgartener Jungfer and Schönhell, the wines have been improving from year to year, both in dry and sweeter styles. The Löwensteins regard Schönhell as their Erstes Gewächs, but also use an "R" designation to signify top reserve wines.

G.H. VON MUMM

Schloss Johannisberg, 65366 Geisenheim-Johannisberg. Tel: +49 (0) 6722 70090. Fax: 700933. 65 ha (160.6 acres). 50,000 cases.

In 1811 a wine merchant and banker, Peter Arnold Mumm, offered to buy the whole Schloss Johannisberg crop in advance, after a succession of poor vintages. His gamble paid off, because the vintage turned out to be excellent. With the profits he bought sites in Johannisberg, and in 1827 founded the eponymous Champagne house in Reims. Financial difficulties accumulated after World War II and in 1958 the Mumm estate was sold. In 1979 it was acquired by Schloss Johannisberg, and now is also part of the Henkell empire.

The same team responsible for the Schloss wines also produces the Mumm range, which is uninspired. There is a generic Riesling in a medium-dry style, and a rather feeble Pinot Noir from Assmannshausen. More impressive is the Erstes Gewächs from Rüdesheimer Berg Rottland, but only 3,000 bottles were produced in 1999.

DR NÄGLER

Friedrichstr 22, 65385 Rüdesheim. Tel: +49 (0) 6722 2835. Fax: 47363.
www.weingut-dr-naegler.de. 8 ha (19.8 acres). 5,000 cases.

Despite an impressive collection of vineyards in the best vineyards of Rüdesheim, this estate has been underperforming for some years. But with a new generation in the form of Tilbert Nägler in charge from 2001 onward, there may well be changes for the better. Certainly the 2001s from Berg Rottland were impressive, especially the exotic and spicy Erstes Gewächs. Prices are very reasonable.

QUERBACH

Dr Rody Str 2, 65375 Oestrich. Tel: +49 (0) 6723 3887. Fax: 87405.
www.querbach.com. 10 ha (24.7 acres). 6,500 cases.

In 1998 Wilfried Querbach and his son Peter launched their own system of classification. The basic wine is a litre bottling; then the quality rises through the tiers of Gutsriesling, No 2 (in effect a chaptalized Kabinett), No 1 (a Spätlese Trocken from top sites but with relatively generous yields), and an Erstes Gewächs with yields of around 45 hl/ha (18.2 hl/acre). The 1998 Oestricher Doosberg Erstes Gewächs was concentrated, mineral, and long.

The Querbachs have had the courage to bottle their wines without cork closures, so customers must trade the satisfying sound of an ejected cork for the certainty that the wine will be untainted.

SCHLOSS REINHARTSHAUSEN

Hauptstr 41, 65346 Eltville. Tel: +49 (0) 6123 676333. Fax: 4222.
www.schloss-reinhartshausen.de. 82 ha (203 acres). 40,000 cases.

It's hard to miss the blocks of the barrack-like estate buildings as you drive along the river road through the Rheingau. Once the property of the princely von Preussen family, it was bought most recently by a consortium named "The Friends of Reinhartshausen." Previous owners had spent a fortune in modernizing and reshaping the estate, and had converted some of the buildings into a hotel and very expensive restaurant. During the latter half of the 1990s August Kesseler of the Kesseler estate was brought in to manage Schloss Reinhartshausen, but the arrangement came to an end in 2000, when Andreas Blaurock was appointed as the new director.

The Schloss has some impressive vineyards, including Erbacher Marcobrunn, and its neighbour Erbacher Schlossberg, as well as vineyards on a rather damp island in the Rhein. Here, in the Erbacher Rheinhell, the Schloss has for many years had a plot of "experimental" Chardonnay. The overall potential here is enormous but has yet to be fully realized. The powerful, almost meaty Marcobrunn Spätlese Trocken in 1999 and 2001 showed what can be achieved.

BALTHASAR RESS

Rheinallee 7, 65347 Eltville-Hattenheim. Tel: +49 (0) 6723 91950.
Fax: 919591. www.ress-wine.com. 33 ha (81.5 acres). 18,000 cases.

The genial helpful Stefan Ress has for decades been a popular figure in the Rheingau, and his son Christian now assists him in what has become quite a sizeable wine business. Most of the vineyard holdings are in Oestrich (including his *Alleinbesitz* site Schloss Reichartshausen) and Hattenheim, but Ress seems to have vineyards scattered from Rüdesheim in the west to Hochheim in the east. Not a great enthusiast for dry wines, Ress bottles them under the Von Unserm label, other than an Erstes Gewächs from Hattenheimer Nussbrunnen.

The Ress wines are reliable and sound, and occasionally exciting; the range of sites and styles makes it difficult to get a fix on their typicity, however. Early tastings of the 2001 wines show racy acidity and excellent fruit.

ABTEI ST HILDEGARD

65385 Rüdesheim. Tel: +49 (0) 6722 4990. Fax: 499185. 5 ha (12.4acres).
3,000 cases.

The large monastic buildings in the heart of the Rüdesheim vineyards belong to a nunnery founded here in 1900. The nuns, dressed in their formal and unreconstructed habits, will be happy to pour you a sample of their wines, which come from both Rüdesheim and Assmannshausen (for Pinot Noir). However, they lack concentration and should be much better than they are.

SCHLOSS SCHÖNBORN

Hauptstr 53, 65347 Hattenheim. Tel: +49 (0) 6723 91810. Fax: 918191.
www.schoenborn.de. 65 ha (161 acres). 25,000 cases.

One of the finest estates in the Rheingau, this has been in the possession of the aristocratic Schönborn family for centuries (the cellars date from 1416) and the estate has existed in its present form since the seventeenth century, with vineyards in just about every village of the region. 15 ha (37 acres) of the less interesting vineyards are leased out, allowing the estate to focus on the best sites, which includes the *Alleinbesitz*, Hattenheimer Pfaffenberg.

Quality has been distinctly patchy, and many wines suffered from blowsiness. However, the arrival of a new director in 1995, Günter Thies, seemed to herald a return to more consistent form. In the 1980s there was a heavy reliance on centrifuges and filters, but the estate nonetheless made some sumptuous nobly rotten sweet wines in vintages such as 1989. The development of the Erstes Gewächs system in the late 1990s allowed the estate to focus on some of its greatest sites, singling out Pfaffenberg and Marcobrunn, as well as Rüdesheimer Berg Schlossberg, for its top dry wines. It also revived an old eighteenth century label for its best Spätlese bottling from Pfaffenberg.

JOSEF SPREITZER

Rheingaustr 86, 65375 Oestrich. Tel: +49 (0) 6723 2625. Fax: 4644.
www.weingut-spreitzer.de. 11 ha (27.2 acres). 7,000 cases.

Brothers Andreas and Bernd Spreitzer have been running this property since 1997, although their father Bernhard is still involved. The principal vineyards are in Oestrich and Hattenheim. The brothers have been quick to absorb modern ideas on quality wine production. Their vineyards are cultivated with green cover, and green harvested to reduce yields; harvesting is selective, with up to four passages through the vineyards, as in 2000. In the winery there is whole-cluster pressing, and no pumping of the must. Fermentation is prolonged, often continuing through the winter months, and the wines stay for some months on the fine lees.

These are delightful wines, not the most powerful or full-bodied in the Rheingau, but racy and elegant. Alcohol levels rarely exceed twelve per cent, and the fruit is always in balance with the fresh acidity of the wines.

SCHLOSS VOLLRADS

65375 Oestrich-Winkel. Tel: +49 (0) 6723 660. Fax: 6666.
www.schlossvollrads.com. 56 ha (138 acres). 32,000 cases.

From the fourteenth century onward, this sprawling Schloss was the home of the Greiffenclau family. In the late nineteenth century the family had no male heirs, so the line was continued by marrying a daughter to the Matuschka family. In 1975 Erwein Graf Matuschka-Greiffenclau took over running the estate, and a few years later he was also in charge of the Löwenstein estate in Hallgarten, which was leased to Vollrads. Tribute has been paid earlier in this book to the enormous contribution Matuschka made to the promotion of Rheingau wines, and, during his stint as head of the VDP, of German wines in general.

Ironically, his own wines from Vollrads were uninspired for many years, often showing rasping levels of acidity. Matuschka's crusading zeal was not translated into the highest quality at his own estate, where such dubious practices as machine-harvesting some of the vineyards were perpetrated. Throughout the 1990s the estate slipped ever deeper into a financial mire. When, in August 1997, Matuschka's bankers refused to bail him out yet again, he committed suicide. The bank, the Nassauische Sparkasse, took over the property and for some time there was anxiety that this noble estate would be broken up, because no purchaser could be found to take on the whole.

Finally, the Sparkasse decided to keep Vollrads intact and in 1999 hired Dr Rowald Hepp, one of Germany's top winemakers, as director. He had a tough time persuading the estate workers to reduce the crop and to harvest selectively. His predecessor had liked to pick early for safety, but Hepp insisted on harvesting as late as possible.

Hepp has abandoned Matuschka's bizarre colour-coding of labels to indicate quality levels, and introduced a Castle Label Riesling, a wine that goes through partial malolactic fermentation and is intended for early drinking. In 1999 and 2000 Vollrads was able to produce some delicious

Beerenauslese, as well as a fine 2000 Eiswein. In October 2001, however, a bizarre tornado and hail destroyed half the crop.

Quality has undoubtedly improved, but there is still a way to go. The vineyards lie relatively far inland, and are tricky to cultivate, so it will take a few years to return them to perfect working order. But at least Vollrads has been able to continue a tradition that dates back six centuries.

GEHEIMRAT J. WEGELER ERBEN

Friedensplatz 9–11, 65375 Oestrich-Winkel. Tel: +49 (0) 6723 99090. Fax: 990966. www.wegeler.com. 55 ha (136 acres). 36,000 cases.

In the 1990s this estate, allied to the Wegeler property in the Pfalz, seemed to be cruising on its reputation, but at the end of the decade there were major changes in personnel, and Oliver Haag (son of Wilhelm Haag in Brauneberg, see p. 182, and brother of Thomas Haag of Schloss Lieser) was taken on as winemaker. The last vintage of the former regime, the 1999, was of good quality, notably the Erstes Gewächs from Rüdesheimer Berg Schlossberg, and the Auslese from Geisenheimer Rothenberg. The 2000s, which I have not tasted, are said to be of excellent quality, so Wegeler is once again an estate to watch.

ROBERT WEIL

Mühlberg 5, 64399 Kiedrich. Tel: +49 (0) 6123 2308. Fax: 1546. www.weingut-robert-weil.com. 65 ha (161 acres). 37,000 cases.

This is now the superstar estate of the Rheingau, largely thanks to its consistent production of ultra-ripe Rieslings that fetch astonishingly high prices. Although managed for many years by the youthful Wilhelm Weil, the property was sold to Suntory in 1988 as the sole way to avoid provisions of the inheritance laws that would have required his father to split the estate. New cellars were built in 1991.

Although Weil says he isn't obsessive about yields, they are decidedly low: around 45 hl/ha (18.2 hl/acre) for most regular bottlings, and 40 hl/ha (16.2 hl/acre) for Erstes Gewächs. Enormous care is taken in cultivating the vineyards, using only organic fertilizers and no herbicides. Any yellow leaves are painstakingly removed, as are imperfect bunches, and whereas most conscientious growers may send their pickers through the vineyards three or four times, Weil will do so up to fifteen times. During an eight-hour day, he explains, a single picker will probably return with the equivalent of three bottles of Auslese, one of BA, and half of TBA. Over a ten to twelve week harvest period, the estate employs seventy pickers. There is a further selection of the grapes in the cellar. So no wonder the wines are expensive.

When the must weight is more than 90 Oechsle, the estate uses whole-cluster pressing; below that level, there is partial crushing of the fruit in order to obtain more extract. All wines are vinified in steel tanks using their own yeast selection. Fermentation is arrested with chilling. Almost eighty per cent of the wines are dry, because there is a huge following for the estate in top German restaurants. On the other hand, the meticulous harvesting, as well as the intrinsic quality of Weil's top vineyard, Kiedricher Gräfenberg, ensures that he is able to make good quantities of Auslese, BA, Eiswein, and TBA each year. Until the late 1980s the estate had produced only two TBAs in 120 years; the 1999 TBA was the eleventh consecutive TBA from the Gräfenberg, a remarkable achievement. There was even a Goldkapsel TBA, picked at 243 Oechsle.

The 2000s were a fine range of wines in a tricky vintage. Particularly impressive were the Gräfenberg Erstes Gewächs, and a lush, smoky Auslese Goldkapsel.

Although the Weil estate fully deserves its acclaim, its achievement has also extracted criticism. One senior figure in the Rheingau told me: "The wines sweep the board at blind tastings because the estate requires extremely high minimum must weights for its wines. Some Auslesen have, in terms of their must weight at harvest, been at TBA level. Few wineries have the vineyards or resources to match this approach. It is fair to ask whether an ultra-rich Auslese is a typical Auslese."

DOMDECHANT WERNER'SCHES WEINGUT

Rathausstr 30, 65324 Hochheim. Tel: +49 (0) 6146 835037. Fax: 835038. www.domdechantwerner.com. 12 ha (30 acres). 7,500 cases.

This estate was founded in 1780, when the property was acquired by the Dean (*Domdechant*) of Mainz Cathedral, who is credited with having saved the cathedral from destruction during the French Revolution. The present owner, Dr Franz Werner Michel, the former president of the German Wine Institute, is the seventh generation to run the property.

All the vineyards are in Hochheim, on gently sloping sites. Half the production is of dry wines, to which the village is well suited. The must is clarified with a centrifuge before fermentation, but the ageing of the wine is mostly in large wooden casks, although Dr Michel also uses steel tanks. No *Süssreserve* is employed. The style of the wines is quite rich and firm, though those from Kirchenstück can be a touch too lean. The 1998 vintage was particularly successful here, showing a raciness and flair not always apparent in 1997 or 1999.

7

Mittelrhein

The Mittelrhein is easy to find. At Rüdesheim, turn your back on the vineyards of the rest of the Rheingau and follow the road as it swings slowly right and skirts the Rhein in a vaguely northwesterly direction. You'll pass Assmannshausen and then Lorch, and everything thereafter for about 100 kilometres (62 miles) as far as Lahnstein belongs to the Mittelrhein. This forms one of Europe's most exquisite riverscapes, an entrancing blend of castles, walled towns, cliffs, rock formations, and, of course, vineyards. There were some vines cultivated here in Roman times, but the terraced vineyards on very steep sites were originally planted around 1000.

It's a region that has had difficulty establishing an image for itself, because it's inevitably overshadowed by the Rheingau. In fact, the wines are quite distinct from those of the Rheingau. Although there are south-facing vineyards, they are not as immense as that great flank from Rüdesheim to Hochheim. The soils, being both quartzite and Devonian slate, are like a blend of those found in the Mosel and Rheingau. The grapes do usually ripen, because the vineyards are sheltered, and the swift-flowing waters of the Rhein beneath them ameliorate the climate. Acidity levels are generally higher than those of the Rheingau, giving sharper, more bracing wines. Riesling is easily the dominant variety, accounting for seventy-two per cent of vineyards; this puts the region in immediate competition with its neighbours.

It used to be different. In the early twentieth century there was a good deal of red wine produced here, just as there still is today in Assmannshausen. About twenty per cent of production used to be red, even though the slate soils are better suited to Riesling. Today, Pinot Noir accounts for about six per cent of plantings, giving wines

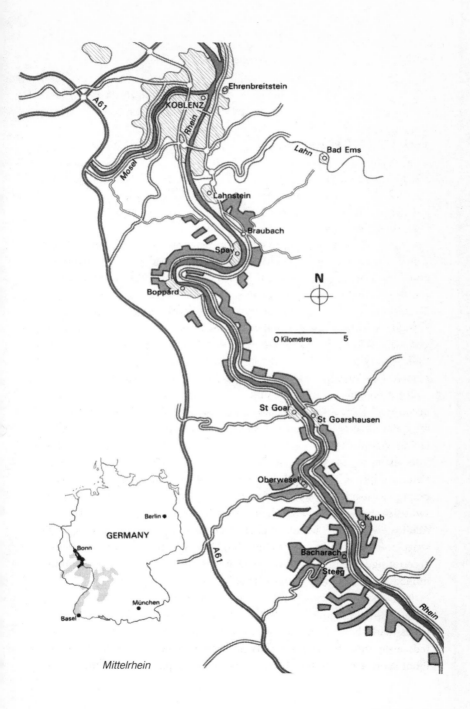

Mittelrhein

that are fruity but low in alcohol, pleasant but lacking in body and weight.

In the past much of the production, like that from the Saar, was vinified by large companies as sparkling wine. Today there are many small producers, some of whom make excellent wines, though they are hampered by the fact that it is very hard to obtain realistic prices. The vineyards tend to be steep and difficult to cultivate, so labour costs are high. The northerly climate presents the same difficulties as the vineyards of the Mosel: grapes will only ripen on steep slopes with a southerly exposure. Such sites can suffer in dry years from drought stress, but in wet years, which are not uncommon, the drainage is excellent. Sites near the river are best; with every kilometre that you move away from it, and with every one hundred metres (328 feet) that you gain in altitude, you lose 1°C of average temperature.

The wines are a challenge to make and can be brilliant, but they simply can't command the prices of good bottles from the Rheingau or Mosel. Peter Jost, one of the best known growers in the Mittelrhein, says that the only way to maintain one's vineyards is to lower costs by intro-ducing whatever kind of mechanization is feasible. He has a winch in some of his vineyards that can lower a tractor onto his parcels; it can also be used during the harvest to transport grapes to a tractor on the road above. (I watched one of these cables in operation in Boppard. A tractor remained stationary on the road, while a cable from the side winched a wagon filled with compost down a steep slopes. A worker ran down the slope to follow the wagon, unloaded the compost at the right spot, then jumped in the wagon and was towed to the top where he filled the next load.)

Jost's harvesting costs are roughly £350/ha (£142/acre); if it all had to be done by hand, it would double. Quite apart from costs, there is a shortage of manual labour, and workers are more tempted by better pay-ing jobs in nearby cities such as Bonn and Koblenz. The region also suffers from a lack of "big names," the equivalent of Prüm in the Mosel or Schloss Johannisberg in the Rheingau. Growers such as Jost are widely respected, but they are hardly household names.

Consequently the area under vine is shrinking fast. A century ago there were some 2,000 ha (5,000 acres) of vineyards. By 1950 that figure was reduced to around 1,200 ha (3,000 acres), and today there are only 550 ha (1,400 acres). However, while it's calculated that the area under vine is diminishing by twenty-five ha (sixty-two acres) every year, the region is probably not in serious risk of extinction as a winegrowing area. This is the most romantic and most photographed stretch of the Rhein, lined on both sides of the river with crags and castles and dotted with charming little towns. Weekenders from Bonn and holidaymakers from further afield come here in droves to enjoy a stroll and a bottle of wine in the garden of an inn. This means there is a steady market for local wines, even if many of those sold to an undiscriminating but thirsty public do little to enhance the reputation of the region.

Vintages are similar to those in the Rheingau, with one significant exception. In 1999 there was significant hail damage, and this did have a deleterious effect on the quality of some of the drier wines. There was also considerable rain late in the season. Even though overall ripeness levels were higher in 1999 than 1998, some growers prefer the latter. 2001 was almost certainly the best vintage here since 1990.

Vineyards

There are two Bereiche, eleven Grosslagen, and more than one hundred Einzellagen. Bereich Loreley is by far the larger of the two.

Bereich Loreley. Grosslagen: Schloss Reichenstein, Schloss Stahleck, Herrenberg, Schloss Schönburg, Loreleyfelsen, Burg Rheinfels, Gedeonseck, Marksburg, Lahntal, Burg Hammerstein.

Bereich Siebengebirge. Grosslage: Petersberg.

Grosses Gewächs vineyards:
Bacharach: Hahn, Posten, Wolfshöhle.
Engehölle: Bernstein.
Oberwesel: Oelsberg.
Steeg: St Jost.

BACHARACH

A famous village with six growers just downstream from Lorch. Its roughly 50 ha (124 acres) of vineyards are almost entirely on steep blue-slate soils. Behind these vineyards are plateaux where there is no slate; there are some vines planted here, and they are mostly machine-picked at high yields. As well as Riesling, Müller-Thurgau and Pinot Noir are planted.

Bacharacher Hahn. Just north of the village. 4.5 ha (11 acres), of which 4.2 ha (10.4 acres) are owned by Toni Jost. A steep site, facing south and southeast. Pinot Noir is planted at the foot of the hill, Riesling higher up. The midslope gives the best and ripest wines.

Bacharacher Heyles'en Werth. These vines are on an island in the Rhein, and are the *Alleinbesitz* of Bastian.

Bacharacher Kloster Fürstental. Ratzenberger owns vineyards here. Spätburgunder is planted as well as Riesling.

Bacharacher Matthias Weingarten. 5 ha (12.4 acres). Inland from Hahn, with loam on the upper slopes. Planted with Riesling and Müller-Thurgau.

Bacharacher Posten. Immediately behind the village and close to the river, a warm site with white quartzite as well as slate, giving mineral wines. Mostly owned by Bastian.

Bacharacher Wolfshöhle. Partly on steep slopes behind Posten, and partly up on the plateau. Fine racy Rieslings.

BOPPARD

90 ha (222 acres). The soils are grey and blue Devonian slate, and average yields are somewhat higher than in Bacharach. The wines are fruity but do not age as well. Growers such as Ratzenberg worry that some neighbours are pushing down prices and giving Boppard a reputation for cheap wines for early drinking. Nonetheless there are excellent wines produced here, and the site is exceptional. All the sites are known collectively as Bopparder Hamm, and consist essentially of a wall of fairly steep south-facing vineyards.

Thomas Perll believes the site was first planted about 2,000 years ago. Before the 1960s there was no road here and grapes had to be carried in hods down the slope to waiting tractors. However, there was *Flurbereinigung* in the 1960s and further adjustments in the 1990s. The best sites are those sheltered by the rock, because the cliffs reflect warmth onto the vines. Vines at the top of the slope ripen up to two weeks later than those lower down. The Hamm is prone to fog, which has the advantage that temperatures never drop too low. The vineyards have diminished in surface area, and there are abandoned sites between the village and the Hamm; vineyards on the opposite side of the river are no longer in production because the only way to transport the bunches during harvest was by boat.

There are some twenty producers. A note of complication is added by the fact that some growers still use individual vineyard names rather than the collective Bopparder Hamm. These vineyards, from the village moving downstream, are Elfenlay, Fässerlay, Weingrube, Mandelstein, Feuerlay, Ohlenberg, and Engelstein. Thomas Perll believes the best sites are Mandelstein, Feuerlay, and Ohlenberg, but Matthias Müller favours Engelstein.

ENGEHÖLL
A side valley close to Oberwesel with two notable sites: Bernstein, 15 ha (37 acres) and Goldemund. There was *Flurbereinigung* here in the 1960s. Lanius-Kalb is a major proprietor.

OBERWESEL
About 75 ha (185 acres). Oberwesel is a pretty walled medieval town. About half the vineyards, which used to account for 150 ha (371 acres), have been abandoned. The soils are slate, and as you move inland from the river there is more grey slate. Sites near the river give lean, elegant wines, not unlike those from the Saar. There are also three south-facing side valleys that produce wines with more body: Römerkrug south of the castle; Engehölle (see above) north of the castle; and further north, St Martinsberg. The village has fifteen per cent red vines, mostly Pinot Noir on soils with more loam. Some Müller-Thurgau remains but is not being replanted. Until the 1940s the vineyards on the other side of the river were also cultivated, but there is no road, so almost all have been abandoned; the terraces are still visible.

Oberweseler Oelsberg. 5 ha (12.4 acres). These terraced vineyards lie north of the village on the bend of the Rhein and thus face south across the river.

Oberweseler Rossstein. On the other side of the river opposite the village. A famous site that belongs to Heinrich Weiler, but it has been leased out and is no longer that good.

Oberweseler St Martinsberg. This has rather heavier soil than the other valleys, and some Kerner and Spätburgunder are planted here as well as Riesling. There was *Flurbereinigung* in the 1970s.

STEEG

This village belongs to Bacharach but the vineyards lie in a side valley. They used to stretch for two kilometres (1.2 miles) beyond Steeg, but have mostly been abandoned.

Steeger St Jost. Inland from Posten and Wolfshöhle, forming a cliff face of vines. Mostly owned by Ratzenberger.

Producers

FRITZ BASTIAN

Oberstr 63, 55422 Bacharach. Tel: +49 (0) 6743 1208. Fax: 2837. 6 ha (14.8 acres). 2,500 cases.

From his Bacharach vineyards, which include those on an island in the Rhein, Friedrich Bastian makes steely racy Rieslings, which are best sampled at his inn, "Zum Grünen Baum." His Grosses Gewächs Rieslings in 2001 were among the best Mittelrhein wines of the vintage.

TONI JOST

Oberstr 14, 55422 Bacharach. Tel: +49 (0) 6743 1216. Fax: 1076. 13 ha (32 acres) of which 3.5 ha (8.6 acres) are in the Rheingau. 6,000 cases.

Peter Jost is the fifth generation of his family to make wines here from the Bacharacher Hahn, although the estate dates back 350 years. Jost is probably the best known producer in the Mittelrhein. He exudes enthusiasm, and enjoys explaining the specificity of the vineyards here. His mother comes from the Rheingau so he has some vineyards in Walluf and Martinsthal, but everything is vinified here.

Almost eighty per cent of the vineyards are planted with Riesling, the remainder with Pinot Noir and Dornfelder. The average yield is 55 hl/ha (22.3 hl/acre). All the grapes are picked by hand over a period of six weeks. The wines are fermented in temperature-controlled steel tanks, and the whites spend a short period in cask before bottling. He finds this an advantage in slightly unripe years, because the gentle oxidation rounds out the wine. Some customers find cask-aged wines old-fashioned, but he likes both styles, treating each wine individually. A very delicate wine wouldn't benefit from wood; a richer wine does. The balance of each wine has to be determined by nature, he insists, not by the needs of his customers.

Jost produces rosé from young Pinot Noir vines, and various cuvées of red, some of which are partially aged in barriques.

The estate is known for a simple Riesling called Jodocus, which is made for restaurants to provide consistency and reasonable quantities. Despite Jost's reputation, I find the 1998 Rieslings, both dry and sweet, somewhat disappointing, lacking elegance and verve. The sweet wines can be exceptional, and he is usually able to make a Beerenauslese every year. He was also able to make TBA in 1989 (2,000 litres), 1993 (300), 1994 (100), 1996, 1998, and 2000, when he could only harvest 60 litres!

WEINGUT DR RANDOLF KAUER
Mainzer Str 21, 55422 Bacharach. Tel: +49 (0) 6743 2272. Fax: 93661. 3 ha (7.4 acres). 1,800 cases.
This organic estate was founded in 1989 by a professor at the Geisenheim wine college. Pursuing an organic regime in this climate keeps the yields low but some tasters discern a lack of ripeness in the fruit grown here. Although I have not encountered the wines, which are almost all dry Rieslings, they have a good reputation.

LANIUS-KALB
Mainzer Str 38, 55430 Oberwesel. Tel: +49 (0) 6744 8104. Fax: 1537. 7 ha (17.3 acres). 3,000 cases.
The lean, good-humoured Jörg Lanius owns very steep sites, all in the Engehöller valley. Most sweeter wines come from Goldemund. Eighty-five per cent of his vineyards are planted with Riesling, the remainder with Pinot Noir and Müller-Thurgau. The must is centrifuged before fermentation in steel tanks at around 13°C; the wine is aged in large casks on the fine lees for four months. Most of the wines are Trocken or Halbtrocken (they use the term Feinherb) and contain no *Süssreserve*. Lanius believes his wines need three years in bottle to show at their best.

His best Rieslings come from Engehöller Bernstein, and from the Oberweseler Oelsberg, which in 2001 produced a full-bodied, spicy Grosses Gewächs. The dry wines as well as the sweet Auslesen are juicy and enjoyable, but the 1998s lack a little raciness and verve, although there is an exquisite 1998 BA from Goldemund. The 1999s have more charm and delicacy. The Pinot Noir, also from Bernstein, is pretty but rather light.

MATTHIAS MÜLLER

Mainzer Str 45, 56322 Spay. Tel: +49 (0) 2628 8741. Fax: 3363. 8 ha (19.8 acres). 6,000 cases.

The Müllers have owned this estate for three centuries, but the primary focus only became wine after 1980. Matthias Müller took over from his parents in the mid-1990s. All vineyards are at Boppard, although the winery is based in the hamlet of Spay, where there used to be vineyards; they were never exceptional and have mostly been abandoned. As well as Riesling, with eighty-five per cent of plantings, Müller also has some Pinot Gris, which he particularly likes as a good alternative to Riesling, and Pinot Noir, which is only used to produce rosé, because he feels it lacks sufficient body for a red wine. Yields seem quite high at 80 hl/ha (32.3 hl/acre), but Müller has tried cropping at both higher and lower levels and feels this is about right.

All his wines go through a slow fermentation in steel tanks using, whenever possible, only indigenous yeasts. There is no use of *Süssreserve* and since 1987 no deacidification either. Forty per cent of the wines are Trocken (but with six to eight grams of residual sugar to keep them fruity) and forty per cent Halbtrocken. He is seeking to produce dry wines that are elegant and mineral, fruity but not too high in alcohol. He was lucky in 1999, because his grapes remained healthy, so healthy that he was unable to make Beerenauslese, which he usually produces every year.

He is happy too with his 2000s, even though it was a difficult vintage. Strict selection allowed him to produce a fair quantity of Auslese too. One house speciality is Riesling Trocken from the Mandelstein; this is labelled *Hochgewächs*, signifying that it was picked at 10 Oechsle above the minimum, and is in effect a chaptalized Kabinett. Tasting the 1999s and 2000s confirmed Müller's own good opinion of his wines. Overall, the wines are well balanced, fresh, quite mineral, but lack some concentration.

AUGUST UND THOMAS PERLL

Oberstr 81, 56154 Boppard. Tel: +49 (0) 6742 3906. Fax: 81726. 7 ha (17.3 acres). 5,500 cases.

Almost half the Perlls' vineyards are in Mandelstein, which the young Thomas Perll rates highly. Most of the vines are Riesling, but they also have Müller-Thurgau, Kerner, Scheurebe, Optima, and Pinot Noir. Almost all the wines are vinified in steel tanks. Forty per cent are Trocken, but Perll says Halbtrocken is very popular with his customers. The Pinot Noir is aged in large casks.

The whites I have tasted have deep colours and seem very evolved given their youth. A 1998 Mandelstein Eiswein also seemed well developed for a young sweet wine. There have been better reports of subsequent vintages, but I have not tasted them.

RATZENBERGER

Blücherstr 167, 55422 Bacharach. Tel: +49 (0) 6743 1337. Fax: 2842.
www.weingut-ratzenberger.de. 9 ha (22.2 acres). 5,000 cases.

The articulate Jochen Ratzenberger is now the front man for this fine estate, although his father still seems to have a hand in the winemaking. Seventy-five per cent of the vineyards are planted with Riesling, and there is also some Pinot Noir, Pinot Gris (only produced in good years), and Müller-Thurgau. Ratzenberger's main vineyard is Steeger St Jost, where they own 3 ha (7.4 acres), and they also have vines in Bacharacher Kloster Fürstental. They believe in selective harvesting by hand, so that the average yield is no more than 60 hl/ha (24.3 hl/acre).

The wines are vinified in both casks and steel tanks. Because the cellars beneath the vineyards are cold, there is no need for temperature control to achieve long fermentations. Seventy per cent of the wines are Trocken and Halbtrocken. Their Gutsriesling is called "Caspar R," a wine with high acidity balanced by high residual sugar. These are among the best Rieslings of the Mittelrhein, made in a lean style with good acidity and mineral structure. I find the young wines often have aromas of pears. They are remarkably long-lived. Jochen Ratzenberger generously poured me Spätlesen from 1969 and 1982, which had lost their sweetness but remained lively and mineral.

Ratzenberger have also been making good quality traditional-method Sekt since 1997. A pure Riesling, it is aged for three years on the lees, and does not go through malolactic fermentation.

WEINGART

Mainzer Str 32, 56322 Spay. Tel: +49 (0) 2628 8735. Fax: 2835. www.weingut-weingart.de. 8.5 ha (21 acres). 7,500 cases.

Florian Weingart produces little else other than Riesling, which comes from vineyards equally divided between holdings in Boppard and Fürstenberg. My experience of these wines is limited, but I have found them to have a light style that lacks some persistence and verve.

8

Ahr

Of all the wine regions of Germany, this is surely the most mysterious. We're accustomed to thinking of northern Germany as white wine country. There just isn't sufficient warmth to ripen most worthwhile red grapes. And yet way up north, between Koblenz and Bonn and close to the uppermost stretches of the Mittelrhein, the Ahr valley wanders off to the west, producing some of Germany's most impressive, and expensive, Pinot Noirs.

The reason why Pinot Noir can ripen here is that the Ahr valley, some twenty-five kilometres (sixteen miles) long, is narrow and sheltered by the Eifel range. Moreover, seventy-five per cent of the vineyards are on steep slopes, thus straining to catch every ray of sunlight. Frank Adeneuer, a leading grower, says it can be surprisingly hot here in summer, with sudden storms and high humidity. The mesoclimate has the added inconvenience of dropping unwelcome rain in September, and outbreaks of rot often need to be monitored and dealt with. Annual rainfall is around 600 millimetres (twenty-four inches).

No one seems to know when Pinot Noir was first planted here, though there are rather implausible claims that it was originally cultivated here by the Romans. As in Burgundy and Champagne, it's the mid-slopes that give the best quality. There is a difference between the east and west end of the valley: the former having more loam, the latter more slate. Pinot Noir is the dominant grape, with fifty-eight per cent of the surface, and the other varieties are Portugieser (eighteen per cent) and Riesling (eight per cent). In all there are 520 hectares under vine, and almost as many proprietors.

The traditional red wine of the Ahr was rather feeble stuff. It was known as *Ahrbleichert*, meaning "bleached," which in practice meant

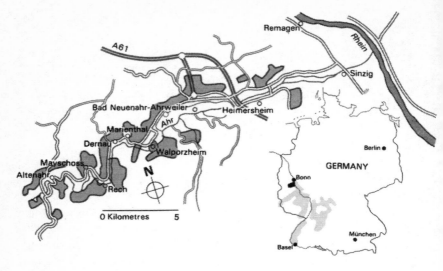

Ahr

minimal maceration. The wines may well have resembled a Weissherbst or rosé. Perhaps it's not surprising that by the 1950s the reputation of the Ahr had plummeted to such an extent that Fritz Hallgarten could write: "The cultivation of red wine on the Ahr is on the wane. The growers are of the opinion that the vineyards are 'burgundy-weary', an opinion based on the discovery that in many places new cuttings lacked vigour in their development, while other species – when planted in vineyards earlier devoted to burgundy vines – bore good fruit. Just as a farmer rotates his crops, so the vine grower must from time to time change the species of vines in his vineyards. As a result of these considerations, the growers on the Ahr have begun to plant grapes that produce white wines. At the present day, red and white wines are being grown in about equal proportions."[1] In 1962 Alfred Langenbach was writing about the "distress and misery" of the Ahr growers and hoping that the region would be replanted with "rejuvenated" vines.[2]

New Pinot vines were planted at that time, and with hindsight the

[1] Hallgarten, p. 85.

[2] Langenbach, pp. 172–3.

choice of clone was far from ideal. A good deal of the Mariafelder clone was selected and planted. Adeneuer has such a low opinion of it that he uses these vines only for rosé.

Like all steep vineyards those of the Ahr are costly to cultivate, and the best wines, which are in short supply, are expensive. Because the quantities are low, and the local clientele includes the prosperous citizenry of Bonn and Koblenz, sales of the top wines are brisk and high prices are no deterrent so long as quality is perceived to be high. "Twenty years ago," Adeneuer told me, "growers from other regions used to mock us for trying to make good red wines. But we've improved our quality, and now a lot of German consumers who used to drink imported burgundies are coming to the Ahr. For them a price of twenty or twenty-five Euros is still good value compared to red burgundy prices."

Of course not all the wine is especially good. Cooperatives are still responsible for seventy per cent of production (down from ninety-four per cent in 1988), although some of them, notably the 112-ha (277-acre) Mayschoss cooperative, do make good wines. And the fact that a fair amount of Portugieser, one of the world's duller red grape varieties, survives in the Ahr suggests that it is often used to stretch Pinot Noir and soften any youthful astringency.

Although the best wines are certainly capable of ageing for many years in bottle, there is little tradition here of keeping Pinot Noir. Thomas Nelles estimates that about half the production of red wine is drunk within a year of release. The best vintages here have been 2001, 1999, 1997, 1995, 1993, and 1990.

Vineyards
There is just one Bereich – Walporzheim/Ahrtal – and a single Grosslage: Klosterberg.

AHRWEILER
Vineyards close to the spa town of Bad Neuenahr-Ahrweiler. The sites are: Daubhaus, 35 ha (86.5 acres); Forstberg, 33 ha (81.5 acres); Riegelfeld, 18 ha (44.5 acres); Rosenthal, 50 ha (123.6 acres); Silberberg, 28 ha (69.2 acres); Sonnenberg; and Ursulinengarten, 24 ha (59.3 acres).

ALTENAHR

54 ha (133 acres). In the far western end of the valley.

Altenahrer Eck. 22 ha (54.4 acres). This is the vineyard that Weingut Dentzerhof considers its best. There has been no *Flurbereinigung*, and it is necessary to use a small cog railway to climb the slope.

Altenahrer Ubigberg. 32 ha (79 acres). Mostly steep. Riesling dominates.

HEIMERSHEIM

The village closest to the Rhein, with impressive cliff-like vineyards.

Heimersheimer Burggarten. 21 ha (51.9 acres). A volcanic hill with thin, very stony soils with basalt and weathered slate. Heat is reflected off the cliffs, warming the vines.

Heimersheimer Kapellenberg. 22 ha (54.4 acres). Mostly planted with Portugieser.

Heimersheimer Landskrone. 26 ha (64 acres). The village's most celebrated south-facing site. It takes in the best portion of the Burggarten, but then stretches to the east around the neighbouring hills. The vineyards were terraced until *Flurbereinigung* in 1965, which helped enormously because before then there was no road.

MARIENTHAL

About halfway along the valley.

Marienthaler Jesuitengarten. 12 ha (30 acres). Steep.

Marienthaler Klostergarten. 10 ha (24.7 acres). *Alleinbesitz* of Staatsweingut.

Marienthaler Rosenberg. 15 ha (37 acres).

Marienthaler Stiftsberg. 12 ha (30 acres). *Alleinbesitz* of Staatsweingut.

Marienthaler Trotzenberg. 8 ha (19.8 acres).

MAYSCHOSS

At the western end of the valley, and home to the oldest cooperative in Germany. The individual sites are Lochmühlerley, 10 ha (24.7 acres); Laacherberg, 49 ha (121 acres); Silberberg, 22 ha (54.4 acres); Burgberg, 14 ha (34.6 acres); Schieferlay, 28 ha (69.2 acres); and Mönchberg.

Mayschosser Mönchberg. 43 ha (106 acres). The best site in the village. Deutzerhof owns vines here.

WALPORZHEIM

Midway along the valley.

Walporzheimer Gärkammer. 0.68 ha (1.7 acres), making it the smallest vineyard in Germany. *Alleinbesitz* of Adeneuer. It is terraced and gives top quality wines.

Producers

J.J. ADENEUER

Max Planck Str 8, 53474 Ahrweiler. Tel: +49 (0) 2641 34473. Fax: 37379. 9 ha (22.2 acres). 6,000 cases.

The Adeneuer vineyards are dispersed, partly on terraces, partly on steep sites, and the rest on flatter land. They line the eastern end of the valley from Heimersheim to Walporzheim, and some of the vines are sixty years old. Twenty years ago the Adeneuers were producing mostly sweet wine, but in the mid-1980s switched to drier styles. Unfortunately they were, by the Adeneuers' own admission, not very good, marred both by rot and by high yields. They realized the only sensible way forward was to improve quality, and they followed the model already being provided by Meyer-Näkel. Adeneuer only make red wines, other than a dry Blanc de Noirs. Apart from Pinot Noir, they grow some Frühburgunder, which they like, and a little Portugieser and Dornfelder. The use of barriques has increased over recent years, although a majority of the wine is usually aged in larger casks for about ten months. Where barriques are employed, there is never more than thirty per cent new oak.

"No 1" is their top barrique-aged Pinot Noir, from a number of sites. The wine from the tiny Walporzheimer Gärkammer is bottled separately, and is not aged in barriques so as to preserve the special character it derives from the slate soils. "No 2" is usually made from grapes harvested at below 100 Oechsle. In exceptional years such as 1999 and 2001, there can also be an Auslese Trocken and an Auslese Trocken Goldkapsel.

These tend to be medium-bodied wines, with more emphasis on fruit than tannin, and a smoky character derived from the oak-ageing. They are not intended for long keeping, and are best drunk at between three and five years. Although not in the very top tier of red wines from the Ahr, they are improving from year to year.

DEUTZERHOF

53508 Mayschoss. Tel: +49 (0) 2643 7264. Fax: 3232. www.weingut-deutzerhof.de. 9 ha (22.2 acres). 5,000 cases.

This highly regarded estate is owned jointly by the Cossman and Hehle families, with the Cossmans tracing their ancestry in the Ahr back to 1574. Wolfgang Hehle, who makes the wine, looks rather like Berthold Brecht.

Pinot Noir dominates the vineyards at sixty-two per cent, but there are parcels of Riesling up to fifty years old, forty-year-old Dornfelder, and some Portugieser that is now eighty years old. Some of their vineyards have not been reshaped, and retain their ancient terracing. Their top sites are Altenahrer Eck and Mayschosser Mönchberg opposite the winery, which is located at its base.

Hehle planted Chardonnay in 1991 from cuttings taken from the South Tyrol; he placed the vines on some limestone soil within Heimersheimer Landskrone. I believe this is the only Chardonnay produced in the Ahr. The 2000, a blend from casks and tanks, was elegant rather than rich, which is the way Hehle wants it.

Saumon de l'Ahr is a Pinot Noir rosé, given a short fermentation and designed to go with salmon. Hehle tells me he has been battling with Dornfelder for twenty years and is convinced that with low yields it can match the tannin levels of Cabernet Sauvignon. So he reduces the yields savagely and ages the wine in barriques. It has a rich chocolatey plummy nose, and is supple and quite concentrated.

Hehle rather grandly calls his Frühburgunder "Alpha and Omega" because the grapes come from opposite ends of the valley. Cuvée Alfred C is from old-vine Portugieser. Although he has planted some new Pinot clones, he considers himself lucky also to have vines that are around fifty years old. He finds these old vines similar to Burgundian Pinot, and they have small berries. Almost all the Pinot Noir from Deutzerhof is aged in small oak, usually medium-toast Allier, ranging from 200–300 litres in capacity, and mostly one to three years old; they never use more than one-third new oak. The wines are aged for nine months, and the top cuvées are bottled without filtration.

The regular Spätburgunder QbA Trocken is aged in older barrels and barriques, with no new oak. Caspar C is a QbA Trocken, blending the production from different vineyards. Grand Duc and Altenahrer Eck are the top reds. Grand Duc comes from old vines on south-facing sites cropped at 30–40 hl/ha (12.1–16.2 hl/acre). Altenahrer Eck is Hehle's favourite site, cropped at 20 hl/ha (8 hl/acre) and in effect an Auslese Trocken. A cuvée from Mönchberg is the wine he sends to auction, where it has fetched €60 (£39.20) per bottle. Both the 1999 Mönchsberg Auslese Trocken and the 1999 Altenahrer Eck Auslese Trocken are superb wines, well structured and built for ageing.

Although Hehle doesn't particularly like botrytized wines, he often makes high-quality Riesling Auslese and, in 2000, no fewer than two Eisweins, from Mönchberg and Eck.

MEYER-NÄKEL

Hardtbergstr 20, 53507 Dernau. Tel: +49 (0) 2643 1628. Fax: 3363.
www.meyer-naekel.de. 13 ha (7.4 acres). 8,000 cases.

Werner Näkel has set high standards, which other growers have been happy to emulate. His wines, almost entirely red, come in the form of numerous cuvées. The Trocken and Trocken "G" are the simplest, followed by the "Blauschiefer", grown, as its name suggests, on blue slate soils. Then there are Gold Capsule and Gold Capsule "S." Finally, there are three single-vineyard Spätburgunders: Bad Neuenahrer Sonnenberg, Dernauer Pfarrwingert, and the wildly expensive Walporzheimer Kräuterberg. I have only tasted a few of these wines. The 1999 Spätburgunder Gold Capsule "S" was unusually harmonious: oaky on the nose, but not excessively so, and then rich and firm yet lively on the palate, with an imposing tannic structure. The Frühburgunder here can also be remarkable: smoky and oaky on the nose, and ripe and full-bodied with fresh acidity giving good length.

Without doubt this is one of the finest red wine producers in Germany.

NELLES

Göppinger Str 13, 53474 Heimersheim. Tel: +49 (0) 2641 24349. Fax: 79586.
www.weingut-nelles.de. 6 ha (14.8 acres). 3,500 cases.

The Nelles label is proudly emblazoned with the date 1497, which is not a vintage but a reference to the year in which a Nelles predecessor was first recorded as owning vineyards here. The current Nelles is Thomas, an urbane man with greying swept-back hair. Only half his vines are Pinot Noir: he also has reasonable quantities of Portugieser, Frühburgunder,

Domina (planted in the 1970s), Regent, Riesling, and Pinot Gris (also planted in the 1970s). He found that in the 1970s there was little public interest in Ahr Riesling, so he planted Pinot Gris as an alternative. He used to make it in a heavy Ruländer style, because there was a market for rich sweet wines, but now the style is dry.

The white wines here lack excitement. "Albus" is an easygoing blend of Riesling and Pinot Gris with a dash of Müller-Thurgau. The pure Pinot Gris is rather dull too, and the dry Riesling is perhaps not helped by being put through malolactic fermentation to tame its acidity.

All red grapes are destemmed and fermented by maceration, not by heating the must. Portugieser is made in Halbtrocken and sweet styles. The Trocken has a varnishy nose, and is light, dilute, and short. The Domina has a sweetish jammy nose, and a little discernible residual sugar. "Clarus" is a Pinot Noir rosé, rounded and pleasant, with a light acidic bite. "Ruber" is a blend of roughly eighty per cent Pinot Noir, and ten per cent each of Portugieser and Domina, resulting in a juicy easy-drinking style with light spiciness. The Frühburgunder is aged in older barriques. In 1999 it exhibited a powerful cooked cherry nose; although a touch jammy, the wine had attractive acidity on the finish.

His best Spätburgunders are given numbers, and there are no vine-yards specified on the labels of any of the wines. Thomas Nelles admitted that his "number" system is a marketing ploy, because it facilitates communication when people ask what it means. The "Classic" is aged in old casks: silky and delicate, but not that concentrated. "B" signifies barriques, although the barrels are French, German, and American, with toasted ends. "B48" is the next tier up, then "B52." Sometimes, as in 1999, there is a B52 Goldkapsel. But in 2000 there were no top cuvées.

I can't help feeling that Nelles tries too hard, making too many wines, and trying to find a commercial angle that will make them acceptable to a not very demanding public. The top wines show that he is capable of making very good red wines, so it's a pity the range is not more consistent.

STAATLICHE WEINBAU-DOMÄNE MARIENTHAL
Klosterstr 3, 53507 Marienthal. Tel: +49 (0) 2641 98060. Fax: 980620. 20 ha (49.4 acres). 8,000 cases.

This domaine began its existence as a Romanesque monastery, which was then partly destroyed during the Thirty Years' War and secularized in 1803. The roofless ruins are still standing and are used for concerts and other events. In 1925 the state of Rheinland-Pfalz took over the domaine, and in 1945 it became part of the viticultural research centre in Ahrweiler. Three per cent of the production is still made for research purposes. Two top sites in Marienthal, Klostergarten and Stiftsberg, are exclusively owned by the domaine, and they also have vineyards in Ahrweiler and Walporzheim. Sixty per cent of production is of Pinot Noir.

Although the winery dates from the 1920s, it was built to operate by gravity and is still efficient and practical. The director, Wolfgang Frisch, aims for a seven-day fermentation followed by maceration of up to two weeks. The wines are aged in large *Fuders* and, for top cuvées, medium-toast German small oak barrels. Herr Frisch doesn't want to ape burgundy, and tries to retain the typicity of Ahr red wines.

The top white wine is called Domäne Blanc, and is a blend of Pinot Blanc and Riesling, deliberately made in a low acidity style. The 1999 was fresh but also rather soft.

The Domäne Frühburgunder is picked at 95–100 Oechsle, before the acidity drops. They find it well suited to barrique-ageing, because the wine is more tannic than Pinot Noir. Yields for Pinot Noir are kept low, in some cases as low as 20 hl/ha (8 hl/acre), though the more basic wine is cropped at around 50 hl/ha (20.2 hl/acre). Their Spätburgunder Domäne Trocken is chaptalized to thirteen per cent, and partly aged in barriques. The domaine's top Spätburgunder is Marienthaler Klostergarten Auslese Trocken. In 1999 it was picked at a very ripe 107 Oechsle. There is also a dry Spätburgunder BA but not even Herr Frisch seems that keen on it.

JEAN STODDEN

Rotweinstr 7–9, 53506 Rech. Tel: +49 (0) 2643 3001. Fax: 3003.
www.stodden.de. 6 ha (14.8 acres). 4,000 cases.

Eighty-three per cent of Gerhard Stodden's vineyards are planted with Pinot Noir on steep vineyards. His principal site is Recher Herrenberg near Mayschoss. He produces numerous cuvées, and those marked "JS" or, as in 1999, "JS***", are aged in barriques and bottled without filtration. I have not tasted them, but they have a good reputation, can be very tannic, and are very expensive.

9

Mosel

For many winelovers it is the wine from the Mosel valley that is the quintessence of Riesling: light, racy, elegant, refreshing, ethereal yet steely. Curiously its renown is relatively recent; only in the twentieth century did these wines begin to be appreciated. It is true that there have been vineyards here since Roman times, and that certain estates, especially church foundations such as Maximin Grünhaus or Karthäuserhof, were highly regarded in the Middle Ages. Nonetheless, there are few if any properties with the pedigree of Schloss Johannisberg or Kloster Eberbach in the Rheingau. The nobly sweet wines from the Mosel, Saar, and Ruwer are among the most prized and costly wines in the world, but they are, in historical terms, an innovation. TBAs were produced at the top estates of the Rheingau throughout the nineteenth century, but the first example of such a wine from the Mosel was as recent as 1921.

Today the wines of the Mosel are grouped with those from the Saar and Ruwer valleys for administrative purposes, and indeed this makes sense, because there is a family resemblance between them. But this chapter will, for practical purposes, consider the Mosel alone, leaving the next to look at the wines and estates of the Saar and Ruwer.

Anyone seeking evidence of the Roman origin of these vineyards will not have to search hard. In Brauneberg, Neumagen, and Piesport Roman wineries have been excavated, and a Roman tomb from the third century portrays a ship navigating the Mosel and bearing casks of wine. Nor was there much of a hiatus between the periods of Roman and ecclesiastical wine production. As early as the fourth century monastic foundations were established and they gradually acquired vineyards, often as gifts. Vineyards such as Josephshof, today the *Alleinbesitz* of the Kesselstatt estate, was of monastic origin, and a dependency of the abbey of St Martin.

The cellarbooks of the British nobility refer to Mosel wines from the early eighteenth century onward, so the wines must have enjoyed some reputation. It is unlikely that they bore much resemblance to the wines produced today. Their modern character was probably established only after a decree by the Prince-Elector of Trier, Clemens Wenzeslaus, in October 1787, requiring all inferior vines to be grubbed up after the vintage and replaced by better quality varieties, which would certainly have included Riesling. But Riesling was never as ubiquitous in the Mosel as in the Rheingau. The state domaines that enhanced the reputation of vineyards in the Rheingau and Nahe had their counterpart here too from the late nineteenth century onward. As in the Nahe, the state domaine, which has recently been broken up, did not acquire vineyards in well established areas, but instead cleared land that viticulturalists suspected were capable of producing fine wine. In the case of the Mosel-Saar-Ruwer, that included sites in the Saar in villages such as Serrig and Ockfen.

The Mosel is a more isolated region than either the Rheingau or Rheinhessen, so the wines tended to be drunk and appreciated locally. It was not until the development of railway networks and, later, good roads, that Mosel wines left the region, and the country, in large quantities. The river was navigable, but could not compare in this respect with the Rhein. Toward the end of the nineteenth century merchant houses began to be set up in the region, in Trier and Traben-Trarbach and Koblenz, and trade in Mosel wines accelerated.

In the nineteenth century the wines were routinely doctored, often with an elderflower potion that was used to disguise the frequent thinness of the wine. Red wines were also produced, including some from Pinot Noir. As has already been mentioned, quality-enhancing practices such as selective harvesting came late to the Mosel. Fritz Hallgarten, writing more than fifty years ago, states that "the grapes are not left on the vines until they reach Edelfäule, but only till they have reached full maturity."[1] Morton Shand, writing in 1929, observes: "Not so very long ago Moselle was considered merely as one of the fashionable wines of the moment, a transient vogue. Even in Germany it was long known as a

[1] Hallgarten, p. 94.

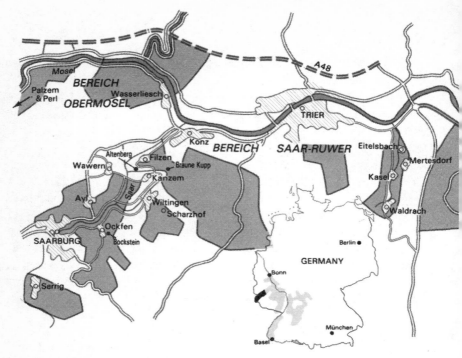

Upper Mosel

Modewein – an unjust aspersion – while in East Prussia it was hardly known at all until a few decades ago. In England those who did not stigmatize it as a fashionable whim considered it in the light of an invalid, or hypochondriac, fad. Certainly it is a wine that is easily digested and wholesome, especially for rheumatic subjects." He clearly did not rate them very highly: "These wines mature very quickly, thanks to their slight body and slender alcoholic content, and do not generally keep well. They should be drunk at latest before their fourth or fifth year as a general rule."[2] Today, of course, we take a very different view, knowing that the Rieslings from the top estates are capable of decades of longevity.

Many of the best growers joined forces to promote their wines by forming an organization called the *Grosser Ring* in 1908. Their most celebrated activity was and remains the annual auction in Trier, where some

[2] Shand, pp. 52–3, 55–6.

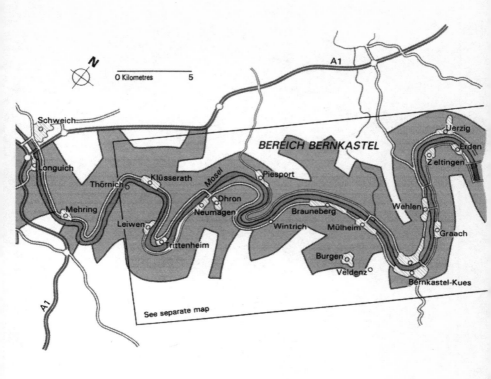

rare wines are regularly sold for high prices in the full glare of publicity. It also organizes tastings of its members' wines throughout the world.

Today the Mosel as a whole has around 11,240 ha (27,770 acres) of vineyards. Riesling is dominant at fifty-four per cent. Müller-Thurgau accounts for twenty per cent, Elbling for nine per cent, and Kerner for seven per cent. Despite the region's renown, its area is shrinking, and recently almost 300 ha (740 acres) were abandoned within a twelve-month period. Not all of them are a great loss, because poor-quality flat vineyards are being abandoned due to the fact that the wine they produce fetches too low a price; however, some steep sites have also been abandoned because of high production costs.

The traditional way to train Riesling vines in the Mosel is on poles, but many recent plantings have been trained along wires. With wire-trained vines, you lose some density, because the vines tend to be 1.2 or 1.4 metres (3.9 or 4.6 feet) apart, compared to one metre (3.3 feet) for pole-trained vines. The reason for retaining the latter is that they get better

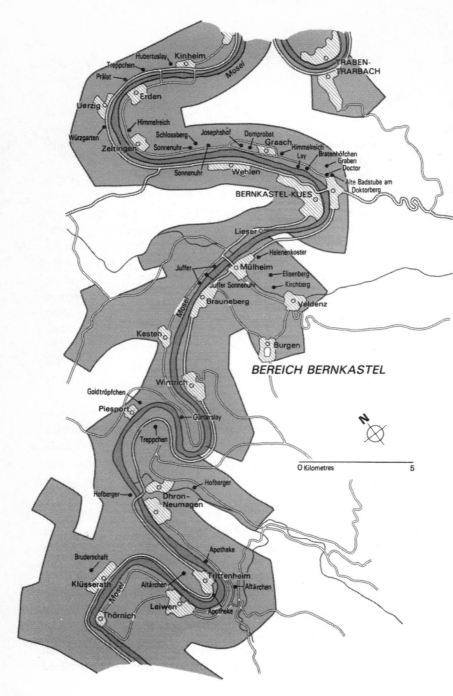

Middle Mosel

exposure to the sun. Dr Manfred Prüm of J.J. Prüm says that binding the shoots to the poles is a lot of work, but it's worth it to obtain optimal exposure.

Training vines on a pole and binding them to it is known as *Pfalerziehung*. Some growers, not only in the Mosel but in other regions with steep hand-worked vineyards such as the Mittelrhein, have also adopted a system known as *Trierer Rad* ("Trier wheel"), which trains the vine vertically, and takes three shoots, which are bent over the edge of what looks like a steering wheel above the vines. As the bunches grow, their weight forces the canes down, so that the bunches remain quite high and well exposed. The advantage of this system is that it is cheap to prune, and uses half the labour of other systems, so costs are generally around one-third of Pfalerziehung. Another system developed over the last twenty years is *Drahtramenziehung*, which trains the canes along wires. This creates a wall of foliage above the bunches. This system is cheap to install and gives good quality fruit, and would be the likely choice for any grower planting a vineyard today, although traditionalists might prefer to retain the more costly Pfalerziehung.

The central stretch of the valley, the Mittel (or Middle) Mosel focused around Bernkastel, has always been the most prized sector. Curiously, there is no legal definition of the Mittel Mosel, but the term can be sensibly applied to the swathe of vineyards between Leiwen and Erden. It is part of the fascination of the Mosel that even within a short stretch of the river, there can be significant variations in soil and microclimate. Graach, for instance, has heavier soils than Zeltingen, just a couple of miles away, with Wehlen probably acquiring its supremacy by being between Graach and Zeltingen, both geographically and stylistically. Then in Erden, just beyond Zeltingen, the blue slate gives way to red slate, which gives different nuances to the wine. The differences are of style rather than quality. Thus Zeltingen grapes tend to obtain higher sugar levels than those from Graach, but the latter produces wines with greater power and minerality.

The Lower Mosel is the more northerly area that almost reaches the suburbs of Koblenz. Long regarded as second-rate, it has recently shown itself capable of producing excellent wines. The region is attempting to acquire a stronger identity by renaming itself as the Terrassenmosel, because many of the vineyards between Zell and Winningen are indeed

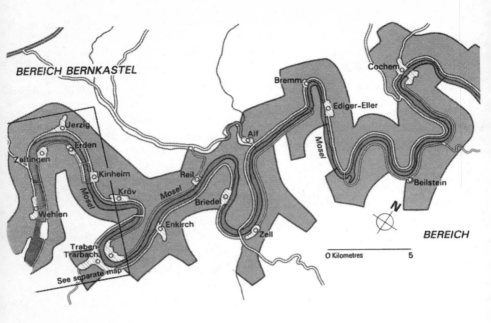

terraced. The Lower Mosel always languished in the shadow of the Mittel Mosel and the Saar and Ruwer because there were few prestigious estates here.

The third section is the Upper Mosel, which takes in the vineyards between Trier and Luxembourg. This is certainly the least interesting part of the region, and it is here that much Elbling, rather than Riesling, is planted. The climate can be harsh, and spring frosts regularly diminish production. Many of the wines are tart and so tend to be used as base wines for sparkling Moselle. But yields can be ridiculously high: 159 hl/ha (64.3 hl/acre) in 1993, 270 hl/ha (109 hl/acre) in 1992.[3]

The best soils, found throughout the Mittel Mosel and in many parts of the Lower Mosel, are of course slate, and the Devonian blue slate is particularly prized. Not only does the slate component in the soil contribute a steely mineral flavour to the wine, but the shards of stone, sometimes as packed and layered as a suit of armour, retain the warmth of the

[3] Clarke, *Wine Atlas*, p. 120.

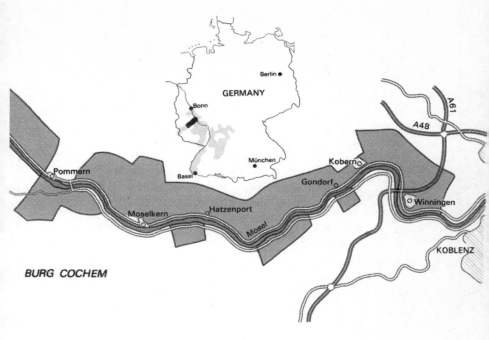

Lower Mosel

sun (when it is shining) and help the grapes to ripen. Slate has brilliant drainage properties too, which are essential in a fairly wet climate.

The whole Mosel valley is a marginal area for viticulture, so every advantage has to be taken of local microclimatic conditions. As you travel up the valley you will see cliff-like vineyards rising to a height of around 200 metres (650 feet), vineyards that vanish as soon as the river bends; sometimes the vineyards lie on the west side of the river, as at Brauneberg, and elswhere, as at Bernkastel or Wehlen, on the opposite bank. It's very simple: grapes will only ripen fully on the steepest sites with the best exposure to the sun. Ernst Loosen tells how, on a visit to the northern Rhône, he was taken to see the steep vineyards of Côte Rôtie by the Chapoutier brothers. Loosen was unimpressed. "You think this is steep?" he said to the Chapoutiers. "To me, this looks like a holiday."

Often the finest parcels lie midway up the best slopes, as in the Côte d'Or in Burgundy. At midpoint the vineyards are sheltered from the cold winds that can hinder ripening at the top of the slopes, and are better protected from the frost that can affect lower portions. The slate cliffs also ensure excellent drainage, which is crucial in the long growing season that Riesling requires. Properly tended vineyards on steep, well drained soils are less likely to succumb to grey rot and other diseases during the rainy spells often experienced in September and October.

The correlation between steepness of site and quality of wine has been well established. Unfortunately, the steepest sites are also the most expensive to cultivate. If you travel up the valley from Trier, you soon come to bands of steep vineyards in villages such as Schweich. It is reasonable to suppose that Schweich is capable of producing good Rieslings, but who has ever heard of them? And the same is true in the Lower Mosel, in villages such as Bremm and Pünderich. It takes more than topography to achieve renown for a vineyard: it takes growers and winemakers too. While distinguished wine-producing families such as the Prüms and the Bergweilers have been established in the Mittel Mosel for decades, even centuries, there are few such counterparts in Longuich or Pünderich. Without famous estates to validate the wine, sites soon become forgotten, which is what has happened to, for example, the entire stretch of vineyards from Trier to Leiwen.

With little public recognition of these forgotten sites, it is almost impossible for even the most conscientious of growers to obtain good prices for the wine emanating from them. Thus a vicious circle begins. Without high prices that can to some extent compensate growers for the costs of production on steep sites, it soon becomes uneconomic to cultivate them. The problem is compounded by high labour costs, so it is not surprising that the more obscure villages and vineyards have become increasingly marginalized. The cultivation of a single ha (2.5 acres) of good land in the Mosel requires about 2,500 to 3,600 hours of labour, compared to 800 in the Pfalz. Of course the figures are much lower in the flatter vineyards away from the river that can be mechanized, where no more than 400 are required. In addition, labour shortages have made it difficult to find workers, especially among the German population, who are drawn less and less to backbreaking work in some of world's steepest vineyards. Legal restrictions also make it harder to find non-German workers. Bert Selbach of Weins-Prüm points out: "Without Polish workers, the cultivation of most steep sites in the Mosel, Saar, and Ruwer would have had to be abandoned. But they are only allowed to stay in Germany for three months in any year. So although there are many workers from Poland who would be only too happy to work for German wine estates, they are only permitted to do so for limited periods. What's more, if we want to hire non-German workers, we have to give the authorities six weeks' notice of an invitation – but who knows precisely when the harvest is going to begin?" So bureaucratic restrictions are hampering the efficient manual cultivation of some of Germany's greatest vineyards. (On the other hand a long-established producer such as Dr Dirk Richter says he has no problems finding workers. "Only I have to pay them wages competitive with those they would receive from industry.")

Yet all is not lost. It is true that many sites have been abandoned in recent years precisely because they are uneconomical to cultivate, but for the most part they are not in the best sectors. Many of the vanishing sites are in side valleys, vineyards that were planted during boom years but which have ceased to be viable. In any event, many of those remoter vineyards were planted with a view to producing bulk wines for which the demand has shrunk.

There are certainly some abandoned parcels even in top vineyards such as Wehlener Sonnenuhr, especially in those corners that are the least accessible to workers and equipment, but such losses are partially balanced by the enterprise of young growers who are demonstrating that fine wine can be made from potentially great vineyards that have lost their renown. Heinz Schmitt in Leiwen has bought sites in Longuich and Schweich, pointing out that there are bargains to be had, and that vineyard prices are about seven times lower in Longuich than in Leiwen, which is itself hardly the most renowned of Mosel villages.

Today throughout the length of the twisting Lower Mosel, in obscure villages such as Kröv, Enkirch, and Winningen, there are estates producing excellent wines, both dry and sweet. Growers such as Reinhard Löwenstein and Reinhard Knebel in Winningen have triumphantly demonstrated the real potential of this region, especially for drier styles. Knebel points out that Winningen, although more northerly than Trier, enjoys a slightly warmer climate. The soils are slate and warm up fast, and acidity levels are rarely aggressive. Monorails installed from the early 1980s onward have made it possible for growers to cultivate the terraced vineyards, and the region is enjoying something of a renaissance. Its proximity to major cities such as Koblenz (a few kilometres away) and

Bonn also means that the Lower Mosel is becoming a magnet for weekend tourists out for a good meal and the opportunity to purchase a few cases of decent wine directly from the growers.

Unfortunately, by no means all wine from the Mosel is of good quality. The wine laws encouraged vineyard expansion onto flatter land that was hardly suitable for the cultivation of Riesling. So lesser varieties, notably Müller-Thurgau, were planted, ensuring regular large crops of the kind of bland wine for which the cooperatives and *Kellereien* thirsted as fodder for their cheap export blends. These mediocre vineyards usually benefited from a misleading prestigious Grosslage name, of which the most notorious is Piesporter Michelsberg. Such wines, alas, still account for about forty per cent of production and do little to enhance the renown of the region as a whole.

Production tends to be polarized, with high-quality private estates on the one hand, and mediocre wholesalers on the other. Moselland is easily the largest and most powerful of the cooperatives. These large Kellereien and cooperatives completely dominate the open market, leaving little room for quality-oriented négociants. Nonetheless, a few of the latter have managed to succeed, the best known being Selbach and Richter.

Despite the efforts of growers such as Heinz Schmitt and Reinhard Löwenstein to rescue forgotten vineyards, the threat to the region must not be underestimated either. In the decade from 1988 to 1998, the region lost 8.5 per cent of its vineyards, although many, perhaps most, of those lost sites were not among the best. In the early 1990s vineyard prices were plummeting. In the late 1980s good sites were priced at 40–50 DM/square metre; by the mid-1990s you could pick them up for round 10 DM. The low point was reached in 1993, when you could buy parcels within esteemed sites such as Erdener Treppchen for 15–20 DM/square metre. The main reason for the lack of demand was the depressed economic climate within Germany itself, and genuine worries about the cost of cultivation. There was little point acquiring a top vineyard if you lacked either the workforce or the means to cultivate it.

However, by the late 1990s the worst seemed to be over, and it was no longer easy to find bargains in the Mittel Mosel, although Heinz Schmitt enjoyed happy hunting in less favoured stretches of the valley. There was a revival in the demand for top Mosel Rieslings both from within

Germany and from crucial export markets such as the United States and Japan, and this meant that the leading estates could sell their production with relative ease and for good, if not always exceptional, prices.

A combination of low prices and a lack of marketing skills has shrunk the number of estates. The structure of the wine business in the Mosel means that an estate with a mere 2 or 3 ha (4.9 or 7.4 acres) of vines can't easily prosper. Willi Schaefer in Graach is atypical in thriving with under 3 ha (7.4 acres) of vines: he does well because the sheer quality of the wines has brought international recognition. Estates also sell up because of changing labour patterns. Children are less wedded than their parents to the land of their birth. In the past it was quite possible for a family to cultivate a couple of hectares, sell the wine to passing tourists or local restaurants, and still find time to hold down jobs in Trier or Koblenz. Today the children of an ageing wine grower are more likely to be working in Cologne or Munich or Paris, and have no need to supplement their income by producing wine from labour-intensive vineyards. Far easier to sell them off or lease them out. The process has been aided by the fact that it is now possible to retire at the age of fifty-eight, so owners are selling off their vineyards earlier than they might otherwise have done, and receiving government subsidies when they do so.

The Napoleonic code applied in the Mosel from the early nineteenth century, one consequence being that estates were constantly subdivided as they passed from generation to generation. Eventually the point was reached when they no longer became viable. This process continues to this day. According to Dr Dirk Richter, there were 7,500 growers in the Mosel in the early 1970s; thirty years later there are no more than 2,500, and the numbers are set to reduce further.

This need not necessarily be a bad thing. *Hobbywinzer*, producing wine in their spare time, do not always produce good wine; indeed, the odds are very much against them doing so. The disappearance of many very small estates gives an opportunity to the likes of Heinz Schmitt and the many burgeoning properties in Leiwen and Trittenheim to acquire good sites at affordable prices.

Johannes Selbach, a grower and négociant in Zeltingen, is not unhappy to see the shrinkage among hobby growers. "These are the kinds of estates that sell cheap and usually mediocre wines to tourists from roadside stands or from the cellar door. Such wines don't do much for the prestige of the region." It would probably be more sensible for the hobby growers to sell their grapes to cooperatives or négociants, and some do exactly that, but many others take pride in bottling and selling their own wines.

When times are bad, however, they have to resort to desperate measures to sell their wines. I am indebted to Ernst Loosen for the following anecdote, which deserves to be true. A certain grower would load his van with wine, drive to a large town, and check in the local newspaper for recent death announcements. Funerals usually take place three days after decease, so he would turn up at the house of the bereaved on the morning of the funeral. He would cheerfully announce that he had arrived with the wine delivery. The grieving family would explain the circumstances, whereupon the grower would say, "Oh, I had no idea, I'm very sorry. I suppose he must have sent me the order just before he died." Embarrassed and with no way of checking the story, the family would take in the wine and pay for it. He would then repeat the scam until the van was empty.

Even though a diminution in the numbers of growers may prove a favourable long-term trend, because it allows greater consolidation under the banner of professional and ambitious producers, some are more troubled by the abandonment of more and more vineyards. Ernst Loosen points out: "When sites are abandoned, the parcels that remain tend to be scattered. The abandoned sectors are much more prone to disease precisely because they are untended, and that poses a threat to the surviving parcels. It would be sensible to consolidate the remaining parcels into the best parts of the site, but that would be too costly for many to contemplate. We're now down to less than 12,000 ha (30,000 acres) and some estimates suggest the area could keep diminishing until only about 6,000 ha (15,000 acres) are left. Unfortunately it's not only the mediocre side valleys that are disappearing. It's the steep sites as well, especially in the Lower Mosel from Traben-Trarbach to Koblenz. Once those sites have been abandoned, they will never be replanted."

In an earlier chapter I reviewed the debate on what constitutes the most authentic style of Rheingau Riesling. There is a similar, but less heated, discussion about the identity of Mosel Riesling. Despite the recent fad for drier wines from the Mosel, it seems fairly clear that "traditional" Riesling here almost always had some residual sugar. The harvest tended to be very late, in October or November when the days were already cool; so fermentations were correspondingly slow and took place in the traditional 1,000-litre Fuder casks. It would not have been unusual, then as now, for fermentations to stop of their own accord before the wines had achieved complete dryness. The absence of cultivated yeasts also meant that fermentations were likely to be haphazard. However, the presence of residual sugar in the wine did not necessarily mean they tasted sweet, because of the pronounced acidity in Mosel Riesling. It is entirely possible to taste a wine with 20 or 30 grams of residual sugar without being able to detect sweetness in the wine, so long as the acidity is firm enough to disguise it. Mosel Riesling, far more so than any other expression of the variety, is all about balance. Wines that have not fermented to dryness will have lower alcohol than those that have done so, and this allows the sheer fruitiness of Riesling to shine through, a fruit quality that is brought into focus by the dazzling interplay of acidity and sweetness.

As in the Rheingau, the introduction of modern technology, notably the filter and the centrifuge and the development of cultivated yeasts, has made it far easier to control the style and balance of the wine. Nothing need be left to chance, as in the past. So when in the 1980s German wine writers and sommeliers started to insist that Riesling ought to be a dry wine (except when made from botrytized fruit), some Mosel growers did their best to respond. I tasted a lot of those wines from the 1980s, and the great majority were dire. Insufficiently ripe grapes were fermented to near dryness, and results were tart and even sour. It took a while for the realization to sink in that if you wanted to make dry wines in the Mosel, you need maximum ripeness for your grapes, otherwise the wines would lack body and the acidity would be accentuated without any balancing sweetness. A wine with 20 grams might easily taste dry, but could not be labelled as such, so producers, bound by the 1971 Wine Law, were forced to keep residual sugar levels below 8 grams, however awful the wine might taste.

By the mid-1990s, however, these lessons had been learned. Although some good dry wines were being made in the Mittel Mosel, it was hard to claim that this the natural forte of the region. In parts of the Saar and Ruwer, however, and in the Lower Mosel, where acidity levels tended to be lower, it was quite feasible to make drier wines, whether officially designated as Trocken or Halbtrocken. Moreover, certain producers, such as Paulinshof and Clemens Busch, went out of their way to establish a reputation for their dry wines, and they understood the need for maximum ripeness. Dry wines tended to be costly, because only good sites would deliver the required ripeness levels, and it was often necessary to leave the grapes on the vine until far into the growing season, and that entailed a level of risk that could backfire. The producers' directory that follows will confirm that many excellent dry Rieslings are now being produced in the Mosel, yet the sweeter styles remain the wines that give Mosel Riesling its uniqueness. In any case, the dry wines can be matched and often surpassed by those from the Pfalz or Rheinhessen; the same is emphatically not true of the styles with residual sweetness. That, of course, is no excuse for wines that are merely sugary or so weakly structured that they are flabby.

Because residual sugar is an important component of many of the wines, the hierarchy of "quality" levels laid down by the Wine Law is still largely followed in the Mosel. At good producers, the ascent from Kabinett to Spätlese and Auslese is not simply a question of sweetness. Many a young Auslese from a top grower tastes no more sugary than his Kabinetts. The sugar level will be higher as one rises through the scale, but so will other components, such as acidity and extract. Quality is essentially defined by intensity.

The quality levels established by the wine law are supplemented by various other categories. *Hochgewächs* wines are still to be found in the Mosel, as well as other regions The wines must be made from Riesling with at least 65 Oechsle, and being chaptalized will often have more body and weight than a Kabinett. The wine is also required to score slightly higher than other wines at the undemanding AP tastings, achieving a total of at least 3.5 out of five. The wines have enjoyed some success in restaurants, but are not that commercially significant.

Some growers use the term *Feinherb* on the label to signify wines at the upper end of the Halbtrocken range, or just beyond it. Halbtrocken has a bad image, with good reason, so some growers such as Kerpen, Kesselstatt, and Pauly-Bergweiler opt for Feinherb. It seems to me to be more of a nuisance than a help.

The thorny issue of classification is also under discussion in the Mosel-Saar-Ruwer, though the debate is even less clear-cut than in the Rhein regions. The stylistic parameters adopted in the Pfalz, for example, can't really apply to the Mosel, where there is no tradition of producing dry wines.

As in the other regions, the basis for classification is the existence of old tax maps, the principal one dating from 1868. The difficulty is that the 1971 Wine Law greatly expanded the historic sites, and the major vineyards of the Mosel – such as Piesporter Goldtröpfchen and Wehlener Sonnenuhr – are not only very large but are divided among many dozens of owners. Whereas it was feasible to classify only the "best" sectors of the Rheingau's vineyards, that would simply be impractical in the Mosel, even though both the historic maps and contemporary experience could be used to define the "best" sectors of the Sonnenuhr. There are simply too many owners with too many dispersed parcels: the boundary disputes would never end. To the argument that classifying an entire vineyard as first growth would open the system to mediocre wines from mediocre producers, Johannes Selbach responds: "The market will soon sort out those who are exploiting a great name but producing lousy wine."

The 1868 map is not the first classification of the Mosel-Saar-Ruwer. A much earlier one was made in 1804, and it was based on the price per 1,000 litres paid for wines from certain sites. Because this Napoleonic classification is almost two centuries old, it is of interest to see which sites were most highly regarded. The top village was Brauneberg (172 francs), followed at some distance (150 francs) by Piesport, Wehlen, Machern, Graach, Zeltingen, and Erden. The third group, valued at 140 francs, included Bernkastel, Grünhaus, Kesten, Oberemmel, Niederemmel, Minheim, and Reinsport. Valued at 129 francs were Kues, Lieser, Wintrich, Ürzig, Kröv, Köwerich, Mülheim, Dhron, Kinheim, Kindel, Wolf, and Neumagen.

A comparison of the tax map of 1868 with later editions such as that of 1904 makes it clear that there was considerable vineyard expansion in the late nineteenth century, mostly into south-facing side valleys. Ernst Loosen, who showed me this map, points out that such expansion would have involved clearing forests and would have been an expensive operation. This confirms that a century ago the wines from the Mosel were selling for good prices and that there was sufficient demand for them to justify expansion.

Any classification of the twenty-first century will almost certainly try to establish a stylistic structure, too. The most likely outcome is that dry wines will be labelled as QbA, thus eliminating categories such as Kabinett Trocken, Spätlese Trocken, and Auslese Trocken. The Prädikat categories would thus be reserved for styles with residual sugar. The major change would be the restriction on the sites that could be identified on the label. This has already begun to happen, especially on the part of estates with an excess of single vineyard sites. Thus Kesselstatt has cut back severely on cited vineyards, and the Pauly-Bergweiler estate now identifies only its two sites in Bernkastel and Urzig. At J.J. Prüm, Manfred Prüm cites only Wehlener Sonnehuhr, Graacher Himmelreich and, occasionally, Bernkasteler Badstube; all other sites are merged into his Gutsriesling.

Indeed, some producers question the necessity for a classification in the Mosel. Dirk Richter observes: "Ideas about classification merely sum up what the market demands anyway: fewer single vineyards on the labels, fewer or no Grosslage names. As for identifying the top sites, that has been achieved ages ago. The problem lies with the secondary vineyards that were once celebrated but have lost their renown because there are no good producers with vines in those sites. Frankly, with strong competition between the best growers of the Mosel, it is by no means clear what a classification will achieve."

No final decisions have been taken on how the classification will work, but in March 2003 the VDP announced the broad outlines. About 4 per cent of the vineyards would be classified. Maximum yields for first growths would be set at 50 hl/ha. The wide variety of wine styles encountered in the Mosel-Saar-Ruwer would be retained, from dry QbAs to fresh Kabinetts and sweeter Spätlesen and Anslesen. It is likely that whatever system is devised will be open to all proprietors who meet the criteria, not just to VDP members.

Vineyards

Within Mosel-Saar-Ruwer there are six Bereiche and twenty Grosslagen, which are listed within each Bereich. There are 523 Einzellagen.

Bereich Burg Cochem (Koblenz to Zell). Grosslagen from east to west: Weinhex, Goldbäumchen, Rosenhang, Grafschaft, Schwarze Katz.

Bereich Bernkastel (from Zell to Trier). Grosslagen from east to west: Vom Heissen Stein, Schwarzlay, Nacktarsch, Münzlay, Badstube, Kurfürstlay, Michelsberg, St Michael, Probstberg.

Bereich Saar (Saar valley). Grosslage: Scharzberg.

Bereich Ruwer (Ruwer valley). Grosslage: Römerlay.

Bereich Obermosel (Upper Mosel). Grosslagen: Königsberg, Gipfel.

Bereich Moseltor. Grosslage: Schloss Bübinger.

BERNKASTEL

The famous vineyards of this town lie clustered beneath or around the ruined castle. Some authorities detect a flintiness or smokiness in the wines, though I can't say I have recognized this character. There are two Grosslagen: Kurfürstlay and Badstube. The former can include wines from Brauneberg and Wintrich and is very large indeed. Badstube, however, must be drawn from the village's top sites (see under Badstube below).

Bernkasteler Alte Badstube am Doktorberg. After seventeen years of legal wrangling, the Pauly-Bergweiler estate was allowed to retain this name, referring to a 2-ha (4.9-acre) parcel within the Badstube. Another parcel here was owned by Deinhard, but Pauly-Bergweiler bought these vines, giving them a virtual monopoly here.

Bernkasteler Badstube. 59 ha (146 acres). A small Grosslage which may only draw on the following vineyards: Lay, Bratenhöfchen, Graben, Matheisbildchen, Alte Badstube am Doktorberg, and Doktor. Some very good wines are bottled under this appellation by, among others, Friedrich Wilhelm Gymnasium, the two Thanisch estates, Markus Molitor, Wegeler, and Selbach-Oster.

Bernkasteler Bratenhöfchen. 18 ha (44.5 acres). Most wines from this site are bottled as Badstube, but Markus Molitor still uses the appellation.

Bernkasteler Doktor. 3.26 ha (8.1 acres). The most famous site in Bernkastel, and possibly in the entire Mosel. It takes its name from a legend concerning Archbishop Boemond II, elector of Trier, who ruled from 1351 to 1362 and owned the castle above Bernkastel. He fell ill while visiting the castle but his doctors were unable to cure him. Everyone was convinced the archbishop was dying, so he was brought a flask of wine from one of the best sites in Bernkastel. After drinking the wine the prelate made a speedy recovery, and as a mark of his gratitude conferred the name Doktor on the curative vineyard. It was here that in 1921 the first TBA in the Mosel was produced, although TBAs were also produced that year in the Saar and Ruwer. In 1971 the vineyard was expanded sixfold, but still remains small. There is no doubt that the wine from the south-facing Doktor can be very good indeed. Whether it is significantly better than the other wines from top Bernkasteler vineyards is arguable, but its proprietors rejoice in the fact that the Doktor is the highest priced agricultural land in Germany. The wines are mineral, of course, and slow to develop. All the vines are trained on poles. The major owners are Wegeler, and the two Thanisch estates. The spelling of Doktor has varied over the years, and is sometimes spelt "Doctor."

Bernkasteler Graben. 13 ha (32.1 acres). This site adjoins the Doktor, but faces southwest. The soil is relatively heavy, with good water retention, and the wines can be quite spicy. Respected growers such as Studert-Prüm and Molitor believe that the quality is almost as high as from its more celebrated neighbour. Owners include Studert-Prüm, Pauly-Bergweiler, Franz Dahm, the two Thanisch estates, and S.A. Prüm.

Bernkasteler Lay. A steep slate site close to the riverbank, planted entirely with Riesling. Owners include the two Thanisch estates, Franz Dahm, Pauly-Bergweiler, and Ernst Loosen, who often produces Eiswein from here.

Bernkasteler Schlossberg. 50 ha (124 acres). Close to the Doktor, and enjoying a southwest exposure. Viewed from Kues, it is just to the left of the castle. The site is steep and slatey but the quality is variable. Owners include Selbach-Oster and Thanisch-Erben Thanisch.

BRAUNEBERG

306 ha (756 acres). A cliff face of magnificent south-facing vineyards across the river from the village. The grapes here can achieve high levels of ripeness. The top-ranking vineyard in the Napoleonic classification.

Brauneberger Juffer. 32 ha (79 acres). This has iron-rich slate soils, giving wines that are rich yet elegant. The presence of some sand in the soil is given as an explanation for its slight inferiority in comparison with Juffer-Sonnenuhr. Owners include Max Ferd. Richter, Fritz Haag, and Willi Haag.

Brauneberger Juffer-Sonnenuhr. 10 ha (24.7 acres). An enclave within

Juffer, consisting of the central and lower parts. It is very well sheltered and also benefits from the reflection of the river just below. In parts the steepness is seventy-eight per cent, and the slate content is very high, making this indisputably a first growth. The site attracts botrytis quite easily, so it is not ideal for dry wines. The wines are rich and high in extract. *Flurbereinigung* in 1990 revealed the presence of a Roman presshouse at the foot of the vineyard. Owners include Fritz Haag, Willi Haag, Max Ferd. Richter, the two Thanisch estates, and Paulinshof.

Brauneberger Kammer. 0.5 ha (1.2 acres). *Alleinbesitz* of Paulinshof since the late 1980s. It lies just beneath a cliff within the Juffer, and the soil is brown slate with iron. The vineyard is very steep and receives excellent day-long exposure to the sun. The Jüngling family replanted the site, so the first crop under their ownership was 1992. The site was acclaimed as long ago as 1788 by Thomas Jefferson.

BREMM
Lower Mosel.

Bremmer Calmont. The steepest site in the Mosel, and, it's claimed, all Europe. The vineyard is terraced. Franzen is the best-known owner.

DETZEM
A village between Mehring and Leiwen, and not highly regarded.

Detzemer Maximin Klosterlay. A steep site with hard slate soils prized by Carl Loewen and Walter Rauen.

DHRON
Adjoins Neumagen.

Dhroner Hofberger. 17 ha (42 acres). A south-facing vineyard on the steepest slopes of the village, though tucked into a side valley. Reddish slate. The Bischöfliches Priesterseminar is a major owner, and Rosch also has vines here.

ENKIRCH
162 ha (400 acres). In the Lower Mosel, just beyond Traben-Trarbach. Blue slate is plentiful here.

Enkircher Batterieberg. 1 ha (2.5 acres). *Alleinbesitz* of Immich-Batterieberg and one of the best-known vineyards of the Lower Mosel. It is located about 2 kilometres (1.2 miles) from Enkirch itself in the direction of Traben-Trarbach.

Enkircher Steffensberg. 82 ha (203 acres). Reddish slate with iron, giving fruity wines.

Enkircher Zeppwingert. 17 ha (42 acres). Adjacent to Batterieberg. Blue slate. Immich-Batterieberg has recently acquired 1.5 ha (3.7 acres).

ERDEN

100 ha (247 acres). A famous village at the northeast end of the Mittel Mosel. The exposure is excellent, so that the vines are bathed in sunshine. The wines are full-bodied and quite spicy, and generally more elegant than those from Ürzig. As well as the celebrated sites listed below, there are flatter vineyards of no distinction where no Riesling is planted. Erden as a whole has soils that cope exceptionally well with wet conditions.

Erdener Prälat. 2.2 ha (5.4 acres). A very steep, south-facing site with red slate. Thanks to the cliffs and outcrops that flank the site, it is very sheltered and probably enjoys the warmest microclimate of any site in the Mosel, making it the source of many outstanding Auslesen, with aromas of exotic fruit. Owners include Dr Loosen (with about twenty-five per cent), Weins-Prüm (with very little, but in the original portion of Prälat), Peter Nicolay, Meulenhof, Mönchhof, and Vereinigte Hospitien.

Erdener Treppchen. 40 ha (99 acres). Often successful in wet years. Recent *Flurbereinigung* means that few old vines remain, but there are some ungrafted vines belonging to J.J. Christoffel Erben. Less opulent wines than Prälat. Other owners include Loosen, Merkelbach, Mönchhof, Peter Nicolay, Meulenhof, Schmitges, and Bischöfliches Priesterseminar.

GONDORF

Lower Mosel, not far from Koblenz. In the 1960s there were 40 ha (99 acres) in production, but by 2002 the surface had shrunk to around 6 ha (14.8 acres).

Gondorfer Gäns. Very varied slate soil with quartzite and some sandstone. Mostly south-facing, at the end of a curved ridge. It produces wines with high extract.

Gondorfer Schlossberg. Adjacent to Gäns and above the village. The site is well ventilated so the grapes tend to stay healthy late into the autumn, when they are susceptible to botrytis. Thus the site is better for sweet wines than for dry.

GRAACH

The soils are somewhat heavier than those of Wehlen, have a subsoil of clay or loam, and the wines tend to be less elegant. On the other hand they can be rich and powerful and long-lived, with a distinct earthy character. *Flurbereinigung* means that there are few old vines.

Graacher Domprobst. 28 ha (69 acres). An extremely steep slatey vineyard downstream from Himmelreich, giving more elegant wines than its neighbour. Curiously the whole site is embraced by Himmelreich, which continues after Domprobst ends. The soils are deeper than Himmelreich, and the wines need some years to show their full potential. It is capable of producing good dry wines. Owners include Schaefer, Weins-Prüm, Friedrich Wilhelm Gymnasium, Kees-Kieren, Kerpen, Kesselstatt, Markus Molitor, Max Ferd. Richter, S.A. Prüm, and Selbach-Oster.

Graacher Himmelreich. 89 ha (220 acres). Modern Himmelreich now incorporates many smaller vineyards of high quality, such as Humberg and Stablay. Owners include Schaefer, Kees-Kieren, Friedrich Wilhelm Gymnasium, Loosen, Markus Molitor, Wegeler, Selbach-Oster, the two Thanisch estates, J.J. Prüm, S.A. Prüm, and Studert-Prüm.

Josephshof. 4.7 ha (11.6 acres). *Alleinbesitz* of Kesselstatt. The seventeenth-century house was part of a monastic foundation secularized by Napoleon and bought in 1803 by a banker from Trier, then sold to Kesselstatt in 1858. Surrounded by Domprobst and Himmelreich, it resembles the former more than the latter. Fine schist-slate soil with good water retention, so it can be very successful in dry years. The vines are either ten or thirty years old. The wines are slow to develop, full-bodied, occasionally earthy, and very long lived. Annegret Reh-Gartner of Kesselstatt compares them to Hochheim in the Rheingau, with their softer acidity.

HATZENPORT

Lower Mosel, between Cochem and Winningen.

Hatzenporter Kirchberg. A site validated by Heymann-Löwenstein, which owns 2 ha (4.9 acres) here.

JOSEPHSHOF
See Graach.

KESTEN
121 ha (299 acres). A rather obscure village between Brauneberg and Piesport, and less well exposed than either.

Kestener Herrenberg. 71 ha (175 acres).

Kestener Paulinsberg. About 40 ha (99 acres). Good site with steepness ranging from twenty-five per cent to sixty-five per cent.

Kestener Paulins-Hofberger. 9 ha (22.2 acres). Faces south and southeast, with deep slate soils giving spicy, racy wines. Probably the best site in the village, being a continuation of Brauneberg-Juffer toward Kesten. Proprietors include Paulinshof and Bastgen.

KINHEIM
An underrated village beyond Erden. The wines tend to be fresh and enjoyable Rieslings.

Kinheimer Hubertuslay. 105 ha (259 acres). A top site, but completely lacking in reputation, thanks to the lack of well-known proprietors other than Mönchhof.

KLÜSSERATH
353 ha (872 acres). An underrated village between Detzem and Leiwen.

Klüsserather Bruderschaft. 250 ha (618 acres). Probably the best site, but given its size, very varied. Kirsten is a major owner, with 5.5 ha (13.6 acres).

KOBERN
Lower Mosel. Village adjoining Gondorf.

Koberner Uhlen. 10 ha (24.7 acres). In effect, a continuation of Winninger Uhlen, with varied slate soils.

KRÖV
Lower Mosel. A village that once enjoyed a high reputation for its wines, until its growers opted for high yields and until the small négociant houses based here were taken over by larger companies less concerned about quality. Today a few conscientious growers are again making good

wines here. There was *Flurbereinigung* in the late 1970s, so there are few old vines.

Kröver Letterlay. 6 ha (14.8 acres). South-facing. A top site.

Kröver Paradies. Although across the river from Letterlay, growers such as Martin Müllen claim that this stony site can produce excellent wines.

Kröver Steffensberg. A top site with reddish and blue slate soils.

LEIWEN

450 ha (1,112 acres). A village that lost its reputation when in the 1950s some of its growers decided to plant more vineyards on flat farmland. Today it is fast recovering its reputation, thanks to a number of quality-conscious producers in the village.

Leiwener Klostergarten. The vineyards immediately surrounding the village. The soil varies from sandy loam to deep stony gravel. However, part of the vineyard is flat and incapable of producing fine wines from low yields. Consequently, the quality from Klostergarten is very inconsistent, but can be good. Owners include Grans-Fassian, Rosch, and Loewen.

Leiwener Laurentiuslay. 9 ha (22.2 acres). The village's best steep site. There has been no *Flurbereinigung* here, and a few parcels planted before World War I are still in production. Owners include Rosch, Sankt Urbans-Hof, Grans-Fassian and Loewen.

LIESER

Close to Bernkastel, with many steep sites. The wines tend to be broader than those from neighbouring Brauneberg. In 1906 a cask of wine produced by the von Schorlemer family, owners of Schloss Lieser, fetched a record price at auction, so the wines clearly were once highly thought of.

Lieserer Niederberg-Helden. 18 ha (44.5 acres). Between the village and Bernkastel. The soils are deep and quite rich. Nonetheless the wines can have an engaging elegance. Schloss Lieser is the main owner, and Thanisch Müller-Burggraef also has vines here.

LONGUICH

A village closer to the Ruwer valley but not known for the distinction of its wines.

Longuicher Maximiner Herrenberg. Mostly blue slate with some red slate, and deep soils that give powerful wines. Heinz Schmitt is an owner.

LÖSNICH
The next village beyond Erden, giving fresh fragrant Rieslings.

MEHRING
290 ha (717 acres). This village between Longuich and Detzem has light soils that can suffer stress in dry years.

Mehringer Blattenberg. 12 ha (29.7 acres). Friedrich Wilhelm Gymnasium has been a major owner here, but recently sold 0.6 ha (1.5 acres) of ungrafted vines from 1925 to Heinz Schmitt.

Mehringer Zellerberg. 185 ha (457 acres). Between Mehring and Trier. Southwest-facing and quite slatey, this is a well regarded but very large site that lacks outstanding growers. Clüsserath-Weiler and Heinz Schmitt have vines here.

MÜLHEIM
Between Brauneberg and Bernkastel.

Mülheimer Helenenkloster. 0.8 ha (2 acres). The *Alleinbesitz* of Max Ferd. Richter, and being fairly flat, it is prone to frost. This has allowed Richter to produce a succession of excellent Eisweine here.

NEEF
Lower Mosel.

Neefer Frauenberg. 40 ha (99 acres). A site validated by Reinhold Franzen of Bremm. The wines have great charm.

NEUMAGEN
An ancient site dating back to Roman times, when it also functioned as a port for shipping the wines of the Mosel.

Neumagener Nusswingert. 0.6 ha (1.5 acres). The *Alleinbesitz* of Markus Milz. The slatey soil is fairly thin.

Neumagener Rosengärtchen. 38 ha (94 acres). Heinz Schmittt has ninety year old ungrafted vines here.

PIESPORT

387 ha (956 acres). True Piesporter is a wine of remarkable finesse, and has nothing to do with the rightly despised Grosslage of Piesporter Michelsberg, which is 1,500 ha (3,707 acres) in size.

Piesporter Domherr. 5 ha (12.4 acres). A very steep enclave within Goldtröpfchen and close to the river and the old part of the village. Kesselstatt is a major proprietor, and Reinhold Haart and Kurt Hain also own vines here.

Piesporter Goldtröpfchen. 120 ha (297 acres). A splendid south-facing site protected from winds by its location on a loop in the river. The soils are slatey and deep, and the wines very mineral in character. Stuart Pigott first pointed out to me their occasional aniseed flavour, which can be pronounced in some vintages. Until 1971 the site was restricted to the site behind the village, but was then expanded sideways to incorporate many other vineyards. Owners include Reinhold Haart, Joh. Haart, Hain, Kesselstatt, Sankt Urbans-Hof, Bischöfliches Konvikt, and Lehnert-Veit. In 1972 O.W. Loeb noted that much wine labelled with the name of this vineyard was in fact produced from neighbouring, and lesser, sites.

Piesporter Kreuzwingert. An enclave within Goldtröpfchen bought as an *Alleinbesitz* by Reinhold Haart in 1993. Long-lived wines.

Piesporter Treppchen. 250 ha (618 acres). The misleading name of the large flat vineyards across the river in Niederemmel.

PÜNDERICH

Lower Mosel. A village between Enkirch and Zell with impressive vineyards.

Pündericher Marienburg. 110 ha (272 acres), but some vineyards have been abandoned. Although there was *Flurbereinigung* here in the 1980s, some of the best sectors, around the rail viaduct, were unaffected, leaving old vines in place. Higher on the slope there are deep slate soils that give very mineral wines. Owners include Clemens Busch.

Pündericher Nonnengarten. 10 ha (24.7 acres). Adjacent to Marienburg. Deep soils of red slate with loam, giving full-bodied wines that need time to open up.

SCHWEICH

Village between Longuich and Mehring, and no longer highly regarded.

Schweicher Annaberg. A famous site in the nineteenth century, with deep soils of red slate and sandstone that rarely suffer from drought. It has some resemblance to Ürziger Würzgarten and can produce very good dry wines in certain vintages. Heinz Schmitt has vines here.

THÖRNICH

An underrated site now being revived thanks to the efforts of the Carl Loewen estate.

Thörnicher Ritsch. The village's best site, with soft slate soil. It has not been subject to *Flurbereinigung*. Carl Loewen is the best-known owner.

TRARBACH

Lower Mosel. The villages of Traben and Trarbach face each other cross the river and maintain a genial rivalry.

Trarbacher Hühnerberg. 15 ha (37 acres), although only 6 ha (14.8 acres) remain in production. Located some six kilometres (3.7 miles) from the town in a well sheltered side valley and highly rated in the late nineteenth century. The terraced vineyards deliver wines that to some palates closely resemble those from the Saar and need many years to evolve. The site is being restored thanks to the efforts of Martin Müllen, who is propagating new vines from old ones.

Trarbacher Ungsberg. Adjacent to Hühneberg and also well thought of in the nineteenth century.

TRIER

370 ha (914 acres). There are some twenty vineyards within the city limits, none of special renown.

Trierer Augenscheiner. The only Trier site that lies on the other side of the river from the town. *Alleinbesitz* of Vereinigte Hospitien.

Trierer Tiergarten. The best-known of the Trier sites, with many owners.

TRITTENHEIM

326 ha (806 acres). At this village, the principal vineyards are on both sides of the river, because the loop of the river means that both sides have

a similar exposure. Thus parts of Apotheke and Altärchen can be first-rate; other parts, on flatter land, middling. There is a proposal to expand Apotheke into Altärchen, while renaming the vineyards across the river now divided between Apotheke and Altärchen as Altärchen only. The village enjoys the dubious distinction of having been the first place in the Mosel where Müller-Thurgau was planted.

Trittenheimer Altärchen. 245 ha (605 acres). Gravel and slate soils. It lies between the Trittenheim bridge and Leiwen, and is adjacent to Apotheke. More than half the site is on steep slopes. Those sections close to Apotheke are just as good as the more celebrated Apotheke, but most parts of Altärchen are not at this level. Owners include Ernst Clüsserath, Franz-Josef Eifel, Grans-Fassian, Friedrich Wilhelm Gymnasium, and Bischöfliches Priesterseminar.

Trittenheimer Apotheke. 55 ha (136 acres). In 1971 this famous site was expanded to its present size. Although the cliff it shares with parts of Altärchen looks fairly uniform, it is in fact quite undulating, so quality can vary substantially from parcel to parcel. Owners include Ernst Clüsserath, Clüsserath-Eifel, Clüsserath-Weiler, Franz-Josef Eifel, Friedrich Wilhem Gymnasium, Grans-Fassian, Milz, Rosch, and the Bischofliches Priesterseminar.

Trittenheimer Felsenkopf. 1 ha (2.5 acres). An *Alleinbesitz* of Milz, located within Altärchen on the other side of the river from the main site. It is unusually steep, up to seventy-two per cent, and the soil is deep blue slate. It used to be known as Laurentiusberg, as a chapel dedicated to St Lawrence tops the site. The Milz family was able to establish that it had owned this site for centuries, so it was allowed to retain its separate identity after 1971. Its wines tend to be rich and powerful.

Trittenheimer Leiterchen. 1 ha (2.5 acres). Also a Milz *Alleinbesitz* and for the same reasons as Felsenkopf. It is located on deep blue slate terraces in the heart of Apotheke. The site is well ventilated and gives delicate elegant wines.

ÜRZIG

61 ha (151 acres). One of the oldest documented wine-producing villages on the Mosel, with evidence of Franconian ownership in the seventh century. It is very distinctive, because much of it is located on red sandstone as well as slate.

Ürziger Goldwingert. 0.5 ha (1.2 acres). *Alleinbesitz* of the Peter Nicolay estate, which was allowed to retain this old name after 1971. It is located between Urziger Würzgarten and Erdener Prälat on red volcanic soil that is rich in iron.

Ürziger Würzgarten. 50 ha (124 acres). A south-facing site, famous for its red sandstone soil to which slate has been added over the years. It retains moisture and fares well in dry years. The wines tend to be a touch spicier and heavier than those from Erden. The parcels added onto the original Würzgarten after 1971 tend to have a higher slate content. Overall the wines, according to Robert Eymael of Mönchhof, take longer to open up than those of its neighbour Erden, but are also longer lived. Ernst Loosen detects aromas of blackcurrant and aniseed. Owners include Christoffel Erben, Weins-Prüm, Bischöfliches Priesterseminar, Peter Nicolay, Dr Loosen, Merkelbach, and Mönchhof.

VELDENZ

Located in a side valley behind Mülheim.

Veldenzer Elisenberg. 4.3 ha (10.6 acres). 2 ha (4.9 acres) are owned by Max Ferd. Richter, and the remaining portions by a cousin of Dirk Richter, making this a virtual *Alleinbesitz*.

WEHLEN

The only important site is the large Sonnenuhr, grouped around the sundial high on the cliff-face. Most of the mediocre vineyards on the flatter land on the other side of the river were removed in the 1990s to make room for a road-widening scheme, to the delight of the best growers.

Wehlener Abtei. Faces north, and not very good. Markus Molitor uses this site for Eiswein.

Wehlener Klosterberg. Tucked into a south-facing side valley opposite Sonnenuhr. The best of the village's south-bank vineyards. Light slatey soil. Markus Molitor owns 6 ha (14.8 acres) here. Other owners include J.J. Prüm and Mönchhof.

Wehlener Klosterhofgut. Faces north, and not very good.

Wehlener Nonnenberg. North-facing, with the usual deficiencies that entails. Owners include J.J. Prüm.

Wehlener Sonnenuhr. 65 ha (161 acres). A classic Mittel Mosel site, packed with weathered blue Devonian slate, and protected from water stress by a profusion of deep underground streams. The wines are clean and elegant and show well when young, although they keep very well. *Flurbereinigung* is due to begin in the early 2000s but will take ten years to complete; it seems certain that this will involve grubbing up many of the old vines here. Fifty years ago the wines from the Sonnenuhr were almost as highly rated as those from the Doktor, although before 1971 the site was considerably smaller, and when it was registered in 1913, it consisted of a mere 10 ha (24.7 acres). Owners include J.J. Prüm, Weins-Prüm, Dr Loosen, Kerpen, S.A. Prüm, Pauly-Bergweiler, Max Ferd. Richter, Selbach-Oster, Studert-Prüm, Thanisch Müller-Burggraef, and Wegeler.

WINNINGEN

148 ha (366 acres). The vineyards are situated on fairly spectacular cliffs close to Koblenz, making it the last outpost, and one of the best, of the Lower Mosel. The soils are light sandy slate that heats up fast. Some of the vineyards were planted on more fertile land in the 1880s, so the village is far from uniform.

Winninger Brückstück. 6 ha (14.8 acres). Close to Röttgen. A terraced vineyard on light slate that gives wines with fresh acidity. Owners include von Heddesdorf.

Winninger Domgarten. 121 ha (299 acres). The vineyard surrounding the village, some of it fairly flat and undistinguished. Sandy loam soils, with varying exposures.

Winninger Hamm. 16 ha (39.5 acres). Very varied in quality, although the terraced sectors can give good wines.

Winninger Röttgen. 7 ha (17.3 acres). An excellent site, with light shale soil with slate and iron, giving mineral wines with considerable elegance. Many growers think it is best suited to sweeter styles. Owners include Heymann-Löwenstein, von Heddesdorf, Richard Richter, and Reinhard Knebel.

Winninger Uhlen. 17 ha (42 acres). Another outstanding site located on the bend of the river approaching the Autobahn bridge. A steep terraced vineyard, facing south and southwest. The reddish soil is slate with clay, and it warms up fast, giving precocious ripening and high must weights. The wines are powerful and broad and many growers think it ideal for dry Riesling. Owners include Heymann-Löwenstein, von Heddesdorf, Richard Richter, and Reinhard Knebel.

WINTRICH
272 ha (672 acres).

Wintricher Ohligsberg. 10 ha (24.7 acres). A seventy per cent steep site with hard slate soils and once the *Alleinbesitz* of Schloss Lieser when the Schorlemer family owned the property. Excellent wines are made from here by Theo Haart, who says the site was highly regarded in the past but has been forgotten.

ZELTINGEN
The largest wine village in the Mittel Mosel, and the continuation of Wehlen.

Zeltinger Himmelreich. 110 ha (272 acres). Exposure determines the quality of various sectors of this large south-facing site. The best parcels are on steep weathered slate soils behind the village, but there are also inferior vineyards on flatter land beyond the bridge. Owners include Mönchhof.

Zeltinger Schlossberg. 50 ha (124 acres). Behind the village and above the Sonnenuhr. The soils are fairly heavy blue Devonian slate over loam. The vineyards are south-facing and have good water retention, which is beneficial in dry years. The wines tend to be robust and comparable to Graacher Domprobst in style. Many ungrafted vines remain.

Zeltinger Sonnenuhr. 40 ha (99 acres). A more homogeneous site than the larger Wehlener Sonnenuhr. It lies lower than the latter, and benefits from its proximity to the river. It still contains a large number of ungrafted vines, as it has not been subject to *Flurbereinigung*. The wines can be very elegant. Markus Molitor is a major owner with 4.5 ha (11 acres); others include Selbach-Oster, Friedrich Wilhelm Gymnasium, and J.J. Prüm.

Producers

BISCHÖflICHE WEINGÜTER

Gervasiusstr 1, 54203 Trier. Tel: +49 (0) 651 43441. Fax: 40253.
www.bwgtrier.de. 107 ha (264 acres). 70,000 cases.

This organization is responsible for managing and marketing the production of three ancient estates: the Bischöfliches Konvikt, the Bischöfliches Priesterseminar, and the Hohe Domkirche. The Konvikt was founded in 1806 as a cathedral school and seminary; it owns 40 ha (99 acres), with good sites in Piesport, Ayl, and Kasel. The Priesterseminar was founded in the sixteenth century and became a Catholic seminary, acquiring substantial vineyards from the elector of Trier, Clemens Wenzeslaus. By 1999 it still owned 34 ha (84 acres), with extensive vineyards in Erden, Ürzig, Trittenheim, Kasel, Wiltingen, and Ayl. The Hohe Domkirche, also an ecclesiastical foundation, now owns 22 ha (54.4 acres), principally in Avelsbach and the Saar. All these institutions were both endowed with vineyards by their founders, and acquired more holdings as the result of legacies and bequests. Almost all their vineyards are planted with Riesling. For many years the director has been Wolfgang Richter, and since 1993 the cellarmaster has been Johannes Becker.

All vinification takes place in Trier, where most of the top wines are still fermented in wooden casks, using mostly natural yeasts. *Süssreserve* is very occasionally used for QbA and Kabinett wines. Despite the large volume of wine produced here, standards are high: yields are far from excessive, and the wines are clean and well made. Most of them are made in a dry or off-dry style.

Because of the huge number of wines produced, it is difficult to taste them all, and on various visits I have only been able to assess a cross-section of the range. Consistently fine are the wines, especially in a sweeter style, from Kaseler Nies'chen, and the 2000 Kabinett from Trittenheimer Apotheke is vigorous and elegant.

The Weingüter's wine list usually includes a good number of mature wines from older vintages. Wolfgang Richter says there is little demand for older vintages, but Riesling fanciers, aware of how beautifully the wines can age, can take advantage of the domestic market's lack of interest in these older bottles and buy them at very attractive prices.

CLEMENS BUSCH

Im Wingert 39, 56862 Pünderich. Tel: +49 (0) 6542 22180. Fax: 1625. 7 ha
(17.3 acres). 3,500 cases.

Clemens Busch and his wife Rita took over the family estate in 1991. The
vineyards are in the village's top vineyards, Marienburg and Nonnengarten, and are cultivated organically. Almost all the wines are dry,
though when conditions permit Busch is keen to make nobly sweet wines
as well. His various parcels in the Marienburg show considerable
differences, so he makes a large range of wines from them, signalling
differences between two or more Spätlese Trocken wines by using a star
system. Particularly precious is the 0.12-ha (0.3-acre) parcel called the
Felsterrasse and located between the cliffs in the Marienburg; here he has
sixty year old vines that have very small berries, producing wines of great
concentration. They also resist drought conditions very well, presumably
because the old vines have sunk their roots deep into the rock.

The wines are often fermented in steel tanks, using only natural yeasts,
but are usually aged in wooden casks. Busch is no fan of malolactic
fermentation for Riesling, and if the wines show high acidity, he will simply give them more time to mellow out in cask and/or bottle.

These dry wines from the Marienburg are very mineral, sometimes
austere and pungent; many of them have a scent of limes. The 2000
Felsterrasse is excellent: full-bodied and peppery, and a touch bitter in its
youth as a result of the high extract; the 1999 Felsterrasse is a touch
broader and more peachy and flowery, but it too has a peppery mineral
finish. In 1999 Busch was able to make an Auslese Trocken from the
Marienburg, but the high alcohol (fourteen per cent) unbalances the
wine, and gives it an oiliness and heaviness that are not attractive. The
2000 sweet Auslesen from the Marienburg are delicious: lean racy wines
with a great deal of finesse; and the style is similar but even more intense
in the creamy Beerenauslese of the same year. This is an underrated
estate, probably because its vineyards are not in a fashionable location.

J.J. CHRISTOFFEL ERBEN

Schanzstr 2, 54539 Ürzig. Tel: +49 (0) 6532 2176. Fax: 1471. 2.2 ha (5.4
acres). 1,800 cases.

This tiny estate, with excellent and mostly ungrafted vineyards in Erdener
Treppchen and Ürziger Würzgarten, is in a state of transition. In 2001

Hans Leo Christoffel turned sixty-five and retired, leasing his vineyards to his neighbour Robert Eymael at Mönchhof. Even though the vineyard area is small, Christoffel used to make a large number of wines, distinguishing between different quality levels with a star system. My personal acquaintance with the wines is patchy, but they have for many years enjoyed a fine reputation, and the 2000 Würzgarten Spätlese is a delightfully racy wine. Under the new regime, the wines will continue to be bottled under the Christoffel label, and it will be no easy task for Eymael to maintain two separate, and in a sense competing, ranges at the very high quality level typical of both estates. Yet to judge from the 2001s, he has done exactly that: Christoffel's Ürziger Würzgarten Kabinett shows much more weight and spice than Mönchhof's, which is leaner and more elegant. The 2001 Würzgarten Auslesen are exquisite.

ERNST CLÜSSERATH

Moselweinstr 67, 54349 Trittenheim. Tel: +49 (0) 6507 2607. Fax: 6607. 3 ha (7.4 acres). 2,000 cases.

The reserved Ernst Clüsserath took over the family estate from his father in 1991 when he was aged thirty-two. All the vineyards are in Trittenheimer Altärchen and Apotheke, but they are divided into no fewer than thirty parcels on both sides of the river. Thirty per cent of the vineyards are steep, and the viticulture is comparable to the French system of *lutte raisonnée*, quasi-organic but prepared to use treatments if absolutely necessary. Yields are low – only 47 hl/ha (19 hl/acre) in 2001, but usually around 60 hl/ha (24.3 hl/acre) – and stylistically the wines are divided equally between Trocken, Halbtrocken, and sweeter styles.

Clüsserath harvests his vineyards selectively by hand. He prefers whole-cluster pressing, and in 2001 substantially increased the number of stainless steel tanks in his cellar in preference to older wooden casks. Natural yeasts are used for fermentation, and the wine spends at least two months on the fine lees before being bottled in the spring.

Having tasted a thorough cross-section of his wines from the 1999 and 2000 vintages, I find them very attractive and often delicate, yet quite a few of them lack concentration and length, despite the low yields. But Ernst Clüsserath is a determined and ambitious grower, so this is an estate to watch.

CLÜSSERATH-WEILER

Der Haus an der Brücke, 54349 Trittenheim. Tel: +49 (0) 6507 5011. Fax: 5605.
www.cluesserath-weiler.de. 5 ha (12.4 acres). 3,000 cases.

Half of Helmut Clüsserath's vineyards (all Riesling) are in the Apotheke, though divided among twenty different parcels. His pride and joy is the very steep 0.25-ha (0.6-acre) parcel called the Färhfels, which is located between Apotheke and Altärchen and planted with one hundred-year-old vines. The total production is a trifling 500 litres so the wine is scarce and expensive. He bought the Fährfels from the Friedrich Wilhelm Gymnasium in 1997 jointly with his neighbour Gerhard Eifel, although only one wine is produced.

Yields are set at around 60–65 hl/ha (24.3–26.3 hl/ha), and the wines are vinified in stainless steel and wooden casks using only natural yeasts. For his dry wines, Clüsserath is keen that the acidity inherent in such a style should never be too obtrusive; he wants his wines to show elegance and minerality.

This they do. These are elegant, finely honed and medium-bodied. The Fährfels is the best of the dryish wines (it has 15 grams of residual sugar that is scarcely discernible on the palate), as indeed it should be. The sweet wines are excellent, even in a difficult year such as 2000, when Clüsserath distinguished between various Apotheke Auslesen with various stars on the label. The 2000 Eiswein is very good, but less sleek and persistent than the Auslesen.

REINHOLD FRANZEN

Gartenstr 14, 56814 Bremm. Tel: +49 (0) 2675 412. Fax: 1655.
www.weingut-franzen.de. 4.5 ha (11 acres). 3,500 cases.

Ulrich Franzen is the best-known owner of the Mosel's steepest site, the Bremmer Calmont. Almost all the wines are dry, and many of them go through malolactic fermentation. This is one of the few estates in the Mosel to offer a red wine from Frühburgunder.

FRIEDRICH WILHELM GYMNASIUM

Weberbachstr 75, 54290 Trier. Tel: +49 (0) 651 978300. Fax: 45480. www.fwg-weingut-trier.com. 28 ha (69 acres). 20,000 cases.

This estate was founded by the Jesuits in 1561 as an adjunct to their school, which still exists. Vineyards were acquired by donations from parents, which explains why today they consist of some 200 parcels dispersed over a wide area from Ockfen to Graach. Fifty-five per cent of the vineyards are on very steep sites, fifteen per cent on fairly steep sites, and thirty per cent on flatter land. The mainstay of the estate are the vineyards in Falkenstein in the Saar, 14 ha (34.6 acres) that were acquired in 1901. Some of these are on flatter sites that make them suitable for mechanical harvesting. Other top sites include Trittenheimer Apotheke and Altärchen, Graacher Himmelreich and Domprobst, Zeltinger Sonnenuhr, and Bernkasteler Badstube.

The cellars in Trier are 400 years old, but the vinification is modern, with minimal use of cultivated yeasts and *Süssreserve*. About forty per cent of the wines are dry, twenty per cent Halbtrocken, and the remainder sweet. Although Riesling is obviously the most important grape variety, the estate also produces Rivaner (Müller-Thurgau) and red wines from Regent and Pinot Noir. Since 1996 the estate has been directed by the affable Helmut Kranich, the former manager of the Langwerth von Simmern estate in the Rheingau. For some reason the gymnasium sold off some outstanding parcels of vines in the late 1990s, such as the Fährfels in Trittenheim, now owned by Clüsserath-Weiler.

The range of wines has been expanded in recent years, because the estate tries to reach out to a younger generation of wine drinkers. Thus wines such as Rivaner and the Regent rosé sport modern packaging, and are fresh, simple, and inexpensive. As for the classic Rieslings, the 1999s and 2000s are delicate, fruity, and have a good acidic structure, although some wines do lack concentration. Standards are quite high, but few wines are outstanding.

GRANS-FASSIAN

Römerstr 28, 54340 Leiwen. Tel: +49 (0) 6507 3170. www.grans-fassian.de. 9 ha (22.2 acres). 6,000 cases.

The urbane Gerhard Grans is the latest of his family to run an estate founded in 1624, and he took over from his father in 1982. More than half his vineyards lie in the Leiwener Klosterlay and Laurentiuslay, but he also has holdings in Trittenheimer Apotheke and Altärchen, and a small area in Piesporter Goldtröpfchen. The wines are fermented in stainless steel, using natural yeasts, and he likes a prolonged fermentation to maintain aromatic complexity. Some are aged in casks, and all are left on the fine lees for two months or more before bottling. About forty per cent of his wines are dry, but he also produces some superb sweet wines and a notable Eiswein, which usually come from Leiwener Kloster-garten.

In 1986 he began to produce a barrique-aged wine called Catharina, using Kerner and Müller-Thurgau as well as Riesling. The wine used to spend four months in new oak and was, frankly, weird. Gerhard Grans saw the error of his ways (and rightly points out that the wine was very marginal in terms of his total production) in 1994. Catharina still exists, but the present-day version is an off-dry blend of Riesling and Weissburgunder with around 12 grams of residual sugar.

These are excellent wines, the best exhibiting an exemplary purity. In 2000 the top dry wine, the Laurentiuslay Spätlese Trocken "S," the Altärchen Kabinett and the Apotheke Spätlese are all good examples of this style. However, some of the wines show a leesy character that may not be to everyone's taste: the 1999 Apotheke Spätlese had this character, which Grans likes but I don't. The sweet wines are exquisite, especially the impeccable Auslesen, which combine richness of fruit (apricot, peach) with racy acidity. The 1999 Goldkapsel Auslesen are brilliant, as is the 1999 Eiswein, with pears on the nose, and an opulence of fruit balanced by high acidity and very good length.

FRITZ HAAG

Dusemonder Str 44, 54472 Brauneberg. Tel: +49 (0) 6534 410. Fax: 1347. 7.5 ha (18.5 acres). 5,500 cases.

When I see Wilhelm Haag moving in my direction, I usually beat a fast retreat. Not because I don't like him – on the contrary – but because he delights in giving the fiercest, most bone-crushing handshake I have ever experienced. This seems to be the sole defect in an otherwise energetic and persuasive personality, characteristics that find their way into his wines. His best sites are in the Juffer-Sonnenuhr, and although he does produce a few dry wines, his forte lies in the superb range of sweeter styles, all produced without *Süssreserve*. The wine-making is traditional, with most wines being aged in *Fuder* casks. A certain connoisseurship is required to navigate the Haag wine list, because there are numerous bottlings, often differentiated by *Fuder* numbers, AP numbers, or length of capsule. Often the price tells you all you need to know.

In about 1990 Haag acquired some excellent parcels, but some of them required replanting, which meant that for some years the vines were very young. Perhaps the 1992 vintage was a tad disappointing – or at least not up to the stellar standards Haag has led us to expect – and the estate has taken a while to return to top form. Overall, the wines are about as complete as any wines from the Mosel can be, having tremendous concentration, a bracing minerality, astounding depth of flavour, fine racy acidity, and great longevity. They are unusual in combining richness and power with a lightness of touch: a Haag wine is never heavy. It seems superfluous to add that when he does produce a BA or TBA, the wines are among the finest of the region.

As well as being one of the top winemakers in Germany, Wilhelm Haag has worked tirelessly for the VDP and Grosser Ring organizations, proudly offering the wonderful wines of the region, and not just his own, to an expanding world of winelovers through the media of tastings and auctions.

WILLI HAAG

Burgfriedenspfad 5, 54472 Brauneberg. Tel: +49 (0) 6534 450. Fax: 689. 5.5 ha (13.6 acres). 4,000 cases.

It is inevitable that the supremacy of the Fritz Haag estate should leave the Willi Haag estate somewhat in the shade. It was the parents of Wilhelm Haag who in the early 1960s divided their Ferdinand Haag estate between Wilhelm (of Fritz Haag) and Dieter (of Willi Haag). Dieter Haag died prematurely in the mid-1990s, leaving his widow and his son Marcus to take over. The vineyards lie in the Juffer and Juffer-Sonnenuhr, and the majority of the wines are made in a sweetish style. They are vinified in both casks and stainless steel, and aged in exceptionally damp cellars. In general, the wines are good, clean, and attractive, but lack intensity and don't seem to be quite as concentrated and persistent as they could be.

REINHOLD HAART

Ausoniusufer 18, 54498 Piesport. Tel: +49 (0) 6507 2015. Fax: 5909. www.haart.de. 6.5 ha (16 acres). 4,000 cases.

For about a decade Theo Haart has reigned supreme as the best winemaker in Piesport. Most of his holdings are within Goldtröpfchen, and include a parcel known as Kreuzwingert that he acquired in 1993. He also bought vines in Wintricher Ohligsberg in 1990. He has used the old vines in his vineyards to propagate massal selections for replanting, ensuring a high standard of raw materials. Yields are no more than 50 hl/ha (20.2 hl/acre). Haart insists on scrupulous harvesting to ensure only healthy grapes go into the press, and he favours a long fermentation, in either steel or wood, at cool temperatures. Only a small proportion of the Haart wines are dry, and his style accentuates the purity of fruit and minerality of Goldtröpfchen at its best. The 1991 vintage, admittedly difficult, was disappointing here, but recent vintages have been superb. The 1997s in particular combined a flowery exuberance with a firm structure that promised an interesting evolution in bottle. The 1999s and 2000s are excellent and consistent.

KURT HAIN

Am Domhof 5, 54498 Piesport. Tel: +49 (0) 6507 2442. Fax: 6879. 5 ha (12.4 acres). 3,000 cases.

Gernot Hain took over this long-established family estate in 1988, consolidating its holdings in some of the best Piesport vineyards, notably Goldtröpfchen. Half the wines are Trocken or Halbtrocken. The 2001s from Goldtröpfchen were packed with fruit and marked by a grapefruity zest.

FREIHERR VON HEDDESDORF

Moselufer 10, 56333 Winningen. Tel: +49 (0) 2606 962033. Fax: 962034. www.vonheddesdorf.de. 4.5 ha (11 acres). 3,500 cases.

Andreas von Canal, the grandson of the last Freiherr von Heddesdorf, runs this all-Riesling estate close to Koblenz. Half the vineyards are in the top site of Winninger Uhlen, and eighty-five per cent of the wines are made in a dry or off-dry style, as is common here. Yields are fairly low and the grapes are harvested selectively. The vinification takes place in stainless steel tanks, using cultivated yeasts. The wines are sound, have good fruit character, but lack complexity and persistence. In 2000 Canal made some quite good Auslesen from Winninger Brückstück and Röttgen. All the wines, whether dry or sweet, seem to share a melony character that renders them somewhat one-dimensional. I suspect it is a yeast character, but it is hard to be certain.

HEYMANN-LÖWENSTEIN

Bahnhofstr 10, 65333 Winningen. Tel: +49 (0) 2606 61919. Fax: 61909. www.heymann-loewenstein.com. 12 ha (29.7 acres). 7,000 cases.

This important estate has vineyards in Winningen's best sites, as well as 2 ha (4.9 acres) in Hatzenporter Kirchberg. Reinhard Löwenstein took over the property in 1980, and since then has gone his own way, forging a path along which a number of other wine producers in the Mosel have eagerly followed. Since 1987 he has dispensed with the categories of Kabinett and Spätlese and focused production on dry wines, sold as QbA, or sweet wines of at least Auslese quality. Viticulture is along organic lines, supplemented by treatments conceived in the 1930s by Wilhelm Reich that are akin to biodynamism.

The spacious cellars are decidedly bizarre. He pumps in water directly from the Mosel so that it flows along a narrow channel through the centre of the cellars, and he has installed organ pipes that link the cellars with the fresh air above. The idea is to give his wines exposure to the elements. The cellarwork is non-interventionist. He used to have some hi-tech equipment, more as a kind of insurance than because it was integral to his winemaking, but now it has all been thrown out. He hasn't used cultivated yeasts since 1993, and no longer makes use of enzymes or bentonite for clarification or fining. The only manipulation of the wine that he employs is chaptalization and temperature control.

Löwenstein does bottle single vineyard wines from Kirchberg and Winninger Röttgen, and Winninger Uhlen is invariably his best wine. In addition there are terroir-based blends of dry wine: Schiefferterrassen (slate terraces) and Von Blauen Schieffer (from blue slate), and sometimes his top sweet wines, such as TBA, are similarly differentiated. All the wines are aged in steel tanks, and they have a pronounced leesy character in their youth. His aim is to communicate the special terroirs and flavours of the region. He admits that 1996 was a tricky vintage, with many bunches that failed to ripen properly; in contrast, 1997 and 1999 were so hot and dry that acidities were rather low. 1998 was very good here, and I was very impressed by the 2000s.

These are very complex wines, and their richness and concentration can be taken for granted. What is surprising is their range of flavours and nuances. The 2000 slate-soil blends were leesy but had additional hints of lemon-rind, banana and wax. The 2000 Kirchberg exudes a whiff of

Scotch and iodine, which is more attractive than it may sound. When a Schiefferterrassen wine stops fermenting a touch too early, leaving some residual sugar, Löwenstein calls the result Sommernachtstraum (summer night's dream), which in 2000 was a juicy yet tight wine with a surprisingly dry finish. As for the sweeter styles, he bottles up to three Auslesen from Uhlen, each reflecting a different soil type within the vineyard (such as fossil soils or red slate). They are all marked by a refreshing acidity, as well as considerable power.

The wines may, like their producer, be somewhat idiosyncratic, but they are without doubt some of the very best dry wines of the Mosel. Other estates may match their brilliance from time to time, but few can rival their consistency. They may not be to everyone's taste, but they are wines that every Riesling lover should make an effort to taste.

CARL AUGUST IMMICH-BATTERIEBERG

Im Alten Tal 2, 56850 Enkirch. Tel: +49 (0) 6541 83050. Fax: 830516.
www.batterieberg.de. 7 ha (17.3 acres). 3,000 cases.

The delightful house in old Enkirch dates back to 850, when it was built on the site of a Roman villa. It was partly destroyed during the war-torn Middle Ages, but some older halls survive. The Immich family owned the property from 1425 until 1989, when it was bought by Gert and Sabine Basten. Basten, a former wine merchant, restored the property and hired as his cellarmaster the enthusiastic Uwe Jostock. The Enkircher Batterieberg, so splendidly depicted on the wine labels, is in the sole possession of the estate, which also owns vineyards on neighbouring slopes: Zeppwingert, Ellergrub, and Steffensberg. Most of the wines are made in a dry style.

Jostock prunes short to ensure low yields, and the grapes are picked selectively by hand. There is some natural yeast fermentation after whole-cluster pressing. The wines are fermented in stainless steel, but also spend a period in cask subsequently. The most distinctive wine is called Renaissance, a late-picked dry Riesling, aged in casks after fermentation with natural yeasts; in 1999 this was particularly successful, combining fullness of body with a long mineral finish. The 1999 Batterieberg Spätlese Trocken was also very good, perhaps a touch broader, reflecting the fact that one third of the berries were botrytis-affected. The sweeter styles are also a touch broad and heavy, with the exception of the very intense, apricotty Batterieberg Auslese No 1, picked at 130 Oechsle.

KARP-SCHREIBER
Moselweinstr 186, 54472 Brauneberg. Tel: +49 (0) 6534 236. Fax: 790. 6 ha (14.8 acres). 3,300 cases.

This estate has had a troubled history. Christian Karp-Schreiber died in 1991, and a power struggle ensued between Alwin Karp and his mother. Karp won control of the estate in 1994. The property, which includes vineyards in Brauneberg and Mülheim, is run along organic lines and yields are modest at around 60 hl/ha (24.3 hl/acre). Two-thirds of the wines are dry or off-dry, and for the sweeter styles Karp favours wines with rather more alcohol and rather less residual sugar than is customary. My recent experience of these wines is limited, but in the mid-1990s Karp produced some very impressive BA and TBA.

HERIBERT KERPEN
Uferallee 6, 54470 Wehlen. Tel: +49 (0) 6531 6868. Fax: 3464. www.weingut-kerpen.de. 6 ha (14.8 acres). 3,500 cases.

The good-humoured Martin Kerpen, the latest of many generations to run this property, is fortunate enough to own 3 ha (7.4 acres) in Wehlener Sonnenuhr as well as vineyards in top sites in Graach and Bernkastel. Many parcels still have ungrafted vines. The winemaking is very traditional, with ageing in large casks that preserve the natural carbon dioxide in the wine. Kerpen was one of the Mittel Mosel's pioneers of dry wines. But his sweeter wines are excellent too and entirely typical of the region in general and Wehlen in particular. He likes to distinguish between various Auslesen by using a star system.

REICHSGRAF VON KESSELSTATT
Schlossgut Marienlay, 54317 Morscheid. Tel: +49 (0) 6500 91690. Fax: 916969. www.kesselstatt.com. 42 ha (104 acres). 22,000 cases.

In the centre of Trier stands a handsome late Baroque palace, the Palais Kesselstatt, where the wines of this noble estate were made from 1746. In 1978 the Graf, unwilling to divide the large estate among his heirs, sold the property to Günther Reh, a very successful wine wholesaler. Five years later Reh handed control of the estate to his daughter Annegret.

After a few years it became apparent that the estate was simply too large and unwieldy to be viable. In the early 1980s it consisted of 100 ha (24.7 acres), spread through the Mosel-Saar-Ruwer and including the *Alleinbesitz* of Josephshof in Graach. But many of the vineyards were either small or not especially distinguished, and Annegret Reh began leasing off vineyards of little interest. There were some little known sites that she knew were capable of producing excellent wine, but they were hard to sell and to promote. She retained, however, the long-term cellar-master, Bernward Keiper, who has been at Kesselstatt since 1972. Annegret Reh is now assisted in running the estate by her husband Gerhard Gartner, who in an earlier career achieved renown as Germany's first chef to win two Michelin stars.

The wines are vinified at Morscheid in the Ruwer, where cellars were renovated in the late 1980s. The wines are fermented using natural yeasts, there is no deacidification, and the use of *Süssreserve* ceased after 1994. All fermentation and ageing takes place in steel tanks. About half the wines are dry, and there is an excellent dry Gutsriesling under the Palais Kesselstatt label. Although released as a QbA, only very ripe and healthy grapes are used. There is also a Sekt labelled as Palais Kesselstatt to distinguish it from a more commercial sparkling wine; this Palais Kesselstatt is sometimes administered its dosage in the form of Eiswein, giving a full-bodied aromatic wine with unusual richness.

Even in its pared-down form, Kesselstatt still releases a large number of wines, so generalizations are hard to make. Personal favourites include the wines from Kaseler Nies'chen and Piesporter Goldtröpfchen, which I usually prefer to the rich, broader Josephshof. But, looking through tasting notes spanning almost two decades, all kinds of wines leap from the page: a robust 1994 Scharzhofberger Spätlese Trocken, delicious 1994 Spätlesen from Graacher Domprobst and Kaseler Nies'chen, a superb 1994 Goldtröpfchen Auslese Goldkapsel, the tight racy 1996 Josephs-höfer Kabinett, the rich, bold, mineral 1990 Josephshöfer Spätlese and the creamy concentrated 1990 Goldtröpfchen Spätlese, the irresistibly lush 1989 Scharzhofberger BA, and many others.

Inevitably, there are disappointments, wines such as many 1992s that failed to deliver their early promise and some slightly vegetal 1996s. Occasionally, the wines have expressive fruit but at the expense of finesse. But such variations and fluctuations are inevitable with such a large range of wines. What is evident, however, is Kesselstatt's determination not to rest on its laurels but to continue to improve the overall quality of its wines. Annegret Reh-Gartner is relentlessly self-critical; her achievement in making the Kesselstatt wines more coherent and more consistent shouldn't be underestimated.

REINHARD KNEBEL

August-Horch-Str 24, 56333 Winningen. Tel: +49 (0) 2606 2631. Fax: 2569. 6 ha (14.8 acres). 3,500 cases.

The Knebel estate was run by Reinhard's father and his two brothers until 1990, when Reinhard set up on his own. He has supplemented his own holdings with sites he has leased and which he cultivates in the same way as his own vineyards. Most of the vineyards are terraced and there are many parcels with vines up to fifty years old. Yields vary from 40 to 60 hl/ha (16.2–24.3 hl/acre) and most of the wines are dry, as is common in Winningen. Knebel is not keen on whole-cluster pressing, and clarifies the wines by sedimentation, not by filtration or centrifuge. The best wines tend to come from Röttgen and Uhlen.

The 2000s here are remarkably good. True, there are some rather earthy wines among the simpler bottlings, but the Uhlen Spätlese Trocken is sleek and elegant, and preferable to the same wine in 1999, which lacks zest. The Halbtrocken wines are very good, with an appealing sweet-and-sour quality and good length. The sweet wines are outstanding, especially the Uhlen Auslese. At the conclusion of my visit, Reinhard's wife Beate presented what looked like two medicine phials; they turned out to be miniatures containing Röttgen TBA from 1999 and 2000. With such wines produced in minute quantities (50 litres in 2000) it was sensible to "bottle" a few samples in miniatures for tasting purposes. Both wines are fabulous, and here the 1999 won out over the 2000. The 1999 TBA was picked at 270 Oechsle, had a syrupy texture reminiscent of Esszencia, and had quite extraordinary weight and richness, and exceptional length.

SCHLOSS LIESER

Am Markt 1, 54470 Lieser. Tel: +49 (0) 6531 6431. Fax: 1068. www.weingut-schloss-lieser.de. 7 ha (17.3 acres). 4,000 cases.

The Schloss Lieser estate and the rambling castle on the edge of this village just a few miles from Bernkastel were the property of the Freiherr von Schorlemer until the 1970s, when these properties were sold. After various changes in ownership, Thomas Haag, the son of Wilhelm Haag of Weingut Fritz Haag, leased the estate in 1992 and bought it five years later. The Schloss itself, however, was not part of the deal, and was sold to a new owner in 2001. Although the estate owns vines in Bernkastel and Graach, only wines from the Lieser vineyards are identified on the label. The best site is the Niederberg-Helden.

Thomas Haag is an insouciant character, radiating casual self-confidence. He could hardly have had a better professional upbringing under his father's tutelage, and ten years of independence as a wine-maker, and the acclaim given to his wines, must have confirmed his conviction of his abilities. The vinification is straightforward. The grapes are pressed, settled, and racked into either steel tanks or casks for a slow fermentation with natural yeasts. No *Süssreserve* is used, and no malolactic fermentation for the dry wines. Almost half the production is of dry Riesling.

My first encounter with Haag's wines in 1999 impressed me: they were youthful and tight, with a fetching raciness. Subsequent tastings have confirmed this impression. The sweeter styles have charm, filigree delicacy and a raciness that gives good length. Perhaps they lack a little flesh, but this seems to be a stylistic choice, because Haag isn't looking to produce wines with a lot of power. He distinguishes between different bottlings of his Auslesen with a star system: the 1999 two-star is a brilliant wine with exquisite peachy fruit. And the 2000 BA, very lean and intense, has the precision and balance that are among the hallmarks of this ever improving estate.

CARL LOEWEN

Matthiasstr 30, 54340 Leiwen. Tel: +49 (0) 6507 3094. Fax: 802332.
www.weingut-loewen.de. 6 ha (14.8 acres). 4,000 cases.

The earnest Karl-Josef Loewen clearly sees himself as something of a visionary, rescuing forgotten vineyards and creating new styles of Riesling. His crusading zeal is somewhat undermined by his marmalade cat Suzi, who steals the show by chasing freshly pulled corks around the tasting room.

Loewen began his career in the early 1980s by specializing in dry wines, but has since expanded his range. He acquired vines in Leiwener Laurentiuslay in 1982, and subsequently bought parcels in the little-known Thörnicher Ritsch and in Trittenheim and Dhron. He prides himself on an intimate knowledge of his vineyards and fears that by expanding further, a commercial temptation, he might lose some of the complete control he enjoys now. As well as vineyard-designated wines, Loewen makes a dry Riesling he calls Varidor, and a QbA called Christopher's Wine that comes from a steep parcel within Detzemer Maximin Klosterlay; this leaves him free to balance the wine as he sees fit, thus dispensing with designations such as Trocken and Halbtrocken. The 2001 Christopher's Wine tasted dry but had 15 grams of residual sugar.

Among his idiosyncrasies is the practice of leaving some bunches on the vine after harvesting for Auslese, so that those grapes can contribute to the other wines made from the site. And rather than pump the grapes into the crusher, he prefers to use a pitchfork. Entirely admirable is his decision to propagate vines for planting in Klosterlay from very old vines in Piesporter Goldtröpfchen, to ensure he obtained the small-berried selection he particularly sought. The vinification is straightforward if conservative.

The wines themselves are impressive. The 1999 Auslese and Auslese Trocken from Laurentiuslay are first-rate, with exemplary length of flavour, and the 1999 and 2000 Thörnicher Ritsch Spätlesen are clean and transparent in their fruit quality, the 1999 having a slight edge over the rather grapefruity 2000. 1998 was a great year for Eiswein, and Loewen's Leiwener Klostergarten, with its apple compote nose, doesn't disappoint.

DR LOOSEN

St Johannishof, 54470 Bernkastel. Tel: +49 (0) 6531 3426. Fax: 4248.
www.drlooosen.de. 12 ha (29.7 acres). 6,000 cases.

When Ernst Loosen comes bounding into a room, one is struck first by his energy and second by his intelligence. It was never his intention to become a winemaker, especially because he did not get on well with his father and had no wish to be under his thumb. Instead he pursued his university studies. Then in the mid-1980s his father fell seriously ill, and it became clear that either Ernst returned to Bernkastel to run the estate, or it would have to be sold. He came back and his first harvest was in

1987. He hired an old friend, Bernhard Schug, as cellarmaster, a position he holds to this day.

Having made the decision to abandon his studies and become a wine producer, he threw himself into the calling with typical energy and determination. His intelligence came into play when he decided to throw everything about the estate into question.

"The problem at the estate was that most of the staff had been there for twenty-five years, and were stuck in their ways. They detested the idea of selections in the vineyard because it meant more work. But I knew from the start that I had to improve quality. I had always loved wines, collected them, drunk them with friends. I knew that winemaking was essentially simple. What was crucial was to improve the quality of the grapes.

"Right in the middle of the 1987 harvest my entire staff walked out. So Bernie Schug and I had no choice but to take over. I had two options: I could either apologise to my staff, in which they case they might return but I would never be able to control them. Or I could call their bluff and let them go. If I fired them I would have to pay a lot of compensation which we couldn't afford. But they had walked out, so I didn't have to pay them anything. Bernie and I decided to make a fresh start. We talked everything over and in a sense learned our winemaking as we went along. We really worked closely together and consulted on every detail, every barrel. By 1992 we really felt we knew what we were doing. Our palate developed together and we still work together."

Loosen knew his vineyards were excellent, representing the finest the Mittel Mosel had to offer: 2.5 ha (6.2 acres) in Bernkastel, almost 1 ha (2.5 acres) in Graacher Himmelreich, 2.2 ha (5.4 acres) in Wehlener Sonnenuhr, 1 ha (2.5 acres) in Ürziger Würzgarten, and smaller parcels in Erden. Right from the start he began reducing yields severely and introducing selective harvesting. Loosen was an early proponent of whole-cluster pressing, and only natural yeasts were used. There is no deacidification, even in a vintage such as 1996 when he had acidities of 13 grams per litre in Erdener Prälat, trusting that bottle age would reveal the wine's balance and harmony. He prefers a slow fermentation in casks for the very gradual oxidation it gives to the wine. With a prolonged fermentation there is a risk of leesy aromas when the wine is young, but it tends to dissipate with bottle-age.

The wines are brilliant, and for some years have been copybook examples of how the wines from individual vineyards should taste. At Dr Loosen the Wehlener Sonnenuhr is invariably racy and zesty and delicate, as it should be, whereas the Ürziger Würzgarten is more spicy, and the Erdener Treppchen is tight and complex. The wines, except for the superb Auslesen, show well in their youth and develop ever more complexity with age. Their *terroir* comes through strongly because the yields are low, allowing the grapes to be infused with whatever cocktail of minerals and fruit flavours are most typical of the site. The TBAs, in vintages such as 1997 and 1999, are among the finest the region can offer.

Ernst Loosen is among the most internationally minded of the Mosel growers. He ventured into the Pfalz to lease the J.L. Wolf estate (*q.v.*), so that he could try his hand at making dry Rieslings. And he has launched a joint venture with Chateau Ste Michelle in Washington state to produce Rieslings in the Columbia Valley. Equally important, he has refused to be cowed by the wretched international image of German Rieslings. He travels constantly to preach the good word and to show his wines, even though he concedes that if there is to be a revival of Riesling, it is more likely to come from Australia or Austria than from Germany. He has also produced Gutsriesling of exemplary quality and in decent quantities, allowing larger retailers in Great Britain and the USA to stock his wines, which have enjoyed a well-deserved success.

Vintages such as 1997, 1998 (especially for sweet wines), and 1999 have been remarkable here, and the 2000 is a great success given the difficulties of the year. Like the 1996s, they are wines that will repay ageing.

LUBENTIUSHOF

Kehrstr 16, 56332 Niederfell. Tel: +49 (0) 2607 8135. Fax: 8425.
www.lubentiushof.de. 5 ha (12.4 acres). 1,800 cases.

The modest Andreas Barth is a rarity among Mosel wine producers: a self-taught grower. His first vintage was 1994, and in moments of crisis he was able to call on his friend Fritz Hasselbach of Weingut Gunderloch in Rheinhessen for advice. Most of his vineyards are in Gondorf, and his top site is Gondorfer Gäns. Yields are kept very low, and eighty per cent of the production is of dry wines. He vinifies in steel tanks, using only natural yeasts. He bottles later than most, sometimes in August. At present only

Gondorfer Gäns and Niederfeller Kahllay appear on the label, and his blended wines are sold under the "Burg von der Layen" label, which is illustrated with a painting by Turner. The dry wines from Gondorfer Gäns are the most successful, although the 2000 is much inferior to 1998 and 1999. The sweeter styles are rather lacklustre, although the 1999 Gondorfer Schlossberg BA is concentrated and creamy. Overall the wines are good but lack flair and complexity. No doubt more experience will bring its rewards in due course, and there is no doubting Barth's commitment to quality.

MILZ (LAURENTIUSHOF)
Moselstr 7, 54349 Trittenheim. Tel: +49 (0) 6507 2300. Fax: 5650. 7 ha (17.3 acres). 5,500 cases.

There was a time when this estate was probably the best in Trittenheim. It is certainly endowed with some excellent sites: not only Apotheke, but monopoly sites in the best corners of Apotheke and Altärchen: Felsenkopf and Leiterchen, as well as Neumagener Nusswingert. Leiterchen is probably Milz's best site, though very small. The wines are mostly vinified in steel tanks, though higher qualities are aged in wood. Having recently tasted a large range from 1998 and 2000, I was puzzled by their lack of excitement. Some showed grapefruity characters, others more mineral tones, while many lacked length, verve and concentration; the dry wines from 2000 are excessively austere. Even the 2000 Apotheke Eiswein lacked concentration and vigour. In the past I have encountered impressive wines from this estate. Today it seems to have been superseded by some of its neighbours.

MARKUS MOLITOR
Klosterberg, 54492 Zeltingen. Tel: +49 (0) 6532 3939. Fax: 4225. www.wein-markus-molitor.de. 35 ha (86.5 acres). 20,000 cases.

This is the largest estate on the Mittel Mosel, embracing vineyards from Ürzig and Zeltingen down to Brauneberg, though when Markus Molitor took over the family property in 1984, it was only half its present size. Molitor's principal holdings are in Zeltinger Sonnenuhr, 4.5 ha (11 acres) and Wehlener Klosterberg, 7 ha (17.3 acres). Half the production is of dry wines, but Molitor also produces splendid Auslesen from the Sonnenuhr, which are ranked by a star system. No cultivated yeasts are used, and most wines are aged on the fine lees in casks and bottled fairly late. Molitor picks as late as possible, which accounts for the body of his dry wines and the intensity of his sweet ones. In 1998, for example, he was still picking Spätlesen in the third week of November. As well as Riesling, a little Pinot Noir (from Graach and Trarbach) and Pinot Blanc are also produced. More controversially, there is also an "Alte Reben" dry Riesling aged in barriques.

I have a marginal preference for the Halbtrocken wines to those that are labelled Trocken, and a 1999 Zeltinger Sonnenuhr Auslese* Feinherb with 20 grams of residual sugar had just the right touch of sweetness and sufficient delicate acidity to balance the wine. 1999 was also a fine year for Auslesen from the Wehlener Klosterberg, and in 1998, a great Eiswein year, Molitor produced an intense, racy example from Wehlener Abtei, with flavours of candied pineapple. Molitor maintains a selection of older BAs and TBAs on his wine list. Indeed, he has developed a fine sideline in nobly sweet wines, and even in a tricky year such as 2000 managed to produce a wide range of Auslesen.

MÖNCHHOF

Mönchhof, 54539 Ürzig. Tel: +49 (0) 6532 93164. Fax: 93166.
www.moenchhof.de. 10 ha (24.7 acres). 5,000 cases.

This lovely old house facing the river (though its lavish Renaissance-style cladding dates from 1898) has been owned by the Eymael family since 1803. Robert Eymael is now in sole control of the property, having bought out his brother in 1994. The cellars date from 1509, and wooden props between the casks and the roof help keep the barrels in place when, as occasionally happens, the river floods the cellars. The vineyards are in excellent steep sites in Ürzig, Erden, Zeltingen, Wehlen, and Kinheim. They were expanded in 2001 when he leased the vineyards of J.J. Christoffel (*q.v.*). Very little dry wine is produced, the wines (other than dry ones) are fermented with natural yeasts only, and the sweet styles are made without recourse to *Süssreserve*. The wines were patchy in the 1980s and early 1990s, though I recall some very elegant 1990 Auslesen, but in recent vintages the quality has become much more consistent, and reasonable prices make this an excellent source of wines from some of the best Mittel Mosel vineyards.

MOSELLAND

Bornwiese 6, 54470 Bernkastel. Tel: +49 (0) 6531 570. Fax: 57127.
www.moselland.de. 2,238 ha (5,530 acres). Case figure not available.

This vast cooperative unites the production of 3200 members, vinifying about one quarter of the entire production of the region. About half the wines are exported. This is not a source for high-quality wines, though it distributes some better bottlings from the Cardinal Cusanus Stift. In 2001 they signed on to the Classic and Selection initiatives of the German Wine Institute, producing versions from both Riesling and Rivaner. At the same time they launched a premium range called Divinum. The 2001 Trocken was rich and firm and had good length. The lesser wines are simple at best, dull at worst. Other brands include the off-dry Riesling Signature, and Gentle Hills Riesling Classic from the Nahe. The Riesling Selection comes from Zeltinger Himmelreich.

MARTIN MÜLLEN

Alte Marktstr 2, 56841 Traben-Trarbach. Tel: +49 (0) 6541 9470. Fax: 813537.
www.weingutmuellen.com. 3 ha (7.4 acres). 1,800 cases.

Müllen, who took over the family property in 1992 as a young man, is an individualist, highly committed to quality. Most of the vineyards are in Kröv and in Trarbacher Hühnerberg, a vineyard being resuscitated by him. His grandfather was a diabetic, so the estate has been producing dry wines since the 1970s, and these represent the majority of his production. Whether for dry or sweeter styles, he is convinced that full physiological ripeness is essential, so he harvests late, and assesses the ripeness of his grapes by tasting as well as by Oechsle levels. He uses natural yeasts for his Rieslings and almost all the wines are aged in casks before being bottled in the early summer. Müllen is in no rush to market the wines, and will sometimes leave a bottling in his cellars for years before offering it for sale. This means he can offer a wide range of vintages, and he sees it as a bonus that the wines on his list can be very varied.

These are not wines for the faint-hearted, and some of them strike me as excessively austere, for all the emphasis on full ripeness. The range of flavours is wide – from apricot to peach to gooseberry – and the wines are seasoned with nuances of spice and pepper, as well as quite marked acidity. They have power and pungency, but are as serious and uncompromising as their maker.

PAULINSHOF

Paulinsstr 14, 54518 Kesten. Tel: +49 (0) 6535 544. Fax: 1267.
www.paulinshof.de. 8 ha (19.8 acres). 6,000 cases.

A monastic property until the Napoleonic era, it was secularized in 1803 and came into the hands of the Jüngling family in 1969. Klaus Jüngling brought the estate to its present high quality level, and he is gradually handing over the reins to his son Oliver, who trained at Geisenheim and made his first vintage here in 2000. The vineyards are located in Kesten and also in neighbouring Brauneberg, where Paulinshof owns an *Alleinbesitz*, Brauneberger Kammer.

Paulinshof is best known for its dry wines. Excessive acidity that can be acceptable in a wine with high residual sugar would mar a dry wine, so the Jünglings harvest very late when the acidities are dropping. Yields are around 50 hl/ha (20.2 hl/acre) in the top sites. There is no malolactic fermentation. From year to year they manage to make delicious dry peachy Rieslings with no trace of harshness. I have encountered outstanding wines such as the 2000 Brauneberger Juffer-Sonnenuhr Spätlese Trocken, the 1999 Kestener Paulins-Hofberger Auslese Trocken, and a 1998 Brauneberger Kammer Spätlese Halbtrocken; even in a high-acidity vintage such as 1996, Paulinshof made a superb Kammer Auslese Halbtrocken. The sweeter wines are very good too – such as the opulent and exotic 1999 Paulins-Hofberger Auslese and the sumptuous and smoky 1999 Juffer-Sonnenuhr BA – but overall it's the dry wines that command admiration.

DR PAULY-BERGWEILER (AND PETER NICOLAY)

Gestade 15, 54470 Bernkastel. Tel: +49 (0) 6531 3002. Fax: 7201. www.pauly-bergweiler.com. 12.5 ha (31 acres). 9,000 cases.

Dr Peter Pauly, having studied at Geisenheim, first made wines at the family estate in 1959, because his parents, whose wealth derived from outside the region, were not that interested in running it. Nonetheless, the Paulys are deeply embedded in the Mosel, being related to the Prüms of Wehlen. Moreover, his wife Helga is the co-owner of the Peter Nicolay estate, which was based in Ürzig. Pauly in effect merged the two estates and in the mid-1980s built a modern winery just outside Bernkastel. The Peter Nicolay label is now essentially a brand for the wines from Ürzig and Erden; the name is easy to pronounce, which helps on the export market. The Pauly-Bergweiler estate is mostly in Bernkastel, where it retains a small portion of the Badstube vineyard under the name Alte Badstube am Doktorberg, which is almost a monopoly. The Nicolay estate has a monopoly site in Ürzig, the small Goldwingert, which, together with Erdener Prälat, is the source of its best wines.

Quite a few Mittel Mosel growers produce a little red wine, but Dr Pauly seems particularly pleased with his, which comes from 0.5 ha (1.2 acres) of Pinot Noir in a sector of Graacher Domprobst where there is no slate. The first vintage was 1989. My experience of the wine is limited, but the 1995 was fragrant though not exactly fruity. Where the estate excels is with some of its sweet wines, such as the sumptuous TBAs from Ürziger Würzgarten and the Eiswein from Bernkasteler Lay.

JOH JOS PRÜM

Uferallee 19, 54470 Wehlen. Tel: +49 (0) 6531 3091. Fax: 6071. 14.5 ha (35.8 acres). 10,000 cases.

No estate better represents the culture and conservatism (and quality) of the Mittel Mosel than J.J. Prüm. Along the quayside at Wehlen stands a group of large imposing mansions, several of them owned by Prüms. Sober in their décor and furnishings, they speak of solid bourgeois comforts derived from generations of winemaking expertise. The owners here are Dr Manfred Prüm and his mostly invisible brother Wolfgang, who looks after the vineyards in Wehlen and Graach.

A visit to Uferallee 19 is a ceremony, because bottles are brought up from the cellars for tasting by the beaming Dr Prüm. There is no tasting room, and visitors are ushered into the drawing room, where they sip the wines under the watchful gaze of portraits of long-deceased Prüms. He gives minimal information about the wine being poured into the glass, wanting his visitors to focus on the wine without preconceptions. Spitting is discouraged. Some years ago I entered the drawing room to find a British wine buyer perched on the sofa, an array of bottles and glasses before her. She gave me an imploring look. From past experience it was easy to interpret. In the course of a prolonged tasting chez Prüm, and there is no such thing as a brief tasting, it is quite easy to consume, in small sips, a total of about one bottle of wine. At the end of a day spent visiting various estates, that can take its toll. My arrival gave the wine

buyer an excuse to flee. Which meant she probably missed out on a con-
cluding bottle of 1964 or 1959 Auslese.

I have never seen the cellars at J.J. Prüm. Has anyone? Manfred Prüm
effects his magic away from the public gaze. In fact, there are no secrets.
Just vines in the finest vineyards, selective harvesting, and slow cold
fermentations. When young, the wines are marked both by their natural
carbon dioxide, which gives them a distinct *pétillance*, and by a character
derived from prolonged lees contact in cask. For this reason, Manfred
Prüm is reluctant to show very young vintages. Any commercial drawback this may have is balanced by the confidence everyone has, whatever
the vintage, that this estate will have drawn the most from it. The wines,
whether a modest Kabinett or an opulent Beerenauslese, are the epitome
of filigree elegance: light in body but intense in flavour, exquisitely
balanced and precisely tuned, and capable of the most extra-ordinary
longevity. With the rise of so many excellent winemakers in the region,
one might have supposed that J.J. Prüm, with its profound conservatism,
might have been overtaken and left behind. Not a bit of it. The estate
remains where it has been for decades: at the summit.

S.A. PRÜM
Uferallee 25–26, 54470 Wehlen. Tel: +49 (0) 6531 3110. Fax: 8555.
www.sapruem.com. 16.5 ha (40.8 acres). 10,000 cases.

After the Prüm estate was divided up among seven children in 1911, this
portion was named after Sebastian Alois Prüm, who died in 1959. The
forward-looking Raimund Prüm has been in charge here since 1971. All
the vineyards are on steep sites in Wehlen, Graach, Bernkastel, and
Zeltingen. Prüm favours whole-cluster pressing and long ageing in casks.
Whereas J.J. Prüm produces virtually no dry wines, S.A. Prüm produces
seventy per cent Trocken and Halbtrocken wines. As well as Riesling, he
makes a sizeable amount of Weissburgunder.

Raimund Prüm has been quite innovative, given his family heritage.
He introduced a Gutsriesling in 1985 and has packaged some of his wines
with breezy modern labels. Given the excellence of the vintage, I found
the 1999s here, whether dry or sweet, rather disappointing: charming
and vigorous in their attack on the palate, but then showing a lack of concentration and complexity.

MAX FERD. RICHTER

Hauptstr 85, 54486 Mülheim. Tel: +49 (0) 6534 933003. Fax: 1211. www.maxferdrichter.com. 15 ha (37 acres). 10,000 cases.

This is the most important estate in Mülheim and has been run for many years by Dr Dirk Richter. As well as producing wines from the estate's vineyards in Mülheim, Brauneberg, Wehlen, Veldenz, and Graach, Richter also buys in grapes from growers with whom he has long-term contracts to supply his négociant business. These wines from purchased fruit are bottled under a different label, although it still bears the Max Ferd. Richter name. Dirk Richter devotes a good deal of time and energy to the export market, undeterred by the unfavourable image of German wines.

The winemaking is traditional. The must is often chilled to encourage a long slow fermentation that can last up to three months, and always takes place in Fuder casks. No *Süssreserve* is used. Nor is there any difference in winemaking techniques between the domaine and the négociant wines.

The estate made an Eiswein by chance in 1961, and since 1985 has produced one almost every year from the Mülheimer Helenenkloster, a Richter *Alleinbesitz*. In 2001 he was able to harvest an Eiswein here with 223 Oechsle. As for the more standard range of wines, those from Brauneberger Juffer-Sonnenuhr are often among the best, such as the fresh elegant 2000 Spätlese, the 1998 Auslese Cask 19, with its delicate flavours of apricots and mandarins, and the sumptuous, mouth-filling 2000 TBA. Overall quality is very good, with a handful of outstanding wines in almost every vintage.

JOSEF ROSCH

Mühlenstr 8, 54340 Leiwen. Tel: +49 (0) 6507 4230. Fax: 8287. 5.5 ha (13.6 acres). 4,000 cases.

The articulate Werner Rosch started bottling the wines from his family estate in 1985, and has gradually acquired more vines in the best parcels of Leiwen, Trittenheim and Dhron. Most of his wines are dry, in response to strong domestic demand. His vines in Leiwener Klostergarten, his largest holding, are used almost entirely for Trocken and Halbtrocken wines. But he also produces a range of fine sweet wines, notably Auslesen. Above all else, Rosch is looking for what he regards as Mosel typicity, which is to say, wines with elegance rather than power or excessive alcohol.

In the vineyard he is rigorous, pruning to a single cane, and green harvesting is common. Two-thirds of the wine is aged in stainless steel, the rest in casks. Rosch never deacidifies or encourages malolactic fermentation. The wines stay on the fine lees until around May. Some of the dry wines can be austere, even the low-yield blend from top sites, the 2000 Spätlese*** Trocken "JR." In 2000 there were good Auslesen from Trittenheimer Apotheke and Leiwener Klostergarten, especially the former in its three-star incarnation, which is very concentrated and exotic. Not all the wines, though, are of this quality, and some of them lack complexity. Nonetheless they all show admirable precision and purity and are very well made.

SANKT URBANS-HOF

Urbanusstr 16, 54340 Leiwen. Tel: +49 (0) 6507 93770. Fax: 937730.
www.weingut-st-urbans-hof.de. 35 ha (86.5 acres). 20,000 cases.

This winery was founded by the grandfather of the present owner, Nik Weis, who took over the running of the estate in 1998, assisted by cellarmaster Rudi Hoffmann. The family also owns one of Germany's most important nurseries. In 1989 the estate, which already owned vineyards in Leiwen, acquired vineyards in Wiltingen and Ockfen in the Saar, and a parcel in Piesporter Goldtröpfchen. The wines are fermented in stainless steel and aged in casks, and no *Süssreserve* is used. The dry and Halbtrocken wines from Leiwener Laurentiuslay and Wiltinger Schlangengraben are sleek and mineral, but it's the sweeter styles that grab one's attention. The 2000 Goldtröpfchen Kabinett is delicious and elegant. The wines from Ockfener Bockstein can be exquisite, such as the 2000 Spätlese with its floral aromas, its grapefruity flavours and transparent structure and minerality. The 1997 Bockstein Auslese is spicy and mouth-watering, a triumph. The same is true of the 1998 Bockstein Eiswein, which also has complex tones of iodine and dried apricots, and the 2000 Bockstein BA, showing flavours of passionfruit as well as dried apricots. There are few estates in the Mosel so adept at capturing the mouth-watering succulence and purity of the Riesling grape.

WILLI SCHAEFER

Hauptstr 130, 54470 Graach. Tel: +49 (0) 6531 8041. Fax: 1414. 2.7 ha (6.7 acres). 2000 cases.

The lean, bearded Willi Schaefer exudes modesty, but in the thirty years that he has been running this property, he has made it into one of the top estates of the Mittel Mosel. His best parcels are in Graacher Domprobst, and there are others in Graacher Himmelreich and Wehlener Sonnenuhr. Schaefer selects his grapes very carefully, and likes a long slow fermentation to retain acidity and aroma in his wines, an aim aided by his very damp cellars. Most of the wines are aged in cask, and only a minority are made in a Trocken or Halbtrocken style. He likes purity and extract, and doesn't want too much botrytis in his regular wines. Somehow, he always manages to make the most of every vintage that presents itself, endowing them with that slatey typicity of the Mittel Mosel. These are exceptionally concentrated wines. If only they were available in larger quantities!

HEINZ SCHMITT

Stephanusstr 4, 54340 Leiwen. Tel: +49 (0) 6507 4276. Fax: 8161. www.weingut-heinz-schmitt.de. 23 ha (56.8 acres). 10,000 cases.

The self-confident, good-humoured Heinz Schmitt is a self-made man. Beginning with just 3 ha (7.4 acres) in 1983, he has expanded his estate by making a series of astute purchases in little known and in his view under-estimated vineyards. Most of them are steep, and lie along a 30-kilometre (18.6-mile) stretch from Longuich to Neumagen. These include Schweicher Annaberg, Mehringer Zellerberg and Blattenberg, Köwericher Laurentiuslay, and Neumagener Rosengärtchen – none of which are household names.

Nonetheless this is quite a commercial operation. Schmitt produces a lot of wines, most of them Trocken or Halbtrocken, some of them in large quantities for airlines and other major customers. He clarifies the must with bentonite and a vacuum filter; since the late 1990s has avoided cultivated yeasts. Most wines are aged in steel tanks. Quality is variable, almost as though a lot of wines are processed into the system in the hopes that a fair number will turn out well. The simpler wines, such as the Weissburgunder and the dry Kabinetts, are disappointing. Of the dry wines I tasted the most impressive was the Annaberg Spätlese Trocken "L"

Fass 5 (need the labels be quite this complicated?). I enjoyed the body and rich extract of a wine from Longuich, the Maximiner Herrenberg Auslese Halbtrocken. The wines from Köwerich all struck me as earthy, however, and it was hard to get excited by the sweeter Rieslings from Annaberg.

Schmitt, and his assistant Andreas Bender, are clearly gifted and resourceful, but at present the range lacks focus and definition. Schmitt is certainly to be applauded for working hard to revive once famous sites that lost their lustre because few, if any, growers were prepared to go to the trouble he has shown.

SELBACH-OSTER

Uferallee 23, 54492 Zeltingen. Tel: +49 (0) 6532 2081. Fax: 4014. 11 ha (27.2 acres). 9,000 cases.

The Selbach family have owned vineyards in Zeltingen since 1661. Their best site is Zeltinger Sonnenuhr, and they also have vines in Schlossberg and Himmelreich, as well as in Bernkastel Schlossberg. Hans Selbach's son Johannes is also a dynamic *négociant* with an international wine business under the name J. and H. Selbach. Johannes is proud of the long-lived Zeltingen wines, many of which are made from ungrafted vines, and attributes their relative lack of renown to the absence in the past of major estates in the village. Today the situation has changed, with Markus Molitor as well as Selbach-Oster based here.

Selbach produces mostly Trocken and Halbtrocken wines. Vinification remains traditional, and viticultural practices are scrupulous: green harvesting and up to three passages through the vineyards during the harvest. Cultivated yeasts are only used for some of the dry wines; simpler qualities are aged in steel tanks, but other wines could be aged in a combination of steel, fibreglass, and wood. Filtration is kept to a minimum, and only used before bottling.

The range of wines is considerable, especially because Selbach likes, vintage permitting, to bottle a number of different Auslesen, using a star system to indicate qualities. In general, the style of the wines is fresh, elegant, and racy. When tasted young there is a distinct similarity between them, because they are all tight and well structured. Selbach is emphatic in his avoidance of flamboyant and exotic flavours, which, he says, can easily be obtained by using commercial yeasts. Some of the dry wines are a touch austere for my taste, but the Spätlesen and Auslesen in particular are exemplary.

STUDERT-PRÜM

Hauptstr 150, 54470 Wehlen. Tel: +49 (0) 6531 2487. Fax: 3920. www.weingut-studert-pruem.de. 5 ha (12.4 acres). 3,500 cases.

The Studert family were growing vines in the Mosel in 1581 and are now in their twelfth generation. After the estate was joined with that of Peter Prüm, it adopted its present name. Stephan Studert is now enjoying a hale retirement, and the estate is run by his sons Gerhard and Stephan. Their main holdings are in Wehlener Sonnenuhr, supplemented by vines in Bernkasteler Graben and Graacher Himmelreich. Eighty per cent of the vines are ungrafted, and all their parcels are on steep sites.

After whole-cluster pressing, the must is vinified in casks or steel tanks. All wines of Spätlese quality upward are aged in wood, because the Studerts are convinced that wood gives the wines more elegance and roundness. There is minimal use of *Süssreserve*. They believe their wines, of which forty per cent are dry, benefit from at least two years of bottle-age.

In the past the Studert wines could be disappointing, but there are some excellent bottles among the wines of the late 1990s. The dry wines are too tart and green for my taste, at least in 2000, and the Graach wines are relatively earthy. But the Wehlener Sonnenuhr wines are delicious, with a delicate elegant 2000 Kabinett, delicate 1998 Auslesen, and a lush, honeyed 1999 Beerenauslese.

WWE DR H THANISCH – ERBEN MÜLLER-BURGGRAEF

Saarallee 24, 54470 Bernkastel-Kues. Tel: +49 (0) 6531 7570. Fax: 7910. 9.5 ha (23.5 acres). 6,000 cases.

The history of the Thanisch estate is complex. Dr Hugo Thanisch was a famous politician and intellectual, who owned an important property in the Mittel Mosel. He died young, aged forty-two, in 1895, and the property was run his widow (*Witwe* – hence the prefix to the Thanisch estates) Katharine for many years. It was this estate that produced the legendary 1921 Bernkasteler Doktor TBA, the first wine in this style in the Mosel. She had a son and a daughter; the daughter had a son who died young, and a daughter, Margrit Müller-Burggraef, who is the present owner of this estate. There were disagreements between this branch of the family and another descendant, Sofia Thanisch-Spier. In the 1980s it was decided to divide the estates between the two families. Hence the existence of two estates with almost indistinguishable names. This estate is now run by Frau Müller-Burggraef's niece Barbara Rundquist-Müller, and managed on a daily basis by Hans Leiendecker. The wines are vinified and aged in 350 year old cellars directly beneath the famous Doktor vineyard, where both Thanisch properties have vines. The other Müller-Burggraef holdings are in various Bernkastel vineyards, in Wehlener Sonnenuhr, Graacher Himmelreich, and in Brauneberg. They also produce a lightly oaked Dornfelder from vines in Brauneberg, and a Sekt from Lieserer Niederberg-Helden.

After mostly whole-cluster pressing, the must is clarified by sedimentation, and fermented in both stainless steel and casks. Some of the dry wines go through partial malolactic fermentation. It seems rather a waste of expensive grapes to produce a Kabinett Trocken from the Doktor, and indeed the wine is somewhat earthy. Like the regular Kabinett, it's quite a full-bodied wine. The 1999 and 2000 Juffer-Sonnenuhr Spätlesen lack some acidity and so taste a touch too sweet. The 2000 Doktor Spätlese is more mineral, with a sweet and sour tone, and less broad than the 1999 Juffer-Sonnenuhr Auslese. The best wine I tasted is the 1999 Doktor BA, with its nose of peaches and honey; it's an unusually flamboyant wine, with crème brûlée flavours. Indeed the overall style of this estate is quite flamboyant: the wines are big and rich, a far cry from the more filigree raciness of many of the Wehlen estates. It's not my preferred style, but the wines do have a distinctive personality and family resemblance.

WWE DR H. THANISCH – ERBEN THANISCH
Saarallee 31, 54470 Bernkastel-Kues. Tel: +49 (0) 6531 2282. Fax: 2226. 6 ha (14.8 acres). 4,000 cases.

The second of the two Thanisch estates can be differentiated from its cousin either by taking a magnifying glass to the small print on the label, or by looking out for the VDP logo. The estate is run by the charming Sofia Spier (née Thanisch) and her husband Ulrich, and the cellarmaster is Olaf Kaufmann. The principal vineyards are in Bernkastel: Graben, Lay, Schlossberg (bottled as Badstube), and, of course, 1 ha (2.5 acres) of

Doktor, where most of the vines are ungrafted. There are also holdings in Brauneberg and Graach. Hardly any of the wines are dry. They are vinified in both stainless steel and casks.

There were some superb wines from the Doktor in vintages such as 1990, and quality has been maintained through the decade, culminating in an excellent range in 1999 and 2000. Some of the 1996s show a slight vegetal tone typical of the vintage. The 1997 Lay Spätlese is delicious, ripe yet mineral, and beginning to show signs of evolution. In 1999 even the Gutsriesling is highly enjoyable, with good length for a basic wine. The Badstube Kabinett is lean and persistent, but is outgunned by the 2000 Doktor Spätlese, which is both powerful and flowery, with a surprisingly dry mineral finish. The Doktor Auslesen from 1999 and 2000 are lush but tangy, and the 1999 Long Gold Capsule bottling has intense and raw flavours that clearly derive from the inclusion of lightly frozen grapes.

The international celebrity of the Doktor vineyard – and most of these wines are exported – means that its wines are expensive. Is the premium worth it? Fine though these wines are, I am not completely convinced.

GEHEIMRAT J. WEGELER
Martertal 2, 54470 Bernkastel-Kues. Tel: +49 (0) 6531 2493. Fax: 8723. www.wegeler.com. 17 ha (42 acres). 10,000 cases.

Quality at this large estate has been gradually improving over the years. It produces a substantial proportion of dry wines for the domestic market, while the sweeter styles, especially the high-priced bottlings from Bernkasteler Doktor, are exported. The 1999 QbA Trocken from the Doktor had a sweet and sour tone and quite good length, but I preferred the 1999 Spätlese, with its spicy mint-leaf nose, and greater persistence on the palate. The 1999 Auslese from Wehlener Sonnenuhr was rather soft and lacked verve. In 2001 Oliver Haag, brother of Thomas Haag of Schloss Lieser, became involved with the winemaking, and it will be interesting to see whether the style will change.

DR F. WEINS-PRÜM
Uferallee 20, 54470 Wehlen. Tel: +49 (0) 6531 2270. Fax: 3181. 4 ha (9.9 acres). 3,000 cases.

I have never managed to work out how Bert Selbach, the rather shy owner and winemaker here, is related to the Prüm family, but there must be a connection. The estate is based in another substantial mansion on the Wehlen quayside, with its furnishings seemingly unaltered since 1952. The vineyards are in Graach, Wehlen, Erden, and Ürzig. An additional 1 ha (2.5 acres) in the Ruwer is used only for Gutsriesling. A majority of the wines is aged in traditional casks, but stainless steel tanks are used for simpler wines. Very few dry wines are produced. This is a highly dependable source for classic Mittel Mosel wines with bracing acidity balanced by a tangy sweetness, and an undertone of *pétillance* to keep the wines fresh and youthful.

In my view the Weins-Prüm wines have long been undervalued. Having tasted them regularly over some fifteen years, they seem to me impeccable examples of what one might call the Prüm style. They are racy and mineral and long-lived. Most recently, tasting through a broad range of 1999s and 2000s I didn't encounter a single disappointing wine. In their youth their stylistic similarity tends to obscure vineyard differences. The 2000 Erdener Prälat Spätlese is marginally more opulent than the Wehlener Sonnenuhr Spätlese from the same year, but I would find it very difficult to identify the vineyard in a blind tasting. These are wines that demand bottle age, because in their youth they are tight and closed, though always packed with delicious Riesling fruit.

10

Saar and Ruwer

Both the Saar and Ruwer Rivers flow into the Mosel on either side of Trier, the Ruwer just east of the city, and Saar at Konz west of the city. The Ruwer valley is tiny, whereas the Saar valley is more dispersed and less sheltered, stretching from Konz down to Serrig. Although the Romans planted vines here, it requires some courage to plant vines in these valleys, where the warming influence of the Mosel river is negligible, and where there is a higher risk of frost. The nights are cooler here than in the Mosel, which gives even greater finesse and higher acidity to the wines — as long as the grapes ripen. It is usually necessary to wait until late October before beginning the harvest. This means the growing season is very long, but it also increases the risk of inclement weather imperilling the harvest. There's usually a higher proportion of QbA here than in the Mosel itself. Wolfgang Richter of the Bischöfliche Weingüter in Trier says it is the extremes of climate and the variations in vintage, which are more pronounced than in the Mosel, that give Saar wines their fascination.

In good years, the wines can have an unrivalled intensity and minerality, and as long ago as the 1920s the top wines fetched higher prices than those from the Mosel, a situation that really hasn't altered much, when one considers the astounding prices attained by rare bottlings from estates such as Scharzhof and Maximin Grünhaus. The English wine connoisseur George Saintsbury, who had little good to say about German wines, not even Bernkasteler Doktor, was impressed by Scharzhofberger, noting an 1893 that he enjoyed in the 1920s.

I have seen differing estimates of the vineyard area in the Saar, ranging from 600 to 950 ha (1,483–2,347 acres). What is clear is that it is diminishing, just as it is in the Mosel. This is not necessarily regrettable, because there are quite a few mediocre sites in the Saar that will never produce great wines. In the 1950s and 1960s much of the crop was used for sparkling wines: Sekt production was an important industry here. Today that is no longer the case, and the still wines from the best vineyards are greatly valued.

As in the Mosel valley, there is a risk that some very good sites, though not those with the most famous names, will be abandoned forever. The problem is the shortage of labour. Luxembourg with its banks and corporate headquarters is not very far away, and offers greater temptation than years of toil on very steep slopes. Heinz Wagner of Saarburg tells me that when a Polish worker knocks on his door seeking work, the first question he poses, using sign language, is whether the vineyards are steep. If the answer is yes, the Polish worker will shrug, smile, and make his way elsewhere.

The Ruwer has slightly different soil to the Mosel, because many of its vineyards have grey or red rather than blue slate. Like the Saar, the area under vine is shrinking. Carl von Schubert of Maximin Grünhaus estimates it at no more than 200 ha (500 acres); Christoph Tyrell is more optimistic, believing that 280 remain. But both agree that the area is dwindling, and in the summer of 2001 I watched a bulldozer grubbing up a steep vineyard near Eitelsbach. Dr von Schubert told me that in 2000, when he lost most of his crop to hail, his costs of production were 10 DM/litre. At the same time he could have bought bulk wine for only 2 DM/litre, and at those prices it makes little economic sense for smallholders to hang on to their vineyards. Heinz Wagner adds that the cooperatives and Kellereien have driven prices down, forcing growers to abandon their vineyards, a trend he thinks it will be difficult to reverse.

There are no significant differences in viticulture between the Saar and Ruwer and the Mosel. Traditionally, vines were trained on poles; as in the Mosel, there is a move toward training them along wires, although this is being resisted vocally by growers such as Heinz Wagner. On the other hand, Hans-Joachim Zilliken, who can hardly be accused of being a slouch when it comes to quality, argues that training along wires encourages the development of a leaf wall which offers the optimal ratio of foliage to bunches. The result is higher ripeness levels; the drawback is the cost of installation, although this is offset by the fact that it is cheaper to maintain and easier to mechanize.

Some growers, such as Egon Müller at Scharzhof and Roman Niewodniczanski at Van Volxem, are increasing the density of the plantings. Niewodniczanski points out that on very steep sites you don't need wide spacing to get optimal exposure to sunlight. Moreover, by pruning to a single cane rather than two, you reduce the amount of space required per vine and can pack them in more closely.

Few would dispute that the level of quality on the Saar and Ruwer today is very high. Vintages such as 1993 and 1997 in particular have shown how beautiful the wines from these valleys can be. The top estates are achieving record prices at auction for their nobly sweet wines. But Heinz Wagner sounds a note of caution, worrying that because the top estates have focused so much on Eiswein and TBA, they have forgotten that nobody can make a living from such wines, and that all estates need to focus just as strongly on improving the quality of more basic wines.

But high quality wine is expensive to produce, requiring low yields and severe selection. Newcomers to the Saar such as Roman Niewodniczanki are hoping to push up prices in order to enhance the renown of the region for dry as well as sweet wines. That might ease the plight of producers such as Heinz Wagner, who feels economically cramped. He can't produce enough wine to satisfy demand, yet he feels unable to raise his prices to a more realistic level.

RUWER

The Bereiche and Grosslagen for both the Ruwer and the Saar are listed on p. 163.

Vineyards

AVELSBACH
These vineyards, which actually lie within the city limits of Trier, were established by the state domaine, and the best known producer today is the Hohe Domkirche, which is part of the Bischöfliche Weingüter. Top sites: Altenberg, 10 ha (24.7 acres) and Hammerstein, 12 ha (29.7 acres).

EITELSBACH

Eitelsbacher Marienholz. Owners include Bischöfliche Weingüter.

Eitelsbacher Karthäuserhofberg. Former monastic property and now the *Alleinbesitz* of Karthäuserhof. Red slate with iron.

KASEL

Kaseler Hitzlay. 22 ha (54.4 acres). Planted with Riesling and Müller-Thurgau.

Kaseler Kehrnagel. 22 ha (54.4 acres). Lean elegant wines. Owners include Bischöfliches Konvikt.

Kaseler Nies'chen. 17 ha (42 acres). Can be an excellent site in hot years. Powerful wines balanced by refinement. Owners include Priesterseminar, Karlsmühle, von Beulwitz, and Kesselstatt, 3.5 ha (8.6 acres).

LORENZHOF

Lorenzhöfer Felslay. 3.5 ha (8.6 acres). *Alleinbesitz* of Karlsmühle. Has light slate soils.

Lorenzhöfer Mäuerchen. 2.5 ha (6.2 acres). *Alleinbesitz* of Karlsmühle. Fairly deep soils that resist drought well.

MERTESDORF

The home of the Maximin Grünhaus estate and its three *Alleinbesitz* vineyards.

Maximin Grünhäuser Abtsberg. 14 ha (34.6 acres). The top site at this monastic foundation. It has mainly blue slate soil and can very occasionally suffer from water stress.

Maximin Grünhäuser Bruderberg. 1 ha (2.5 acres).

Maximun Grünhäuser Herrenberg. 19 ha (47 acres). Richer, deeper soil than Abtsberg, with softer red slate. It warms up more slowly than the Abtsberg.

WALDRACH

The most southerly wine village of any importance, a source of good if not exceptional wines. The best site is probably Hubertusberg.

Waldracher Sonnenberg. 4 ha (9.9 acres). Weins-Prüm owns 1 ha (4.7 acres).

SAAR

Vineyards

AYL

Ayler Herrenberger. 7 ha (17.3 acres). Partly owned by Bischöfliches Konvikt.

Ayler Kupp. 80 ha (198 acres). A top site. Owners include Priesterseminar, Reinert, and Bischöfliches Konvikt.

FALKENSTEIN

Falkensteiner Hofberg. 13 ha (32.1 acres). Ninety-eight per cent owned by Friedrich Wilhelm Gymnasium. Only twenty to thirty per cent of the vineyards are steep, so the vineyard can be partially mechanized.

FILZEN

52 ha (128 acres). The northernmost wine commune in the Saar.

Filzener Herrenberg. 6 ha (14.8 acres). *Alleinbesitz* of Reverchon. Planted not only with Riesling but with Spätburgunder and Schwarzriesling.

Filzener Pulchen. 5 ha (12.4 acres). The best site in the village. Piedmont is the best-known owner.

Filzener Steinberger. Reverchon is the most important proprietor.

KANZEM

Kanzemer Altenberg. 20 ha (49.4 acres). One of the few steep south-facing sites plunging down to the riverbank. The soil is pure grey slate with some quartz. Racy wines. Owners include Priesterseminar, Le Gallais, Reinert, and von Othegraven.

KONZ

Konzer Falkenstein. Cited by Langenbach as an outstanding site, once the *Alleinbesitz* of Friedrich Wilhelm Gymnasium.

OBEREMMEL

Relatively broad wines for the Saar.

Oberemmeller Hütte. 5 ha (12.4 acres). *Alleinbesitz* of von Hövel. In effect a long hump, the prolongation of Scharzhofberg with Oberemmel village between the two. Fifty-five per cent steep. Faces south and south west. Has many old vines, so yields are low.

Oberemmeller Karlsberg. 42 ha (104 acres). 3.5 ha (8.6 acres) owned by Kesselstatt.

Oberemmeller Raul. 2.4 ha (5.9 acres).

Oberemmeller Rosenberg. 10 ha (24.7 acres). A good site for dry wines. 1.2 ha (3 acres) owned by Friedrich Wilhelm Gymnasium, 3.4 ha (8.4 acres) by Kesselstatt, 2 ha (4.9 acres) by von Hövel, 0.6 ha (1.5 acres) by Van Volxem.

OCKFEN

101 ha (250 acres).

Ockfener Bockstein. 55 ha (136 acres). Much enlarged after 1971. Gravelly slate over yellow loam and quartzite. 4.5 ha (11 acres) owned by Sankt Urbans-Hof. Other owners include Dr Fischer, Zilliken, Heinz Wagner, and Weinhof Herrenberg. Gives relatively broad wines because it has fairly heavy soil.

Ockfener Herrenberg. 7.5 ha (18.5 acres). Owners include Dr Fischer.

SAARBURG

56 ha (138 acres).

Saarburger Kupp. Close to the river in the direction of Trier. Very slatey, with large slabs. Wagner likes it for dry Rieslings.

Saarburger Rausch. 14 ha (34.6 acres). A steep south-facing site looming over the town, with thin Devonian slate over red loam with iron. It also has a volcanic stone called Diabas that gives mineral tones. Zilliken owns 8 ha (19.8 acres), and Heinz Wagner is the other major proprietor. He finds that it provides high levels of tartaric acid, which gives the wines a mouth-watering character, and making them very long-lived.

SCHARZHOFBERG

28.2 ha (70 acres). Originally 18 ha (44.5 acres), it was expanded in 1971 to 27, and some of the added parcels at the top of the hill are not first-rate. Deep slate, with *Grauwacker* (grey slate) on top and in the direction of Oberemmel. Rarely suffers from water stress. The top of the hill is cooler and less good than the slopes, and some parcels at the bottom are also not exceptional. Curiously, one section belonging to Egon Müller is above Wiltinger Braunfels. Owners include Scharzhof (Egon Müller), von Hövel, 3 ha (7.4 acres), Hohe Domkirche, 6 ha (14.8 acres), Kesselstatt, 7 ha (17.3 acres), Van Volxem, 1.7 ha (4.2 acres), and Vereinigte Hospitien, 2 ha (4.9 acres). Only Egon Müller has very old vines. For further discussion of this site, see under Egon Müller, below.

SCHODEN
Schodener Herrenberg. Owners include Weinhof Herrenberg.

SERRIG
84 ha (208 acres). This village has a particularly cool microclimate and it can be a struggle for Riesling to ripen.

Serriger Herrenberg. 6 ha (14.8 acres). *Alleinbesitz* of Bert Simon.

Serriger Schloss Saarsteiner. 9 ha (22.2 acres). *Alleinbesitz* of Schloss Saarstein.

Serriger Vogelsang. 22 ha (54.4 acres). The Bischöfliche Weingüter is the major owner.

Serriger Würtzberg. 6.5 ha (16 acres). *Alleinbesitz* of Bert Simon. Slate and clay soils.

WAWERN
21 ha (51.9 acres).

Wawerner Herrenberger. 7.7 ha (19 acres). *Alleinbesitz* of Dr Fischer.

WILTINGEN
Wiltinger Braune Kupp. 5 ha (12.4 acres). There used to be three owners, but Vereinigte Hospitien sold its parcels in 1992. The other owners are Egon Müller and Le Gallais, so in effect an *Alleinbesitz*.

Wiltinger Braunfels. 58 ha (143 acres). Eighty per cent slate, twenty per cent Grauwacker. A continuation of Scharzhofberg, but the wines have a different character. Owners include Kesselstatt, 3.1 ha (7.7 acres) and Van Volxem 3.8 ha (9.4 acres).

Wiltinger Gottesfuss. 4 ha (9.9 acres). Very steep, up to eighty-five per cent. Red soil and slate. There are parcels of 120-year-old ungrafted vines owned by Van Volxem. In the late nineteenth and early twentieth centuries, Appolinar Koch and Müller achieved the highest auction prices for Scharzhofberg and Gottesfuss. The two producers were great rivals and the wines fetched huge sums. Other owners include Reverchon.

Wiltinger Kupp. 7 ha (17.3 acres). Priesterseminar, Van Volxem, and von Othegraven own vines here.

Wiltinger Schlangengraben. 54 ha (133 acres). Not that deep but well-drained slate soil; however, the exposure is not ideal. A good but not exceptional site. Owners include Sankt Urbans-Hof, Weinhof Herrenberg, Reinert, Resch, and Van Volxem.

SAAR AND RUWER

Producers

ERBEN VON BEULWITZ

Eitelsbacher Weg 4, 54318 Mertesdorf. Tel: +49 (0) 651 95610. Fax: 9561150. www.von-beulwitz.de. 5 ha (12.4 acres). 3,500 cases.

In 1982 Herbert Weis bought a property that consisted not only of 5.5 ha (13.6 acres) of vineyards and wine cellars, but a hotel too. He has maintained all of them, apart from selling off a few parcels of vines he didn't like, and has won a growing reputation for the wines. The cellarmaster is Stefan Rauen. The wines are vinified in steel tanks using only natural yeasts. Some of the simpler dry wines go through partial malolactic fermentation, because he doesn't want more than 8 grams of acidity for a dry wine. Weis likes to give the wines prolonged ageing on the fine lees, often until May.

Although the estate is based in Mertesdorf, his best vineyard is Kaseler Nies'chen. Some of the bottlings are differentiated by a star system which Weis inaugurated in the late 1990s. The wines have excellent fruit, an almost broad peachiness. For my taste they lack some vigour, zest and minerality. I tasted extensively from the 1999 and 2000 vintages, and the best wine was the 1999 Nies'chen Auslese***, which showed botrytis on the nose, yet was lean, racy, and concentrated, with exquisite fruit and excellent length.

LE GALLAIS
See Scharzhof. 4 ha (9.9 acres). 2,000 cases.
Le Gallais is sometimes thought of as a second label of Scharzhof, though it is in fact a separate property. It is jointly owned by a descendant of the Le Gallais family called Gerard Villanova, and by Egon Müller of Scharzhof. The vineyards are in Warwern, and Wiltinger Braune Kupp and Braunfels. The only vineyard designation I have come across is Braune Kupp. Because the estate buildings have been sold off, all wine-making takes places at Scharzhof. My experience of them is very limited.

WEINHOF HERRENBERG
Hauptstr 80, 54441 Schoden. Tel: +49 (0) 6581 1258. Fax: 995438. 2 ha (4.9 acres). 8,000 bottles.
This minute, organically cultivated estate is the property of Claudia and Manfred Loch, who founded it in 1992 and, as winemakers, are self-taught. It must be hard to make a living from 2 ha (4.9 acres), and the couple hope eventually to double the size of the property. The vineyards are in Schodener Herrenberg and Ockfener Bockstein; in Wiltinger Schlangengraben they have a tiny parcel of vines planted in 1892. The Lochs are fanatical about controlling yields, and employ severe pruning, green harvesting and selective harvesting to bring the yields down to between 30 and 35 hl/ha (12.1–14.2 hl/acre).

The winemaking is very reductive and only stainless steel tanks are used. Natural yeasts are almost always used and there is minimal filtration. They are not afraid of high acidity in their wines, which they say is not a problem, so long as the wines have sufficient body and extract.

In 1999 almost the entire production consisted of Auslesen. In 2000, however, all the wines were Trocken and Halbtrocken. It is admirable to match the style of the wines so closely to what nature provides each year, but it must be a marketing nightmare. Still, the Lochs seems untroubled. Their wines are reasonably priced, have been praised by the German wine press, and sales to their mostly private customers seem brisk. Many of the wines are distinguished by different *Fass* (cask) numbers on the labels, because many parcels are vinified separately. One of the wines bears the presumably punning name Contes Saar (Contessa?); it is an Auslese from a single parcel with a heavier slate soil, and is only made when the grapes attain a high level of ripeness.

Some of the dry wines from 2000 are vegetal and austere, and I greatly prefer the No 4 Halbtrocken, which is spicier and better balanced, and the Schlangengraben "Alte Reben" Halbtrocken, with its apricot fruit and fine length. The 1999 Auslesen are all very good, and the Contes Saar is unusually exotic. The range is capped with a supple, peachy 1999 Schodener Herrenberg BA.

VON HÖVEL
Agritiusstr 5–6, 5439 Oberemmel. Tel: +49 (0) 6501 15384. Fax: 18498. 12 ha (29.7 acres). 4,000 cases.

The jovial Eberhard von Kunow is the sixth generation to run this fine property, a monastic estate that came into his family after secularization in 1803. It boasts an Alleinbesitz in Oberemmeller Hütte and holdings in Scharzhofberg and Oberemmeller Rosenberg. Yields are around 50 hl/ha (20.2 hl/acre). Von Kunow believes in pressing as fast as possible to minimize any skin contact with mediocre or rotten grapes that may have been harvested. Centrifuging is very rare, and he prefers to use filtration to stop fermentation; no *Süssreserve* is employed. Some of the wines are vinified in stainless steel, but the best wines all spend time in oak casks.

He produces hardly any dry wines, for the sensible reason that he himself doesn't like them very much and believes Saar wines need some residual sugar to bring out their primary fruit character. There is a Gutsriesling called Balduin von Hövel, which is made in three styles: Trocken, Halbtrocken, and regular QbA.

I have been following these wines for fifteen years, almost always with considerable pleasure. Yet tasting recent vintages at the winery in 2002, I was troubled by a lack of verve in the wine and by a wet-wool character that seemed akin to mustiness. It occurred in vintages as diverse as 1997 and 2000, so perhaps this character emerged from the glasses or from aromas in the tasting room. Nonetheless, the quality of the Auslesen Goldkapsel wines from Hütte came through beautifully, the 1997 intense, appley, and spicy, and with excellent length; the 1999 vivid and racy and creamy in texture.

KARLSMÜHLE

In Mühlengrund 1, 54318 Mertesdorf. Tel: +49 (0) 651 5124. Fax: 561 0296.
www.weingut-karlsmuehle.de. 12.5 ha (31 acres). 5,000 cases.

For many years Peter Geiben led a dual life as hotelier and winemaker. In 1999 he leased out his hotel, allowing him to devote all his energies to his wines, regarded since the late 1980s as among the finest from the Ruwer. Two of his vineyards, Lorenzhöfer Mäuerchen and Felslay, are monopoly sites. Mäuerchen has deeper soils and excels in dry years; Felslay has a light slate soil. Just as important, Geiben has since 1994 owned vineyards in Kaseler Nies'chen.

Two-thirds of the wines are Trocken and Halbtrocken, and all wines are vinified in stainless steel tanks. 2000 was a difficult year, and some of the simpler wines are a touch green. But the Lorenzhöfer Auslese has great intensity and length, and there is a delicious Lorenzhöfer Eiswein, racy and delicate, with a sherbety finish. The 2001s are a triumph, from a pungent, limey Mäuerchen Kabinett, to an exquisite Kaseler Nies'chen Auslese Long Gold Capsule and the ultra-spicy Kaseler Kehrnagel Eiswein.

KARTHÄUSERHOF

54202 Eitelsbach. Tel: +49 (0) 6511 5121. Fax: 53557. 19 ha (47 acres).
12,000 cases.

This former Carthusian estate was secularized in 1811, when it came into the possession of the present owners. As a wine estate it went through a bad patch in the 1970s and early 1980s until the lawyer and passionate game-hunter Christoph Tyrell took control in 1987. During his father's time the magnificent Karthäuserhofberg, a monopoly site that rears up behind the house and winery, was divided into five vineyards, but Tyrell decided to use a single label for the entire production, thus giving him more flexibility and making life a bit simpler for the consumer. Karthäuserhof is unusual in that the bottle bears only a neck label, which somehow manages to cram in all the required information. Tyrell also got rid of varieties such as Ortega and Optima that had been planted earlier, but he has planted some Pinot Blanc on heavier soil at the foot of the vineyard. Although some growers in the Saar and Ruwer are increasing plant density, he removed every third row, partly to give the roots more space in which to search for nutrients, and partly to allow tractors access to this very steep site. Average yields are around 55 hl/ha (22.2 hl/acre).

The grapes are given a very light crushing before being pressed, and the must is clarified by sedimentation and filtration. Vinification takes place in steel tanks, because Tyrell likes reductive winemaking. No *Süssreserve* is used.

Tyrell is convinced that his 1999 range is among the best he ever produced. Unfortunately, in 2000 his vineyards were damaged by hail in May and June, and he told me it felt like being a boxer knocked out in the third round. The vine-stocks as well as the leaves suffered damage and needed time to recover. Despite this setback, the 2000s are good, including the assertive, minerally Weissburgunder. Tyrell produces a lot of dry wines and the 2000 Halbtrockens, in particular, are powerful and spicy. The Kabinett is concentrated yet delicate. With the exception of one Spätlese and an Eiswein, there were no higher Prädikat wines in 2000.

As for the 1999s, the dry wines are powerful, but rather too extracted and assertive for my taste. The Auslese Trocken "S" has 12.7 per cent alcohol and is almost too concentrated and pungent. Among the sweeter styles, the Spätlese has charm yet lacks some persistence, the acidity level being on average one gram lower than in 2000. Tyrell produced a large number of Auslesen in 1999, of which I only tasted the No 22, a lean, tight, apricoty wine with good length and potential. The 2002 show great promise, especially the elegant Spätlese.

GUTSVERWALTUNG VON SCHUBERT – MAXIMIN GRÜNHAUS

Maximin Grünhaus, 54318 Mertesdorf. Tel: +49 (0) 651 5111. Fax: 52122. www.vonschubert.com. 34 ha (84 acres). 15,000 cases.

This is one of the most fascinating estates in Europe, because its monastic origins are so visible. It was a dependency of the St Maximin monastery from the tenth century onward, and there are traces of eleventh century workmanship in the two estate manor houses that stand side by side. In 1882 it came into the hands of the von Schubert family, and for many years it has been owned and managed by Dr Carl von Schubert. Like his neighbour Christoph Tyrell of Karthäuserhof, he is a keen hunter, and when I arrived for dinner one January night, I went into the cloakroom to find six wild boar suspended from the ceiling.

Opposite the manor stands the immense hill that constitutes the

Alleinbesitz vineyards of the property. It is divided into three sectors. The finest is the Abtsberg; as its name suggests, its wines were reserved for the abbot. The other large vineyard is the Herrenberg (the lord's hill) and the smallest is the Bruderberg (the brothers' hill). Von Schubert only uses the Bruderberg for simpler qualities.

The vineyards are planted with a range of clonal selections, and yields are kept low, rarely exceeding 50 hl/ha and often far lower. Harvesting is highly selective, and at one time von Schubert devised a system whereby his pickers could harvest six different quality levels simultaneously. Today he prefers to send out pickers to focus on a single quality, such as Beerenauslese, rather than making complex selections in the vineyard.

Once the grapes are in the winery, they come under the control of Alfons Heinrich, who has been the cellarmaster here for more than thirty years. He is also the vineyard manager, so he knows exactly what to expect when the grapes arrive. Different parcels and qualities are vinified separately, and any blending required takes place shortly before bottling. Treatments are minimal, with natural sedimentation and natural yeasts. The best wines are vinified in casks, the simpler qualities in steel tanks. The cellars are very cold, so fermentations tend to be prolonged.

About half the production is of dry wines, for which the estate has an excellent reputation. The sweeter wines are made without *Süssreserve*. The wines are bottled in May or June, but there was one vintage, 1982, when the dry wines required two years' ageing in casks. The sweet wines can be utterly exquisite. 1964, 1976, 1983, and 1988 were all excellent vintages here, and 1989 gave the richest wines. Beerenauslese was produced every year from 1993 to 1997, but in 1998 only Eiswein was made at the very top level. 1999 was a fine year, but 2000 was disastrous, because on 11 May hail destroyed half the vineyards; the silver lining, says von Schubert, is that this gave better aeration within the vineyard that proved beneficial.

So many different qualities and styles are produced each year, and so many casks are bottled separately to preserve their distinctive character, that to provide individual tasting notes would be tedious. On my most recent visit to the estate, in June 2001, I tasted at least sixteen wines from 1999 and 2000; earlier visits and tastings in London have yielded notes that run into the hundreds. It must be said that recent vintages have come in for some stick from certain quarters of the German wine press, somewhat to my surprise. In a tricky year such as 2000 I find the dry wines too austere, but in other vintages they can be excellent. The top wines from the most recent vintages – Auslesen, Eiswein, BA – have been as intense and elegant as I have come to expect, with fine length, and a flavour spectrum that ranges from apricot and apple to quince. When tasted very young the wines can have a leesy character that is disturbing; but these are wines that need to be cellared for a few years. Good vintages here can age for twenty or thirty years without difficulty, achieving a magical balance between their delicacy of structure and their wealth of flavour. At their best these are among the supreme wines of Germany.

EGON MÜLLER – SCHARZHOF

54459 Wiltingen. Tel: +49 (0) 6501 17232. Fax: 150263. www.scharzhof.de. 8 ha (19.8 acres). 5,000 cases.

As you drive from Oberemmel toward Wiltingen, you pass on your right the great whale-like hump of the Scharzhofberg. At its foot stands the lovely Scharzhof manor house, its pale yellow façade broken by numerous windows and dormers. A visit here was, and to some extent still is, a step back into the nineteenth century. The late Egon Müller III, a moustachioed man with a slightly military bearing, would greet his visitor with courtesy, and you would be invited to sling your coat over an antlered rack. In the hall a round table was placed by the window, and on it eight or so bottles of recent vintages. Scharzhof produces wine only from the Scharzhofberg, so the tasting was not too arduous. Stage two of the tasting, if you were fortunate enough to be invited to it, would take place in the drawing room in greater comfort. Herr Müller would disappear to the cellars and bring up the bottles for which this estate is really prized: precious old Auslesen, an Eiswein or two, perhaps a 1971 Beerenauslese. It was like being in wine heaven.

Herr Müller retired in 1991 and his place has been taken by Egon Müller IV. The tasting ceremony has hardly altered, except that you are more likely to trip over a blue battery-powered car or a teddy bear, signifying the arrival of the next generation of Müllers.

Scharzhof is an institution, and for some lovers of German wine, the finest estate in the land. It is, like Maximin Grünhaus, coherent in that it produces wine from a single site, although that site is shared with a number of other growers. The Müllers' blocks of vines include a parcel behind the house with one hundred-year-old ungrafted vines. They have recently engineered a complicated exchange with the Kesselstatt estate, so that both proprietors can benefit from larger single parcels.

I once asked Egon Müller IV what made Scharzhofberg so special. "Good question. It's not a site that brings in grapes with high Oechsle levels, and it's very hard to put our finger on what its defining feature is, other than the fact that it has a deep subsoil. The exposure to the sun is good, and the site is steep, but that's true of other vineyards too. It must be a combination of factors. I'm convinced that *terroir* is behind the greatness of the site, but we can't always explain what that means. But even estates with substantial holdings in other parts of the Mosel as well as in Scharzhofberg admit that there is something special about the hill.

"The vineyard was almost certainly planted by the Romans. The name *Scharzhof* derives from a Latin word for newly cultivated land, and given the nature of the land – steep slopes – it could only have referred to grapes. It became a monastic property in around 700. There were many other similar estates around but Scharzhof was unusual in that it consisted only of vineyards, and not of forests and farmland as well. So it must have been of outstanding quality to have been worth conserving on its own.

"In 1797 it was secularized by the French, at which time it was bought by my great-great-great grandfather. After he died it was subdivided among seven children, which is why there are multiple owners today. The house has always belonged to us, but there are other buildings on the estate that are the property of the Bishop of Trier."

The grapes are always picked late so as to ensure optimal ripeness that will support the natural high acidity of Scharzhofberg wine. In 2001, Müller told me, he started picking relatively early, just to get his bearings in the vineyard, so to speak. Gradually his selections became more focused. "Then I had to judge the day when I would go for the ultimate: TBA. There are only a couple of days when you can pick for TBA, because picking individual berries makes great demands on the harvesters. Keep them at it for too long and they grow weary and less careful." Such efforts pay off, in more senses than one. In 2001 a case of 1994 TBA was sold at the annual wine auction in Trier for the equivalent of more than $42,000 (€44,940).

Müller explains how he harvests: "Usually we send our pickers into the vineyards with a basket, and attached to it is another small basket. Any botrytis grapes go into the smaller basket. On a single day we'll have about forty pickers at work, and the result will be about 1,000 litres of regular wine and 50 litres of botrytis wines. We can't really do the selective harvesting you find in Sauternes, because our vintage starts so much later than in Bordeaux. Often we only start picking in late October or November, and we know that it is only a matter of time before the bad weather arrives and puts an end to the harvest. So we're pressed for time. I remember that in 1989, 1997, and 1999 it rained at the end of the harvest, and any remaining botrytis fruit had to go into our Kabinett or Spätlese, because the grapes had lost concentration and acidity by the time they were picked."

Scharzhof is also famous for its Eisweine, although Egon Müller III was never that keen on Eiswein as a category. He insisted, rightly, that it was harder to make a fine BA than a good Eiswein, because BA grapes had to be selected from the best sites, whereas you could make Eiswein from any old grapes, as long as they were healthy and frozen. Egon Müller IV concurs. Nonetheless, it's Eiswein that has captured the public imagination and taste. It was first made here in 1929, and again in 1942: they were aberrations. It was not until 1961 that they were sold commercially. More were made in 1962, 1966, and 1970, and thereafter the estate began to plan for their production. Müller observes: "I find it's not always easy to distinguish BA from Eiswein. In 1995 our BA had very high acidity, which gave it an Eiswein character. And in 1973, 1985, and 1992 our Eiswein didn't have very high acidity and could easily be mistaken for BA. BA fetches slightly higher prices than Eiswein, and in our view is the more complex wine because of the botrytis and concentration."

At the other end of the scale, some dry wine was made from 1980 until 1996, but the Müllers themselves often found these wines disappointing, so they ceased production.

The wines are aged in casks and bottled relatively early to escape oxidation. In the 1980s I often found the simpler wines of the estate, such as his Kabinetts, lacked interest. In the 1990s that seems to have changed, and even in a difficult vintage such as 2000, the Kabinett and Spätlese have precisely the mineral tone and extract one looks for from such a great site. Nonetheless, it's the riper styles that show the real class of Scharzhof. The Auslese Goldkapsel is a declassified BA, because there wasn't sufficient must of BA quality to justify a separate bottling; it is both intense and creamy, and has very good length. The 2000 TBA is already a deep copper-gold in colour, and more raisiny than most Scharzhof TBAs, although it also has very high acidity and excellent length. In 1999 there was a profusion of single cask bottlings. Everything I have tasted from this vintage here has been delicious: what could be finer than the Auslese Goldkapsel No 33, with its terrific attack, its butter-cream texture, and its racy acidity? Delicious now, but promising decades of ever greater complexity.

It would be tedious to catalogue the great older Scharzhof wines I have tasted. Suffice it to say that BAs and Eiswein from vintages such as 1971 and 1976 are among the most stupendous Rieslings I have ever encountered, and it was a privilege to be admitted to old Herr Müller's drawing room to taste them.

VON OTHEGRAVEN

Weinstr 1, 54441 Kanzem. Tel: +49 (0) 6501 150042. Fax: 18879. www.von-othegraven.de. 8 ha (19.8 acres). 3,500 cases.

Until 1986 this estate was run by Maximilian von Othegraven. After his death his widow Maria von Othegraven continued until her death at the age of ninety-six. Since 1995 it has been run by their niece Dr Heidi Kegel. The top site is Kanzemer Altenberg. Maximus is a cuvée for grapes not of sufficient quality for a first growth. For some reason I have never encountered the wines, but in recent years the estate has won a good reputation for its dry Rieslings.

REVERCHON

Saartalstr 2–3, 54329 Konz-Filzen. Tel: +49 (0) 6501 923500. Fax: 923509. 20 ha (49.4 acres). 8,000 cases.

Eddie Reverchon focuses on dry and off-dry wines, mostly from Riesling, but also from Weisser Burgunder. Filzener Herrenberg is his Alleinbesitz, and he also has old vines in Wiltinger Gottesfuss. I have not tasted the wines in many years.

SCHLOSS SAARSTEIN

54455 Serrig. Tel: +49 (0) 6581 2324. Fax: 6523. 10 ha (24.7 acres). 6,000 cases.

A long drive up from the village of Serrig brings you to the hilltop mansion of Schloss Saarstein. It was bought by Dieter Ebert in 1956 and has been run for many years by his son Christian. Most of the wine comes from the *Alleinbesitz* of Serriger Schloss Saarsteiner, where some of the vines are sixty years old. In 1999 Ebert bought 2 ha (4.9 acres) more in Serriger Antoniusberg to provide more wine for his Gutsriesling. More than half the wines are made in a dry or off-dry style, and most of it is released as Gutsriesling. However, in a fine vintage such as 1999 he will also make a Spätlese Trocken from Schloss Saarsteiner.

Ebert employs mostly whole-cluster pressing and ages the wines predominantly in casks. He does use *Süssreserve*, but produced from his own vineyards. He doesn't like to interfere too much with the fermentation process, so if the fermentation stops with a level of residual sugar he feels is insufficient to balance the wine, then he will add some *Süssreserve* – but not for Auslese or higher qualities.

In general, these are wines with high acidity, which gives them a distinct raciness. Except in relatively low-acidity years such as 1999, they benefit from bottle-age. The 1999 Spätlese Trocken had 12.5 per cent alcohol and is a full-bodied wine with ample richness and extract. The regular Spätlese is delicious and elegant, a wine with real charm, and the Auslese Goldkapsel is racy, intense, and pineappley. The 2000s are much leaner, and taste quite dry on the finish thanks to the high acidity and extract.

VAN VOLXEM

Dehenstr 2, 54459 Wiltingen. Tel: +49 (0) 6501 16510. Fax: 13106. www.vanvolxem.de. 13 ha (32.1 acres). 3,000 cases.

This long-established estate near the church in Wiltingen has had a troubled history in recent years. In 1991 the Van Volxems sold it to a purchaser who after two years sold it on to the Jordan family. The Jordans were well intentioned, but a mixture of financial and health problems obliged them to put the estate back on the market. In the meantime an imposing young man called Roman Niewodniczanski had been looking for a property at which he could make top quality dry Rieslings. He was influenced by Reinhard Löwenstein of Heymann-Löwenstein (q.v.) and knew it was possible to make outstanding dry wines even in the seemingly unpromising climate of the Mosel. Failing to find what he was looking in the Lower Mosel, he heard that Van Volxem was on the market. As an heir to the Bitburg brewery fortune, Niewodniczanski had the resources required for the purchase, and in January 2000 he became the new owner.

He resuscitated the old name of the estate, sold off some lesser sites that did not interest him and hired Gernot Kollmann, who had previously worked with Loosen and Castell, as cellarmaster. He also signed contracts with good local growers to supply him with additional fruit which will be used to produce a Gutsriesling from 2002 onward. He pays very high prices to ensure the growers follow his viticultural dictates.

Van Volxem is certainly endowed with magnificent vineyards: 2 ha (4.9 acres) of Scharzhofberg, 3.8 ha (9.4 acres) of Wiltinger Braunfels, 1.5 ha (3.7 acres) of Wiltinger Gottesfuss, as well as other sites in Wiltingen and Oberemmel. In 2001 Niewodniczanski exchanged 1.5 ha (3.7 acres) of red vines for Riesling in Wiltinger Kupp. He is particularly proud of the parcel of 120 year old vines in Gottesfuss; it delivers tiny grapes which in 2000 resulted in a pitifully low yield of 14 hl/ha. He was unfazed, low yields being exactly what he was looking for.

He harvests up to three times, starting with the ripest grapes. Almost all the wines are vinified in casks with natural yeasts. Fermentation is prolonged, and the wines stay on the fine lees and are stirred until the summer, when they are bottled.

All the dry wines are labelled QbA, although they are, in terms of their must weights, all Spätlese or Auslese level. Niewodniczanski wants the customer to focus on the vineyard site, not on bureaucratic verbiage on the label. He has instituted an internal hierarchy for his wines. Wiltinger Riesling is the most basic, followed by Wiltinger Braunfels, and with Braunfels Vols as the top bottling, Vols being a parcel with sixty-year-old vines. Another parcel is bottled separately: Pergentsknopp from within Scharzhofberg.

The dry wines from the tough 2000 vintage are remarkable. Low yields and severe selection have allowed the Van Volxem team to make wines with no harshness or greenness; indeed, wines that taste fully ripe as well as mineral. They are all excellent. Some other wines, such as Scharzhofberger and the Gottesfuss Alte Reben, have some residual sugar (15 to 20 grams), but their sheer concentration of flavour overwhelms any suggestion of sweetness. These are powerful wines with amazing length.

The range is capped with an intense, firm Scharzhofberger Auslese Goldkapsel, and a peachy, highly concentrated Scharzhofberger Eiswein.

So Niewodniczanski has succeeded in doing what he set out to do: prove that top sites in the Saar, even in a tricky vintage such as 2000, are capable of producing powerful and harmonious dry Rieslings, as well as resplendent sweet ones. To achieve this he has had to reduce yields severely and practice the kind of selection that most growers cannot afford. Moreover these 2000 wines were modestly priced, as befits a "new" estate. I would not be surprised if Van Volxem is running at a loss. At the same time that is surely not the owner's intention. He has a larger programme in mind. He plans to increase his prices substantially for the 2001 range. This, he knows, will lose him some customers, but he hopes the quality of the wines will win him new ones. He wants to show that for dry wines as for sweet wines, high prices are no impediment if the quality is evident. This in turn, he hopes, will encourage other growers to follow his lead.

DR HEINZ WAGNER

Bahnhofstr 3, 54439 Saarburg. Tel: +49 (0) 6581 2457. Fax: 6093. 9 ha (22.2 acres). 5,000 cases.

This well-known estate is lucky to enough to possess excellent steep sites in some of the best villages of the Saar: Saarburg, Ockfen, and Ayl. Almost all the vines are old. Heinz Wagner, now in his mid-sixties, is a staunch traditionalist, and none the worse for that, although he can be quite defensive about his style of winemaking. He has no need to be. The business has seen more glorious days. In the 1880s his great-grandfather built the imposing cellars that reflect the days when exports to East Prussia required much larger volumes than are sold today. His grandfather founded the estate of Schloss Saarfels, which became famous for its sparkling wines. But the property was sold long ago.

Wagner begins his harvest by picking about one-third of the crop for his QbA wines, then leaves the rest to ripen further for at least two weeks. The vineyards are traditionally planted on poles, and the wines are vinified in casks, staying on the lees for about two months. Stylistically, he likes wines that taste clean and pure, and is not a fan of high levels of botrytis for his Auslesen.

About half his production is Trocken and Halbtrocken. His dry wines in 2000 were rather austere, but he managed to produce a fine range of sweeter wines that are piquant and elegant. His best wines usually come from Saarburger Rausch, which gives classic Saar Rieslings; the wines from Ockfener Bockstein are as carefully made but perhaps a touch broader. Nonetheless, the 1999 Bockstein Auslese is a lovely wine, and the 2000 Bockstein Eiswein is brilliant: intense, grapey, appley, and very concentrated. Eiswein, indeed, is something of a Wagner speciality. I recall a superb 1971, still rich and vibrant twenty years later, and another good example in 1985.

FORSTMEISTER GELTZ-ZILLIKEN

Heckingstr 20, 54439 Saarburg. Tel: +49 (0) 6581 2456. Fax: 6763.
www.zilliken-vdp.de. 10 ha (24.7 acres). 5,000 cases

Strolling past the modern house on a slope above the town of Saarburg, one would never suspect what lies beneath. Hans-Joachim Zilliken lives above three tiers of cellars cut into the rock, and as you descend the chill increases. Water drips from the ceiling and the level of humidity is such that the wines never seem to evolve down here, retaining their youthful freshness for decades.

Zilliken is fortunate enough to own about two-thirds of the splendid Saarburger Rausch vineyard that looms over the town. He also has vines in Ockfener Bockstein but his best wines come from the Rausch. In the southeast corner of the vineyard, which is the least sheltered and most prone to frost, he reserves a parcel for Eiswein, for which he has become famous. Yields are low, at around 50 hl/ha, and the vines are mostly trained to a single cane. There is strong demand for his wines on the export market, so Zilliken makes about two-thirds of his wines in sweeter styles. When he is unhappy with the quality of any of his wines, he has no qualms about selling off certain casks to wholesalers. This happened in 1986, for example, when a third of the crop was sold off, and in 1987, when only half was retained.

Zilliken says he wants his wines to resemble butterflies, and that's a good encapsulation of his style: light and delicate, but rich in flavour. There was a time when his Eisweine in particular were too extreme. I recall the 1988, which had 15 grams of acidity and 200 grams of residual sugar: the acidity was so pronounced I found the wine impossible to taste. But in the 1990s the style moderated and the Eisweine are better balanced. In 1994 he produced no fewer than four different Eiswein bottlings.

Because he harvests late and is keen on Eiswein, Zilliken sometimes ends up with frozen grapes that are not sufficiently chilled to make the top grade. These grapes are often blended into other wines. Thus a failed Eiswein in 1987 ended up as a Spätlese Goldkapsel, and the Lange Goldkapsel AP9 in 1989 was half composed of frozen grapes and half of grapes of BA quality.

1999 was a superb year here and even the dry wines were rounded and showed no aggressivity. From Rausch alone he produced nine Auslesen! In 1998 he produced another of his sensational Eisweine (AP 1), and 1997 was another excellent vintage, with some wines showing notes of exotic fruits such as mango. The few 2000s I have tasted were somewhat raw and fierce. The wines overall are always tightly structured and notable for their intensity and length. They are among the most consistent Rieslings the Saar has to offer.

11

Nahe

If the Nahe region, which was established administratively in 1930, seems to lack identity, that is surely because it does lack identity. Indeed, until the 1930s hardly any wine was bottled locally, because most of it was shipped to wholesalers for blending. Despite a surface area of 4,600 ha (11,367 acres), it is not a cohesive winegrowing district. Its vineyards mostly overlook the River Nahe as it flows toward Bingen and the mighty Rhein. It's a meandering river; from Sobernheim to Bad Kreuznach it flows from west to east, and after Bad Kreuznach it turns north toward Münster-Sarmsheim and Bingen. The section west of Bad Kreuznach, which includes ˙Schlossböckelheim, Niederhausen, and Oberhausen, is the Upper Nahe, where there is a good deal of slate in the soil. This is mostly Riesling territory, and the wines can have a raciness and elegance reminiscent of a good Mosel wine. And because of the course followed by the river, many vineyards have an ideal southerly exposure. Indeed, these can be as superlative as any other Rieslings from Germany, with a perfect balance between intensity and elegance, between fruitiness and minerality.

Around Bad Kreuznach, where the vineyards are less stony and mineral, the Rieslings have more body and weight. This tendency increases as one moves north toward the Rhein, because the vineyards have a much higher clay content. Nor is the Lower Nahe, north of Bad Kreuznach, pure Riesling territory; many other varieties are grown and bottled, not always with happy results. Here many of the best vineyards are in the side valleys on south-facing hills rather than directly along the north-flowing river. The wines are decidedly fruity rather than mineral.

The image of the Nahe was given a major boost in the very early twentieth century, when a state domaine was created close to Schloss-böckelheim. This decision was taken after the Royal Prussian Survey completed its examination of the region in 1901. Many new vineyards were created by using convict labour to cut down forests and plant vines on sites that had long been abandoned. The most famous of these is the Schlossböckelheimer Kupfergrube on the site of a former copper mine. For decades the state domaine produced magnificent and long-lived wines, but in the 1990s it was sold and is now in private hands.

Only one-quarter of the vineyards of the Nahe are planted with Riesling. Müller-Thurgau occupies nineteen per cent and Silvaner, which can give good wines here, about nine per cent. Other varieties with between six and eight per cent are Kerner, Bacchus, and Scheurebe. The area devoted to red-wine production is also increasing.

Classification is a live issue in the Nahe, especially since the re-publication of the 1901 Prussian tax map. As in the other Rhein regions, the best sites are clearly identified, with the exception of some of those established by the fledgling state domaine. As presently constituted, wines aspiring to first growth status must be pure Riesling, hand-picked at no more than 50 hl/ha – an earlier version stipulated 48 hl/ha, but this has been slightly increased. Minimum must weights far higher than the legal minimum have been set, and there is a tasting panel to ensure the wines are of high quality. Armin Diel of Schlossgut Diel was a leading proponent of the new system from 1997 onward, but he faced opposition from other VDP estates that were not willing to accept the criteria. Reichsgraf von Plettenberg actually left the VDP as a consequence. However, the system is not limited to VDP members. At the same time, some top estates of the Nahe, including Diel and Kruger-Rumpf, have adopted the new Wine Institute category of Selection, so it's possible that for some years this may confuse customers rather than enlighten them.

Vineyards

There is a single Bereich: Nahetal. (Before 1993 the region had two Bereiche: Kreuznach and Schloss Böckelheim.) There are seven Gross-lagen (Kronenberg, Pfarrgarten, Schlosskapelle, Sonnenborn, Burgweg, Paradiesgarten, and Rosengarten) and 328 Einzellagen.

Grosses Gewächs vineyards:
Münster-Sarmsheim: Dautenpflänzer, Pittersberg.
Niederhausen: Hermannsberg, Steinberg.

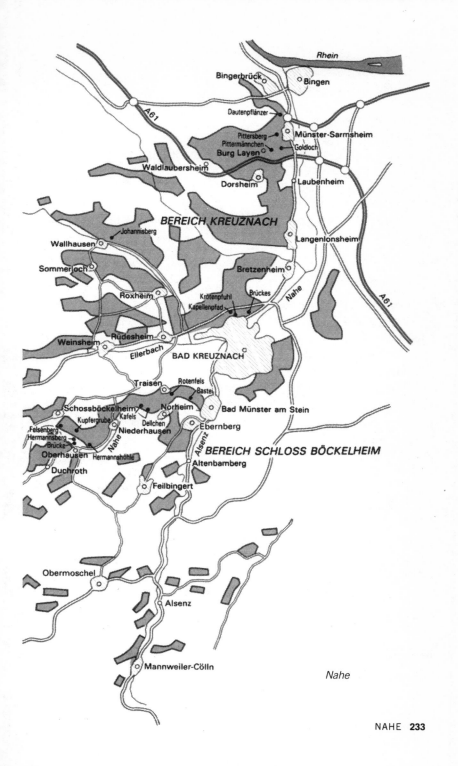

Nahe

Schlossböckelheim: Felsenberg.
Wallhausen: Johannisberg.

ALTENBAMBERG

Many of the village's vineyards, which lie in a side valley south of Bad Kreuznach and Bad Münster, were uprooted after phylloxera in the nineteenth century. Porphyry soils.

Altenbamberger Kehrenberg. 16 ha (39.5 acres). A very good Riesling site.

Altenbamberger Rotenberg. 17 ha (42 acres). Steep reddish sandstone. 6 ha (14.8 acres) are owned by the Gutsverwaltung Niederhausen-Schlossböckelheim.

BURG LAYEN

A village in a side valley west of Münster-Sarmsheim.

Burg Layer Hölle. 28 ha (69 acres). South-facing. Slate and clayey loam.

Burg Layer Johannisberg. 67 ha (165.6 acres). Mostly steep south-facing slope with clay, loam and slate.

Burg Layer Rothenberg. 68 ha (168 acres). Gentle south-facing slope. Clayey, weather-worn red sandstone.

Burg Layer Schlossberg. 21 ha (51.9 acres). A mainly steep, south-facing slope. Slate with clayey loam and gravel.

DORSHEIM

Like Burg Layen, a village in a side valley west of Münster-Sarmsheim.

Dorsheimer Burgberg. 6 ha (14.8 acres). Brown soil, with some slate and iron. Diel owns half the site.

Dorsheimer Goldloch. 11 ha (27.2 acres). Clay over rock, with a mix of clay and pebbles above. Good in wet years. Owners include Diel and Kruger-Rumpf.

Dorsheimer Honigberg. 15 ha (37 acres). Above Goldloch, with warm stony soil. Diel has Pinot Gris planted here.

Dorsheimer Jungbrunnen. Sloping down to bottom of Trollbach valley. Loamy grit.

Dorsheimer Laurenziweg. Partly steep slope, with gritty loam of sandstone and quartzite. A warm site.

Dorsheimer Pittermännchen. 8 ha (19.8 acres). The name refers to a silver coin. A kind of *Flurbereinigung* took place as long ago as 1929, so there are many old vines. The subsoil has a higher gravel and slate content than Goldloch. Worn conglomerate of sandstone and quartzite. Diel likes it best for fruitier wines because the vineyard gives racy acidity.

BAD KREUZNACH
This spa town has some thirty vineyards, of which the best all face south and are sheltered. Mostly deep loam soils, so the style of the wines is fairly rich and broad.

Kreuznacher Brückes. 19 ha (47 acres). Aromatic Riesling from a steep site with deep loam soils.

Kreuznacher Kahlenberg. 14 ha (34.6 acres). A top Riesling site. Rich accessible wines.

Kreuznacher Kauzenberg. A small site producing excellent Riesling.

Kreuznacher Krötenpfuhl. 10 ha (24.7 acres). A top site for Riesling.

LANGENLONSHEIM
Between Bingen and Bad Kreuznach. A good deal of red wine is produced nowadays in the Nahe, but there has long been a red wine tradition in this village.

Langenlonsheimer Berghorn. 26 ha (64.2 acres). Sandy, loamy clay. Good for Silvaner.

Langenlonsheimer Königsschild. 23 ha (56.8 acres). Light loam soil giving elegant fruity Rieslings. Also Gewürztraminer.

Langenlonsheimer Löhrer Berg. 50 ha (124 acres). Stony site giving fruity wines. Tesch is a major owner.

Langenlonsheimer Steinchen. 140 ha (346 acres). The village's largest site. Loess-loam.

LAUBENHEIM
Between Bingen and Bad Kreuznach, and just north of Langenlonsheim.

Laubenheimer Karthäuser. 27 ha (66.7 acres). Light reddish loess-loam soil, faces southwest. This site gives Tesch's best dry Rieslings with good acidity.

Laubenheimer Krone. 26 ha (64.2 acres). Light loam soil with gravel. Gives powerful structured dry Rieslings. Tesch is a major owner.

Laubenheimer St Remigiusberg. 5 ha (12.4 acres). Faces southeast, it has red soils, with chalk and clay too. Tesch owns ninety-five per cent. It attains very good ripeness.

Laubenheimer Vogelsang. Partly steep south-facing slopes, with clayey, loamy gravel.

MONZINGEN
Upper Nahe.

Monzinger Halenberg. Blue slate soils, giving refined Rieslings. Emrich-Schönleber owns most of the site.

Monzinger Frühlingsplätzchen. 120 ha (297 acres). Reddish loam soils with stone and slate, giving readily accessible wines.

MÜNSTER-SARMSHEIM
In the twentieth century much farmland around the town was converted into vineyards, and today it is a vine monoculture. The vineyards are planted on very varied soils. The wines can resemble those from Rüdesheim and Bingen. Kruger-Rumpf and Göttelmann are replanting some abandoned sites, but only those accessible by tractor.

Münsterer Dautenpflänzer. 6 ha (14.8 acres). Slate below loess-loam. No water stress. Less steep than Kapellenberg above. Göttelmann regards it as a top site and find it better than Pittersberg in lesser years, and Kruger-Rumpf says it offers good early-drinking wines.

Münsterer Kapellenberg. 30 ha (74.1 acres). Some quartzite on the higher sections. Kruger-Rumpf has parcels here.

Münsterer Königsschloss. 100 ha (247 acres). South- to southeast-facing slope on a plateau. Clayey loam and grit, with quartzite conglomerate.

Münsterer Pittersberg. 6.5 ha (16 acres). Grey slate. A top site, giving wines that need time to open up. Owners include Kruger-Rumpf.

Münsterer Rheinberg. 6 ha (14.8 acres). Some Devonian slate. South- and southeast-facing. Almost all Riesling. Gives lean refreshing wines. Göttelmann is a major owner, and Kruger-Rumpf also has vines here.

NIEDERHAUSEN
120 ha (297 acres), and about 20 ha (49.4 acres) abandoned. The soils have a lot of slate, which warms up fast, and retains good acidity. The best

sites are south-facing and sheltered. There are eight growers, but there used to be eighty.

Niederhäuser Hermannsberg. 5.5 ha (13.6 acres). *Alleinbesitz* of Gutsverwaltung Niederhausen-Schlossböckelheim. South-facing, with porphyry and slate over loam, so the wines have ample body and good acidity.

Niederhäuser Hermannshöhle. 8 ha (19.8 acres). The best portion of Hermannsberg, south-facing and receiving sunlight all day long, and thus one of Nahe's top sites. Slate, sandstone and loam. Above the river, following the bend. Lighter soil than Schlossböckelheimer Kupfergrube, but perhaps the wines are more elegant. Owners include Gutsverwaltung Niederhausen-Schlossböckelheim, Dönnhoff, and Sitzius. Dönnhoff believes this is the best site of Niederhausen and indeed of the Nahe. Long-lived wines.

Niederhäuser Kerz. 5.4 ha (13.3 acres), half abandoned. All Riesling. Beneath Klamm. Very steep. Black-grey and red slate mixed with porphyry. Terraced above the river; very sheltered.

Niederhäuser Pfaffenstein. About 50 ha (124 acres). Up on the plateau. A new name for a number of merged pre-1971 sites. Up to a steepness of twenty per cent, so not much Riesling. Mathern has 1 ha (2.5 acres).

Niederhäuser Pfingstweide. 3 ha (7.4 acres). Riesling only.

Niederhäuser Rosenberg. 12 ha (29.7 acres). A mix of porphyry and slate above the village, with some fifty-year-old vines. Mathern has 1 ha (2.5 acres).

Niederhäuser Rosenheck. Between the plateau and the village. Steep slate soils.

Niederhäuser Steinberg. Steep and stony, southwest and southeast facing. Porphyry soils. Gutsverwaltung Niederhausen-Schlossböckelheim has 5.5 ha (13.6 acres).

Niederhäuser Steinwingert. Flatter site with loam. Best for Pinot Noir and Pinot Blanc.

NORHEIM

Between Niederhausen and Bad Münster. Very steep vineyards with porphyry and stony soils.

Norheimer Dellchen. 7 ha (17.3 acres). Slate and porphyry. A terraced site, gives high ripeness. Mathern has forty-year-old vines. Other owners include Dönnhoff.

Norheimer Kirschheck. 10 ha (24.7 acres). South-facing, porphyry with some slate. Crusius has 0.5 ha (1.2 acres). Other owners include Dönnhoff.

OBERHAUSEN
Just south of Niederhausen.

Oberhäuser Brücke. 2 ha (4.9 acres). *Alleinbesitz* of Dönnhoff. Slate, porphyry, and sandstone soils, with loam above. Minerally wines.

Oberhäuser Felsenberg. Dönnhoff owns vines here.

Oberhäuser Kieselberg. Porphyry and slate. Sitzius has vines here.

Oberhäuser Leistenberg. Pure slate. Dönnhoff owns vines here.

ROXHEIM
South-facing vineyards northwest of Bad Kreuznach.

Roxheimer Berg. Red slate and loess-clay. A warm site, giving broader wines. Salm is a major owner.

Roxheimer Höllenpfad. A good Riesling site.

SCHLOSSBÖCKELHEIM
Upper Nahe, just west of Niederhausen.

Schlossböckelheimer Felsenberg. 25 ha (61.8 acres). Crusius has vines in this excellent and very stony site, as do Dönnhoff, Gutsverwaltung Niederhausen-Schlossböckelheim, Paul Anheuser, and Plettenberg.

Schlossböckelheimer Kupfergrube. 14 ha (34.6 acres). Former *Alleinbesitz* of Gutsverwaltung Niederhausen-Schlossböckelheim. South-facing, with weathered volcanic soil, with high copper content from the mines below. Gives steely mineral wines.

Schlossböckelheimer Steinberg. Porphyry soils. Gutsverwaltung Niederhausen-Schlossböckelheim owns 5.5 ha (13.6 acres).

TRAISEN
About 35 ha (86.5 acres). Thirty years ago there was no red wine here; now there is even some Merlot.

Traisener Bastei. 1.5 ha (3.7 acres). The Rotenfels, at 214 metres (702 feet) is said to be the highest cliff in Europe north of the Alps. The vineyard was 2.5 ha (6.2 acres) a century ago but rockfalls have diminished it. One hundred per cent Riesling, planted at the foot of the cliff on rubble soils. The site is two degrees warmer than Rotenfels and flowers earlier, but this can be dangerous in cold springs. Ripeness levels are high thanks to good exposure, but acidity can sometimes be low. Gutsverwaltung Niederhausen-Schlossböckelheim, Crusius and Voightlander in Bad Münster are the three owners.

Traisener Rotenfels. 15 ha (37 acres). Porphyric, with various degrees of red sandstone and clay. Some of the vineyard has been abandoned. The south-facing slopes are planted with Riesling; elsewhere there are other varieties, including red. Very varied slopes and exposures. There are many owners, including Crusius.

WALLHAUSEN

Northwest of Bad Kreuznach. 400 ha (988 acres). Fifty growers. Not mentioned in 1901 classification. Very varied soils. The best sites face south. On the other side of the village are vineyards on flatter land which the growers find easier to cultivate. Red grapes grown here too: Pinot Noir, Dornfelder, Dunkelfelder, Portugieser.

Wallhäuser Felseneck. Between Wallhausen and Dalberg. Much enlarged in 1971. Green slate. Salm says it is capable of producing racy mineral wines.

Wallhäuser Johannisberg. The top site, though partly abandoned. Red slate. Salm owns forty-five-year-old vines.

Wallhäuser Kirschheck. Salm is one of the owners but doesn't use the name on his labels.

Producers

PAUL ANHEUSER

Stromberger Str 15–19, 55545 Bad Kreuznach. Tel: +49 (0) 671 28748. Fax: 42571. www.anheuser.de. 67 ha (166 acres). 40,000 cases.

This enormous estate is run by the powerfully built Peter Anheuser, whose family has been involved in wine production since 1627. His vineyards are dispersed throughout the Nahe, and many of them are on steep sites. For some time quality has been patchy, with wines made in a rather broad flat style.

DR CRUSIUS

Hauptstr 2, 55595 Traisen. Tel: +49 (0) 671 33953. Fax: 28219. www.weingut-crusius.de. 13.5 ha (33.4 acres). 8,000 cases.

The Crusius family can trace their winemaking roots back to the sixteenth century. Today the estate is run by Dr Peter Crusius, following in the respected footsteps of his father Hans. They own vineyards throughout the Upper Nahe, but their pride and joy is the tiny holding in the Traisener Bastei. Not only is the parcel tiny, but yields are minute.

All the Rieslings are vinified in casks, employing mostly natural yeasts. Many of the dry wines are made from varieties other than Riesling, such as Pinot Blanc. As for the Rieslings, they are made in quite a rich style that at Kabinett and Spätlese level can lack some vigour and verve. They are much better at Auslese level and above, in part perhaps because the grapes come from very good sites such as Schlossböckelheimer Felsenberg and Traisener Bastei. Certainly, wines such as the 1998 Felsenberg Auslese AP 22 have both delicacy and minerality, and the 2000 Bastei Auslese is lush without being cloying, with an elegant apricot finish.

SCHLOSSGUT DIEL

55452 Burg Layen. Tel: +49 (0) 6721 96950. Fax: 45047. www.schlossgut-diel.com. 16 ha (39.5 acres). 7,500 cases.

The charming house and its ruined castle lie on the edge of the village, and have belonged to the Diel family since 1802. Armin Diel has been in charge here since the mid-1980s, when he introduced significant changes. He eliminated the crossings that had been planted in some of the vineyards, introduced barrique ageing for some wines, especially Burgundian varieties, and eliminated the use of *Süssreserve*. Diel is a well known figure in German gastronomic circles, having been an influential restaurant critic for many years. He is also co-author of the annual Gault-Millau guide to German wine, although he scrupulously avoids any assessment of his own wines! He is a leading light in the Nahe VDP and was an early advocate of classification here.

The vineyards lie in a broad band of south-facing slopes in a side valley. The best sites are Dorsheimer Pittermännchen, 1 ha (2.5 acres), Burgberg, 1.8 (4.4 acres), and Goldloch, 4.5 ha (11 acres). Pittermännchen was replanted in 1986, so the vines are not especially old.

Goldloch has dry stony soil and old Riesling vines. Burgberg is a recent acquisition, having been bought in 1997. There are also some lesser sites such as Dorsheimer Honigberg, where Pinot Gris is planted, and various vineyards in Burg Layen.

Diel offers a number of ranges of wines. He is one of the few important producers in Germany to have adopted the new Classic and Selection system, producing the latter as essentially dry wines from his top sites. There are barrique-fermented wines from Pinot Gris and Pinot Blanc, a range of Riesling Spätlesen and Auslesen from his best sites, and occasional nobly sweet wines. There was a time when Diel thought barrique-aged Riesling was a worthwhile idea, but this was fortunately abandoned in 1989. One of his most expensive wines, however, is Cuvée Victor, a blend of Pinot Gris and Pinot Blanc aged in new barriques. The Burgundian varieties tend to be picked at high ripeness levels, and even in 2000 Victor attained an alcohol level of 13.5 per cent. There is also a Riesling Brut, first introduced in 1989, a wine that spends two years on the lees.

The 2000 Selection Rieslings are very successful, especially the somewhat exotic Goldloch. Among the sweet Spätlesen in 2000, the Pittermännchen had the edge, being zesty and mineral, whereas the Goldloch has more hints of tropical fruit such as pineapple. The Auslesen are surprisingly racy, because most of the wines from this part of the Nahe tend to be broad. Both the 2000 Goldloch Auslese and the Burgberg Auslese Goldkapsel have zesty pineapple fruit and are sleek and stylish. Despite the early aberrations with barrique-aged Riesling, the barrique wines from Diel are very good, especially the Weissburgunder, though they are expensive.

HERMANN DÖNNHOFF

Bahnhofstr 11, 55585 Oberhausen. Tel: +49 (0) 6755 263. Fax: 1067. www.doennhoff.com. 14.5 ha (35.8 acres). 8,000 cases.

Oberhausen is a pretty village, slightly off the beaten track. Helmut Dönnhoff took over the family property in 1971 at a young age, and has brought it to the pinnacle of Nahe estates. He has excellent vineyards in Niederhausen, Oberhausen, Norheim, and Schlossböckelheim, mostly on volcanic soils with porphyry. Oberhäuser Brücke is a small but highly rated *Alleinbesitz*. Yields are low at around 50 hl/ha, and the harvest can be as late as mid-November. Most of the wines are aged in casks, fermentation in his cold cellars is prolonged, and Dönnhoff prefers a hands-off approach once the wines are maturing in wood. No *Süssreserve* is used.

Although Dönnhoff has a fine reputation for his brilliant Eisweine, the quality shines through across the board. What the wines have in common is a tremendous purity of fruit, and a richness that never comes over as heavy or fatiguing. In short, they are beautifully balanced. 2000 proved an excellent year here, and Dönnhoff thinks it may prove better than 1999. The dry Riesling and Weissburgunder are delicious, with surprising concentration for such basic wines. The Norheimer Dellchen Kabinett shows just how good this site can be, and the Oberhäuser Leistenberg Kabinett is equally fine. The Schlossböckelheimer Kupfergrube lacks a little zest. The Brücke Eisweine, harvested just before Christmas 2000, are about as good as Eiswein gets. The 2001s show the same level of brilliance, with some exquisite Auslesen from Hermannshöhle and Brücke.

EMRICH-SCHÖNLEBER

Naheweinstr 10A, 55569 Monzingen. Tel: +49 (0) 6751 2733. Fax: 4864.
www.emrich-schoenleber.com. 14 ha (34.6 acres). 10,000 cases.

Monzingen has never been a name to conjure with but Werner Schönleber has produced a string of delicious Rieslings from his vineyards here. Both Monzinger Frühlingsplätzchen and Halenberg are Grosses Gewächs. The grapes are whole-cluster pressed and often fermented with the indigenous yeasts. These are concentrated Rieslings, with a fine acidic backbone, and a peppery vigour. My experience of these wines is, regrettably, limited, but they enjoy the highest reputation, especially the Eisweine, which, together with those from Dönnhoff, must be counted among the best in the Nahe, and indeed the best in Germany. A 2001 Halenberg Auslese Gold Capsule showed a perfect balance between sweetness and acidity.

GÖTTELMANN

Rheinstr 77, 55424 Münster-Sarmsheim. Tel: +49 (0) 6721 43775. Fax: 42605.
12 ha (29.7 acres). 6,000 cases.

The friendly Götz Blessing, who is married to Ruth Göttelmann, has been running this family estate since 1984. He admits that he prefers working in the vineyards to cellar work, so he has devised an elaborate sound system to pipe jazz music into the cellars to inspire him. He concedes readily that not all his vineyards are in top sites. The most important is Münsterer Rheinberg, where Göttelmann own 4 ha (9.9 acres), and they also have 0.8 ha (2 acres) in Dautenpflänzer. Roughly half the production is of Trocken wines, and a quarter Halbtrocken. The dry wines include not only Rieslings, but Grauer Burgunder, which he personally doesn't like very much, and Chardonnay. Most of the wines are made with cultivated yeasts and sometimes he uses a centrifuge to stop fermentation for the sweeter styles.

I like the Grauer Burgunder more than Blessing does, and although it is aged in barriques, the oak is not too dominant. The 2000 Riesling Kabinett Trocken wines are undernourished, but the Spätlese Trocken from Dautenpflänzer is excellent, full-bodied and with a nutty finish. The sweet Spätlesen from the Rheinberg are somewhat slack and broad in 1999, and the 1998s are distinctly better. The same is true of the Auslesen, which in 1998 have juicy quince flavours. I am less keen on the Beerenauslesen, which are solid and lack zest and length.

KRUGER-RUMPF

Rheinstr 47, 55424 Münster-Sarmsheim. Tel: +49 (0) 6721 43859. Fax: 41882. www.kruger-rumpf.com. 19 ha (47 acres). 10,000 cases.

The best place to enjoy the wines from this estate is at the charming inn run by the Rumpf family on the main street in Münster-Sarmsheim in the house where Stefan Rumpf was born. The property has been in the family since 1790 and seventy per cent is planted with Riesling in some of the best sites in the village, such as Dautenpflänzer and Pittersberg. In 2001 he acquired 1 ha (2.5 acres) of vines in Binger Scharlachberg; although the vineyard is in the Rheinhessen region, he says the soils are identical to those in the Nahe, and it's true that the vineyards are very close to each other. In 2000 he produced three wines under the new Classic category, but he feels the upper limit of residual sugar is too high at 15 grams, and he keeps the levels lower to make sure they taste properly dry.

The Rieslings are easily the best wines. Some bottlings such as the 2000 Weissburgunder Classic have too much residual sugar to maintain the clarity of the fruit. The dry Kabinetts in 2000 are fairly light, but none the worse for that. The best of them is from Dautenpflänzer, and the same is true of the 1999 Spätlese Halbtrocken, which has more finesse than any other wine in this category. The 2000 Kabinetts are very attractive: Pittersberg is the most delicate, Rheinberg is the most refreshing, Kapellenberg juicier but a touch broad. In 1999 the Spätlesen were particularly successful, both Pittersberg and Rheinberg showing excellent fruit and clean acidity. The 2000 Pittersberg Auslese Goldkapsel is very closed, but has creamy apricot fruit, and fine acidity that gives very good length.

MATHERN

Winzerstr 7, 55585 Niederhausen. Tel: +49 (0) 6758 6714. Fax: 8109.
www.weingut-mathern.de. 12 ha (29.7 acres). 9,000 cases.

The jovial and articulate Helmut Mathern runs this up-and-coming estate, which has a fine selection of vineyards in Niederhausen. He retains some parcels of minor grape varieties such as Würzer, Optima, and Kerner, but all his best wines are Rieslings grown on steep slopes. The Rieslings are vinified in stainless steel, and all the sweeter styles are made using natural yeasts. Mathern does not seem that focused on nobly sweet wines, because the last BA here was in 1994.

The Halbtrocken wines seem better balanced than the Trocken bottlings, which can be austere and even tart. The Rosenheck Auslese Halbtrocken from 1999, with its white pepper nose, is the best wine in this style I have tasted from Mathern. The sweeter styles are quite rich and ample for Upper Nahe wines. The exceptions are the very elegant 1999 Auslesen from Norheimer Dellchen and Niederhäuser Rosenberg.

GUTSVERWALTUNG NIEDERHAUSEN-SCHLOSSBÖCKELHEIM

55585 Niederhausen. Tel: +49 (0) 6758 925010. Fax: 925019. www.riesling-domaene.de. 32 ha (79 acres). 18,000 cases.

This important estate is the new incarnation of the former state domaine, which was created in the early twentieth century. The first vintage was 1907. In 1948 the property came into the hands of the state of Rheinland-Pfalz. Endowed with superb vineyards in Niederhausen and Schlossböckelheim, as well as Traisen and Altenbamberg, the estate made brilliant wines in the 1970s and 1980s. The 1983 Hermannsberg Eiswein was magnificent, and in 1987 the estate must have been one of the earliest in the region to green harvest, thinning out the Steinberg vineyard by one-third. Then the wines went through a bad patch, though I don't know the reason for this. The property was put up for sale and bought in 1998 by Erich Maurer, an agricultural products manufacturer from the Pfalz. He invested heavily in the cellars and in replanting some of the vineyards. His son Thomas and daughter-in-law Gudrun help him to run the estate on a daily basis. Kurt Gabelmann became cellarmaster in 1993 and has stayed on under the new regime.

Eighty-five per cent of the vines are Riesling, but small parcels of Burgundian varieties have also been planted, notably 1 ha (2.5 acres) of Pinot Noir in Hermannsberg. The most important site is the famous Schlossböckelheimer Kupfergrube, named after the nearby copper mine. Unlike the Kupfergrube, the Niederhäuser Hermannsberg remains an *Alleinbesitz*, and the other Niederhausen site is Hermannshöhle. In Schlossböckelheim, the estate owns parcels in Felsenberg, Steinberg, and Kertz; and in Traisen, 1 ha (2.5 acres) of the famous Bastei. There are also 6 ha (14.8 acres) in Altenbamberger Rotenberg. Finally, the vineyards in Münster-Sarmsheim, at some distance from the winery, have been leased out.

Under Maurer, the harvesting strategy is to wait as long as possible before beginning, and then to pick very fast to ensure the grapes stay perfectly healthy. They are fermented with natural yeasts and aged in both casks and stainless steel. The cellars are equipped with a centrifuge, but it is hardly ever used. Sixty per cent of the wines are dry. The minerality of the vineyards comes through strongly on the 2000 dry Rieslings, though they lack a little charm. The Halbtrocken wines are a mixed bunch, though both the 1998 Rotenberg Spätlese and the 2000 Hermannshöhle Spätlese in this style are delicate and persistent. As for the sweeter wines, the 35 grams of residual sugar is scarcely perceptible in the 2000 Kupfergrube Kabinett, and the 1998 Bastei Auslese has wonderfully ripe acidity and good length. 1998 was a great year in the Nahe, and there can be few finer wines than the Hermannsberg Eiswein AP 36, with its amazingly complex nose of raisins, peaches, and iodine, its tremendous concentration of flavour, and an impeccable balance that somehow absorbs effortlessly the 16 grams of acidity.

PRINZ ZU SALM-DALBERG'SCHES WEINGUT

Schloss Wallhausen, Schlossstr 3, 55595 Wallhausen. Tel: +49 (0) 6706 944411. Fax: 944424. www.salm-salm.de. 11 ha (27.2 acres). 8,000 cases.

Prince Michael Salm is a powerful figure on the German wine scene, having been president of the VDP for many years. He helped to run the Castell estate in Franken in the 1980s; while there he met and married Philippa zu Castell-Castell. He now occupies himself only with his organic estate in the Nahe, with its headquarters in the centre of Wallhausen in the fine old seventeenth-century Schloss, its slate texture enlivened with black diamonds painted onto white shutters to jazz up an otherwise formidable façade. The Salms also own the ruined castle up the valley in Dalberg, which was built to guard the salt route that ran through the valley.

Prince Salm inherited the property from his grandmother, and when he took it over there were only 3 ha (7.5 acres) of vines, which he has subsequently expanded. There are also extensive forests under family ownership. The vineyards are in Wallhausen, Sommerloch, Dalberg, and Roxheim. About ten per cent of production is of red wine.

The estate has established its own quality hierarchy, beginning at the most basic level with the Der Salm range of easy-drinking blends. Then there is the Prinz Salm range of varietals, mostly from bought-in fruit and not necessarily organic. Then there are the estate wines from Schloss Wallhausen, and at the top level the single-vineyard wines: dry and nobly sweet from Wallhauser Johannisberg, Kabinett from Wallhäuser Felseneck, and Spätlese from Roxheimer Berg. The wines are vinified using mostly natural yeasts, and Grauer Burgunder and some Spätburgunder are aged in barriques.

My visit to Schloss Wallhausen unfortunately coincided with a meeting of the VDP regional directors. The kindly Philippa Salm did her best to entertain me in the drawing room, where we tasted a few wines, while I could hear raised voices from another room where the bosses, including Wilhelm Weil from the Rheingau and Armin Diel from the Nahe, were gathered. At 1.30 pm they emerged for a bowl of soup before resuming their discussions. Prince Salm made a brief appearance in the drawing room during this short lunch break, where, inevitably, we talked more about the VDP and its classification schemes than about his own wines. Then he excused himself and returned, as *capo di tutti capi*, to his meeting.

Although I have only tasted a limited range of recent vintages from this estate, I was less than enthralled. The 1998 Riesling Trocken is unacceptably austere, and the 2000 Halbtrocken only marginally more supple. The 2000 Felseneck Kabinett is much better: full-bodied for Kabinett, but balanced by good acidity. The 1999 Roxheimer Berg Spätlese is pleasant but lacks concentration, and the Spätburgunder from 2000, both the regular bottling and the barrique version, is medium-bodied, neutral, and earthy.

SITZIUS

Naheweinstr 87, 55450 Langenlonsheim. Tel: +49 (0) 6704 1309. Fax: 2781. www.sitzius.de. 15 ha (37 acres). 8,000 cases.

The courteous Wilhelm Sitzius had to take over the family estate when he was eighteen, following the early death of his father. Just under half the vineyards are planted with Riesling, and twenty per cent of production is of red wines such as Spätburgunder and Portugieser. The dry QbA wines from Riesling, Weisser Burgunder, and Rivaner in 2000 are pleasant but hardly exceptional. The 1999 Spätlese Trocken are mineral and concentrated, both from Hermannshöhle and from Oberhäuser Kieselberg. The 1999 Grauer Burgunder Spätlese Trocken, aged in small German oak barrels, is somewhat oily and alcoholic, and high alcohol and some sweetness mar the 1999 Chardonnay Auslese Trocken. The Spätburgunder can be good here: the 1999 Langenlonsheimer St Antoniusweg Auslese Trocken, also aged in German oak, is ripe, sleek, and graceful.

TESCH

Naheweinstr 99, 55450 Langenlonsheim. Tel: +49 (0) 6704 93040. Fax: 930415. www.weingut-tesch.de. 19 ha (47 acres). 13,000 cases.

Founded in 1723, this estate used to be very well known in Britain, and five generations of the Tesch family sold their wines there. Then the estate's renown faded. Dr Martin Tesch, a biochemist by training who took over running the estate in 1996, is determined to return to past glories. In the 1970s about half the production was of Müller-Thurgau, but today there is none, and eighty per cent of the wines are from Riesling. The vineyards are divided between Langenlonsheim and Laubenheim, both of which give wines that are relatively rich and full bodied.

Because most of the Tesch wines are dry, the ripeness and body routinely attained in these vineyards suit the style well. The best Spätlesen Trocken come from Laubenheimer St Remigiusberg and Karthäuser, and from Langenlonsheimer Lohrer Berg, where there are parcels of very old vines. These wines are fruity and easy to enjoy; perhaps they lack some finesse but they are rounded, modest in acidity, and accessible. There is nothing austere about the dry wines from Tesch. The Laubenheim vineyards also give good sweet wines, such as the consistently rich and juicy BA from St Remigiusberg.

In 2001 the usually cautious Dr Tesch leapt into the dark and produced a wine he called Riesling Unplugged, a wine made without any treatments such as chaptalization and stabilization. Bone dry, it's an excellent, invigorating, pungent Riesling.

12

Rheinhessen

The Rheinhessen, which produces about one-quarter of all German wine, is the most maligned of Germany's wine regions. And with good reason. Although there are some districts that are capable of producing magnificent wines, there are also vast tracts of vineyards planted on flat fertile soils that are only suited to the churning out of utterly nondescript wines. This particularly applies to the southern part of the region, known as the Wonnegau. Growers tempted to go for volume rather than quality have had a field day in Rheinhessen, although it is widely accepted that there is no future for this kind of viticulture, because the prices for such overcropped wines are rock bottom. In 1992, according to a top grower in Nackenheim, the crop was so large that growers had insufficient tank space to store the must, which was sold off to French wineries who turned it into Euroblends. One can imagine how good such wines must have tasted. The main customers for high-volume wines were the large Kellereien in search of blending material. Cooperatives, rather surprisingly, are not prominent in the Rheinhessen, and in recent years some of them, such as Nierstein and Westhofen, have merged. They market only three per cent of the region's entire production.

On the other hand, the Rheinhessen is often underrated. The Romans planted vineyards here, and during the early Middle Ages the church, in particular the archbishop of Mainz, was a major proprietor, although later overtaken in influence by the princes of the Palatinate.

The Rhein flows along the northern and eastern fringes of the region, and the most esteemed sites are almost all close to the river. Administratively, the region is divided into three Bereiche: Bingen covers the northwest, near the Nahe, Nierstein the northeast, and Wonnegau the rest.

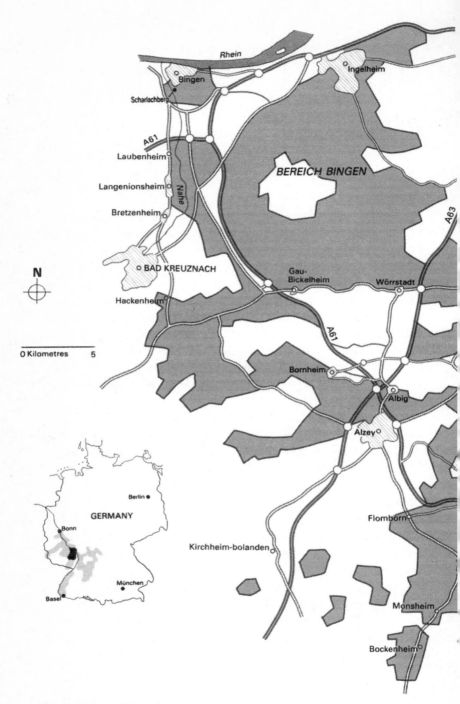

Rheinhessen

It is interesting to look at a survey of the Rheinhessen made by Morton Shand in the early 1920s. In those days the area under vine was 14,400 ha (35,582 acres); today it has almost doubled to 26,450 ha (65,358 acres), with some 8,000 growers. Shand's assessment of the wine's character does not require a great deal of modification eighty years later: "The Hessian wines are decidedly milder and softer than those of the Rheingau, and though seemingly lighter in taste are usually of rather higher alcoholicity. The fullness of and sweetness of Rheinhessen wines is conspicuous, though it is never of a cloying and sugary kind as often in Sauternes . . . Rheinhessen Hocks are not usually very long-lived, nor do they improve sensibly after three or four years in bottle. The province comprises wines of markedly different flavours, such as the delicate and elegant Niersteiner, the premier wine of Rheinhessen; the full, grapey, rather luscious wine of Oppenheim, with its excellent fire and body; the famous Scharlachberger growth of Büdesheim, very like Rüdesheimer both in flavour and colour, made as it is from the selfsame Green Orleans grape; the glorious breed and finish of a Nackenheimer, which often approximates to the best Rheingau Riesling types; the briskness and fine bouquet of Bingen, and the highly individual, wildflower scent and taste of the true unalloyed Liebfraumilch like a far-off and rarefied memory of Tokay. Alas, it has been laid down officially that this picturesque appellation is but a 'Phantasy Name' for a particular quality and flavour of wine, which may be blended from any suitable pure Rhenish wines without much of a name to boast of."[1]

The "true unalloyed" Liebfraumilch originated in Worms, from the vineyards of the Liebfrauenkirche. It was already cited as a distinguished wine in 1744, but having tasted recent examples from this vineyard, it is hard to see what the fuss was about (see Vineyards below). Today, the glory that is Liebfraumilch mops up one-quarter of all Rheinhessen production.

The finest sector of the Rheinhessen is the so-called Rheinfront, a five-kilometre (3.1-mile) band of vineyards above the villages of Nierstein and Nackenheim. Here the soil is a reddish combination of clay, slate, iron, and sand, and the vineyards are known as the *Rote Hang* or red slope. Although some of the colour may derive from the iron content of the soil,

[1] Morton Shand, pp. 48–9.

there is also a theory that 250 million years ago red algae were deposited here. The mineral character of the wines grown on red soils means that they are slow to open up, and invariably benefit from a year or more in bottle.

The vineyards around Bingen, notably the Scharlachberg, are also capable of producing excellent wine, although most growers will acknowledge that their full potential is not at present being realized. As is widely known, the renown of Nierstein in particular has been gravely damaged by the most cynical feature of the 1971 Wine Law: the appropriation of respected names to label junk. Thus the good name of Nierstein was snatched for the Grosslage Niersteiner Gutes Domtal. Nierstein itself is included within the zone, of course, but its total production comprises no more than two per cent of the Grosslage's. Originally the Grosslage was known simply as Niersteiner Domtal: the word "Gutes" was added later to add lustre. The ploy failed.

Silvaner was probably the dominant grape variety in the nineteenth century. It was said by viticulturalists such as Scheu that it was poorly suited to limestone soils, so it was gradually replaced in the course of the twentieth century by the new crossings developed by Scheu and his disciples. Today the dominant variety, rather depressingly, is Müller-Thurgau (twenty-one per cent), followed by Silvaner (twelve per cent), and Riesling (ten per cent). The Pinot family is gradually becoming better established in the Rheinhessen, but the major expansion has been the quadrupling of the area given over to Dornfelder in the past decade. Today red grapes, mostly Portugieser and Dornfelder, account for around eighteen per cent of the entire area.

The southern part of Rheinhessen – broadly speaking, the vineyards around Worms, Westhofen, Alzey, and Wöllstein, at some distance from the river – have been much derided for the wretched quality of much of the wine produced there, much of it on loess and chalk soils. The main problem, though, is not the absence of parcels with excellent soils and microclimates, but the choice of overfertile soils. The Pfannebecker brothers, whose own vineyards lie in such a zone, told me that there is a local saying that if you stick a finger in the ground here, you'd better pull it out fast before it grows roots. Low acidity can also be a problem in the Wonnegau, so many wines, especially from varieties other than Riesling and Silvaner, can be flabby.

As in other wine regions looked down upon by traditionalists, there are certain producers who have studied their soils and found out how to make the most of them. Rather to the dismay of the Rheinfront establishment, the top growths of Rheinhessen are no longer confined to the shores of the Rhein. Much depends on the attitude and approach of individual growers. I find it telling that in Flörsheim-Dalsheim, Weingut Schales doesn't bother with vineyard designations because it finds them of little interest or significance, while the neighbours at Weingut Keller argue the exact opposite.

In part, the fact that certain growers in the derided Wonnegau are clawing their way over the parapet to escape the slough of mediocrity all around them is no more than a means of ensuring economic survival. There is no long-term future for rubbish, a rule that applies just as much to parts of the Languedoc or Spain as to Rheinhessen. Nonetheless, it isn't always easy to make the leap from mass producer to high quality producer, even if the spirit is willing. Because of the poor image of Rheinhessen wines, prices are low, and that in turn means that even ambitious growers find it hard to make the necessary investments – severe reduction of yields, for a start – that would improve the quality of their wines.

Not that the Rheinfront producers can afford to rest on their laurels. Although their Rieslings can be among Germany's greatest, their wines still tend to be underrated. Over the years they have made various efforts to promote the unique qualities of the Rheinfront. I recall the Rhein-Terrasse association, later followed by the Am Strom marketing group. Both, to the best of my knowledge, are defunct or at least moribund. Of course, the energies that went into such endeavours have now been channelled into the cause of classification.

This has been spearheaded, as elsewhere, by the VDP, using old tax maps as the basis for classification. Briefly, the rules are as follows: the vineyards must be cultivated without use of chemical fertilizers, the grapes must be selectively harvested by hand; the maximum yield is 50 hl/ha; and there are minimum Oechsle levels for both Riesling (90) and Pinot Noir (95). (The eventual inclusion of Silvaner as a permitted variety is still under discussion.) Chaptalization is permitted. Pinot Noir must be aged in casks for at least twelve months, and then in bottle for a further twelve. Wines must be approved by a tasting panel before they have the right to be labelled as Grosses Gewächs. At the time of writing the participating wineries are Heyl zu Herrnsheim, Kühling-Gillot, St Antony, Villa Sachsen, Keller, and Wittmann. Gunderloch participated initially, but has withdrawn, as explained in chapter 2, much to the regret of the other producers.

The situation is further confused by the prior existence since 1992 of Rheinhessen Selektion, although with an annual production of around 2,000 cases, it is not commercially significant. This required a maximum yield of 55 hl/ha from older vines of classic varieties. In one respect the criteria were stricter than for Grosses Gewächs, in that chaptalization was not permitted. A few growers still produce Selektion, because they have the right to do so, although the German Wine Institute introduced in 2001 its own nationwide Selection criteria.

Vineyards

The region is divided into three Bereiche, twenty-four Grosslagen and 434 individual sites.

Bereich Wonnegau. Grosslagen from south to north: Domblick, Liebfrauenmorgen (Worms), Burg Rodenstein, Sybillenstein, Bergkloster, Pilgerpfad, Gotteshilfe.

Bereich Nierstein. Grosslagen from south to north: Petersberg, Rheinblick, Krötenbrunnen, Vogelsgärten (around Guntersblum), Güldenmorgen, Spiegelberg, Auflangen, Gutes Domtal (Nierstein hinterland), Rehbach (around Nackenheim), Domherr, Sankt Alban (near Mainz).

Bereich Bingen. Grosslagen from south to north: Adelberg, Rheingrafenstein, Kurfürstenstück, Abtey, Sankt Rochuskapelle (around Bingen), Kaiserpfalz (around Ingelheim).

Grosses Gewächs vineyards:
Bingen: Scharlachberg.
Bodenheim: Burgweg.
Dalsheim: Bürgel, Hubacker.
Nackenheim: Rothenberg.
Nierstein: Pettenthal, Brudersberg, Ölberg.
Oppenheim: Kreuz, Sackträger
Westhofen: Aulerde, Kirchspiel, Morstein.

ALSHEIM

Twelve kilometres (7.5 miles) south of Oppenheim.

Alsheimer Fischerpfad. 35 ha (86.5 acres). Well known site that gives full-flavoured Riesling and Grauer Burgunder.

ALZEY

"The district is cold and windy and therefore unfavourable for the production of quality wines."[2]

Alzeyer Kapellenberg. 47 ha (116 acres). A vineyard with, unusually, slate soils.

BINGEN

The town lies just south of Rüdesheim in the Rheingau, divided, of course, by the river, while to the immediate west, its neighbour is the Nahe region. The soils are varied, ranging from clay-slate to Devonian quartz.

Binger Rosengarten. 47 ha (116 acres). A good deal of Pinot Noir is planted here.

Binger Scharlachberg. 27 ha (66.7 acres). The top site of Bingen, and the only one well suited to Riesling. Its steep south-facing slope has slatey soil with high iron content. The historic heart of the vineyard overlooked the Rive Nahe and faced southwest, but part of this section was grubbed up in the 1980s and has not been replanted. The slopes bear the brunt of winds blowing off the Hunsrück mountains, so in wet weather the grapes dry out quickly and are less prone to rot. These winds can also cause a loss of acidity, so the wines do not share the acidic structure of those from Rüdesheim. Villa Sachsen is the major owner with 12 ha (29.7 acres). Kruger-Rumpf from the Nahe has acquired 1 ha (2.5 acres), and believes the soil has more in common with the Nahe than with Rheinhessen. Because there is plenty of flatter land in the Rheinhessen that is easier to cultivate, the Scharlachberg has been somewhat neglected by its growers and some argue that its potential has yet to be realized.

[2] Hallgarten, p. 65.

BODENHEIM
About 500 ha (1,236 acres). North of Nackenheim and just south of Mainz. This has heavy soils that give full-bodied wines.

Bodenheimer Burgweg. A vineyard that dates back to 1364. Faces east and southeast, with sandy loam soils that warm up fast. Kühling-Gillot produces a Grosses Gewächs from Pinot Noir here.

Bodenheimer Mönchspfad. Kühling-Gillot are among the owners here.

DALSHEIM
In the deep south, west of Worms.

Dalsheimer Bürgel. 30 ha (74.1 acres). Limestone soil. Keller believes that only one-third of the site is of good quality, and designates 2 ha (4.9 acres) for Grosses Gewächs. A lot of Pinot Noir planted here.

Dalsheimer Hubacker. 28 ha (69 acres). Clay with some limestone. Keller has 4 ha (9.9 acres) in the best sector, which is a Grosses Gewächs.

Dalsheimer Steig. 155 ha (383 acres). Largely planted with new crossings.

DIENHEIM
550 ha (1,359 acres). Just south of Oppenheim.

GUNDERSHEIM
A village just west of Westhofen.

Gundersheimer Höllenbrand. Planted mostly with Gewürztraminer and red vines. Refreshed by winds that keep the grapes healthy.

GUNTERSBLUM
Village just south of Oppenheim. Best known sites are Eiserne Hand, Kreuzkapelle, 89 ha (220 acres), Steig, 75 ha (185 acres), and Vögelsgärtchen.

INGELHEIM
Traditionally, a red wine village between Bingen and Mainz. The soils are light and sandy, and the red wines and rosés tend to be light and fresh. The best vineyards are Burgberg, Pares, Rheinhöhe, Schloss Westerhaus, and Sonnenhang.

MONSHEIM

A southern village west of Worms.

Monsheimer Silberberg. Clay-loam soil with gravel subsoil. Planted with Riesling, Rieslaner, and Kerner.

NACKENHEIM

About 150 ha (371 acres). Village on the Rheinfront to the north of Nierstein. Known for its red soils.

Nackenheimer Engelsberg. 60 ha (148 acres). Lies behind Rothenberg and thus further away from the river. The slopes have similar soils to Rothenberg but give lighter wines. Up on the plateau the soil is heavier and better suited to Silvaner.

Nackenheimer Rothenberg. 20 ha (49.4 acres). Very steep, with more slate and a thinner soil than most sites in Nierstein. The best site in Nackenheim, with Gunderloch, 6.5 ha (16 acres), the principal owner.

NIERSTEIN

The most famous village in Rheinhessen, backed by the tremendous vineyards on the "Rote Hang" band high above the Rhein. There are twenty-two individual sites.

Niersteiner Brudersberg. 1.3 ha (3.2 acres). *Alleinbesitz* of Heyl zu Herrnsheim. South-facing, very steep, and close to the river. Replanted in early 1980s and one hundred per cent Riesling.

Niersteiner Glöck. 2 ha (4.9 acres). Documented since 742.

Niersteiner Heiligenbaum. Loam soil, giving light wines for early drinking.

Niersteiner Hipping. 31 ha (76.6 acres). A sheltered site. Rieslings here can have a fairly exotic character. Heyl zu Herrnsheim has some Pinot Blanc here. Other owners include St Antony, 1.7 ha (4.2 acres), Schneider, Strub, Balbach, and Seebrich.

Niersteiner Kranzberg. 16 ha (39.5 acres). Not much red soil, and mostly loess, with a limestone subsoil.

Niersteiner Ölberg. 60 ha (148 acres). Just north of the village and facing due south. A steep site planted with Riesling, Silvaner, and, lower down, Pinot Blanc. Red slate is found only on the slopes. *Flurbereinigung* in the early 1990s means that most of the vines are young, though Heyl managed to retain a fifty year parcel. The soils are relatively deep and the wines tend to be powerful and long-lived. Other owners include St Antony, 3.4 ha (8.4 acres), Schneider, Guntrum, Strub, Seebrich, and Heinrich Braun.

Niersteiner Orbel. 19 ha (47 acres). Often gives wines that are racier and more citric than wines from closer to the river. St Antony a major owner with 3.2 ha (7.9 acres), replanted in 1992.

Niersteiner Paterberg. 148 ha (366 acres). South of the village bordering Oppenheim. No red soil. Gunderloch have some fifty year old Pinot Gris here.

Niersteiner Pettenthal. 32 ha (79 acres). Borders Nackenheim and faces east onto the river at a height of 90–170 metres (295–558 feet). One hundred per cent Riesling. The site now includes fertile land between the railway line and river that should have been excluded. More opulent Rieslings than those, say, from Brudersberg. Major owners are Heyl zu Herrnsheim, 3.5 ha (8.6 acres), Balbach, St Antony, 1.6 ha (4 acres), Braun, Guntrum, and Schneider.

OPPENHEIM

Village just south of Nierstein. Much loess and marl, and the Rieslings have less finesse than those from the Rote Hang. Eleven single vineyards.

Oppenheimer Herrenberg. 29 ha (71.7 acres). Planted principally with Riesling and Silvaner.

Oppenheimer Kreuz. 5 ha (12.4 acres). Loess soil with some limestone. Faces southeast, and has good ventilation. A Grosses Gewächs for Kühling-Gillot.

Oppenheimer Sackträger. 22 ha (54.4 acres). The best-known site here, with loam and clay soils. Owners include Koch, Kühling-Gillot, and Guntrum.

Oppenheimer Schützenhütte. *Alleinbesitz* of Guntrum. Loess and sandy loam.

WESTHOFEN

700 ha (1,730 acres). Fairly deep soils. Limestone and clay-loam. Seven individual vineyards.

Westhofener Aulerde. Faces south and southeast. Heavy clay-loam and some loess with very little limestone.

Westhofener Bergkloster. Best known for Pinot Noir and Silvaner.

Westhofener Kirchspiel. A sheltered amphitheatre of vines faces east and southeast. Clay-loam with some limestone.

Westhofener Morstein. Faces south and southeast. Limestone subsoil, with clay-loam above. Gives quite mineral wines, and Wittmann considers this its best Grosses Gewächs.

WORMS

Cathedral city on the Rhein with seventeen vineyards.

Wormser Liebfrauenstift. The original source of Liebfraumilch. Once a highly regarded site, though its wine has an earthy taste that has few admirers today.

Producers

ANTON BALBACH

See Gunderloch. 18 ha (44.5 acres). 9,000 cases.

Established in 1654, this venerable estate has vineyards in some of Nierstein's best sites. But in the early 1990s it ran into difficulties and in 1996 was leased by Gunderloch, who immediately set about reducing the yields, which previously had been as high as 120 hl/ha. Some of the vineyards have been absorbed into the Gunderloch estate, at least in terms of production, and Fritz Hasselbach has tried to give a completely different identity to the wines he bottles under the Balbach label. These are now jazzily labelled cuvées intended to appeal to a younger generation of wine drinkers who are unconcerned about vineyard sites and grape varieties.

Floréal is a blend of Pinot Blanc and Pinot Gris, a cleanly made, frankly commercial wine. Silvana Nova is a juicy, straightforward Silvaner intended for rapid consumption while its fruit is fresh. Curiously, there was also a 1999 Ölberg Riesling Eiswein in a broad appley style.

BRÜDER DR BECKER

Mainzer Str 3–7, 55278 Ludwigshöhe. Tel: +49 (0) 6249 8430. Fax: 7639. www.brueder-dr-becker.de. 11 ha (27.2 acres). 6,000 cases.

Established early in the twentieth century by two brothers, as the name suggests. The property is now run by Lotte Pfeffer and Hans Müller. For almost twenty years the estate has been farmed organically. The most important varieties are Riesling, Silvaner, and Scheurebe, as well as Burgundian varieties. The best wines, from various sites in Dienheim, notably Tafelstein, are aged in oak casks and show a fresh, crisp, invigorating character. Even the basic Silvaner is aromatic and lively. One curiosity here is the barrique-aged Riesling Auslese.

HEINRICH BRAUN
Glockengasse 5–9, 55283 Nierstein. Tel: +49 (0) 6133 5139. Fax: 59877. 25 ha (61.8 acres). 16,000 cases.

Peter Braun has vineyards in some top sites in Nierstein, two-thirds of them planted with Riesling. Vinification is very traditional, with a heavy reliance on wooden casks. He has never been a fan of Halbtrocken styles, so the wines tend to be either fully dry or nobly sweet. The Grosses Gewächs Rieslings from Hipping and Pettenthal, especially the latter, tend to be full-bodied, gutsy wines, yet not without a certain elegance. His BAs can be extremely rich, oozing with tropical fruit flavours.

GUNDERLOCH
Carl-Gunderloch Platz 1, 55299 Nackenheim. Tel: +49 (0) 6135 2341. Fax: 2431. www.gunderloch.de. 13 ha (32.1 acres). 7,000 cases.

This fine estate, the best in Nackenheim and one of the best in all Rheinhessen, was inherited by Agnes Gunderloch, who married winemaker Fritz Hasselbach. Half their vines lie within the Nackenheimer Rothenberg, a classic Rote Hang vineyard.

As long ago as 1989, the Hasselbachs instituted a kind of classification system. The basic wine was a Gunderloch Riesling or Silvaner, followed by a Nackenheim Riesling (in various styles), and topped by the wines from Rothenberg, either a Spätlese Trocken or a nobly sweet style. In addition there is a wine called Jean-Baptiste, which is technically a Rothenberg Kabinett Halbtrocken, though the Hasselbachs could see that those words would go down like a lead balloon on restaurant wine lists and in the export markets they were developing.

Yields here have always been punishingly low, and in the mid-1990s they averaged between 32 and 40 hl/ha. Hasselbach doesn't use cultivated yeasts and is opposed to deacidification, though with yields as low as this, lack of ripeness is unlikely to be a problem. Although the wines are fermented in steel tanks, they are aged on the fine lees in casks until April, and sometimes the wines are only bottled in the summer. About eighty per cent of the wines are dry.

The best wine here is usually the dry Rothenberg, which is powerful and boldly flavoured – not a wine of great finesse, but one with real character and pungency. The sweet Rothenberg wines can be excellent too: the racy, spicy Auslesen, and in top years the creamy, peachy BA and TBA, such as the outstanding 1999. TBA and 2000 BA.

LOUIS GUNTRUM

Rheinallee 62, 55283 Nierstein. Tel: +49 (0) 6133 97170. Fax: 971717.
www.guntrum.com. 25 ha (61.8 acres). 25,000 cases.

Despite a wealth of modern vinification equipment, and good vineyards on the Rheinfront, Guntrum's wines usually fail to excite. The Rivaner is earthy, and the Rieslings, which account for sixty per cent of production, sappy.

GERHARD GUTZLER

Rossgasse 19, 67599 Gundheim. Tel: +49 (0) 6244 905221. Fax: 905241.
www.gutzler.de. 10 ha (24.7 acres). 5,000 cases.

Gutzler's vineyards are dispersed among various villages of the Wonnegau: Westhofen, Alsheim, Gundheim, and even Worms, where he owns a parcel in the Liebfrauenstift. Most whites are vinified in stainless steel, but some richer whites, picked at more than 100 Oechsle, are barrel-fermented. Red wines are either aged in large casks or in medium-toast barriques.

The simpler whites are somewhat neutral, but the top whites can be exciting wines. Even the Riesling from the Liebfrauenstift, a Spätlese Trocken, is robust and full-bodied. The Chardonnay is straightforward, but there is an appealing barrel-fermented Auxerrois, which may lack elegance but has ample power and richness.

The reds are a mixed bunch. Precisely why Gutzler ages one of his Dornfelder wines for three years in barriques is a mystery. He says he does it to give the wine more tannin, but what is the point? The outcome is a rather bitter wine. The Spätburgunder, which is cropped at around 40 hl/ha (16.2 hl/acre) and punched down during fermentation, is far better, though too extracted for my taste. Gutzler admits that Cabernet Sauvignon doesn't always ripen properly here, and even in a good year such as 1997, this was an austere, charmless wine. Far better is the Cuvée R98, a blend of Cabernet, Pinot Noir, and Dornfelder, which has some elegance.

HEYL ZU HERRNSHEIM

Langgasse 3, 55283 Nierstein. Tel: +49 (0) 6133 57080. Fax: 570880.
www.heyl-zu-herrnsheim.de. 35 ha (86.5 acres). 16,000 cases.

In 1969 Peter von Weymarn, a former physicist, inherited this estate and astonished the estate team by introducing a range of dry wines. He also converted the estate to organic viticulture. Von Weymarn sold the property in 1994 to the Ahr family, and the estate is now directed by Markus Ahr, who has continued in the path that Von Weymarn forged. Heyl has excellent sites in Nierstein that are the basis of its renown.

Von Weymarn, and Markus Ahr subsequently, simplified the commercial structure. Today, the range consists of simple Estate bottlings, a *Rotschiefer* (Red Slate) range of Silvaner, Weisser Burgunder, and Riesling, and then Grosses Gewächs from Brudersberg (*Alleinbesitz*) and Pettenthal. They also consider Ölberg a top site, but the vines are too young at present to justify a Grosses Gewächs designation. Yields are low: around 55 hl/ha in 2000, and 30–40 hl/ha in top sites.

The winemaker Bernd Kutschick has retained wooden casks for vinification, and uses cultivated yeasts to ensure the long slow fermentation that he seeks. The wines can spend ten to twelve months in cask before being bottled. Sweet wines finish their ageing in steel tanks.

The Rotschiefer range of wines have the characteristic earthiness derived from these soils. The Weisser Burgunder is particularly good, rich and full-flavoured, and the Riesling has the sweet and sour tone that I find very characteristic of these vineyards. The two Grosses Gewächs are magnificent: very ripe aromas, even honeysuckle in 1999 from Pettenthal, and tremendous power and persistence on the palate. Of the two growths, Pettenthal is the more voluptuous, Brudersberg the tighter and more overtly mineral, and consequently slower than Pettenthal to strut its stuff. I am less impressed by Heyl's regular Spätlesen and Auslesen, although nobly sweet wines, such as the delicious and exotic 1999

Pettenthal BA and the impeccable and highly intense 2000 Brudersberg TBA, are superb.

KELLER

Bahnhofstr 1, 57692 Flörsheim-Dalsheim. Tel: +49 (0) 6243 456. Fax: 6686. 12 ha (29.7 acres). 8,000 cases.

The rise of the Keller estate to its present position as one of the top wine producers in Germany would have been hard to predict. After all, Flörsheim-Dalsheim is not one of Rheinhessen's top villages. The Kellers would admit that not all their vineyards are capable of producing exceptional wines, but they have made the effort over the years to identify the parcels that do indeed have the potential to rise to great heights.

The Kellers have been here since 1789, when they emigrated from Switzerland. Klaus Keller is the present owner, and in 2000 he turned over the running of the estate to his son Klaus-Peter, then in his late twenties. It remains a family business, with four generations of Kellers involved in one way or another. It was in the early 1990s that Klaus Keller began to reduce yields and focus on quality above all.

They have two top sites: Dalsheimer Hubacker and Dalsheimer Bürgel. Riesling is planted on the former, Pinot Noir on the latter. Klaus-Peter's mother came from the Saar, and so does some of the plant material in Hubacker, which he thinks might account for the wines' unusual raciness. He prunes severely, and leaf removal and bunch thinning ensure that yields rarely exceed 40 hl/ha. There is also a little Weisser Burgunder and Grauer Burgunder, and about 1 ha (2.5 acres) of Rieslaner, which the Kellers adore. The white wines are vinified in steel with natural yeasts, and the Kellers don't mind if the grapes receive some skin contact before fermentation, so long as they are healthy.

I took a walk through Bürgel in September 2001, after days of steady rain. The Kellers have planted new Pinot clones here, and they looked in impeccable condition despite the soggy weather. These are clones selected for their small berries and thus low yields. The grapes for their basic Pinot Noir are cropped at around 60 hl/ha, those for the top wine at 30–40 hl/ha. Their top Pinot is called "Felix," their top dry Riesling, "Max."

As well as the estate Riesling, there is a bottling called Von der Fels from grapes grown on limestone soils: in 2000 the wine was a touch earthy and lacked a little zest. The dry 2000 wines from Hubacker are brilliant. The "Max" was picked very late at ludicrously low yields of 11 hl/ha (4.5 hl/acre) and it attained more than thirteen degrees of alcohol. Despite this ripeness level, the aromas of the wine are intensely citric, but the palate is completely different: far more exotic and explosive and sumptuous. The "regular" Hubacker Spätlese Trocken is excellent too, quite phenolic in character and both mineral and elegant. The Halbtrocken and sweeter wines are good but less exciting, though 1999 yielded some delicious Riesling Auslesen. The Rieslaner 1999 Auslese and 2000 TBA are fabulous, with aromas of pineapple and woodsmoke and amazing complexity and length.

KLAUS KNOBLOCH

Saurechgässchen 7, 55234 Ober-Flörsheim. Tel: +49 (0) 6735 344. Fax: 8244.
www.weingut-klausknobloch.de. 30 ha (74.1 acres). 30,000 cases.

This old family estate has been organically cultivated since 1988. A wide range of wines is produced, including reds from Pinot Noir, Dornfelder, Portugieser, St Laurent, Regent, and Lemberger. The barrique-aged 1999 Lemberger has an appealing spiciness to it. The best white from 2000 I have tasted is the Weisser Burgunder, with its rich fruit and white pepper zestiness.

KÜHLING-GILLOT

Ölmühlstr 25, 55294 Bodenheim. Tel: +49 (0) 6135 2333. Fax: 6463.
www.kuehling.gillot.com. 9 ha (22.2 acres). 6,000 cases.

In 1970 two families were joined in marriage and the first offspring was this wine estate, although both families had been involved in wine production for two centuries. Riesling is the dominant variety but there are also many others, notably the Burgundian varieties. Roland Gillot is not averse to a hard sell, and has come up with many marketing initiatives over the years, such as the "Rhapsody in Blue" and "Matinée Selection", which sounded more like a box of chocolates than a range of dry and off-dry wines.

The vineyards are in Bodenheim, Nackenheim, and Oppenheim. The soils are quite rich and heavy, and so are the wines. This suits the Silvaner and Chardonnay better than some of the Rieslings, which can be broad and lacking in verve. The style often comes into its own with the very sweet wines, and the estate has released some fine TBA in the past. The Grosses Gewächs sites here are Oppenheimer Kreutz and Bodenheimer Burgweg (both for Pinot Noir), and Oppenheimer Sackträger and Nackenheimer Rothenberg for Riesling.

MICHEL-PFANNEBECKER
Langgasse 18, 55234 Flomborn. Tel: +49 (0) 6735 355. Fax: 8365. www.micel-pfannebecker.de. 11 ha (27.2 acres). 6,000 cases.

The hospitable Pfannebecker brothers, Heinfried and Gerold, only started bottling their wines in the 1970s. The structure of the estate was typical of that time, and there were many crossings planted that are now being replaced by better quality varieties. Chardonnay was planted here in 1992, and even Cabernet Sauvignon.

The vines are mostly planted on loess-loam soils at relatively high elevations, up to 200 metres (656 feet), which means they are well ventilated and less prone to rot than many other vineyards in the area. All white wines are fermented in stainless steel, and only the Chardonnay and some of the Silvaner are aged in small oak barrels. As for Pinot Noir, they are switching to French clones that will give better concentration than their German ones; the wines are fermented in tanks that press down the cap mechanically.

The Rieslings are sound, with some elegance and length, but the Silvaners are better, especially those with the quality designation Rheinhessen Selektion. However, the Silvaner aged in American oak is oily and dull. The Weisser Burgunder is less complex and zesty than the Grauer Burgunder and the Chardonnay. The 1999 Scheurebe Eiswein is rather too fruity for my taste, with a piercing aroma that is likely to find admirers only among Scheurebe fans. Most of the Spätburgunders, alas, lack fruit, although the 1999 Gundersheimer Höllenbrand Selektion has better concentration with more elegance and length.

SANKT ANTONY
Wörrstädter Str 22, 55283 Nierstein. Tel: +49 (0) 6133 5482. Fax: 59139. www.st-antony.com. 23 ha (56.8 acres). 15,000 cases.

This estate is owned by the MAN company, which manufactures trucks and industrial machinery, and for some years the director has been Dr Alex Michalsky. In 2001 he hired a young winemaker called Naoki

Nakatani. The property was founded in the 1920s and expanded over the years, and it was renamed in 1985. Two-thirds of the vineyards are planted with Riesling, and St Antony has an excellent portfolio of Roter Hang sites: Pettenthal, Hipping, Ölberg, and Orbel. These are steep and low-yielding. The wines are fermented slowly in stainless steel and then aged in casks. All the wines are dry, with the exception of nobly sweet bottlings.

Although I have tasted older vintages such as 1993 from this estate with considerable pleasure, I found the 2000 Rieslings disappointing. Admittedly, this was a very difficult vintage, but other reputable estates in the region managed to produce clean vigorous wines. Here the overall character is tight and austere, with some odd briny aromas; the Pettenthal is the best of the range. Perhaps they need more time to open up and develop complexity.

SCHALES
Alzeyer Str 160, 67592 Flörsheim-Dalsheim. Tel: +49 (0) 6243 7003.
Fax: 5230. www.schales.de. 52 ha (128 acres). 40,000 cases.

This large estate has seventeen grape varieties in its vineyards, and makes numerous wines from all of them. Unlike its neighbour Keller, Schales sees little point trying to validate vineyard sites, which do not appear on the labels. Anything goes at Schales, and the estate claims to be the first property to have made a sparkling Eiswein, which does seem rather a waste. I have not tasted it, but I have tasted the Grauer Burgunder, which is a speciality of the house, Weisser Burgunder, Müller-Thurgau Classic, Silvaner Classic, and some Chardonnays; among red wines, there's Portugieser and Spätburgunder. Indeed, red wines are a growing segment here. Sweet wines tend to be made from grape varieties such as Huxelrebe and Siegerrebe.

The wines are never great but they are usually enjoyable and highly drinkable. Schales is not ashamed to be a commercial winery, but one with flair, as is evident from its modern packaging and labels, and from its zesty self-promotion.

GEORG ALBRECHT SCHNEIDER
Wilhemstr 6, 55283 Nierstein. Tel: +49 (0) 6133 5655. Fax: 5415. 16 ha (39.5 acres). 7,500 cases.

Albrecht Schneider took over the family estate at the age of eighteen, and it has developed into one of the most reliable sources of elegant Nierstein Rieslings, in dry, half-dry, and lightly sweet styles. He is, of course, assisted by the fact he owns parcels in some of the village's top sites.

VILLA SACHSEN

Mainzer Str 184, 55411 Bingen. Tel: +49 (0) 6721 990575. Fax: 17386. www.villa-sachsen.com. 20 ha (49.4 acres). 10,000 cases.

This handsome villa was built in 1843, but it often changed hands. It won its present name after a businessman from Leipzig bought the property in 1899 and began producing wine here. In the 1990s the vineyards were sold to a consortium that include Prinz Salm and the Schregel family; the consortium leases but does not own the villa itself. Most of the wines are dry, and all wines are vinified in stainless steel. The top Rieslings come from the Scharlachberg, much of which is owned by the estate. At the basic, more commercial level the wines are simple, cleanly made, and attractive. Easily the best wines are the Grosses Gewächs from the Scharlachberg. There are also nobly sweet wines from this site, but they can be a touch broad.

WITTMANN

Mainzer Str 19, 67593 Westhofen. Tel: +49 (0) 6244 905036. Fax: 5578. www.wittmannweingut.com. 20 ha (49.4 acres). 12,000 cases.

As soon as you walk into the Wittmann winery it is plain that the family are avid collectors of modern art, some of which creeps on to their labels. It is also a wine estate in the vanguard. It has been organic since 1990, and although the wines have been very good under Günter Wittmann, they are set to improve even further now that son Philipp has taken over running the cellar. He has reduced yields further to scarcely economic levels of 20–30 hl/ha. The range has been simplified: estate wines, village wines, and Grosses Gewächs. The outstanding bottlings in any vintage are designated "S", which stands for Selektion.

The winemaking is far from high-tech, although the winery is well equipped. Philipp Wittmann uses indigenous yeasts and has acquired more wooden casks, for Burgundian varieties. The single-variety range is clean and fresh, if a touch too tart in the difficult year of 2000. The best of these wines are the "S" from Weissburgunder and Chardonnay. The Rieslings are from three single vineyards, of which I prefer Kirchspiel and Morstein. These are outstanding wines, whether as dry Grosses Gewächs or as concentrated, yet delicate, nobly sweet wines.

13

Hessische Bergstrasse

There isn't much to the Hessische Bergstrasse, a thirty-kilometre (18.6-mile) string of vineyards in a valley just south of Darmstadt. It lies just east of the southern Rheinhessen. Most of the vineyards are around Bensheim and Heppenheim. An additional 50 ha (124 acres) are located just east of Darmstadt in a subregion known as Gross-Umstadt. The Bergstrasse is warmer than the Rheingau and the vines flower earlier. Indeed, its climate resembles that of part of the Pfalz. The nearby Odenwald hills provide shelter from rainfall. The soils are very varied, with yellow sandstone, loess-loam, and sandy loam, and near Bensheim some weathered granite. The 450 ha (1,112 acres) of vineyards face west, southwest, and south. About one-third of these vineyards are on steep slopes. Many of them used to be terraced, but various phases of reorganization led to a change in planting patterns, and most vines are now planted vertically.

Cooperatives are very powerful here, controlling around ninety per cent of the vineyards. Fifty-four per cent of them are planted with Riesling, and there is also a fair amount of Müller-Thurgau (eleven per cent), Pinot Gris (seven per cent), and Silvaner (six per cent). Red wine only accounts for around eight per cent of production. It's not easy to get Pinot Noir to ripen here, unless it is planted in outstanding sites with loess soils.

Most of the consumption is local, because there are large towns nearby, and the region is often visited by weekenders and day-trippers who stock up with wines. The Staatsweingut sells one-third of its production directly to visitors. I doubt that any of the wines are exported.

The best wines here are Rieslings, and they are milder versions of those from the Rheingau, with less firm acidity and less longevity. The

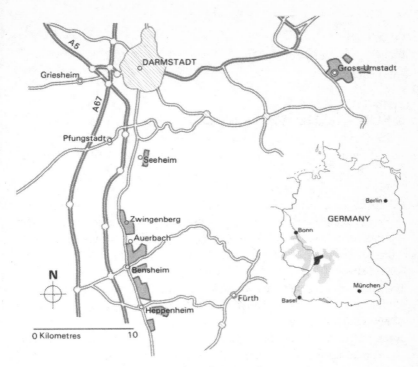

Hessische Bergstrasse

best recent vintages have been 2001, 1999, 1993, and 1990. The 1999s
had rather low acidity, so they are not for long keeping; but they had an
immediate charm and drinkability. The 2000s are patchy, because there
was some rot, and everything depended on the care taken in the vineyard
to reduce yields and remove rotten berries. There are also some good
wines from 1998.

Vineyards

There are two Bereiche.

Bereich Starkenburg. Grosslagen are Schlossberg (Heppenheim),
Wolfsmagen (Bensheim), and Rott (Bensheim).

Bereich Umstadt. No Grosslage, but six Einzellagen.

AUERBACH
Immediately north of Bensheim. There are two vineyards here: Höllberg and Fürstenlager.

BENSHEIM
Bensheimer Hemsberg. Mostly Riesling, Müller-Thurgau, and Silvaner.

Bensheimer Kalkgasse. The Staatsweingut owns 6 ha (14.8 acres). This was the only site to undergo *Flurbereinigung* in the 1970s. The wines, mostly Riesling, tend to have assertive acidity.

Bensheimer Kirchberg. 9 ha (22.2 acres). In effect the *Alleinbesitz* of Stadt Bensheim. Mostly Riesling.

Bensheimer Streichling. Loess-loam. The Staatsweingut has only Riesling here. Stadt Bensheim also thinks it excellent for Riesling.

GROSS-UMSTADT
There are two vineyards here: Steingerück and Herrnberg.

HEPPENHEIM
Loess and yellow sandstone soils.

Heppenheimer Centgericht. 17 ha (42 acres). *Alleinbesitz* of the Staatsweingut. Loess-loam. Gives rounder, more harmonious wine.

Heppenheimer Eckweg. Loam and loess-loam.

Heppenheimer Guldenzoll. Sandy loam.

Heppenheimer Maiberg.

Heppenheimer Steinkopf. 16 ha (39.5 acres). Weathered sandstone. 3.5 ha (8.6 acres) of the steepest south-facing part belongs to the Staatsweingut.

Heppenheimer Stemmler. Loess.

KLEIN-UMSTADT
Only one vineyard in this village: Stachelberg.

SCHÖNBERG
Only one vineyard in this village: Herrenwingert, 11 ha (27.2 acres). Sand and sandy loam. *Alleinbesitz* of Staatsweingut.

SEEHEIM

Only one vineyard here: Mundklingen, 20 ha (49.4 acres), but not all planted.

ZWINGENBERG

There are two vineyards in this village: Alte Burg, 8 ha (19.8 acres) and Steingeröll, 22 ha (54.4 acres).

Producers

WEINGUT DER STADT BENSHEIM

Darmstädter Str 6, 64625 Bensheim. Tel: +49 (0) 6251 580017. Fax: 64970. www.bensheim.de. 13 ha (32.1 acres). 8,000 cases.

Since 1987 Axel Seiberth has run this winery with a firm hand. In the sixteenth century the townspeople of Bensheim were permitted to pay their taxes in the form of grapes if they wished, and this is how the town winery came into existence. Riesling dominates, of course, but the winery also produces Grauer Burgunder in unoaked and oaked versions, and is one of the few estates with plantings of Rotberger.

All white wines are fermented in small steel tanks, and although the winery is equipped with a centrifuge, it is rarely employed. No *Süssreserve* is used. Seiberth likes to bottle relatively early but is in no hurry with Riesling. I have tasted a large number of Rieslings from 1997 to 1999, and find that they are severely marred by a softness on the palate and a lack of length. The fruit is pleasant enough, but this is not my idea of Riesling. For what appear to be purely commercial reasons, Seiberth introduced systematic malolactic fermentation for Riesling in 1995, because his clientele seemed to prefer a rounder style of wine. To give the wine some attack, they retain a good deal of carbon dioxide, but once that initial attack is over, there is little to sustain the wine on the palate. The sweet wines, such as 1997 BA and 1999 Eiswein, both from the Kirchberg, are good but not outstanding, with pronounced appley flavours.

The house rarity is the Rotberger, vinified as rosé; it's flowery but slightly sweet. The Kalkgasse Grauer Burgunder Trocken is reasonably fresh and fruity, but has no complexity.

Spätburgunder is aged in older barriques for twelve months, and in order to ripen here it must be cropped at no more than 30 hl/ha. The

1999 barrique-aged wine from Kalkgasse, aged in older barrels, is reasonably concentrated and not overoaked. It's far preferable to the rather jammy, coarse Dornfelder.

BERGSTRÄSSER WINZER

Darmstädter Str 56, 64646 Heppenheim. Tel: +49 (0) 6252 799411.
Fax: 799450. 263 ha (650 acres). 150,000 cases.
This cooperative has 500 members, with half the vineyards planted with Riesling, as well as Müller-Thurgau, Grauer Burgunder, Silvaner, and Spätburgunder. It vinifies more than half the production of the entire region. I have tasted very few of the wines, and only at the simplest level. The Rieslings seem well made and straightforward.

SIMON-BÜRKLE

Wiesenpromenade 13, 64673 Zwingenberg. Tel: +49 (0) 6251 76446.
Fax: 788641. 12 ha (29.7 acres). 7,000 cases.
In 1991 two young graduates of Weinsberg wine college, Kurt Simon and Wilfried Bürkle, established this estate. Based in the northern part of the region, it has a steadily growing reputation, both for Rieslings and for red wines such as St Laurent.

STAATSWEINGUT BERGSTRASSE

Grieselstr 34 36, 64625 Bensheim. Tel: +49 (0) 6251 3107. Fax: 65706. 38 ha (94 acres). 12,000 cases.
Until 2001 the director of this well-regarded winery, which was founded in 1904, was Heinrich Hillenbrand, the last of three generations from the same family to run the property. His successor is the former cellarmaster, Volker Hörr. Sixty-five per cent of the vineyards are planted with Riesling. Yields are commendably low, averaging 57 hl/ha in recent years, thanks to scrupulous green harvesting.

The Rieslings here are excellent at all levels: racy, stony, and beautifully balanced between a touch of sweetness (except for Trocken wines, of course) and vigorous acidity. The 2000 Bensheimer Kalkgasse Spätlese Trocken is particularly impressive, and shows the potential of this region. The winery is renowned for its Eiswein, which is higher priced than its TBA. Herr Hörr explains that this is because the auction system has pushed up the prices for their Eiswein.

The Grauer Burgunder from the Centgericht is successful too, in a complex dry style, and there are some succulent peachy Auslesen.

Spätburgunder is vinified in open-top fermenters. It can be rather hard and earthy. Pinot Noir is also used to produce Weissherbst Eiswein, delivering a rich honeyed creamy wine that perhaps lacks a little Eiswein typicity.

The Rieslings alone confirm this winery's position as the top producer of the Bergstrasse.

VIA MONTANA

Darmstädter Str 6, 64625 Bensheim. Tel: +49 (0) 6251 580017. Fax: 64970. (Brand name). 2,000 cases.

This is a cooperative venture between four producers (Diehl, Rothweiler, Simon-Bürkle, and Stadt Bensheim) to help make the region better known by producing larger volume cuvées. The first vintage was 2000 and the concept was the brainchild of Axel Seiberth. The wines are blends (red, white, rosé) that are unashamedly commercial in style, their modern packaging aimed at younger wine drinkers.

14

Pfalz

This immense region, often known in English as the Palatinate, is a southern continuation of the Rheinhessen. The Unterhaardt is the northern section, from just southwest of Worms to Bad Dürkheim. Between Bad Dürkheim and Neustadt is the Mittelhaardt, while south of Neustadt is the largest of all the sub-regions, the Oberhaardt, which descends almost as far south as Karlsruhe and the French border. In all this is a distance, from north to south, of more than 80.5 kilometres (fifty miles), through which threads the *Deutsche Weinstrasse*, allowing visitors to combine tourism with visits to wine estates.

Until about fifteen years ago there was little reason to concern oneself with any of the Pfalz other than the Mittelhaardt, where the most renowned vineyards are located. The rest of the region was dedicated to mass-production wines of little distinction, though inevitably there were a few quality-conscious estates that worked hard to show that the less prestigious areas were also capable of producing good wines. In 1951 Fritz Hallgarten was able to conclude of the Oberhaardt: "Nowhere are such record harvests garnered as here."[1] Today this has all changed, and the southerly region, also known as the Südliche Weinstrasse, is heaving with changes, almost all for the better. If the Mittelhaardt remains the homeland of Pfalzer Riesling, in the southern areas the benign climate makes it possible to grow other varieties, notably the Pinot family, with considerable success. There have even been some (usually misguided) attempts to grow Cabernet Sauvignon here.

The Pfalz enjoys a balmy climate, protected from cold winds and rain by the eastern slopes of the Haardt Mountains. Indeed, the Mittelhaardt

[1] Hallgarten, *Rhineland Wineland*, p. 58.

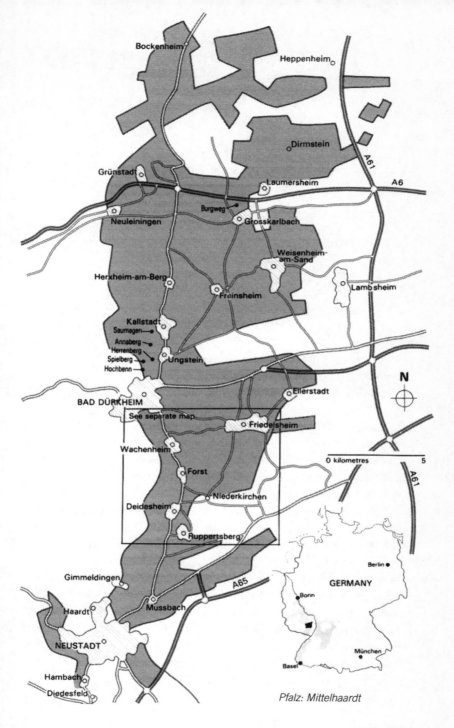

Pfalz: Mittelhaardt

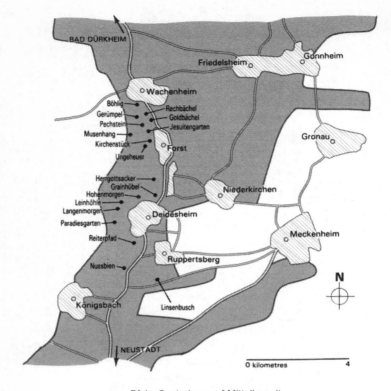

Pfalz: Central area of Mittelhaardt

is one of the driest areas within the whole of Germany. It is hardly surprising, given the size of the Pfalz, that soils are extremely varied, ranging from limestone to loess to basalt, not to mention sand, sandstone, loam, and gravel. Riesling is by no means the major player that it is in the Mosel or Rheingau, and accounts for just more than twenty per cent of plantings. Müller-Thurgau is almost as popular with growers. Red varieties are far more common than further north. In 1979 about ten per cent of the surface was planted with red grapes, mostly the nondescript Portugieser; twenty years later that proportion had more than doubled, and varieties such as Pinot Noir and Dornfelder were making advances. Cooperatives are very important in the Pfalz, as the members own almost thirty per cent of all the vineyards. But there are a huge number of private estates. Unlike other regions such as the Rheingau, there were few properties owned by either the Church or by state domains.

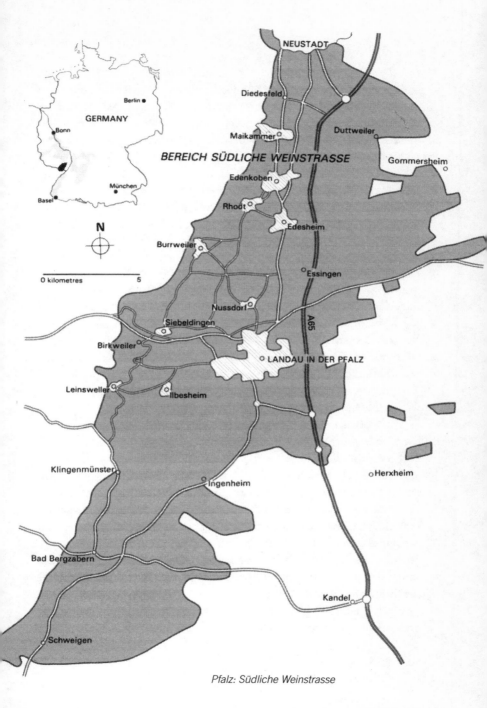

Pfalz: Südliche Weinstrasse

The area under vine has steadily expanded. In 1923 there were 16,000 ha (40,000 acres)[2]; by the early 2000s there were almost 24,000. Certain varieties that were once very popular – such as Silvaner, Traminer, and even Gutedel – are now marginal, and in large part their place was taken by the new crossings, which were adopted with enthusiasm in the southern half of the region, where their resistance to disease and high yields made them well suited to the high-volume (and low quality) wines for which the area was known. More recently, many of those crossings have been replaced by the red varieties mentioned earlier, for which there is a steady domestic demand. There is no record of Riesling having been a dominant variety until the very end of the eighteenth century, when a grower called Andreas Jordan took up the cause of selective harvesting.

The resurgence of the Südliche Weinstrasse was no accident. It was clear that the low prices for bulk wines would soon drive more and more growers out of business. In the 1980s the cooperatives were sitting on huge stocks of high-volume wines for which there was little demand, or not at prices that made financial sense. The mistake had been the expansion of vineyards into flatter sites that would never produce wines of good quality. The only solution for growers with aspirations to quality was to pull out of the local cooperative and bottle their own production. That in turn meant investing in winery equipment and in marketing the wine. Only the best have succeeded.

Many of them were fortunate in having Hans-Günther Schwarz as their mentor. Schwarz is the long-time winemaker at Müller-Catoir and much will be said about his wines later. What made his achievement remarkable in propelling the estate to the very top ranks of Pfalz producers is that Müller-Catoir does not have vineyards of legendary quality. Good sites, yes, but not usually counted among the best. Schwarz essentially argued for low yields and for a non-interventionist style of winemaking quite at odds with the reliance on hi-tech wizardry that prevailed in the 1970s and 1980s at so many Pfalz wineries. For decades young winemakers – such as Hansjörg Rebholz, Helmut Darting, and Frank John – came to Müller-Catoir to work alongside Schwarz. They then dispersed throughout the Pfalz, either to their family properties or to jobs at other prestigious estates, carrying with them the Schwarz

[2] Shand, p. 50.

philosophy. It is rare that in any one wine region one individual should have such extraordinary influence, all of it beneficial.

Certain marketing initiatives have proved successful. Five of the best estates in the south – Becker, Kessler, Rebholz, Siegrist, and Wehrheim – teamed up amicably in a group called *Fünf Freunde* ("five friends"). Each grower has a different focus but each is determined to produce wines of outstanding quality. They present their wines together at important wine shows, but also cooperate in other ways, such as by teaming up to present a single large order to their favourite Burgundian cooper. They also produce a Burgundian blend each year that is composed of the best barrel from each of them. This blend is known as "V Amici" and the 1999 white, from Pinot Blanc and Pinot Gris, and the 1997 Pinot Noir were of excellent quality.

Other groupings such as the "Barrique Forum", which unites most leading producers of barrique-aged wines, have also done much to promote this style of wine, internationally as well as domestically. In the early 1990s there were some fairly awful barrique-aged wines, thanks to a widespread misconception that an oaked wine should taste of wood rather than fruit. Nonetheless, the basic premise of the barrique movement – that certain grape varieties, notably the Burgundian Pinot group, are well suited to barrel-ageing and lees-stirring – is fundamentally correct. Not every producer wants to age his Chardonnay or Pinot Blanc in barriques, but at least the consumer is very receptive to those who favour this style.

Although huge strides have made in improving the reputation of the less well-known parts of the Pfalz, there is still a long way to go; there are still far too many undistinguished wines, such as the tanker-loads of Portugieser Weissherbst (rosé) sold each year. And although Dornfelder can produce attractive wine if yields are kept low, it is in the nature of Dornfelder to produce huge crops, and not every grower feels obliged to impose any constraints on its fecundity. The resulting wine is inevitably insipid.

With its generally warm climate, it should be relatively easy to produce decent quality wine in the Pfalz. Many growers in the south place a heavy reliance on Burgundian varieties, such as Chardonnay, Pinot Blanc and Pinot Noir. But the path to commercial success has proved thornier than expected. The acidity that gives Riesling its vigour and zest is not nearly so desirable in a Burgundian variety. Too many Pinot Blancs and Chardonnays are marked by uncomfortably sharp levels of acidity. The German palate may be accustomed to this kind of balance in a white wine, but it has made it harder for the wines to compete successfully in the international market.

The move toward vineyard classification in the Pfalz has already been discussed, and it is broadly to be welcomed if only because it will reduce the individual internal classifications introduced by many leading estates which, with their minor variations, only added to the confusion to which most consumers were already subjected. In 1994, for instance, Bürklin-Wolf introduced a four-tier system that may have seemed logical in terms of its production and philosophy, but which was not easy to master. The identification of the finest sites as Grosses Gewächs will at least make it possible for the consumer to know which wines, in the eyes of each producer, are considered the finest. The decision by the VDP to admit vineyards in the southern Pfalz to the ranks of Grosses Gewächs is also welcome, despite the fact that there are an awful lot of sites in the Oberhaardt that are simply mediocre.

Inevitably, many of the leading producers of the Pfalz are based in the Mittelhaardt, which unquestionably has the finest vineyard sites. (It also has some exceptionally pretty villages, which draw tourists to their inns and wine bars.) From Bad Dürkheim south to Neustadt a string of villages huddle against the slopes of the Haardt Mountains: Wachenheim, Forst, Deidesheim, and – to a lesser extent – Ruppertsberg. Here varied soils and microclimates all come together to support Riesling wines of uncommon richness and power. Some sites just north of Bad Dürkheim – such as Ungstein and Kallstadt – and some just south of Ruppertsberg such as Gimmeldingen are also capable of giving wines of staying power and individuality.

The great estates of the Mittelhaardt are helped by their ability to focus on a single variety from a series of vineyards that at least enjoy a family resemblance. The problem that still bedevils a number of other potentially excellent estates is that many of their vineyards are either undistinguished or planted with varieties such as Ortega, Portugieser, and Huxelrebe. Consequently they produce too many wines of fluctuating quality and interest. At Bergdolt, in contrast, an estate in Duttweiler, well to the south of Neustadt, Rainer Bergdolt has long specialized in

Pinot Blanc as well as Riesling. Whether you like his wines or not, at least he has given them a clear focus and identity.

Despite the various problems that continue to dog the region, it can plausibly be argued that the Pfalz is now Germany's most dynamic wine region, geared up in a way that, say, Württemberg is not, to produce wines of international appeal. The best dry Rieslings from the Mittelhaardt can easily bear comparison with the top wines in this style from Alsace and Austria, and there is with every year that goes by a growing mastery of the Burgundian varieties. This renaissance of the Pfalz, especially the Mittelhaardt, is a fairly recent phenomenon. In the mid-1980s the largest estates of the region – Von Buhl, Bassermann-Jordan, and Bürklin-Wolf – were underperforming, even though they tended to own the best sites. Their proprietors tended not to live on the property, which was managed by a professional director. As in the Rheingau, these estate managers, although undoubtedly competent, were not always ready to take the risks required to make truly outstanding wines. But ten years later, all this had changed. Christian von Guradze, married to Bettina Bürklin, proved a dynamic director of his wife's property and an ardent proponent of vineyard classification. Von Buhl hired the brilliant Frank John as its head winemaker. And Bassermann-Jordan hired another fine winemaker, Ulrich Mell, to improve on its hitherto lacklustre performance. Within a few years the "Big Three" were back on form, pushing the renown of the Mittelhaardt to ever greater heights. Further south in Neustadt, Müller-Catoir continued to produce wines of unflagging brilliance, and throughout the region numerous estates followed the example set by Müller-Catoir and the "Big Three." Overall standards of wine quality in the Pfalz have surely never been higher than they are today.

Vineyards

There are twenty-six Grosslagen and 330 Einzellagen.

Bereich Südliche Weinstrasse. Grosslagen from south to north: Guttenberg (around Schweigen), Kloster Liebfrauenberg, Herrlich, Königsgarten (around Siebeldingen), Bischofskreuz (around Walsheim), Trappenberg, Ordensgut, Schloss Ludwigshöhe, Mandelhöhe.

Bereich Mittelhaardt/Deutsche Weinstrasse. Grosslagen from south to north: Pfaffengrund (around Neustadt), Rebstöckel, Meerspinne,

Hofstück (Deidesheim), Mariengarten (Forst), Schnepfenflug (Forst), Schenkenböhl (Wachenheim), Hochmess (Bad Dürkheim), Honigsäckel (Ungstein), Feuerberg (Bad Dürkheim), Kobnert (Kallstadt), Rosenbühl (Freinsheim), Schwarzerde (Kirchheim), Höllenpfad, Grafenstück, Schnepfenflug vom Zellertal.

Grosses Gewächs vineyards:
Birkweiler: Mandelberg, Kastanienbusch.
Deidesheim: Kalkofen, Grainhübel, Hohenmorgen, Paradiesgarten.
Bad Dürkheim: Michelsberg.
Dirmstein: Mandelpfad.
Forst: Pechstein, Jesuitengarten, Kirchenstück, Ungeheuer.
Kirrweiler: Mandelberg.
Gimmeldingen: Mandelgarten.
Königsbach: Idig, Ölberg.
Laumersheim: Mandelberg.
Leinsweiler: Sonennberg.
Ruppertsberg: Gaisböhl, Reiterpfad.
Siebeldingen: Im Sonnenschein.
Ungstein: Weilberg.
Wachenheim: Gerümpel, Rechbächel.

BIRKWEILER
Südliche Weinstrasse. This village is situated a few kilometres west of Landau.
Birkweiler Kastanienbusch. Reddish slate soils that warms up fast. Southeast-facing and one of the highest vineyards in the Pfalz. In dry years it can suffer from water stress. A Grosses Gewächs site for Rebholz. Wehrheim has Pinot Noir planted here.
Birkweiler Mandelberg. Loam soil with good water retention. A Grosses Gewächs site for Wehrheim.
Birkweiler Rosenberg. Some Chardonnay is planted here.

BURRWEILER
Südliche Weinstrasse. A village northwest of Landau.
Burrweiler Altenforst. Recently went through *Flurbereinigung* so the vines are very young.

Burrweiler Schäwer. Unusual grey slate soil, probably unique in the Pfalz. Messmer is a major proprietor.

DEIDESHEIM

Mittelhaardt. Complex soil, primarily sandstone with some chalk and volcanic primary rock and basalt. Sandstone walls were built in the early twentieth century to divide the vineyards, and those facing the village reflect sufficient warmth to allow fig trees to grow. Some growers rate the village more highly even than Forst, but this view is by no means unanimous.

Deidesheimer Grainhübel. 12 ha (29.7 acres). Limestone subsoil. Half the site is steep and is very highly regarded by some growers, such as Mosbacher. Other owners include Bassermann-Jordan, Biffar, Deinhard, and Siben.

Deidesheimer Herrgottsacker. 122 ha (301 acres), making it one of the largest vineyards, very diverse in soil and quality. Von Buhl claim to have some of the best parcels. Biffar owns 2.4 ha (5.9 acres).

Deidesheimer Hohenmorgen. 2 ha (4.9 acres). Above the village, and marked by its limestone subsoil. Bassermann-Jordan and Bürklin-Wolf are among the owners (and both consider it Grosses Gewächs), and Christmann leases from Bassermann-Jordan.

Deidesheimer Kalkofen. 5 ha (12.4 acres). Meagre soil, with limestone, sand, and loam. Owners include Deinhard and Bassermann-Jordan (Grosses Gewächs). Highly regarded by Mosbacher.

Deidesheimer Kieselberg. 16 ha (39.5 acres). This vineyard has been documented since 1234. The soil is weathered sandstone, mixed with loam, sand, and weathered limestone. Von Buhl owns twenty-three per cent but admits it is best at producing wines for everyday drinking. Biffar owns 1.4 ha (3.5 acres).

Deidesheimer Langenmorgen. 7 ha (17.3 acres). Light sandy soil above a subsoil of limestone and sandstone. Gives relatively soft wines.

Deidesheimer Leinhöhle. 18 ha (44.5 acres). Red sandstone with loam. Can suffer from stress in very dry years. Owners include Von Buhl with fifteen per cent. The wines are full-bodied and J.L.Wolf and Bassermann-Jordan regard it as a top site.

Deidesheimer Maushöhle. 20 ha (49.4 acres). Has a light sandy soil, with some loam and lime, giving delicate and elegant wines. Owners include Von Buhl, Biffar, 1.1 ha (2.7 acres), and Bassermann-Jordan. Mosbacher and Bassermann-Jordan are not convinced that it is an outstanding site.

Deidesheimer Nonnengarten. Not highly rated.

Deidesheimer Nonnenstück. 125 ha (309 acres).

Deidesheimer Paradiesgarten. 30 ha (74.1 acres). Formerly known as Waldberg, but after World War II it was given a more romantic name. Loam and loamy sand; southeast-facing. Much of the vineyard is located at the top of the slope fringing the forest, so the microclimate is cooler. Owners include Von Buhl and Deinhard. It's a Grosses Gewächs site for Von Buhl.

BAD DÜRKHEIM

Mittelhaardt. Known as much as a tourist and festival centre as for its wines. The main vineyards are Abtsfronhof, 3.2 ha (7.9 acres), *Alleinbesitz* of Fitz-Ritter, Hochbenn, 56 ha (138 acres), Michelsberg, 5 ha (12.4 acres), Nonnengarten, 395 ha (976 acres), and Spielberg, 24 ha (61.8 acres). The best (Michelsberg, Spielberg) have limestone soils and good exposition.

DUTTWEILER

Südliche Weinstrasse. A village southeast of Neustadt.

Duttweiler Kalkberg. 20 ha (49.4 acres). The soil is light sand and loam, and Bergdolt regards this as its best site for Riesling and Pinot Noir.

FORST

Mittelhaardt. 204 ha (504 acres). The vineyards cover the slope between the village and the forest, which offers a great deal of shelter. The top sites tend to be those at between 120 and 150 metres (400 and 500 feet). The soils are rich in potassium and basalt. Mosbacher argues that most of the best vineyards face south or southeast and, being sheltered, give wines with power and elegance. Basalt rubble from nearby quarries has long been scattered over the vineyards, and these stones retain warmth well. The vineyards are deep and rarely suffer from drought.

Forster Bischofsgarten. 43 ha (106 acres). Lies to the east of the railway line, and is of indifferent quality. Von Buhl owns seventeen per cent.

Forster Elser. 10 ha (24.7 acres). Its most southerly vineyard, with dark sandy soil, giving rounder and less mineral wines. Mosbacher is a major owner.

Forster Freundstück. 3.67 ha (9.1 acres). A band of vines close to the village. Von Buhl is the major owner with almost half, and the others include Spindler and Bassermann-Jordan. Not quite as highly regarded as Jesuitengarten and Kirchenstück, but Mosbacher regards it as a Grosses Gewächs site.

Forster Jesuitengarten. 6.8 ha (16.8 acres). In the 1828 classification this was regarded as the second best site in the Pfalz. The soil is basalt and sandstone and good water retention allows it to produce good wine in poor vintages too. One hundred per cent Riesling. Bassermann-Jordan and Von Buhl each own more than 2 ha (4.9 acres). Other proprietors include Eugen Müller, Werlé, Spindler, and Bürklin-Wolf. Unquestionably a top site, but giving slightly more forward wines than the other outstanding vineyards here.

Forster Kirchenstück. 3.67 ha (9.1 acres). The valuations of the early nineteenth century assessed this Riesling site at a higher value than any other, simply because the grapes consistently reached greater maturity here. In the early twentieth century its wines were just as expensive as those from the top Rheingau growths. The wines are not the most fullbodied of the Pfalz, but they have immense finesse and complexity and are very long-lived. Recent replantings, how-ever, mean that the average age of the vines is not that old. Owners of this Grosses Gewächs include Eugen Müller with 1 ha (2.5 acres), Von Buhl with 0.86 ha (2.1 acres), Bürklin-Wolf with 0.55 ha (1.4 acres) Bassermann-Jordan with 0.44 ha (1.1 acres), as well as Spindler and Werlé.

Forster Musenhang. 8.65 ha (21.4 acres). This site lies high on the slope beneath the woods. The soil is weathered sandstone. Cooled by air descending from the forest, it gives leaner, racier wines. Von Buhl owns ten per cent. Mosbacher says it can excel in dry years, because it retains moisture well.

Forster Pechstein. 17 ha (42 acres). Sandy loam, but the presence of basalt in the soil gives mineral, even flinty, wines with a good acidic structure. Von Buhl owns 5 ha (12.4 acres), Eugen Müller 2.5 ha (6.2 acres). A Grosses Gewächs site for Von Buhl and Bürklin-Wolf.

Forster Stift. 56 ha (138 acres). This lies on the east side of the village and thus is not an outstanding site. Riesling, Pinot Blanc, Rieslaner, and Pinot Noir are planted here.

Forster Ungeheuer. 39 ha (96.4 acres). Has a rich mineral soil with limestone, basalt, and loess-loam. The lower parts can be prone to fog and damp; the central part of the slope gives the best quality. Because of *Flurbereinigung* the vines are less than twenty years old. The vineyard was enlarged in 1971, and Von Buhl claims to have some of the best original portions, as does Mosbacher. Mosbacher characterizes the site by saying that whereas Pechstein can taste mineral at the expense of fruit, Ungeheuer always exhibits both. Major proprietors are Müller, 2.5 ha (6.2 acres), Von Buhl, Mosbacher, Deinhard, Werlé, Spindler, and Bürklin-Wolf (Grosses Gewächs).

FREINSHEIM
Unterhaardt. North of Bad Dürkheim.

Freinsheimer Goldberg. Sandy soil, partly terraced, with poor water retention. Lingenfelder values this site for its Riesling and Scheurebe.

Freinsheimer Musikantenbuckel. Enormous vineyard, with 180 ha (445 acres). Sandy soil with gravel.

GIMMELDINGEN
Mittelhaardt. A village just north of Neustadt.

Gimmeldinger Bienengarten. 30 ha (74.1 acres). Sandstone. Christmann has Riesling planted here.

Gimmeldinger Mandelgarten. Weathered sandstone and sand. Grosses Gewächs for Christmann.

GLEISWEILER
Südliche Weinstrasse. Village northwest of Landau, renowned for its exceptionally warm micro-climate.

Gleisweiler Hölle. Red sandstone, making it a very warm site.

GROSSKARLBACH
Unterhaardt. North of Bad Dürkheim.

Grosskarlbacher Burgweg. A sloping site, with loess-loam over limestone. Owners include Knipser and Lingenfelder.

HAARDT

Mittelhaardt. Just north of Neustadt and known as the "the balcony of the Pfalz", because the views from here spread out over much of the Rhein valley. Mostly Riesling is planted, but other varieties are not uncommon. The Rieslings can be quite exotic.

Haardter Bürgergarten. 33 ha (81.5 acres). On the south aside of the village and one of its best sites. Many varieties are planted here. Müller-Catoir, a major owner, often produces outstanding Rieslings from the site.

Haardter Herrenletten. 12 ha (29.7 acres). Loam soil over a limestone subsoil with good water retention, giving long-lived wines. On the mid-slope beneath Herzog.

Haardter Herzog. 48 ha (119 acres).

Haardter Mandelring. 69 ha (170 acres). Müller-Catoir has Scheurebe here.

Haardter Mönchgarten. 33 ha (81.5 acres).

KALLSTADT

Mittelhaardt. 280 ha (692 acres). The soils contain much chalk and retain warmth overnight. The flatter sites used to be planted with red vines, especially Portugieser.

Kallstadter Annaberg. 6 ha (14.8 acres). Yellow sandstone. South-facing. Well known for Scheurebe. Owners include Henninger.

Kallstadter Kronenberg. Light gravelly soil, producing light spicy wines.

Kallstadter Saumagen. 50 ha (124 acres). There were limestone quarries here in Roman times, and some remained until the 1950s. The holes left after quarrying ceased were filled in with gravel and loess-loam soil before vines were planted. The site is a heat trap, and there are fig trees growing here too. The flatter part of the vineyard has more loam, which made it desirable in the eyes of many growers, leaving Kallstadt's best estate, Koehler-Ruprecht, delighted to obtain the better quality slopes, which have more limestone and give better wines. The Protestant church is the major proprietor, leasing out parcels to various growers.

Kallstadter Steinacker. 125 ha (309 acres). The village's largest site.

KIRRWEILER
Südliche Weinstrasse. Village south of Neustadt.

Kirrweiler Mandelberg. 60 ha (148 acres). Loess soils. Bergdolt has Riesling and Pinot Blanc planted here.

KÖNIGSBACH
Mittelhaardt. Village between Haardt and Ruppertsberg.

Königsbacher Idig. 20 ha (49.4 acres). Clay-limestone soils that are warm and aid ripening. A Grosses Gewächs site for Christmann.

Königsbacher Ölberg. 34 ha (84 acres). Clay-limestone. Christmann has Riesling planted here, as well as Grosses Gewächs Pinot Noir.

LAUMERSHEIM
Unterhaardt. A northerly but sheltered village between Bad Dürkheim and Worms. Knipser is the leading producer.

Laumersheimer Kapellenberg. Sandy soils, which are helpful in wet years.

Laumersheimer Kirschgarten. Mostly planted with red grapes.

Laumersheimer Mandelberg. Loess-loam over limestone. South-facing. Much Riesling planted. Knipser is a major proprietor.

LEINSWEILER
Südliche Weinstrasse. Village west of Landau.

Leinsweiler Sonnenberg. Stony soil, with clay, limestone, and sandy loam. Can suffer from water stress in hot years.

MUSSBACH
Mittelhaardt. Village between Neustadt and Ruppertsberg. Mostly flat vineyards.

Mussbacher Eselshaut. Sandy soils. A major site for Müller-Catoir, which has 14 ha (34.6 acres) of Riesling, Scheurebe, Rieslaner, and Pinot Blanc here.

Mussbacher Johannitergarten. Planted with, among other varieties, Rieslaner.

RUPPERTSBERG

Mittelhaardt. Sandstone and loam soils, relatively shallow. The wines can have a slightly earthy character usually absent from Wachenheim and Forst.

Ruppertsberger Gaisböhl. 8-ha (19.8-acre) *Alleinbesitz* of Bürklin-Wolf. South-facing, red and yellow sandstone soils, with underlying sand and clay; well drained. Part of the site recognized as Grosses Gewächs.

Ruppertsberger Nussbien. 80 ha (198 acres).

Ruppertsberger Linsenbusch. 175 ha (432 acres). Most of this huge site is mediocre, and the best parcels are in the northerly section.

Ruppertsberger Reiterpfad. 87 ha (215 acres). Calcareous soil, with loam and sandstone. Not outstanding, but a Grosses Gewächs site for Bergdolt, Christmann, and Von Buhl.

SCHWEIGEN

Sudliche Weinstrasse. Most southerly village in the Pfalz. Its best-known vineyard is the Sonnenberg, 145 ha (358 acres).

SIEBELDINGEN

Südliche Weinstrasse. Village west of Landau.

Siebeldinger Im Sonnenschein. Stony sandy soil. Rebholz declares it as one of its Grosses Gewächs vineyards.

UNGSTEIN

Mittelhaardt. Village just north of Bad Dürkheim.

Ungsteiner Herrenberg. 45 ha (111 acres). A top site, where Pfeffingen has Riesling and Scheurebe. Sand, loam, and limestone.

Ungsteiner Osterberg. Planted with, among other varieties, Chardonnay and Gewürztraminer.

Ungsteiner Weilberg. 10 ha (24.7 acres). Aromatic wines from a well exposed vineyard. Reddish clay and loam. A Grosses Gewächs site for Riesling from Pfeffingen.

WACHENHEIM

Mittelhaardt. Village between Forst and Bad Dürkheim. Its wines are known for purity and elegance rather than power. Thirteen individual vineyards.

Wachenheimer Altenburg. 10 ha (24.7 acres). Biffar has thirty year vines here.

Wachenheimer Belz. J.L. Wolf is a major owner, but does not regard it as a top site.

Wachenheimer Böhlig. 9 ha (22.2 acres). Mostly flat land. Bürklin-Wolf owns vines here.

Wachenheimer Fuchsmantel. Undistinguished site on the southern fringes of Bad Dürkheim.

Wachenheimer Gerümpel. 13 ha (32.1 acres). Owners include Bürklin-Wolf and Biffar. A Grosses Gewächs site for Biffar, which has old vines here.

Wachenheimer Goldbächel. 4.3 ha (10.6 acres). Owners include Bürklin-Wolf and Biffar. Not perceived as a top site.

Wachenheimer Luginsland. 26 ha (64.2 acres). Von Buhl is an owner here.

Wachenheimer Rechbächel. 3 ha (7.4 acres). *Alleinbesitz* of Bürklin-Wolf, which regards it as Grosses Gewächs. Red and yellow sandstone, above chalk and clay. Usually gives broad and forward wines.

Producers

ACHAM-MAGIN

Weinstr 67, 67147 Forst. Tel: +49 (0) 6326 315. Fax: 6232. www.acham-magin.de. 6 ha (14.8 acres). 4,000 cases.

This small estate, with good vineyards in Forster Pechstein, Ungeheuer, and Kirchenstück, as well as Ruppertsberger Reiterpfad (these last two the source of its Grosses Gewächs), focuses almost entirely on dry wines, which are pure and mineral. There is also a small production of Pinot Blanc and Chardonnay.

BASSERMANN-JORDAN

Kirchgasse 10, 67142 Deidesheim. Tel: +49 (0) 6326 6006. Fax: 6008. www.bassermann-jordan.de. 42 ha (104 acres). 25,000 cases.

This major estate oozes history. Within its maze of cellars, dating from 1545 to 1822, are niches filled with Roman amphoras and other treasures that were discovered in the region. Its renown dates from the early nineteenth century, when Andreas Jordan, whose family had owned the property since 1718, replanted the estate with Riesling and introduced an element of monoculture to the Mittelhaardt. The fourth-generation owner, Dr Ludwig von Bassermann-Jordan, was widely respected in the region, but in his old age – he died in 1995 – the estate stagnated. Although it was still capable of producing outstanding wines, this was not happening consistently.

After his death there was a swift realization by his widow Margrit and her daughter Gabriele that the estate was lagging behind its illustrious neighbours, such as Bürklin-Wolf. Ulrich Mell, the gifted winemaker at Biffar, was hired to turn things around – which he has done. As recently as 1995, the average yields were a fairly generous 65 hl/ha, many of the vineyards were machine-harvested, and a centrifuge was employed to clean up the must before fermentation. I noted, after tasting a range of wines from 1992 to 1994, that overall they were rather dull and flabby, lacked concentration, and showed odd sappy melony flavours.

Under Mell yields have been reduced, and the Grosses Gewächs sites (Kalkofen, Hohenmorgen, Kirchenstück) are often cropped at no more than 30 hl/ha. Mell is highly selective in the vineyard and in the disastrous 2000 vintage he obtained no more than 4,000 bottles from 4 ha (9.9 acres) of their top sites. Mell uses both steel tanks and wooden casks to age the wines, and there is no use of *Süssreserve*. As for the vineyards, 18 ha (44.5 acres) lie in Ruppertsberg, 14 ha (34.6 acres) in Deidesheim, and 10 ha (24.7 acres) in Forst.

It wasn't hard to produce excellent wines in 1998 and 1999, but the rain and rot in 2000, especially in the best sites, proved a real test for even the most gifted and conscientious winemaker. The 2000s here were very good. Among the dry wines, the Gutsriesling was fruity and clean, and the Hohenmorgen Spätlese Trocken ripe and mineral, more zesty than the Kalkofen. Among the sweet wines the Hohenmorgen Auslese, picked at 135 Oechsle, showed clear signs of botrytis on the nose, and although a tad heavy on the palate, has fine potential and an appealing juicy, apricoty character. The Ruppertsberger Reiterpfad TBA (picked at 210 Oechsle) is a triumph, with its heady, tarry nose, and a complex palate of stewed peaches and figs, all underpinned by a fine acidic backbone that gives stupendous length. Only the Kabinetts and Spätlesen were rather disappointing, soundly made and balanced but lacking verve and length.

FRIEDRICH BECKER

Hauptstr 29, 76889 Schweigen. Tel: +49 (0) 6342 290. Fax: 6148.
www.weingut-friedrich-becker.de. 14 ha (34.6 acres). 7,500 cases.

You can't get much further away from the Mittelhaardt than Schweigen, in the far south of the Pfalz close to the French border. Until 1973 Otto Becker sent all his grapes to the local Weintor cooperative. Curiously, half the vineyards lay in Alsace in France, and the Chardonnay vineyards still do.

Otto's son Fritz has been running the estate, which belongs to the Fünf Freunde association, for many years. He has done away with vineyard designations on the label, with the exception of Schweigener Sonnenberg. Although Becker, and his long-time winemaker Stefan Dorst, do produce Riesling, the main emphasis is on Burgundian varieties. All the wines are dry, and some of them are labelled as Tafelwein to give Becker maximum flexibility in vinification and barrel-ageing.

Becker first worked with barriques for red wines in 1989 (and with great success), and for whites in 1992. As he has grown in experience and confidence, Becker has gradually evolved a quality structure for his wines. There are three tiers of Pinot Noir: regular, reserve, and the wine he calls simply Pinot Noir. This last is immensely expensive, and the 1996 was priced at 115 DM. Barriques are used not only for Pinot Noir and Chardonnay, but for Weisser Burgunder and Schwarzriesling (Pinot Meunier). There is also an inexpensive red blend he calls Cuvée Guillaume, which combines Pinot Noir, Schwarzriesling, Dornfelder, and Portugieser.

The basic wines – from Riesling, Pinot Gris, Silvaner – are clean and zesty. The 1999 Chardonnay aged in older barriques was rich yet austere after two years, with ample youthful promise. The Cuvée Guillaume can be nondescript, and the 1996 Schwarzriesling, aged in fifty per cent new barriques, had a cherry brandy nose and some jamminess on the palate. The 1997 Spätburgunder Barrique was beautifully scented, and nicely concentrated on the palate, if a touch too extracted. Much more new oak is used for the Reserve, which I have not tasted in many years.

BERGDOLT

Dudostr 24, 67435 Duttweiler. Tel: +49 (0) 6327 5027. Fax: 1784.
www.weingut-bergdolt.de. 23 ha (56.8 acres). 12,000 cases.

As you walk through the gate of the Sankt Lamprecht monastic dependency that is home to this winery, you can see the name Bergdolt and the date 1757 on the keystone. This makes Rainer Bergdolt the eighth generation of his family to run the property.

Although the estate produces attractive Rieslings, Bergdolt has long concentrated on Weisser Burgunder. A few of the wines are barrique-fermented, but ninety-five per cent of them are unoaked. None of the wines goes through malolactic fermentation.

The Riesling is good but somewhat neutral in character, which may be related to the nature of the soils here, or possibly to the fairly generous yields. I tasted a range of Kirrweiler Mandelberg Weisser Burgunder from 1990 to 2000, and can't help feeling that Bergdolt slightly over-rates the potential of the wine. The dry Spätlesen can be delicious (as in 1999, 1997, and 1990), but they seem at their refreshing best within five years. The 1999 Mandelberg Grosses Gewächs was certainly the best of the range. Bergdolt courageously opened a 1992 Auslese Trocken aged entirely in new oak, which was not only hideously oily from the oak but incandescent from the fifteen degrees of alcohol. An aberration.

As for the Rieslings, the 2000s were very successful here, as is the 1999 Ruppertsberger Reiterpfad Grosses Gewächs. The 1998s have a slightly vegetal character, as do the Weisser Burgunders.

All Pinot Noir comes from Duttweiler Kalkberg. Bergdolt first produced the wine in 1990 and it has grown in importance over the years. The Mariafelder clone gives good colour, which is prized in Germany, but perhaps the fruit lacks some Pinot typicity. The Bergdolt style is quite tannic and robust, though vintages such as 1996 and 1997 also show considerable finesse in the Spätlese Trocken bottlings.

JOSEF BIFFAR

Niederkirchener Str 13, 67146 Deidesheim. Tel: +49 (0) 636 967629.
Fax: 967611. www.biffar.de. 12.5 ha (31 acres). 7,000 cases.

The Biffars came to Deidesheim from Lyon in 1723. Their main business is the production of chocolates, dried fruits, and other sweetmeats. They achieved celebrity as wine producers after 1990, when Ulrich Mell joined the estate as cellarmaster. In the late 1990s he left to join Bassermann-Jordan, and his replacement Dirk Roth departed in 2001, to be replaced in turn by the present cellarmaster, Günter Braun, who used to work for Christmann. This is a typical example of Pfalzer musical chairs.

Their vineyards are dispersed among the top villages of the Mittelhaardt, with Deidesheimer Grainhübel and Wachenheimer Gerümpel as their Grosses Gewächs sites. More than two-thirds of their wines are dry. Mell was responsible for reducing average yields from around 75 hl/ha to 55 hl/ha (30.4 to 22.3 hl/acre). Under Braun, there is no rule about pressing: sometimes whole-cluster pressing is employed, sometimes not. It all depends on the quality of the fruit. Half the crop is aged in stainless steel, the other half in casks, which can be temperature-controlled. There is no centrifuge or other hi-tech equipment in the cellars, other than a Kieselguhr filter. No *Süssreserve* is used, and fermentation is arrested by chilling and filtration. Braun does not like to bottle too early, because he wants lees-aged wines that will be long-lived and not merely charming in their youth.

The Rieslings here are of excellent quality, especially the dry wines from Herrgottsacker, Gerümpel, and Maushöhle in vintages from 1997 to 2000. The Auslesen from Grainhübel and Kieselberg have lively acidity and good length, and will be delicious when mature. The dry Weisser Burgunder is also worth looking out for.

Despite the lack of continuity that three cellarmasters in five years can entail, Biffar has maintained the high standards it attained under Mell, and Braun seems determined not to rest on the estate's laurels.

REICHSRAT VON BUHL

Weinstr 16, 67146 Deidesheim. Tel: +49 (0) 6326 965010. Fax: 965024.
www.reichsrat-von-buhl.de. 53 ha (131 acres). 30,000 cases.

This large estate was founded in the mid-nineteenth century, and Felix Mendelssohn was one of its admirers. Today it is owned by Freiherr Georg Enoch von und zu Gutenberg. This gentleman, who by profession is a musician, has little interest in wine and in the late 1980s leased his estate to a Japanese company, which has invested substantially in the property. About one-third of the wine is exported to Japan.

In the 1980s the estate was lacklustre. The cellarmaster in those days tended to harvest early, and the wines often lacked depth and concentration. The Japanese not only invested in the cellars but acquired a new cellarmaster, Frank John, who has been here since 1994. John worked with Hans-Günther Schwarz at Müller-Catoir but has also had wide experience outside Germany, in Beaune and at Château La Tour Blanche in Sauternes. John keeps yields down to around 50 hl/ha, in top sites – they were between 80 and 100 hl/ha, in the 1980s – and has no qualms about risking a late harvest. This paid off spectacularly in 1994, when sixty per cent of the crop was of Auslese quality. He is a great believer in selection, and is opposed to deacidification, because he argues that a winemaker should work with what nature delivers. (It helps to give nature a leg up by harvesting at full maturity, of course.) No *Süssreserve* is used.

Von Buhl is fortunate to have a wonderful array of vineyards in all the major villages of the Mittelhaardt. Viticultural practices are essentially organic, and when replanting is necessary, it is done at a greater density. Frank John is no fan of whole-cluster pressing, except when the must is destined for the estate's not inconsiderable sparkling wine production. In the cellar most of the vinification is done in steel tanks, though some top wines are fermented in temperature-controlled casks with especially thick staves to avoid oxidation during prolonged lees contact.

The estate takes red wine production quite seriously. Pinot Noir was planted in 1990, with the first crop harvested in 1992. The wines have become more serious as the years have gone by, and in 2001 the top Pinot Noir had enough richness to be aged in new barriques. Regular bottlings, however, are aged in older barrels.

In 1992 Von Buhl created a range of Rieslings specifically for the export market: Armand (Kabinett), Julie (Halbtrocken), and Von Buhl (Trocken). In most years I have found the Armand the best of the three.

The 2000 vintage was cruel to Von Buhl and other owners of top sites. They produced no wine at all from Jesuitengarten, Maushöhle, and Reiterpfad. John did make a superb Kirchenstück Grosses Gewächs, a wonderfully concentrated wine with a long mineral finish, but there are only 200 bottles of it. The Pechstein Grosses Gewächs is of comparable quality, and fortunately the quantities were a touch more generous at 2,000 bottles.

When conditions are right, John makes fabulous sweet wines here. In 1994, there were gorgeous Auslesen from Ungeheuer, a brilliant BA from

Jesuitengarten and an extreme Scheurebe TBA, picked at 280 Oechsle, showing an acidity of 20 grams per litre and a near impossible 500 grams of residual sugar. In 1997 the Ungeheuer Riesling TBA was more modest, picked at a trifling 240 Oechsle and retaining a miserable 340 grams of residual sugar. I was dazzled by the same wine in 1998, which had a wonderful intensity. The best vintage for Eiswein was probably 1996, when the grapes were picked in December at a temperature of −17°C. Look out too for the occasional Rieslaner Auslesen.

I tend to think of Bürklin-Wolf as the leading estate of the Mittelhaardt, but as I recall some of the great wines of the past eight years from Von Buhl, I have my doubts. Fortunately, there is no need to declare a winner.

DR BÜRKLIN-WOLF

Weinstr 65, 67157 Wachenheim. Tel: +49 (0) 6322 993355. Fax: 953330.
www.buerklin-wolf.de. 86 ha (213 acres). 50,000 cases.

This huge estate (by Pfalz standards) can trace its history back to the late sixteenth century. It took on its present form in 1875 when Luise Wolf married Dr Albert Bürklin, who built it up into the largest private estate in Germany. Bürklin was also a politician, who rose to become the vice president of the German parliament. Like the other great estates of the Pfalz, it allowed quality to slip in the 1980s. I recall the then general manager telling me in the mid-1980s that yields and quality were not necessarily linked as long as they were kept below 100 hl/ha. Today average yields have been reduced to around 60 hl/ha. Bettina Bürklin trained at Geisenheim, so she knew a thing or two about wine when she inherited the estate; her husband, Christian von Guradze, has shown tremendous energy and determination in helping her to restore its reputation.

The estate's portfolio of vineyards includes just about every good site in the Mittelhaardt, with Ruppertsberger Gaisböhl an *Alleinbesitz*. Viticulture is essentially organic.

In 1994 Bürklin-Wolf became one of the first estates to initiate a classification system, though it was applied only to its own wines. At the basic level there are regional bottlings, then village wines, then a series of wines from the sites regarded as Premiers Crus: Ruppertsberger Hoheburg, Wachenheimer Gerümpel, Goldbächel, Böhlig, Altenburg, and Rechbächel. At the top level are dry Rieslings from the Grands Crus: Jesuitengarten, Ungeheuer, Pechstein, and Kirchenstück in Forst; Gaisböhl and Reiterpfad in Ruppertsberg; and Hohenmorgen, Langen-morgen, and Kalkofen from Deidesheim. The list of Grands Crus has been adjusted after conversion into the Grosses Gewächs classification, which here includes Pechstein, Ungeheuer, Kirchenstück, Hohenmorgen, and Gaisböhl. The present system here is that Erstes Gewächs A denotes Grand Cru, and Erstes Gewächs B denotes Premier Cru.

The winemaking is exacting. There is a sorting table to eliminate unsuitable grapes (it no doubt worked overtime in 2000). Whole-cluster pressing is used, but not systematically. Not only the steel tanks, but many of the casks can be temperature-controlled, which is important because they are used for the fermentation of the top wines. The centrifuge has been banished from the cellar, and clarification is now by sedimentation.

As well as Riesling, there is some Pinot Noir, partly aged in barrique; Dornfelder, primarily for local restaurant sales; and a barrique-aged estate red that blends Bordeaux varieties with some Sangiovese thrown in for good measure.

Of course, it's the Rieslings on which the Bürklin-Wolf reputation rests. 1998 and 1999 were both excellent vintages here, but in 2000 none of their wines was classified as Grand Cru. I don't detect a serious weakness among the range, just different characters, with some of the wines showing a racy grapefruity flavour, others being more peachy, others exhibiting varying degrees of spice and white pepper. They are all concentrated, vigorous, and exciting. Bürklin-Wolf has rather lost interest in its sweet wines, which have been repackaged as "R" or "RR" to denote different levels of intensity, and are offered for sale after about ten years of bottle age.

CHRISTMANN
Peter-Koch Str 43, 67435 Gimmeldingen. Tel: +49 (0) 6321 66039.
Fax: 68762. 14 ha (34.6 acres). 10,000 cases.
This constantly improving estate was founded in 1845. Since 1994 Steffen Christmann has been in charge, and from the outset he has simplified the offerings and the labelling, creating a roughly Burgundian-

style hierarchy. Most of the wines are dry. Although Riesling represents two-thirds of production, there are also some wines from the Burgundian varieties, especially Pinot Noir, and from St Laurent. Although many of the vines are young and thus vigorous, Christmann tries hard to keep Riesling yields down to around 50 hl/ha and less for his top sites, and at 60–70 hl/ha for the Burgundian varieties, other than Pinot Noir, which is cropped at 45 hl/ha. He tends to make a preliminary selection in the vineyard for the "village" wines, and then leave the remaining bunches for later harvesting at optimal ripeness.

The vineyards cover the lower Mittelhaardt, from Deidesheim to Ruppertsberg to Königsbach. His Riesling Grosses Gewächs come from Linsenbusch and Reiterpfad in Ruppertsberg, from Königsbacher Idig, and from Gimmeldinger Mandelgarten. Königsbacher Ölberg and Idig are the source of his Pinot Noir Grosses Gewächs.

Since 1996 Christmann has been equipped with a sorting table, one of the first in the region. Whole-cluster pressing is an option, but not necessarily exercised. The wines are vinified in stainless steel, and Christmann likes a long slow fermentation, even into the spring following the vintage. The only filtration takes place just before bottling.

The Pinot Noir is punched down mechanically during fermentation in open-top fermenters, with limited pumping over. The proportion of new barriques can be as high as two-thirds.

Christmann produces quite a few Rieslings, mostly dry, from his various sites, and though there are discernible differences between them, they do add up to an awful lot of wines: Kabinett, Spätlese, and then Grosses Gewächs. It is a measure of Christmann's skill that even in the dire 2000 vintage he produced a range of clean, invigorating Rieslings underpinned by ripe acidity. Grosses Gewächs from Reiterpfad and Idig from the 1997 vintage seemed relatively soft and forward in comparison, but the 1999s are excellent. Christmann dispenses with lightly sweet styles, but does produce Auslesen and higher qualities when conditions permit. Even the 2000 vintage yielded a mandarin-flavoured BA from Reiterpfad and a full-bodied TBA from Idig.

More than most in this part of the Pfalz, Christmann has got to grips with Pinot Noir. 1998 was a disappointment, but in 1997 and 1999 he made some rich, svelte, elegant Spätburgunder from Ölberg and

Idig. But yields are extremely small – as uneconomically low as 18 hl/ha in Ölberg in 1999 – to achieve this level of intensity.

KURT DARTING

Am Falltor 4, 67098 Bad Dürkheim. Tel: +49 (0) 6322 979830. Fax: 62303. 18 ha (44.5 acres). 12,000 cases.

After a spell at Müller-Catoir, Helmut Darting decided in 1989 to stop selling his grapes to the local cooperative and began bottling his own production. It is difficult to characterize this estate, because its vineyards, with the exception of Ungsteiner Herrenberg, are not that well known, and Riesling only accounts for forty-five per cent of plantings, the rest being divided between a wide range of varieties. Most of the vineyards are fairly flat, allowing machine-harvesting.

The wines are, by Pfalz standards, inexpensive, and the winemaking is aimed at producing clean aromatic wines that are enjoyable young. Few of the grapes are crushed before fermentation, and must is clarified, if necessary, by filtration. Darting is a believer in reductive winemaking, and the whole process takes place in steel tanks. *Süssreserve* is used when the balance needs fine-tuning, although almost half the wines are dry. They are bottled in the early spring.

The range of wines is all over the place. The domestic market wants dry wines, and, increasingly, red wines, of which production has been increasing. Darting has acquired a reputation for producing nobly sweet wines in surprisingly large quantities, and some of them are excellent: the 1992 Rieslaner TBA and 1998 Muskateller TBA stand out. He has created a substantial export market in the US and Japan for these wines.

The Rieslings are good but rarely first-rate, and often the Scheurebe is more interesting. I find the Gewürztraminer consistently disappointing. Like his mentor Hans-Günter Schwarz, Darting is keen on Rieslaner, and makes some delicious Auslesen (and TBAs) from this variety.

There may be strong domestic demand for red wines, but they are scarcely of international interest. The St Laurent is dilute, the Schwarzriesling too confected, and the new crossing Cabernet Cubin soft and simple.

DR DEINHARD

Weinstr 10, 67146 Deidesheim. Tel: +49 (0) 6326 221. Fax: 7920. 30 ha (74.1 acres). 17,000 cases.

Most of the vineyards once owned by the Deinhard estate, founded by the Deinhards of Koblenz in 1849, have been leased to the Wegeler family. The estate has no close connection with either the Deinhard company or family. Its vineyards are dispersed among excellent sites in Forst, Deidesheim, and Ruppertsberg.

The vinification is traditional, with fermentation in steel tanks, followed by a spell of ageing on the fine lees in wooden casks, with relatively late bottling in May. The Rieslings are sound rather than thrilling, and a good deal of natural carbon dioxide in the wine gives them freshness and good attack. Yet there seems to be a lack of concentration, weight and complexity beneath the glittering surface, and this applies to the dry wines as well as the sweeter ones. I can muster up little enthusiasm for the estate's Weisser Burgunder or bitter Gewürztraminer. But the Rieslaner Auslese from Reiterpfad can be attractive.

FITZ-RITTER

Weinstr Nord 51, 67098 Bad Dürkheim. Tel: +49 (0) 6322 5389. Fax: 66005. www.fitz-ritter.com. 21 ha (51.9 acres). 12,000 cases.

Konrad Fitz is the eighth generation of his family to run the estate. The best vineyard is Ungsteiner Herrenberg, but most of the wines come from Hochbenn, Abtsfronhof (*Alleinbesitz*), and Spielberg in Dürkheim. No herbicides are used, and the viticulture is close to organic. My experience of the wines is limited, but I have found the dry Rieslings somewhat earthy, and the unwooded Chardonnay bland. Fitz ages not only Pinot Noir but Dornfelder in Allier barriques, and both these wines are attractive, perfumed and reasonably concentrated.

KNIPSER

Hauptstr 47, 67229 Laumersheim. Tel: +49 (0) 6328 742. Fax: 4377. 22 ha (54.4 acres). 12,000 cases.

This estate is well regarded in Germany, but little known outside it, and brothers Werner and Volker prefer to stay home with their vineyards rather than travel the world persuading export markets of the merits of their wines.

Rather surprisingly, given the northerly location of this estate, most of the production is of red wine, and 7 ha (17.3 acres) of Pinot Noir are planted. But Werner Knipser is an inveterate dabbler, so he also planted Cabernet Sauvignon and Merlot in 1991, and some Syrah in 1994. He points out that Laumersheim is a sheltered village with low rainfall, making it well suited to red wine production. He is keen on experimentation, and has planted many different clones of both Pinot Noir and Chardonnay. There's a little Sauvignon Blanc, which the Knipsers like to drink with asparagus, and a rarity, Gelber Orleans, once an important variety in Rüdesheim.

Knipser doesn't use insecticides and favour low yields, between 50 and 60 hl/ha for Riesling and far less for Pinot Noir. Vinification is very traditional; Werner Knipser doesn't like very cool temperatures for fermentation, because he doesn't want overaromatic wines that will fade away after a few years.

Riesling only accounts for one fifth of production, but both in 1999 and 2000 Knipser produced excellent results, especially at Spätlese Trocken level. I prefer them to the Auslesen Trocken, which are too burly. The 1996 Eiswein from Laumersheimer Mandelberg has too much alcohol, and the Gelber Orleans Eiswein from the same vintage did not seem phenolically ripe, and showed a fierce acidic structure.

There are unoaked and oaked versions of many other varieties, and in general I find the unoaked Chardonnay and Weisser Burgunder preferable to the barrique-aged versions; nor does Silvaner and barrique seem a marriage made in heaven.

The red wines vary in quality, the best Spätburgunder being at Spätlese Trocken level, the Auslesen being too overpowering and alcoholic. At their best, these Spätburgunder wines are quite concentrated, vigorous, and spicy – wines with character. The 1998 Syrah lacks typicity, and the 1997 St Laurent is unexciting. The 1998 Lemberger is attractive, but there are better examples in other regions. The 1999 Cuvée X (a disguise for the Cabernet/Merlot blend) has firm supple tannins and shows surprising promise.

KOEHLER-RUPRECHT

Weinstr 84, 67169 Kallstadt. Tel: +49 (0) 6322 1829. Fax: 8640. 12 ha (29.7 acres). 8,000 cases.

The gravel-voiced Bernd Philippi not only runs this excellent estate, which dates back to 1680, but has found the time over the years to set up a winery in Michigan, and to establish, with Bernhard Breuer, a vineyard in the Douro Valley, and to consult for wineries in Madeira, China and Canada.

Here in Kallstadt he runs a very traditional estate, with all his wines aged in wooden casks of varying sizes. Yields are around 55 hl/ha for Riesling and there is no use of cultivated yeasts and no chaptalization. He bottles unusually late, shortly before the next harvest. About eighty per cent of the wines are dry.

The best wines come from the remarkable Kallstadter Saumagen vineyard. It lies within a former quarry and the soil is limestone beneath gravel. The Rieslings here manage to be both mineral and exotic, and they age magnificently. Philippi finds there is no need to chaptalize, because the grapes routinely ripen to Spätlese level and potential alcohol levels of fourteen per cent or more are not unusual. He makes a full range of wines from Saumagen, of which the most impressive are the dry wines at Spätlese and Auslese level. In top vintages he produces a reserve wine labelled "R" from Saumagen, only released about five years after the vintage. Very occasionally he makes a double selection labelled "RR." My most recent tastings of these wines, which I have followed for ten years, stimulated a string of superlatives for all the wines from 1996 to 1998.

There's a playful side to Bernd Philippi too, and he claims to have produced the first ever red Eiswein in 1983, from Pinot Noir grapes. The 1991 version of this wine was creamy and intense, and its fine texture may have well have derived in part from its having been barrel-fermented.

Philippi is keen on barriques, and has produced barrel-fermented wines from Riesling, Pinot Blanc, and Pinot Gris. Because these are so different from his regular wines, they are released as Tafelwein under the Philippi label. The amount of new oak varies from fifty per cent to one hundred per cent. He finds that by retaining the wine on the fine lees throughout the ageing, which is from twelve to fourteen months, the overt oakiness of the wine is reduced.

Occasionally he produces sweet wines too, and his Elysium is a multi-varietal blend of grapes at Beerenauslese level, aged in new oak for three years. Philippi likes a good deal of alcohol (usually fifteen per cent) and no more than 80 grams of residual sugar. There is a vogue for this kind of wine in Germany, though I find the alcohol too obtrusive. There are also TBAs from time to time, and both the 1989 and 1990 were outstanding.

His Philippi label Pinot Blanc and Chardonnay can be delicious, but the Pinot Noir is probably the best of the barrique wines. About two-thirds of the grapes are destemmed, the remainder given a cold soak for four days. The wines are bottled without filtration and only occasional fining. As with the Saumagen Riesling, there are "R" and "RR" bottlings, which are usually a barrel selection. The 1997 and 1998 are good wines, but the 1999s are superb, with intense raspberry aromas, highly concentrated on the palate, and with excellent length.

Inevitably, given Bernd Philippi's penchant for experimentation, some of the wines are hit and miss. They demand patience, being, in a sense, intellectual wines, short on aroma and youthful charm but built to last, impressively structured and balanced, and finished with pungency and length of flavour.

LERGENMÜLLER
Weinstr 16, 76835 Hainfeld. Tel: +49 (0) 6341 96333. Fax: 96334.
www.lergenmueller.de. 65 ha (161 acres). 32,000 cases.

This large estate near Landau is run by brothers Stefan and Jürgen Lergenmüller. The former trained in France and South Africa and has a more international perspective than most. The wines are bottled without vineyard designations, because the estate consists of 250 separate parcels. The range includes straightforward dry wines from the Burgundian varieties, as well as a strange Riesling/Chardonnay blend called Del Vino. The Dornfelder No 1 is made in a Nouveau style, there's a good solid Merlot, and Philipp L, usually the top wine, is a blend of Cabernet Sauvignon, St Laurent and Merlot, aged in barriques for twenty months. I have been unimpressed by the simpler bottlings of Grauer Burgunder, Dornfelder, and St Laurent.

LINGENFELDER
Hauptstr 27, 67229 Grosskarlbach. Tel: +49 (0) 6238 754. Fax: 1096. 15 ha (37 acres). 13,000 cases.

Rainer Lingenfelder has always made a point of cultivating export markets, and his wines enjoy a strong international following. In his youth he worked in California and New Zealand, was also a blender at Sichel and thus not unfamiliar with the recipe for Blue Nun.

His main vineyards are in Grosskarlbacher Burgweg and Freinsheimer Goldberg. Those in Burgweg are gently sloping, and in Goldberg there are some old Riesling vines which often attain high maturity levels.

The winemaking is non-interventionist, with no centrifuging, no cultivated yeasts, no bentonite fining. But Lingenfelder has been known to use malolactic fermentation for his Riesling and Scheurebe, as in 1996. This may explain why some of his Rieslings can be a touch soupy. One of his innovations is a Silvaner called Ypsilon, which is aged in new ovals from Pfalz oak, but I have found the wine at thirteen per cent too buttery and alcoholic for my taste.

Lingenfelder was one of the first Pfalz producers to take Pinot Noir seriously, fermenting on the skins from 1983 onward (at a time when heat extraction was the favoured method of fermentation), and buying barriques from a well-known Pauillac estate. For some years the wine was never as impressive as it should have been, and this may be due to the Mariafelder clone, which is loose-clustered and less intense than most Burgundian clones, or to fairly high yields. In the late 1990s he introduced a richer, oakier style of Pinot Noir called Ganymed. For many years Lingenfelder's Dornfelder has been one of the better, juicier versions from the Pfalz.

HERBERT MESSMER

Gaisbergstr 5, 76835 Burrweiler. Tel: +49 (0) 6345 2770. Fax: 7917. 26 ha (64.2 acres). 18,000 cases.

The estate was founded in 1960 with the intention of focusing on Riesling, especially from Burrweiler Schäwer. The business must have prospered. The present winery is ultra-modern and the tasting room is often thronged with visitors. Gregor Messmer is another disciple of Hans-Günter Schwarz. The fairly warm climate here in Burrweiler means that almost all the wines can be made in a dry style. Riesling is still important here, and 10 ha (24.7 acres) are planted with the variety. Messmer is keen on the slaty soils of Schäwer, but admits the soils are fairly light and this is inevitably reflected in the wines. In other locations where there is more limestone in the soil, Messmer has planted Burgundian varieties.

All the white wines have hitherto been vinified in stainless steel, but soon the Burgundian varieties will be aged in barriques, as long as the musts are sufficiently ripe to support the oak. The reds have for some time been aged in barriques, of which one-third are new. The best wines in the range are denoted as Selection, which has nothing to do with the new Selection system introduced by the German Wine Institute (see pp. 52–3).

The Rieslings here are very good, lean tangy wines with a surprising raciness and vigour. The same is true of the Weisser Burgunder, which is among the best I have encountered in the Pfalz, and far more stylish than the Grauer Burgunder. The Scheurebes I have tasted here have been disappointing, especially the cloying 1999 Kabinett. The reds, both the St Laurent and the Spätburgunder, strike me as overextracted.

THEO MINGES
Bachstr 11, 76835 Flemlingen. Tel: +49 (0) 6323 93350. Fax: 93351. 16 ha (39.5 acres). 8,000 cases.

Theo Minges's best site is northwest of Landau, at Gleisweiler Hölle, where he grows Riesling, which is limey and attractive. He produces many other wines too. Cuvée Libelle is an unoaked blend of Weisser Burgunder, Grauer Burgunder, and Chardonnay – a fresh fruity wine. The Gewürztraminer can be surprisingly delicate, but the oaked Weisser Burgunder and Grauer Burgunder are just too woody for my taste. New oak also marks, and mars, some of his top red wines, such as the Flemlinger Vogelsprung Spätburgunder, aged in seventy per cent new barriques, and the rather bitter 1997 Flemlinger Herrenbuckel Dornfelder. He also produces Cabernet Sauvignon and Cabernet Franc, which I have not tasted.

GEORG MOSBACHER
Weinstr 27, 67147 Forst. Tel: +49 (0) 6326 329. Fax: 6774. 13.5 ha (33.4 acres). 11,000 cases.

Richard Mosbacher's daughter Sabine married a fellow graduate from Geisenheim, Jürgen Düringer, and today the three of them run this excellent estate jointly. Their best sites are in Deidesheim as well as Forst, and their Grosses Gewächs wines come from Forster Freundstück and Ungeheuer, and from Deidesheimer Kieselberg. The viticulture is essentially organic. When I first visited the estate in 1995 I was told the average yields were 72 hl/ha, but today they are considerably lower. The centrifuge has also been banished from the cellar, and replaced by Kieselguhr filtration. Düringer uses partial whole-cluster pressing, followed by an eighteen-hour sedimentation; the must is racked off the lees, which are filtered. Both stainless steel tanks and oak casks are used to age the wines, the former being in the majority. The wines stay on the fine lees for about two months before bottling. Until the advent of classification, Mosbacher used a three-star marking to designate their top wines.

They keep the barrique-aged portions of their red, both Dornfelder and Pinot Noir, down to no more than fifteen per cent. In 1999 they planted some Merlot on flat sandy soil on the eastern side of the main road.

The dry Rieslings are excellent here, wines that are both flowery and mineral. Until 2001, 1998 was probably the most successful of recent vintages here. The 1996 and 1998 from Ungeheuer stood out in particular, but even in 2000 some good wines were made. The Auslesen usually come from Forster Elser, and are both pretty and persistent. The nobly sweet wines can be exceptional, such as the 1994 and 1999 Ungeheuer BAs, though I was less taken by the rather broad 1998 Eiswein from Freundstück.

Mosbacher also has a good reputation for its Sauvignon Blanc, but I have not tasted it. Riesling dominates, as indeed it should, accounting for more than ninety per cent of plantings.

EUGEN MÜLLER

Weinstr 34, 67174 Forst. Tel: +49 (0) 6326 330. Fax: 6802. www.weingut-eugen-mueller.de. 17 ha (42 acres). 12,000 cases.

This estate, now run by Kurt Müller and his son Stephan (who, for better or worse, spent a year working in the Barossa), is fortunate in possessing a substantial proportion of Forster Kirchenstück as well as 2.5 ha (6.2 acres) in Ungeheuer. The winemaking is traditional here, with the Rieslings aged in large casks. One oddity is the drawing off in good years of a few hundred litres of free-run juice from Kirchenstück in order to make a wine relatively free of phenolics. The 2000 dry Rieslings were rather tough and earthy, but the 1999 Kirchenstück and Ungeheuer were opulent and peachy without being in any way blowsy or broad. In their youth, the Ungeheuer was showing slightly better.

MÜLLER-CATOIR

Mandelring 25, 674333 Neustadt. Tel: +49 (0) 6321 2815. Fax: 480014. 20 ha (49.4 acres). 11,000 cases.

Although this estate is known for its influential winemaker, Hans-Günther Schwarz, the owner is Jakob Heinrich Catoir, whose Huguenot family has owned the estate since 1744. His mother, who died in 1968, was the third woman in succession to run the property.

The most remarkable feature of the estate, which many regard as the outstanding wine producer of the entire Pfalz, is that it does not own exceptional vineyards. Indeed, only about thirty per cent of them are on slopes. The most important sites are Haardter Mandelring, 1.5 ha (3.7 acres) and Bürgergarten, 2.5 (6.2 acres), and 14 ha (34.6 acres) in the much larger Mussbacher Eselshaut. The soils are gravel, loam, and sand, which can warm up fast and give a more exotic tone to the wines than the more mineral and sandstone soils further north in Deidesheim and Forst. Riesling is dominant, but there are significant parcels of Scheurebe, Muskateller, Grauer Burgunder, Gewürztraminer, and Rieslaner too. The viticulture is close to organic.

Schwarz himself is a courteous, outwardly modest man who takes a charming pleasure in the quality of his own wines. Yet behind this gentle exterior there must be a steely determination, because from the outset his philosophy was diametrically opposed to the prevailing orthodoxy of the time. During a period when much German oenology was aimed at minimizing risk by "cleaning up" musts and wines, Schwarz argued for leaving the wines alone. He had no truck with centrifuging the must, with deacidification, with cultivated yeasts. His winemaking was essentially reductive, yet the wines were aged on the fine lees until just before bottling in the spring. He opposed fining the wine, although a light filtration was unavoidable. In the vineyard too he was rigorous: planting green cover to help water retention, pruning severely to limit yields, eliminating fertilizers, and ploughing the soil to stimulate micro-organisms and to prevent the roots from drawing their nourishment only from the topsoil. And, of course, late and selective harvesting were essential.

Such practices were, of course, labour-intensive and costly, so he was fortunate in having a proprietor prepared to bear the financial burden that they entailed.

All the wines from Müller-Catoir are outstanding, effortlessly combining an intensity of flavour with an undeniable exoticism. The Rieslings can be brilliant, their richness balanced by a vibrant acidity, and the Scheurebe can usually persuade me that I like Scheurebe. And it was here, many years ago, that I learned how marvellous Rieslaner can be. It is something of a house speciality, at its best at Auslese level or above. It has higher acidity than Riesling, so sweet Rieslaner is never cloying, and always has an invigorating raciness and zest. The BAs and TBAs can be among the great sweet wines of Germany.

If one had to level a criticism at the estate's wines, it might be that they are sometimes rather high in alcohol, especially with varieties such as Gewürztraminer and Grauer Burgunder. There is a small production of Pinot Noir, aged for two years in 1,000-litre casks, although I have not tasted the wine for many years.

The outstanding vintages of recent years were 1998 and 2001, and 1999 was very impressive too. The 2000s are undeniably lighter and less complex, but no less limpid and invigorating than the preceding vintages.

MÜNZBERG

76829 Landau-Godramstein. Tel: +49 (0) 6341 60935. Fax: 64210.
www.weingut-muenzberg.de. 13 ha (32.1 acres). 8,000 cases.

Lothar Kessler bought this property in 1974, and it was developed by his sons Rainer and Gunter. Münzberg is also the name of the once excellent vineyard in Godramstein. "Originally around 20 ha [49.4 acres]," explains Rainer Kessler, "it was expanded in 1971 to around 450 [1,112 acres], so it became meaningless as a vineyard designation, even though the best parcels are still capable of producing some excellent wines." Overall, the soils are heavier here than in the Mittel-haardt, so they are probably better suited to Burgundian varieties than to Riesling. Indeed, the Pinot family has been grown in this area for decades, and accounts for sixty per cent of the estate's plantings. They have a massal selection from old Pinot Blanc vines, and planted Chardonnay in 1990.

All vineyards are hand-picked. The Riesling and Weisser Burgunder are vinified in steel; the Chardonnay, however, is barrique-fermented. The best reds are released as Spätlese Trocken; all the rest are QbA and chaptalized. Barrique-ageing for red wines was introduced in 1989. There is also a blend of Pinot Noir and Dornfelder known as Cuvée Gustav.

Almost all the wines are dry. The dry Weisser Burgunder Kabinett can be rather tart, but the Spätlese and occasional Auslese are delicious. In 1999 the Chardonnay Auslese Trocken weighed in at fourteen per cent, which helped it support the fifty per cent new oak – a rich appley wine with good length. The 1999 Riesling Auslese Trocken managed to retain a fresh minerality despite the richness of the wine. I don't much care for the jamminess in the barrique-aged Dornfelder and Cuvée Gustav, but the Spätburgunder Spätlesen Trocken from 1997 and 1999 are attractive and reasonably concentrated, although not exactly complex.

NECKERAUER

Ritter von Geissler Str 9, 67256 Weisenheim am Sand. Tel: +49 (0) 6353 8059. Fax: 6699. www.weingut-neckerauer.de. 16 ha (39.5 acres). 10,000 cases.

Weisenheim lies northeast of Bad Dürkheim, and the soils are sandy loam. This isn't ideal Riesling territory, and the estate fares rather better with varieties such as Grauer Burgunder. They are proud of their Portugieser, which is attractive; however, the barrique-aged Spätburgunder is not that concentrated and has a slightly dry finish from the oak. Müller-Thurgau is not usually the stuff of which TBA is made, but I have enjoyed a splendid caramelly example from here.

KARL PFAFFMANN

Allmendstr 1, 76833 Walsheim. Tel: +49 (0) 6341 61856. Fax: 62609. 30 ha (74.1 acres). 25,000 cases.

The history of this property is typical of that of many estates around Landau. Until the 1970s the Pfaffmanns practiced polyculture, wine production being just one of many agrarian activities. With the change of generations, a growing emphasis was placed on viticulture. Helmut Pfaffmann has recently been joined by his son Markus, who completed his studies at Geisenheim in 1999. The vineyards lie in Nussdorf and Walsheim, but they have been enlarged to such an extent that their names no longer mean very much.

Many of the grapes are machine-harvested and only lightly crushed before being pressed. All vinification of white wines is in steel tanks, as Markus Pfaffmann likes a reductive style. About one-third of the production is of red wine. Although they have some Regent and St Laurent, they are not that keen on them, and will focus more on Spätburgunder.

The 2000s are very good: tangy Rieslings with good acidity, a lean, slightly neutral Chardonnay Kabinett, a delicate dry Gewürztraminer, and a somewhat vegetal Grauer Burgunder Spätlese Trocken. The Huxelrebe grape delivered a fresh if rather simple BA in 1999, and the 1999 Ortega TBA is too candied and cloying for my taste. However, the 1998 Riesling Eiswein is racy and elegant and very well balanced. Perhaps the wines overall lack some complexity, but 2000 was a taxing year, and this is clearly an estate to watch.

PFEFFINGEN – FUHRMANN-EYMAEL

Pfeffingen an der Weinstr, 67098 Bad Dürkheim. Tel: +49 (0) 6322 8607. Fax: 8603. www.pfeffingen.de. 11 ha (27.2 acres). 8,000 cases.

This estate is located just north of Bad Dürkheim. Its present owner, Doris Eymael, is the daughter of Karl Fuhrmann, and she looks after the property with her son Jan while her husband Gunter pursues a political career. The vineyards surround the winery, and the best known is the Ungsteiner Herrenberg. Most of the sites are fairly flat, and have alluvial soils, so the wines are quite rich. Many of the vineyards were replanted in the 1980s, so the average age is still rather young. Although Pfeffingen makes good Rieslings, the estate also enjoys a very good reputation for its Scheurebe and Gewürztraminer. Although I have not tasted the wines in a few years, I found their sweeter styles more successful than many of the dry and half-dry wines, with spicy Rieslings and sappy plump Scheurebe from Herrenberg.

PHILIPPI

See Koehler-Ruprecht.

PROBSTHOF

Probstgasse 7, 67433 Neustadt-Haardt. Tel: +49 (0) 6321 6315. Fax: 60215. 11 ha (27.2 acres). 7,500 cases.

This is a traditional estate run by the Zimmermann family. I find the wines rather broad, even the 1998 Rieslaner BA, but they have a growing reputation.

REBHOLZ

Weinstr 54, 76833 Siebeldingen. Tel: +49 (0) 6345 3439. Fax: 7954. www.oekonomierat-rebholz.de. 12 ha (29.7 acres). 6,000 cases.

For some time this has been a leading estate of the Pfalz, arguably the best in the southern part of the region. Hansjörg Rebholz took over running the estate as a young man in 1978, after the death of his father. He is a very serious man, and his personality is reflected in the wines, which can have a certain austerity.

The winemaking here is non-interventionist. There is hardly ever any chaptalization, and Rebholz won't even produce any Chardonnay unless the grapes attain a natural potential alcohol of thirteen per cent; if less potent, the must is turned into Sekt. There is no deacidification and no use of *Süssreserve*. The latter is not especially surprising, because all the wines (other than some Gewürztraminer and Muskateller) are dry, unless there is a stuck fermentation, in which case Rebholz will just live with it.

He began producing barrique wines in 1989, and these are distinguished from the traditional wines by bearing a handsome black-banded label. These barrique wines now represent about ten per cent of production.

The Rieslings can be an endurance test to taste when young. I once tasted the 1994s from tank before bottling, and found their acidity hard to take. But Rebholz insists that they need time to develop, and are capable of great longevity. The Weisser Burgunder, fermented in older barriques, can be delicious, and so is the flowery Muskateller.

In 1998 the estate introduced two Grosses Gewächs: Birkweiler Kastanienbusch, where it has 2 ha (4.9 acres), and Siebeldinger Im Sonnenschein. For Riesling I find the Kastanienbusch more exotic, the Sonnenschein more classic. Grosses Gewächs wines are also made from Weisser Burgunder and Spätburgunder.

Any qualms I had about the Rieslings in 1993 and 1994 have been completely dispelled by the brilliant range of wines from 1998 to 2000 here. These are classic Rieslings: the Kastanienbusch touched with passion-fruit and aniseed, the Sonnenschein more opulent and apricoty.

And all the wines have tremendous extract and length of flavour and will surely keep for a decade or two without difficulty.

As for the other varieties, the 2000 Weisser Burgunder Sonnenschein Grosses Gewächs smells of pears and has a powerful austerity on the palate. The Spätburgunder "R" is concentrated and extracted, hardly Burgundian but none the worse for that. One of the finest Pinots from the Pfalz I have encountered is the 1997 Gold Label, with its rich sumptuous plummy nose, yet without a trace of jamminess on the palate; instead it is rich, supple, and concentrated, with ripe tannins and a svelte texture. Indeed, the barrique wines as a whole retain a Germanic typicity because of their acidity; the raw material for the wines designated "R" is sufficiently weighty and concentrated for the almost two years in eighty per cent new oak to be sustainable.

KARL SCHAEFER
Weinstr Süd 30, 67098 Bad Dürkheim. Tel: +49 (0) 6322 2138. Fax: 8729. www.weingutschaefer.de. 17 ha (42 acres). 6,500 cases.
This is a traditional estate, planted with eighty-five per cent Riesling. The grapes are picked by hand and fermented slowly in oak casks. There has been a change of generation recently. The owner, Dr Wolf Fleischmann, died, and his daughter Gerda Lehmeyer has taken over, assisted by long-time cellarmaster Thorsten Rotthaus. The vineyards are in Ungstein, Dürkheim, Forst, and Wachenheim. Although the estate has a good reputation, I found the 1999 Rieslings rather too supple and dilute, and I didn't care for the dill tones on the barrique-fermented Chardonnay. Nor did the 1999 Pinot Noir from Wachenheimer Fuchsmantel impress.

EGON SCHMITT
Am Neuberg 6, 67098 Bad Dürkheim. Tel: +49 (0) 6322 5830. Fax: 68899. www.weingut-egon-schmitt.de. 13.5 ha (33.4 acres). 9,000 cases.
The speciality here is red wine, which accounts for half the production. Less than one-third of the estate is planted with Riesling. The white wines are vinified in steel; the reds are macerated for up to four weeks, before being aged in both French and American oak. The main red varieties here are Pinot Noir, Regent, and Dornfelder, but Schmitt has also planted Cabernet Sauvignon, Cabernet Mitos, St Laurent, and Acolon, most of which are employed only in his blends such as Duca XI and Thor.

Overall, he has twenty-three grape varieties in his vineyards, which seems excessive for a small estate.

The best of the 2000 Rieslings is the vigorous and spicy Spätlese Trocken from Dürkheimer Spielberg. Also from 2000 the Grauer Burgunder Spätlese Trocken, with just a touch of new oak, was lively and peppery. The Regent is too soft and jammy for my taste, and I prefer the Spätburgunder cuvée known as Xero, although it is quite oaky in 1998.

GEORG SIBEN ERBEN

Weinstr 21, 67146 Deidesheim. Tel: +49 (0) 6326 989363. Fax: 989365. 17 ha (42 acres). 10,000 cases.

Wolfgang Siben was one of the first Pfalz producers to espouse the cause of dry Rieslings with enthusiasm. In 1997 he retired, handing the reins over to his son Andreas, making him the eleventh generation to run the estate, which was founded in 1710. Andreas Siben has introduced some steel tanks; his father preferred to age the wines in cask. They own 12 ha (29.7 acres) in Deidesheim and Ruppertsberg, the remainder being in Wachenheim and Forst. Eighty-five per cent of the vines are Riesling, the rest being Burgundian varieties. In the 1980s I found the wines rather light, but they have gathered in strength over the years. The 1999 Rieslings are very good, especially the Forster Ungeheuer Spätlese Trocken. A 1999 Grauer Burgunder Kabinett from Ruppertsberger Reiterpfad had a rich hazelnut character which is attractive. Although sweet wines have never been a Siben forte, the 1999 Riesling Auslese from Kalkofen is juicy and spicy.

SIEGRIST

Am Hasensprung 4, 76829 Leinsweiler. Tel: +49 (0) 6345 1309. Fax: 7542. www.weingut-siegrist.de. 13 ha (32.1 acres). 7,000 cases.

Thomas Siegrist was a Pfalz pioneer of barrique-aged red wines, first making such wines in 1985. He continues to do so, aided by his cellar-master and son-in-law Bruno Schimpf. Most of the oak is local, the rest being from Allier. Grauer Burgunder and Chardonnay are also usually aged in oak. In 1990 Siegrist created his Cuvée Johann Adam Hausch, which is seventy-five per cent Pinot Noir, the rest being Dornfelder; this is aged for sixteen months in fifty per cent new Allier. It's a sleek oaky wine, with a hint of jamminess. In 1999 he and Schimpf added a new top cuvée called Bergacker, from the best lots of Pinot Noir, Dornfelder, and Cabernet Sauvignon. They have resisted the temptation to produce a pure Cabernet, because the variety does not always ripen properly here. The wine is slightly jammy on the nose, but on the palate it is distinctly oaky and hefty, and in its youth, at any rate, lacked finesse.

I much prefer the Spätburgunder. The regular 1998 bottling, aged in older barriques, is somewhat astringent, but the two-star bottling, aged in sixty per cent new oak for sixteen months, is more sleek and stylish, with a firm acidic backbone to give length. The three-star bottling has more weight and flesh, and the acidity is properly integrated; nor is it too apparent that the wine has been aged entirely in new oak. The 1997 Auslese Trocken is even more impressive, with a sweet smoky nose, and ample power and concentration on the palate.

With so much emphasis on red wines, there is a tendency to overlook the whites. I have enjoyed good unoaked Chardonnay, peachy vigorous Weisser Burgunder, and a piquant 2000 Leinsweiler Sonnenberg Riesling Kabinett Trocken. Only the full-throttle 1999 new-oaked Chardonnay was a serious disappointment, with the almost oily oak not harmonizing with the assertive acidity of the wine.

HEINRICH VOLLMER

Gönnheimer Str 52, 67158 Ellerstadt. Tel: +49 (0) 6237 40030. Fax: 8366. www.weingutvollmer.de. 126 ha (311 acres). 40,000 cases.

When Heinrich Vollmer founded this estate in 1972, he bought 30 ha (74.1 acres), mostly Portugieser. Today he has many more, making this one of the largest estates in Germany. Sixty per cent of the production is of red wine. Bizarrely, he decided to plant Cabernet Sauvignon, which has rarely proved worthwhile, though the 1996 wasn't bad: a supple wine with good acidity. To his credit he has always tried to make a decent red wine from the much maligned Portugieser.

WEEGMÜLLER

Mandelring 23, 67433 Neustadt. Tel: +49 (0) 6321 83772. Fax: 480772. www.weegmueller-weine.de. 14 ha (34.6 acres). 9,000 cases.

This estate is run by the exuberant Stephanie Weegmüller-Scherr and her husband Richard Scherr. The family is of Swiss origin, and has been here since 1685. The vineyards are scattered around Haardt, Mussbach, and Gimmeldingen, and Riesling represents just more than half the plantings. Two-thirds of the wines are dry, and the sweeter styles are made without *Süssreserve*. She has recently bought some temperature-controlled steel tanks to supplement the wooden casks.

With so many grape varieties and so many vineyards, it is hard to find a consistent thread uniting this range of wines. The best Rieslings are the Spätlesen Trocken from Haardter Herrenletten; some of the other wines seem to lack verve and length. Herrenletten is also the source of good dry Grauer Burgunder. The nobly sweet wines are a touch thick and heavy, such as the 1998 Bürgergarten Riesling Eiswein and the 1998 Herren-letten Ruländer BA, with its flavours of figs and stewed peaches.

WEHRHEIM
Weinstr 8, 76831 Birkweiler. Tel: +49 (0) 6345 3542. Fax: 3869. www.weingut-wehrheim.de. 12 ha (29.7 acres). 6,000 cases.

Karl-Heinz Wehrheim has simplified his list by eliminating vineyard designations except for the two Grosses Gewächs: Birkweiler Mandelberg and Kastanienbusch. Riesling occupies forty per cent of his vineyards, the other important varieties being Pinot Blanc, Pinot Noir, and Chardonnay, which he first planted on an experimental basis in the late 1980s. St Laurent was planted here as long ago as 1974. There is also some Cabernet Sauvignon, which has to be severely bunch-thinned to be per-suaded to ripen, and Wehrheim blends it with Merlot to produce his Cuvée Carolus, which was first made in the mid-1990s.

Weisser Burgunder is particularly successful here, finding its richest expression in the 1999 Mandelberg Grosses Gewächs. The Rieslings are quite citric, and the 2000 Birkweiler Spätlese Trocken is admirably fresh and assertive. I find the St Laurent fairly light, and the 1999 Carolus ripe but overtannic and lacking in flesh and succulence. Far better is the 1998 Kastanienbusch Spätburgunder Grosses Gewächs, perfumed and oaky on the nose, and on the palate refined and sleek, if a touch over-extracted.

WERLÉ ERBEN
Weinstr 84, 67174 Forst. Tel: +49 (0) 6326 8930. Fax: 6777. 12 ha (29.7 acres). 7,000 cases.

Claus and Hardy Werlé, whose family settled here in 1794, have excellent vineyards in Forst, Deidesheim and Ruppertsberg. They operate a very traditional estate, nurturing their wines in casks. The style is powerful and well structured, and the wines take time to develop. They have many admirers, but I have never tasted the wines.

J.L. WOLF

Weinstr 1, 67157 Wachenheim. Tel: +49 (0) 6322 989795. Fax: 981564. www.drloosen.de. 10 ha (24.7 acres). 5,000 cases.

Not content with developing his family property in Bernkastel into one of the top estates of the Mosel, Ernst Loosen grabbed the opportunity to lease this Pfalz estate in 1996, because it allowed him to produce the dry Rieslings that are not the forte of the Mosel vineyards. The Wolf estate had become quite run down and Loosen and his partners had to invest considerable sums in the cellar. Fortunately the vineyards are excellent. Loosen has devised his own hierarchy of quality, beginning with simple Wachenheim Riesling, then the equivalent of premiers crus such as Wachenheimer Belz, and at the top level, the first growths such as Forster Jesuitengarten, Pechstein, and Ungeheuer. In addition to the Rieslings, there is a little Pinot Gris under the Villa Wolf label, one-third of it aged for six months in older barriques.

The wines are splendid, with a purity and zest not unrelated to the classic Mosel style of Riesling, although of course these are dry wines with far more body and alcohol. The 1998s were an admirable collection, and Loosen's first vintage here. The 1999s were uniformly successful with the Ungeheuer, and the Wachenheimer Goldbächel and Gerümpel particularly rich and tangy.

15

Baden

The wines from Baden are appreciated within Germany but little known outside it. This is not surprising, because the region is so large that it lacks unity and consistency, and it has struggled to find an image on the back of which its wines can be marketed. Moreover, it remains dominated by cooperatives, which are responsible for at least seventy-five per cent of production. Some of them work to a high standard, but it is in the nature of German cooperatives to produce too many wines, and this in turn poses enormous problems when marketing overseas. Only about half of Baden's 120 cooperatives actually bottle and market wine; the remainder sell either to négociants or to mega-cooperatives such as the Badische Winzerkeller.

Baden is most closely identified with the Burgundian family of grape varieties, and its Pinot Noir, Pinot Gris, and Pinot Blanc can be very good indeed. And so they should be, because the vineyards are just across the Rhein from those of Alsace. But Baden also has pockets of vineyards that produce delicious and elegant dry Rieslings, as well as swathes of vineyards that churn out large quantities of Gutedel, a wine with an avid local appeal that seems to pall as soon as you leave southern Baden.

There are some 15,900 ha (39,289 acres) under vine, and some 28,000 growers tending them – which works out at around 0.6 ha (1.5 acres) per grower. Hence the central role of cooperatives, because one hectare or two of vines are an insufficient base for a grower to bottle and market his own wines. Müller-Thurgau was dominant until a few years ago, but has been surpassed by Pinot Noir, which occupies thirty-two per cent of the surface. Müller-Thurgau still accounts for twenty-six per cent.

Broadly speaking, the Baden vineyards stretch from near Würzburg southwest toward Basel. The confusingly named Badische Frankenland

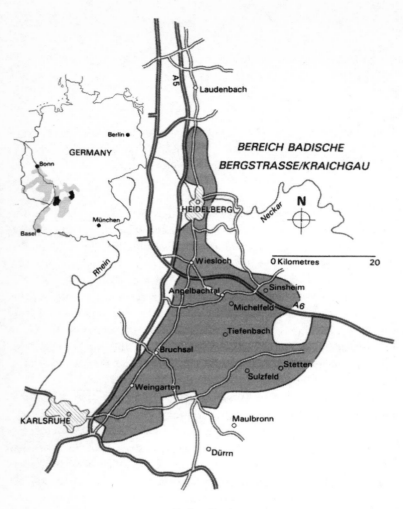

Baden: North

lies just west of Würzburg, which is of course the main city of Franken. Between Heidelberg and Karlsruhe is a large band of vineyards known as the Badische Bergstrasse-Kraichgau. These two regions are far less well known than those that stretch from Baden-Baden in the north to Basel in the south. These in turn are subdivided, from north to south, into three regions, the Ortenau, Breisgau, and Markgräflerland. About midway down this almost continuous band of vineyards, and about 19.3 kilo-

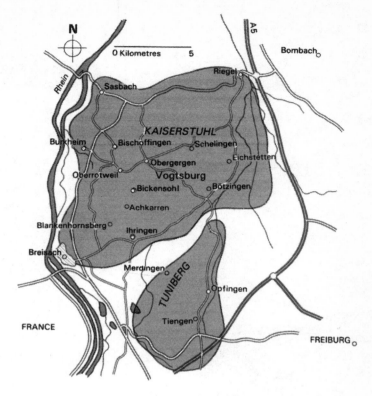

Baden: Central

metres (twelve miles) northwest of Freiburg, is Baden's most renowned region, the Kaiserstuhl, and tucked beneath it is the Tuniberg. There is one more region, some distance to the east of the Markgräflerland: Bodensee. As its name suggests, it consists of vineyards that border the Bodensee (Lake Constance).

The Badische Frankenland, which is also known as the Tauberfranken, is a region of some 700 ha (1,730 acres), with Müller-Thurgau easily the dominant variety. The wines are not unlike those of Franken, and are often marketed in a *Bocksbeutel*. The Badische Bergstrasse-Kraichgau, with vines planted mostly on west-facing slopes, is significantly larger, with around 1,700 ha (4,201 acres) under vine, 385 ha (951 acres) belonging to the Bergstrasse, the remainder to the Kraichgau. The stony clay soils suit Riesling well, giving quite a full-bodied style. There are also

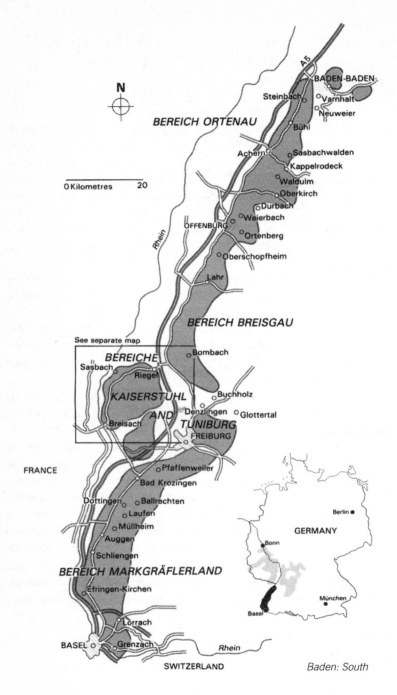

N

BEREICH ORTENAU

BADEN-BADEN
Steinbach
Varnhalt
Neuweier

Bühl

Achern
Sasbachwalden
Kappelrodeck

Waldulm

Oberkirch

Durbach

OFFENBURG
Weierbach

Ortenberg

Oberschopfheim

Lahr

0 Kilometres 20

BEREICH BREISGAU

See separate map

BEREICHE
Sasbach
Riegel
Bombach

KAISERSTUHL
Buchholz

AND
Denzlingen
Glottertal

Breisach
TUNIBURG
FREIBURG

FRANCE

Pfaffenweiler

Bad Krozingen

Dottingen
Ballrechten

Laufen

Müllheim

Auggen

Schliengen

BEREICH MARKGRÄFLERLAND

Éfringen-Kirchen

GERMANY

Berlin

Bonn

München

Basel

BASEL
Lörrach

Grenzach

Rhein

SWITZERLAND

Baden: South

some chalky loess soils better adapted to the Pinot family. Auxerrois is one of the specialities of the Kraichgau.

The Ortenau is a region of exceptional potential. About one-quarter of its 2,600 ha (6,425 acres) is planted with Riesling, which thrives on granitic soils and tolerates the relatively high rainfall of the region. Riesling is sometimes bottled under its regional synonym of Klingelberger. It acquired this name after authorization was given to plant Riesling at Schloss Klingelberg in 1776.[1] The best known wine village of the Ortenau is Durbach, surrounded by steep slopes and twisting valleys. Durbach is known not only for its racy, dry Rieslings but for good Traminer. The villages of Varnhalt, Umweg, Steinbach, and Neuweier have the historic right to use the *Bocksbeutel*. Close to Baden-Baden is a subregion known as Rebland, some 300 ha (741 acres) very much dominated by Riesling.

South of Offenberg the Ortenau turns into the Breisgau, although the vineyards are continuous. There are 2,600 ha (6,427 acres) of vineyards, most of them at an elevation of 200–300 metres (656–984 feet). The main varieties here are Müller-Thurgau, Pinot Gris, and Pinot Noir, which do well on the mostly loess soils. The wines overall are less interesting than those from the neighbouring regions, but usually have good acidity.

South of Freiburg the Breisgau becomes the 3,000-ha (7,413-acre) Markgräflerland. Despite its southerly location, the wines are fairly light, probably because of the chalky loess-loam soils. Although many grape varieties are planted here, it is best known for Gutedel, which is identical to the Swiss Chasselas. And like the Swiss Chasselas, it produces a rather neutral, indeed boring, white wine. It was brought here from Switzerland in 1780 by Margrave Karl Friedrich and has thrived ever since. Gutedel is a simple quaffing wine, pleasant enough when served chilled on a hot summer afternoon, but seemingly incapable of rising to great heights. I am intrigued by a description of the Markgräflerland wine given by Morton Shand in 1929 as "a round, decidedly full-bodied wine of a rich dark colour, and of quite unique and potent flavour. Made from the Gutedel vine . . . its lasting powers are proverbial."[2] This description

[1] Langenbach, *German Wines and Vines*, p. 165.

[2] Shand, p. 61.

bears no relation to the modern-day Gutedel, which is light in colour and flavour, and best drunk very young. One other speciality of the region is Nobling, a crossing between Gutedel and Silvaner.

Without question, the Kaiserstuhl gives the most flamboyant of Baden's wines. Despite a surface of 4,200 ha (10,378 acres), it's a compact region, planted around the stump of an extinct volcano that rises moodily from the broad and flat Rhein valley. It is distinctive both because of its climate and its soils. These are loess soils over a volcanic subsoil rich in minerals. The microclimate is exceptionally warm. Figs and apricots can be grown here, and rare butterflies flitter over the sheltered south- and west-facing slopes, which are warm enough for orchids to grow. Varieties such as the Pinot family and Gewürztraminer do well here, but so do Riesling and Silvaner, even though one might suppose the Kaiserstuhl too warm for them. With the exception of some nobly sweet wines, all the wines are dry and because of their high ripeness levels, alcohol levels can be high too: 13.5 per cent or fourteen per cent are by no means exceptional.

The Tuniberg, with 1,000 ha (2,471 acres) under vine, used to be part of the Kaiserstuhl but has been separated from it. As a *berg* it is unimpressive, never rising much higher than one hundred metres (328 feet). The soils are loess over limestone, and Müller-Thurgau is the dominant variety, with some Pinot Noir too. Almost the entire production is vinified by the Badische Winzerkeller at nearby Breisach.

Finally, there's the Bodensee. The lake ensures a mild climate, although both lake and vineyards are quite high, at up to 570 metres (1,870 feet). There have been vineyards here for at least a thousand years, and today some 500 ha (1,236 acres) are under vine. The production is almost equally divided between Müller-Thurgau and rosé made from Pinot Noir. The state domaine at Meersburg is the largest producer.

Over the past fifteen years or so great efforts have been made to improve the quality of wines such as Pinot Noir. In the past, many red wines from Baden were scarcely distinguishable from rosé. This is because they used to be vinified by heating the must. This would extract some colour and flavour from the grapes quite rapidly, but the speed of the process robbed the wines of complexity and depth. The reason why heating the must was routinely employed was that cooperatives in particular could not afford to tie up tank space for weeks. Each fermentation tank might have to serve for three or four wines in the course of the harvest. It was imperative to complete the fermentation as rapidly as possible – but this was done at the expense of the quality of the wine. Today the best producers use Burgundian techniques, macerating the wine on the skins (*Maischegärung*), with pumping over and/or punching down as additional methods of extraction.

Grauer Burgunder (Pinot Gris) has proved a success story in Baden. It is closer in style to Alsatian Pinot Gris than to other expressions such as north Italian Pinot Grigio, and none the worse for that. Throughout the 1990s there was a fad for fermenting Pinot Gris in barriques, but the musky, heady, exotic flavours of the variety did not always marry well with the flavours of new oak. Apart from the issue of oak-ageing, there are two distinctive styles of Pinot Gris. The first is essentially dry, and is labelled as Grauburgunder or Grauer Burgunder. The wine is made in the usual hierarchy of the German wine law, but Kabinetts often lack body and richness. Like Gewürztraminer, Pinot Gris demands high ripeness levels to display typicity, so the best wines tend to be Spätlese or even Auslese Trocken. As in Alsace, Pinot Gris can easily develop botrytis in certain vintages, resulting in splendidly honeyed, figgy sweet wines. They can be rather overpowering and finesse is not the term that springs to mind when describing them, but they can be utterly hedonistic. In such cases Grauer Burgunder undergoes a name change, and such wines are almost always labelled under another German synonym, Ruländer. However, many producers have found that Ruländer is harder to sell than Grauburgunder, so the name on the label is no longer a reliable guide to the style of the wine in the bottle.

Chardonnay is a newcomer to Baden, having only been authorized in 1992, although a number of growers had planted the variety surreptitiously before then. It clearly has considerable potential here, and despite the youth of the vines, there are some impressive wines from Huber and other producers.

Together with Württemberg, Baden is a region dominated by coopera- tives. As has already been mentioned, most vineyards are smallholdings, and there are only a few of the large aristocratic estates found in the Rheingau. Many vineyard owners are weekend gardeners, cultivating a parcel or two of vines in their spare time, and selling the grapes to the local cooperative.

There is no doubt that many cooperatives do their best to produce a range of wines of good quality, but many of them seem to suffer from weak management. It can't be easy to run a cooperative: by their nature, grape farmers are more interested in quantity than quality. Some coops, such as Sasbachwalden, have persuaded their members to reduce yields in order to cut down on inexpensive but dilute wines for which there is a shrinking market and to focus instead on better quality wines at higher prices. Correcting the plantings of grape varieties to match both adaptability to the terroir and commercial requirements is a protracted process. If grower Schmidt has 2 ha of Scheurebe, then the co-op to which he belongs has to produce some Scheurebe, whether or not there's any demand for it. Even if a dynamic co-op director acknowledges the need to change and has a plan to bring it about, he must still secure the agreement of boards of directors and the more important individual growers. The independent private estate is far more flexible.

A former sales director of the Badische Winzerkeller told me that growers take pride in the sheer variety of wines and styles of wine that their cooperative offers. If a grower delivers Spätlese grapes, then he'll expect to be able to recover a Spätlese wine after vinification. Co-op directors fear that if they try to diminish the profusion of wines on offer – a profusion that can only cause endless headaches to the winemakers and the sales team – then they will lose those customers who have always preferred specific wines. Most co-ops lack the vision or ability to create vibrant new markets to replace moribund ones. With sometimes hundreds of wine on a co-op list, export becomes a near impossibility. Except at the lowest level of quality, volumes are too small to secure large orders.

The one cooperative with the clout to succeed internationally is the Badische Winzerkeller (BWK), which vinifies a substantial proportion of Baden's production. Its sales directors recognized that the future for mass-market wines lay in varietal wines, as Australia and Chile have so profitably discovered. The problem was that Baden had the wrong varietals. Nonetheless, in 1995 the BWK made a deal with a large British supermarket chain for a range of varietal wines. A few months later a broker approached the supermarket buyers with a similar range but at lower prices. The supermarket reneged on the deal with the BWK. Six months later the new range was dropped too. With all the emphasis on price points, it is not surprising that the few wines that have penetrated the export market, such as the BWK's "Baden Dry" blend, have been of uninspiring quality.

Inevitably, younger, more ambitious growers have been leaving the bosom of the cooperatives and launching out on their own. With many hobby growers giving up their family vineyards either because of low grape prices or because they are too much trouble to cultivate, there have been ample opportunities for private estates to expand their holdings, and many have snapped up excellent parcels. A few of them, such as Joachim Heger, have secured an international as well as domestic reputation for their wines. Some cooperatives too are well run and clearly focused. Even so, the wines of Baden have had far less impact than their quality deserves.

Marketing has been fairly chaotic, with too many uncoordinated initiatives. In 1992 the region inaugurated a Baden Selection range, stipulating quality criteria such as low yields and vines at least fifteen years old. But by this time many cooperatives had already set up their own "Selection" programmes, in some cases with criteria stricter than those required for Baden Selection. Thus two similarly named labelling systems came into being, with no clear way for the consumer to distinguish between them. Moreover, Baden Selection wines had to be sold as QbA, which put them at a commercial disadvantage against many Prädikat wines from other growers, because the consumer understandably thought the latter were supposed to be superior. Even more daft, vineyard names couldn't be used on the label. Now there is a nationwide "Selection" system, as has already been discussed in chapter 2, to confuse matters further. A category specific to Baden is "Chasslie," which is a Gutedel aged *sur lie* to give the wine more body and complexity. It was introduced in 1995 and has been adopted by a few producers.

During my first visit to Baden in the early 1990s, I was intrigued to find many good-quality wines being sold in restaurants in 50 cl bottles. At first this idea was welcomed and seemed to be enjoying some success. By 1995 it had been abandoned. Another marketing concept had bit the dust. German wine bureaucrats have also not helped. For many years it was illegal to put the word "barrique" on the label, even though many wines were being aged in small oak barrels. Some producers such as the cooperative at Königsschaffhausen got round this by drawing little barrels on the label. In 1996 the feared word was allowed on the label, but only if the wine itself had a detectable aroma or flavour of wood, thus ignoring the fact that many winemakers use barriques to give their wines depth and flesh and subtlety, not simply to impart a particular flavour to the wine.

Classification is not a burning issue in Baden, even though old maps identify the most highly regarded sites, just as they do in other regions. The main reason for this is that the all-powerful cooperatives are more interested in producing cuvées than single-vineyard wines. Moreover, some "single" vineyards, as in Rheinhessen, are so large as to make their designation on the label virtually meaningless. The VDP, so keen on the idea in other regions, was initially less enthusiastic in Baden, possibly because some of its members make good wine but do not own prestigious sites. Some growers, such as Franz Schmidt of Bercher Erben & Schmidt, use a star system to identify wines from their best sites. The Bischoffinger Enselberg, for example, is 140 ha (346 acres), but, in Schmidt's view, the *filetstück* that really is of exceptional quality amounts to no more than 2.5 ha (6.2 acres). A star on the label signifies a wine from that top sector. "The problem of not having any classification," he told me, "is that the consumer has no way of knowing, other than by price, which are likely to be the best wines." In 2001, however, the VDP inaugurated the use of Grosses Gewächs sites, but took care to ensure that only the outstanding sectors of enlarged vineyards were granted that status.

Baden wines and Baden wine marketing are, in short, a bit of a mess. No one is particularly motivated to sort it out. Individualist growers simply go their own way and trust in the quality of their wines to secure a share of the market. Karl-Heinz Johner has simply abandoned all vine-yard and "quality" designations and focuses instead on well-crafted and expensive varietal wines aged in barriques. He has no problem selling them. Other growers, such as Huber or Schloss Neuweier, produce entirely different styles of wine from Johner, or indeed each other, and both are highly regarded and successful, even if they are little known outside Germany. It seems probable that the stern demands of the market will eventually impose some discipline on a fairly chaotic region. Until that happens, the search for ever better quality rests firmly in the hands of independent growers.

Vineyards

There are nine Bereiche and sixteen Grosslagen.

Bereich Bodensee. Sole Grosslage: Sonnenufer

Bereich Markgräflerland. Three Grosslagen: Vogtei Rötteln, Burg Neuenfels, Lorettoberg.

Bereich Kaiserstuhl. Sole Grosslage: Vulkanfelsen.

Bereich Tuniberg. Sole Grosslage: Attilafelsen.

Bereich Breisgau. Three Grosslagen: Burg Zähringen, Burg Lichteneck, Schutterlindenberg

Bereich Ortenau. Two Grosslagen: Fürsteneck, Schloss Rodeck

Bereich Badische Bergstrasse. Two Grosslagen: Stiftsberg, Rittersberg.

Bereich Kraichgau. Two Grosslagen: Hohenberg, Mannaberg.

Bereich Tauberfranken. Sole Grosslage: Tauberklinge.

Grosses Gewächs vineyards:

Burkheim: Feuerberg

Glottertal: Eichberg

Ihringen: Winklerberg.

Neuweier: Mauerberg.

Oberrotweiler: Eichberg

Sulzfeld: Burg Ravensburger Husarenkappe.

Tiefenbach: Spiegelberg.

Zell-Weierbach: Neugesetz.

As has already been explained, many ancient vineyard sites have been expanded to such an extent that they have lost much of their identity as Einzellagen. Every grower or cooperative takes pride in one or two vineyards in their possession, but it is extremely difficult to provide a meaningful evaluation of such sites. Tastings suggest that some sites truly are better than others, but it would be rash to lay down the law about which are the top vineyards. And because no classification is presently in existence, it seems pointless to give detailed information about individual vineyards. However, it is worth singling out Baden's best-known sites.

ACHKARREN

Kaiserstuhl.

Achkarrer Castellberg. 20 ha (49.4 acres). Mostly Pinot Gris.

Achkarrer Schlossberg. 85 ha (210 acres). Steep volcanic vineyard. Gives perfumed and well structured wines from Burgundian varieties.

AUGGEN
Markgräflerland.
>Auggener Letten. 30 ha (74.1 acres). Steep site. Best for Pinot varieties.
>Auggener Schäf. 171 ha (423 acres). Mostly planted with Gutedel.

BICKENSOHL
Kaiserstuhl.
>Bickensohler Herrenstück. 53 ha (131 acres). Excellent for Pinot Gris.
>Bickensohler Steinfelsen. 115 ha (284 acres). Best for Pinot Gris and Pinot Blanc.

BISCHOFFINGEN
Kaiserstuhl.
>Bischoffinger Enselberg. 160 ha (395 acres). Planted with a wide range of varieties. Johner has vineyards here but does not use the name.
>Bischoffinger Rosenkrantz. 34 ha (84 acres). Good site for Silvaner.

BURKHEIM
Kaiserstuhl.
>Burkheimer Schlossgarten. 71 ha (175 acres). Planted with many varieties. Bercher a major owner.

DURBACH
Ortenau.
>Durbacher Bienengarten. 5 ha (12.4 acres). Small but excellent vineyard.
>Durbacher Josephsberg. 10 ha (24.7 acres). A good Riesling site.
>Durbacher Kochberg. 105 ha (260 acres). Best for Pinot Noir.
>Durbacher Plauelrain. 120 ha (297 acres). Steep south-facing site, the source of some of Baden's best Rieslings.
>Durbacher Schlossberg. 45 ha (111 acres). Good white grape site, especially Riesling.

EHRENSTETTEN
Markgräflerland.
>Ehrenstettener Ölberg. 60 ha (148 acres). Gutedel and other varieties.

IHRINGEN
Kaiserstuhl. About 600 ha (1,483 acres).
Ihringer Winklerberg. 150 ha (371 acres). The vines are planted on heat-retaining volcanic soils. Although the site has only been planted since the 1820s, when explosives were used to break up the volcanic soil, it is so well exposed that the grapes often ripen two weeks earlier than those in neighbouring sites. However, the Winklerberg was enlarged three-fold in 1971, so the site is less consistent than it used to be.

KAPPELRODECK
Ortenau.
Kappelrodecker Hex vom Dasenstein. 105 ha (260 acres). Famous vineyard, as much for its lurid labels as for its Pinot Noir.

KÖNIGSCHAFFHAUSEN
Kaiserstuhl.
Königschaffhauser Hasenberg. 60 ha (148 acres). Excellent Gewürztraminer.
Königschaffhauser Steingrüble. A good Pinot Noir site.

MALTERDINGEN
Breisgau.
Malterdinger Bienenberg. 135 ha (334 acres). Mostly Müller-Thurgau, but also planted with Pinot Noir and the rare Freisamer (see p. 63). Huber has made the vineyard well known.

NEUWEIER
Ortenau.
Neuweierer Altenberg. 37 ha (91.4 acres). Good Riesling site.
Neuweierer Mauerberg. 39 ha (96.4 acres). A steep site, giving outstanding Riesling.
Neuweierer Schlossberg. 3 ha (7.4 acres). Excellent Riesling site.

OBERROTWEIL
Kaiserstuhl.
Oberrotweiler Eichberg. 83 ha (205 acres). Planted with Silvaner and Pinot Noir.

Oberrotweiler Henkenberg. 53 ha (131 acres). Very warm site, ideal for Pinot varieties.

Oberrotweiler Käsleberg. 262 ha (647 acres). Vast site, but Pinot Noir can give good results.

Oberrotweiler Kirchberg. 6 ha (14.8 acres). Outstanding Pinot Noir site for Salwey and other growers.

SASBACH

Kaiserstuhl.

Sasbacher Rote Haide. 10 ha (24.7 acres). Village's top site, almost entirely planted with Pinot Noir.

SASBACHWALDEN

Ortenau.

Sasbachwaldener Alde Gott. 180 ha (444 acres). Leading Pinot Noir vineyard, mostly vinified by the local cooperative.

SCHLIENGEN

Markgräflerland.

Schliengener Sonnenstück. 223 ha (551 acres). Best for Gutedel and Pinot Noir. Blankenhorn an important producer.

UMWEG

Ortenau.

Umweger Stich den Buben. 30 ha (74.1 acres). Well-known Riesling site.

Producers

W.G. (WINZERGENOSSENSCHAFT) ACHKARREN

Schlossbergstr 2, 79235 Achkarren. Tel: +49 (0) 7662 93040. Fax: 930493.
145 ha (358 acres). 140,000 cases.

With substantial holdings in the Kaiserstuhl, divided among 320 growers, this cooperative produces a wide range of wines from the volcanic Schlossberg and the loess/loam Castellberg. Grauer Burgunder ripens well here, so well that much of the Kabinett is in fact of Spätlese quality. The microclimate also allows botrytis wines to be made almost every year. The top Grauer Burgunder bottlings can be very good but watch out for their high levels of alcohol. The top selection within any category is labelled *Bestes Fass* (best cask).

W.G. AUGGEN
An der B3, 79424 Auggen. Tel: +49 (0) 7631 36800. Fax: 368080. www.auggener-wein.de. 280 ha (692 acres). 200,000 cases.
As befits a Markgräflerland cooperative, the emphasis here is on Gutedel, which accounts for more than half the vineyards. These are divided between two sites: three-quarters on Auggener Schäf, the remainder on Auggener Letten. There is also good Weisser Burgunder and Spätburgunder Weissherbst.

BADISCHE WINZERKELLER
79206 Breisach. Tel: +49 (0) 7667 900221. Fax: 900232. Case figure not available.
It is impossible not to be awed by the sheer scale of this winery, which is the largest in Europe and claims to be the fourth largest in the world. This mega-cooperative was created in 1952. Its new winery in Breisach is filled with enormous steel tanks that can hold one hundred million litres, and that's in addition to the sixty million stocked elsewhere. The largest tank has a capacity of 1.2 million litres.

In the mid-1990s, however, the BWK began to reduce its stock, because it was by no means clear that there was a market for all this wine. Indeed, much of it was not of exceptional quality. The BWK buys the entire production of forty-five Baden cooperatives, and part of the crop of forty-five others. This represents the labour of 25,000 individual growers and about one-third of the entire Baden crop. The result is an annual output of around 500 wines, which includes sparkling wines, own-label wines for supermarkets in Germany and abroad, and small ranges of wines of higher quality.

So diverse is the production that it is impossible to make any sensible assessment of quality. Certainly, some top-of-the-range wines, such as the Martin Schöngauer brand of Pinot varieties, can be good; on the other hand, the winery's best-known brand, the Müller-Thurgau-based Baden Dry, does no favours to the reputation of Baden wines as a whole.

BERCHER

Mittelstadt 13, 79235 Burkheim. Tel: +49 (0) 7662 90760. Fax 8279. 23 ha
(56.8 acres). 12,000 cases.

Two brothers, Rainer and Eckhardt Bercher, run this excellent Kaiserstuhl
estate, and are now aided by the tenth generation in the shape of Martin
Bercher, who for some reason speaks English with a strong Glaswegian
accent. Their estate is based in the heart of Burkheim, one of the prettiest
of the Baden wine villages, and has 130 (321 acres) of vineyards on loess
and volcanic soils.

Eckhardt looks after the vineyards, of which 12 ha (29.7 acres) are
within Burkheim, and he does so with great sophistication. He employs
no herbicides, has been green harvesting since 1987, and has planted five
different clones of Pinot Noir. Yields are fairly low by local standards: 60
hl/ha on average, but often considerably lower, at around 45 hl/ha. The
whites, mostly Riesling and Pinot Blanc, are very dry. The grapes are
picked early to conserve acidity, but yields are severely reduced to ensure
that the fruit is fully ripe. The style is undoubtedly lean and racy, but perhaps the wines would benefit from rather more weight. The Chardonnay
is quite acidic and is generally less successful than the Pinot Blancs. There
are a number of different styles to choose from, and the Auslese Trocken
is barrel-fermented and aged in thirty per cent new oak, but the results
can lack the freshness of the unoaked versions.

The Berchers began punching down the cap of their Pinot Noirs in
1995, and the wine is aged partly in barriques and partly in larger casks.
The wines are good but lack some stuffing. After years of experiments,
they came to the conclusion that a light filtration gave a Pinot Noir that
was fresher and fruitier. There is also a Cabernet Sauvignon that I have
not tasted.

The brothers exude a complete confidence in what they are doing, in
their mastery of their vineyards and their competence in the cellar. No
poor wines ever seem to emerge under the Bercher label.

BERCHER-SCHMIDT

Herrenstr 28, 79235 Oberrotweil. Tel: +49 (0) 7662 372. Fax: 6233. 10 (24.7
acres). 5,000 cases.

This Kaiserstuhl estate is a joint venture between winemaker Franz
Schmidt and his jolly wife Beate Wiedemann, who is a dynamic modern

painter. The vineyards are in Bischoffingen as well as Oberrotweil, and Schmidt is keen on those sectors that were the core vineyards before their expansion in 1971. These he signals on the labels by using a star system. The white wines are exceptionally fresh and attractive; they are unoaked and do not go through malolactic fermentation. But Pinot Noir is the wine Schmidt is most proud of. He has planted Burgundian clones in the Oberrotweiler Henkenberg, his preferred vineyard for this variety. The wines are aged in French oak, of which a sizeable proportion – and in a few cases one hundred per cent – is new. These can be exceptional: the 1999 Spätlese Trocken from Henkenberg stands out in recent years. The icing on the cake is the handful of ultra-sweet wines. In 2001 Schmidt made a TBA from Muskateller that miraculously retained its varietal character despite its intense sweetness and acidity.

W.G. BICKENSOHL
Neulindenstr 25, 79235 Bickensohl. Tel: +49 (0) 7662 93100. Fax: 931150.
175 ha (432 acres). Case figure not available.

Bickensohl in the Kaiserstuhl claims to have more Pinot Gris than any other German wine village, so it is not surprising that the former cooperative director Christian Henninger decided to focus on this variety, which is planted on one-quarter of the 210 growers' vineyards, the best sites being Herrenstück and Steinfelsen.

Grauer Burgunder is aged in casks and vinified to dryness. Parcels that attain very high ripeness or that attract botrytis are, of course, left with residual sugar and sold as Ruländer. In 1982 Henninger realized that much of this Ruländer could be heavy and cloying, and thus difficult to sell. So he decided that any Grauer Burgunder grapes that would be vinified sweet would have to be grown on volcanic rather than loess soils. Rootstocks and yields were adapted to these different *terroirs*. Yields were in some places kept as low as 40 hl/ha and Henninger insisted on selective harvesting. This kind of fine-tuning soon established the cooperative's reputation for this variety, which became its best-selling wine.

Riesling is markedly less successful. In 1990 the winery began to experiment with fermenting Pinot Gris and Pinot Blanc in new barriques, though these are not to my taste. Despite the high reputation of this cooperative, I find the wines strong on flavour but low in acidity, which gives them a certain softness that can be cloying. Perhaps the climate is against it, but they lack finesse.

W.G. BISCHOFFINGEN

Bacchusstr 14, 79233 Bischoffingen. Tel: +49 (0) 7662 93010. Fax: 930193. www.wg-bischoffingen.de. 214 ha (529 acres). 200,000 cases.

In the 1990s this cooperative, located in a prime sector of the Kaiserstuhl, enjoyed a new lease of life under an enthusiastic new director, Michael Oxenknecht, and a young cellarmaster, Werner Hassler. Oxenknecht has left, but Hassler remains. The list was rationalized into three quality segments, and fewer individual vineyard names were designated on the label. It was only in 1992 that red wines were encouraged to go through malolactic fermentation, so this too represented a considerable advance. Over the years I have found that quality is good, with many delicious dry Pinot Gris. Barrique-aged wines from Pinot Gris, Pinot Blanc, and Chardonnay are hit and miss, with too many of them exhibiting oily textures and flavours. But the range is so diverse that generalizations are unreliable. The top wines – Spätlese and Auslese Trocken – are certainly concentrated and at best can be splendid, vigorous, and long-lived. Pinot Noir, however, rarely achieves the right balance between fruit, tannin, and acidity.

BLANKENHORN

Baslerstr 2, 79418. Schliengen. Tel: +49 (0) 7635 82000. Fax: 820020. www.gutedel.de. 22 ha (54.4 acres). 14,000 cases.

Founded in 1847, this Markgräflerland estate is run by Frau Rosemarie Blankenhorn and specializes in Gutedel and Spätburgunder. Some of the vineyards are cultivated organically. Schliengener Sonnenstück is the most important site and accounts for most of the wines. Many of the wines have been rather soft, lacking in verve and concentration. The whites, such as Weissburgunder, are better than the reds, although the Cabernet Sauvignon is surprisingly fleshy and attractive.

W.G. BRITZINGEN

Markgräfler Str 25–29, 79379 Britzingen. Tel: +49 (0) 7631 17710. Fax: 4013. www.germanwine.de/wg/britzingen. 182 ha (450 acres). 130,000 cases.

Some eighty-five per cent of Britzingen's vineyards are owned by the 210 members of this Markgräflerland cooperative. Almost half of this is Gutedel, some of it produced in the style known as "Chasslie", which means it is aged for some months on the fine lees to give a richer wine. The top range is called Exclusiv, from lower-yielding vines. In general, the wines are rather characterless, correct but unexciting.

W.G. BÜHL
Betschgraeblerplatz, 77815 Bühl. Tel: +49 (0) 7223 989813. Fax: 989830. www.affentaler.de. 250 ha (618 acres). 165,000 cases.
Founded in 1908, this large cooperative, with 1,000 members, draws on grapes from a number of villages in the northern Ortenau, just south of Baden-Baden. These are all marketed under the cooperative's trademark Affentaler. Half the vineyards are planted with Riesling, and at one time the cooperative dabbled in barrique-aged Riesling too. Pinot Noir is aged in barrique if the grapes are of at least Spätlese quality. In the 1990s the cooperative director, Georg Huschle, made decisive efforts to improve quality, by instructing growers to green harvest and thus reduce yields. The only wines I have tasted recently are the 1997 and 1999 Spätburgunders, which have richness and vigour, yet tail off on the finish. Forbidden by law from using the Franconian Bocksbeutel, the cooperative has opted instead for an ugly dumpy bottle called a *Buddelflasche*, which should effectively kill off any international ambitions the director may entertain.

HERMANN DÖRFLINGER
Mühlenstr 7, 79379 Müllheim. Tel: +49 (0) 7631 2207. Fax: 4195. 20 ha (49.4 acres). 11,000 cases.
This estate supplements its own grapes with an equal quantity of purchased fruit. About half the production is of Gutedel, which is clean, fresh, and dry. Pinot Blanc and Gewürztraminer are of fine quality, and some of the Pinot Gris is aged in new oak.

DUIJN
Hohbaumweg 16, 77815 Bühl-Kappelwindeck. Tel: +49 (0) 7273 21497. Fax: 83773. www.weingut-jacob.duijn.de. 6 ha (14.8 acres). 1,500 cases.
This small estate just south of Baden-Baden is a rarity in Baden, because it produces only Pinot Noir (a small amount of Riesling will soon join the

list). Jacob Duijn, who is Dutch and a former sommelier, is a disciple of Bernhard Huber. The three wines, which I have not tasted, are aged almost entirely in new barriques for up to twenty-one months and neither fined nor filtered. They are predictably expensive.

W.G. DURBACH
Nachtweide 2, 77770 Durbach. Tel: +49 (0) 781 93660. Fax: 36547.
www.durbacher.de. 330 ha (815 acres). 250,000 cases.
This large and enterprising cooperative, directed by Konrad Geppert, focuses on Riesling and Pinot Noir. The steep slopes around Durbach are excellent for Riesling, and the 320 members of this institution own most of them. The best lots of Pinot Noir are aged in Allier barriques. Spätburgunder Weissherbst represents a sizeable proportion of production to satisfy a local clientele. Some Chardonnay too is oaked, often excessively, but the Sauvignon Blanc, something of a rarity in Baden, can be excellent.

EHRENSTETTER WINZERKELLER
Kirchbergstr 9, 79238 Ehrenstetten. Tel: +49 (0) 7633 95090. Fax: 50853.
www.ehrenstetter-winzerkeller.de. 130 ha (321 acres). 100,000 cases.
If you want a wine from Ehrenstetten in the Markgräflerland, then you had better head here, because the cooperative vinifies almost the entire crop from this village. This is a good source of white wines: even Gutedel can be good here, and Weissburgunder and Auxerrois can be satisfying too, especially at the higher quality levels. Some new oak is used to age Pinot Noir and Chardonnay, and local purchasers seem to enjoy a richly oaky style. The barrique-aged Pinot Noir can have bitter tones. In the late 1990s a new red wine was introduced: the barrique-aged Camenot from Cabernet Franc, Merlot, and Spätburgunder. I have not tasted it. From time to time there are some superb sweet wines here, such as the 1989 Ruländer TBA and a 1992 Gewürztraminer Eiswein.

FISCHER
See Dr Heger.

FREIHERR VON UND ZU FRANCKENSTEIN

Weingartenstr 66, 77654 Offenburg. Tel: +49 (0) 781 34973. Fax: 36046. 14 ha
(34.6 acres). 7,000 cases.

This property, which dates back to the fourteenth century, came into the
hands of the Franckenstein family in 1710, and they remain the owners,
although the vineyards are leased to Hubert Doll. It's located in the
Ortenau, so there is a good deal of Riesling, which is planted on steep
sites, of which the estate's pride and joy are the 3.2-ha (7.9-acre)
Alleinbesitz Zell-Weierbacher Neugesetz, a granitic site, and the 5.4-ha
(13.3-acre) *Alleinbesitz* Berghauptener Schützenberg, which has gneiss
soils. Franckenstein also excels with dry Pinot Gris, which it has been
producing for many years. The style of the wines is quite rich and supple,
and the barrique-aged 1997 Spätburgunder Spätlese Trocken is rounded,
plump and enjoyable.

FREIHERR VON GLEICHENSTEIN

Bahnhofstr 12, 79235 Oberrotweil. Tel: +49 (0) 7662 288. Fax: 1856.
www.gleichenstein.de. 24 ha (61.8 acres). 12,000 cases.

This Kaiserstuhl estate concentrates its efforts on dry white wines, which
are robust and assertive. Even simpler wines such as Müller-Thurgau and
Spätburgunder Weissherbst are of very good quality. A new cellarmaster
with international experience, Odin Bauer, was hired in 1999, so quality
is likely to improve further.

DR HEGER

Bachenstr 19, 79241 Ihringen. Tel: +49 (0) 7668 205. Fax: 9300. www.heger-
weine.de. 15 ha (37 acres). (Plus 20 ha (49.4 acres) for Weinhaus Heger and 16
ha (39.5 acres) for Fischer.) 8,000 cases. (Plus 12,000 for Weinhaus Heger and
7,500 for Fischer.)

This outstanding Kaiserstuhl estate was founded in 1935 by Dr Max
Heger, and the present owner (since 1992) and winemaker, Joachim
Heger, is his grandson. The Heger cellars are crowded with barrels, and
such is the proliferation of wines that tasting here can be a prolonged
but enthralling experience. There are two principal sites: the well
known Ihringer Winklerberg and the steep volcanic Achkarrer Schlossberg. Heger points out that Winklerberg has been doubled in size, so
generalizations about its overall exceptional quality are now somewhat

suspect. Joachim Heger claims to have the oldest Gelber Muskateller in Baden, because it was planted in 1951 on the Winklerberg. New plantings of the Heger vineyards are made to a much higher density than in the past: 7,000–8,000 vines/ha (2,833–3,238 vines/acre) is now the norm.

In 1997 Heger bought the 16-ha (39.5-acre) Fischer estate in Bottingen, thus doubling the vineyard area of the Heger estate. Production is divided between two labels, and the Fischer wines are bottled separately. The top wines, mostly from the Winklerberg and Schlossberg, are labelled as Weingut Dr Heger. Those from lesser or leased vineyards, including those on loess soils, are bottled as Weinhaus Joachim Heger. This is not to say that the Weinhaus range is modest in quality; Heger is keen to ensure that very good wines also appear under this label. Indeed, some of the Weinhaus Pinot Noirs from the Tuniberg can be excellent. Joachim Heger doesn't mind complication, so it is worth bearing in mind that he also makes a range of wines from Freiburger Schlossberg, and has a brand called Mimus, a white, first made in 1996, from a blend of Pinot Gris, Pinot Blanc, and Chardonnay.

With the exception of nobly sweet wines, the Heger range is completely dry. Nor does he ever deacidify. Among the white wines, one of his specialities is Silvaner, a variety widely planted in Ihringen. Heger stresses that you need to avoid malolactic fermentation to keep good acidity levels in the wine. The top bottling is the Silvaner from fifty year vines in Achkarrer Schlossberg.

Heger prefers long macerations for his Pinot Noir, and in the exceptional 1990 vintage the wine spent twenty-eight days on the skins. He tends to use cultivated yeasts, because he finds them more reliable, and the wines are pumped over and punched down, in varying permutations. No more than forty per cent new oak is used for Pinot Noir, and Heger uses German as well as French oak. He tends to begin ageing the best wines in new oak, and then transfers them to older barrels. He is now replanting with Burgundian clones, so the Pinot Noir may be even better in years to come.

Joachim Heger aims for elegance in his wines, and largely succeeds, though it can't be easy given vineyards that deliver rich ripe fruit with high must weights. One can depend on Heger for excellent Pinot Noir and Pinot Blanc, though it can require careful study of the wine list to sort out the different bottlings. Riesling from the Winklerberg can be surprisingly good, but good Riesling is not hard to find. So I tend to give more applause to the Muskateller, Pinot Blanc, and Silvaner, which can be exceptional, though I can't work up much enthusiasm for the oaky, liquorice-scented Mimus. Very occasionally Heger produces some stunning TBAs from Muskateller and Riesling.

WINZERKELLER HEX VOM DASENSTEIN
Burgunderplatz 1, 77876 Kappelrodeck. Tel: +49 (0) 7842 99380. Fax: 8763.
140 ha (346 acres). 110,000 cases.
More than two-thirds of production at this Ortenau cooperative, which is named after the village's principal vineyard, is of Pinot Noir. The main marketing ploy is the gaudily painted bottling of the legendary witch after whom the cooperative is named; it apparently goes down a treat in Japan. In the early 1990s the wines were cheap but dire, but I gather quality has improved and the wines are now much fruitier.

REICHSGRAF UND MARQUIS ZU HOENSBROECH
74918 Angelbachtal-Michelfeld. Tel: +49 (0) 7265 911034. Fax: 911035.
www.weingut-graf-hoensbroech.com. 17 ha (42 acres). 10,000 cases.
The Hoensbroech family, now represented here by the willowy Adrian Graf Hoensbroech, is of Flemish origin and came to Germany in the seventeenth century. Their north Baden wine estate, however, is of more recent origin, having been founded in 1966. There is a wide range of grape varieties, including some, such as Lemberger and Schwarzriesling, more often encountered in Württemberg. One of the house specialities is Pinot Blanc, which is tangy and fruity.

BERNHARD HUBER
Heimbacher Weg 19, 79364 Malterdingen. Tel: +49 (0) 7644 1200. Fax: 8222.
22 ha (54.4 acres). 11,000 cases.
Malterdingen is a small village in the southern Breisgau, and most of its grapes, which are grown on limestone and loess soils, are sold to the local cooperative. Bernhard Huber did the same until 1987, when he began bottling his own wines. About one-quarter of the vines are in neighbouring Hecklingen, where some thirty-five year old Riesling is planted. Huber is best known for his formidable Chardonnay and for Pinot Noir,

which is by far the dominant variety here. For some reason there has been some Chardonnay here since 1956, when it was interplanted with Auxerrois.

The Chardonnay is made in a full-blown style, aged in barriques with *bâtonnage*. The Reserve is made from the oldest vines, and aged in a higher proportion of new oak. The wines used to be overoaked, and although I have not tasted recent vintages, I gather that the oak is now less forceful. A white wine I particularly like here is called Malterer – a blend of sixty per cent Pinot Blanc and forty per cent Freisamer – which is a locally nurtured crossing of Pinot Gris and Silvaner, that can give weighty wines when cropped at low levels, as Huber does. Malterer is aged in seventy per cent new oak, but has splendid concentration.

The Pinot Noir, like the Chardonnay, is made in a bold style. The must is chaptalized to bring it up to around thirteen per cent, and tanks are bled to give the wine greater concentration. Since 1995 the cap is punched down during fermentation, and some wines are given a "cold soak" before fermentation to gain greater extraction. Seventy per cent of Huber's vineyards are of Pinot Noir, so there are four cuveés: Junge Reben ("Young Vines"); the regular Pinot Noir which is aged for around nine months in older barrels; the Alte Reben, which is from older vines, cropped at no more than 40 hl/ha and aged twenty months in one-third new oak; and the Reserve "R," scrupulously selected from old vines and given longer oak-ageing. The top Pinots are greatly admired, but I have often found them too woody and austere; there is power and concentration, but not the finesse of great Pinot. But Bernhard Huber is not someone to rest on his laurels, so I expect any such imbalances in the wines will be corrected from vintage to vintage.

W.G. IHRINGEN

Winzerstr 6, 79241 Ihringen. Tel: +49 (0) 7668 903630. Fax: 5556.
www.ihringerwein.com. 365 ha (902 acres). 400,000 cases.

The 280 members of this large cooperative have holdings that include half of the renowned Winklerberg. About one-quarter of the production is of Pinot Noir. Despite the excellent vineyards, the wines are often thin and bland.

W.G. JECHTINGEN

Winzerstr 1, 79361 Jechtingen. Tel: +49 (0) 7662 93230. Fax: 8241.
www.jechtinger-wein.de. 200 ha (494 acres). 150,000 cases.
The vineyards of this Kaiserstuhl village show the usual range of soil types: mostly volcanic and loess. Marketing here is focused on simple wines, mostly from the Pinot family, in attractive packaging, with names such as Vision and Nostalgie. Quality is variable.

KARL-HEINZ JOHNER

Gartenstr 20, 79235 Bischoffingen. Tel: +49 (0) 7662 6041. Fax: 8380.
www.johner.de. 17 ha (42 acres). 8,000 cases.
Karl-Heinz Johner is one of the most radical of German winemakers. After working for some years as winemaker at Lamberhurst vineyards in England he set up his own estate here in 1985, and now operates out of a smart modern winery.

The venture was radical for a number of reasons. Johner abandoned vineyard designations, and decided to age all his wines in barriques. Although counter to the usual German approach, the suppression of individual sites on the label had an obvious commercial advantage. It gave Johner reasonable quantities of wine from each varietal, allowing him to build up a coherent marketing strategy. In any case his vineyards were dispersed over a number of villages in the Kaiserstuhl, so it made sense to blend them. The Pinot varieties are the most important here. He has replanted his 3 ha (7.4 acres) of Pinot Noir with Burgundian clones, which he considers the only ones capable of producing great wine. Yields are exceptionally low: about 20 hl/ha for Chardonnay, and 30 hl/ha for Pinot Noir. About one-quarter of his vineyards are still planted with Müller-Thurgau, so he calls it by its more chic synonym Rivaner and ages it in barriques.

This is a modern winery, employing modern techniques, such as whole-cluster pressing and lees-stirring. He also practices must concentration for Pinot Noir, though he insists it should only be employed when the raw material is of good quality. At one time Johner used a very high proportion of new oak, but by the mid-1990s had diminished it to around fifty per cent. However, the toasting is relatively light, so the wines are not too woody. Not all the oak is French: Johner also likes Swabian oak, and barrels of around 300 litres, slightly larger than traditional barriques.

There are two tiers of wines: the regular bottling and "SJ," which stands, I assume, for Selektion Johner. The proportion of SJ can vary from vintage to vintage. In a good year for red wine such as 1993, about two-thirds of the Pinot Noir was bottled as SJ.

These are wines of very high quality, carefully made, and restrained in their overt oakiness. The whites retain their freshness, despite wood-ageing of up to twelve months. Johner likes to experiment so there are occasional oddities, such as a barrel-fermented Riesling, which on tasting I failed to recognize as Riesling. He has made a white cuvée called Bianca, a delicious but fat wine based on Pinot Blanc.

His reputation for quality and consistency means that he can obtain high prices for his wines, which are greatly sought after. They are unashamedly international-style wines, and could be criticized for lacking Baden typicity. This, I imagine, would not bother Johner greatly, because he is content to march from vintage to vintage, producing his excellent wines and fine-tuning the techniques as he goes along. His son Patrick, who has also made wine in Burgundy and Australia, is now working alongside him.

FRANZ KELLER: SCHWARZER ADLER
Badbergstr 23, 79235 Oberbergen. Tel: +49 (0) 7662 93300. Fax: 719.
www.franz-keller.de. 20 ha (49.4 acres). 30,000 cases.
Oberbergen is in the very heart of the Kaiserstuhl. Franz Keller and his son Fritz run not only this well known estate, but an even better known restaurant of the same name. The sites, mostly top vineyards in Oberrotweil, are steep, and the soils basically of weathered volcanic stone, but with varied layers of loess, loamy sand, and some limestone. The wines are predominantly from Burgundian varieties. The best are aged in wood and labelled as "Selection", usually "Selection S" but, in exceptional years, as "Selection A." All barrique wines are aged in fifty per cent new oak. Production is greatly expanded by the purchase of grapes from neighbouring vineyards.

W.G. KIRCHHOFEN
79238 Ehrenkirchen. Tel: +49 (0) 7633 9089 690. Fax: 7029.
www.winzergenossenschaft-kirchhofen.de. 115 ha (284 acres). 100,000 cases.
Gutedel is the mainstay at this Markgräflerland cooperative, even though

its former sales director once told me: "Gutedel tastes likes water, but it grows on you." The 290 members receive a bonus if they reduce yields, so there is an attempt here to improve quality with their Exklusiv range. In general, the wines are snazzily packaged but lack flair. The reds, which represent ten per cent of production, can be thin and do not have the body of those from the Kaiserstuhl.

W.G. KÖNIGSSCHAFFHAUSEN

Kirchlinsberger Str 2, 79346 Königsschaffhausen. Tel: +49 (0) 7642 90846. Fax: 2535. www.koenigschaffhauser-wein.de. 180 ha (445 acres). 115,000 cases.

Until the retirement of its ascetic but shrewd director, Willi Merkle, in 1997, this Kaiserstuhl cooperative could well claim to be the leading Winzergenossenschaft in Baden. For many years the management imposed strict viticultural standards on the 370 members, and it showed in the wines. Unlike many Baden cooperatives, this one has learned how to handle new oak. Even Grauer Burgunder, which is not always a success when oaked, can be excellent, though some vintages have an unpleasant oily character. The Chardonnay vines are fairly young (they were planted in 1989 and 1990), and barriques have sometimes imparted slight bitterness. The Pinot Noir, especially the top cuvées aged in barriques, are concentrated and elegant, and remarkably consistent. Merkle only released wines when he considered they were ready to drink, so he had the opportunity to monitor quality carefully while the wines were being bottle-aged. His successor, Edmund Schillinger, is maintaining Merkle's high standards, and a Cabernet Sauvignon has been added to the range.

The cooperative is also very well known for outstanding sweet wines. Indeed, it was the first property to produce an Eiswein in Baden in 1962. Both Beerenauslese and Eiswein are often produced from Spätburgunder Weissherbst, and in certain vintages such as 1985 and 1995 there have been magnificent Ruländer TBAs, and fine Eiswein in 1998.

ANDREAS LAIBLE

Am Bühl 6, 77770 Durbach. Tel: +49 (0) 781 41238. Fax: 38339. 6 ha (14.8 acres). 3,000 cases.

Since the late 1990s, Laible has secured his reputation as a masterly producer of Riesling from the Durbacher Plauelrain vineyard in the Ortenau. In their intensity and raciness they are stylistically akin to the Mosel, but are fermented to near dryness and have a broader structure. There are numerous bottlings of Riesling, but his best wine is known as Achat. Other bottlings such as Alte Reben and SL are also of excellent quality, and there are some sweet wines from the Traminer grape.

LÄMMLIN-SCHINDLER

Müllheimer Str 4, 79418 Mauchen. Tel: +49 (0) 7635 440. Fax: 436. www.laemmlin-schindler.de. 20 ha (49.4 acres). 11,000 cases.

Since the late 1980s Gerd Schindler has run this Markgräflerland property on organic principles. This is not a particularly well-known estate, but I have always found the white wines, even the Gutedel, to be refined, and those from Pinot Blanc and Pinot Gris enjoyably stylish. I have been less impressed by the rather thin Pinot Noir. I have not tasted the wines in some years, but recent reports suggest that the wines have been gaining in richness and complexity.

HEINRICH MÄNNLE

Sendelbach 16, 77770 Durbach. Tel: +49 (0) 781 41101. Fax: 44010. 5.5 ha (13.6 acres). 3500 cases.

This Ortenau estate is best known for its Klingelberger (Riesling), its Burgundian-style Pinot Noir, a Cabernet Sauvignon aged twenty months in barriques, and for lush Auslesen from a range of varieties. Unusually for Baden, Männle also offers some Halbtrocken red and white wines.

SCHLOSS NEUWEIER

Mauerbergstr 21, 76534 Neuweier. Tel: +49 (0) 7223 96670. Fax: 60864. www.weingut-schloss-neuweier.de. 10 ha (24.7 acres). 5,000 cases.

In 1992 this well-known property was bought by the Joos family of Frankfurt. Alexander Spinner is the winemaker. There is a restaurant on the ground floor of the castle, but this is rented out. For many years it refused to stock the estate's wines, which robbed Spinner of an excellent showcase. There are two main sites close to the castle: the all-Riesling Mauerberg, at one time an *Alleinbesitz*, and the Schlossberg. The Schlossberg gives slightly heavier wines, the Mauerberg more mineral ones. Average yields are a modest 50 hl/ha.

Schloss Neuweier is unusual in that eighty-four per cent of its vineyards are planted with Riesling, which are invariably fermented to dryness. Aged only in steel, they are lean, racy, and stylish. Spinner stresses that he is not looking for overtly fruity wines, and even the Weisser Burgunder is made in the same zesty style as the Rieslings. This Ortenau property is now the source of some of Baden's top Rieslings.

BURG RAVENSBURG

Hauptstr 44, 75056 Sulzfeld. Tel: +49 (0) 7269 91410. Fax: 914140.
www.burg-ravensburg.de. 28 ha (69 acres). 16,000 cases.

This ancient property has been in the hands of the von Göler family since the thirteenth century. The vineyards, which are closer in character to those of Württemberg than those further south in Baden, are divided among three principal sites in the Badische Bergstrasse, 19 ha (47 acres) of them in *Alleinbesitz*: Husarenkappe (planted with Riesling), Dicker Franz (planted with Schwarzriesling, Lemberger, and Silvaner), and Löchle, which is planted with a miscellany of varieties including Riesling and the Pinot family. There is not a great deal of complexity or richness to these wines, but the Schwarzriesling is unusual and enjoyable. Ravensburg's top wine refers to the castle name. Called Corvus, it signifies Lemberger from vines at least thirty years old that have been aged in barriques for twenty months. It's concentrated and peppery, but shows far too much wood.

SALWEY

Hauptstr 2, 79286 Oberrotweil. Tel: +49 (0) 7662 384. Fax: 6340.
www.salwey.de. 20 ha (49.4 acres). 12,000 cases.

The Salwey family has owned this property since 1763, and the present incumbent is the jovial Wolf-Dietrich Salwey. Like Ihringen, Oberrotweil has exceptionally warm and sheltered vineyards, and most of Salwey's face due south. The soils are diverse, with loess, decomposed volcanic soils, and gneiss. Kirchberg is the hottest site; Eichberg has deeper soil and delivers well-structured Pinot Noir; Käsleberg is loess, and gives lighter but fruitier wines. Pinot Noir, whether vinified as Weissherbst or as red wine, is the most important variety here, and has pronounced cherry aromas. The Grauer Burgunder can also be excellent: spicy, full-bodied, and with a firm acidic backbone.

At one time Salwey could be counted among the top estates of the Kaiserstuhl, but today the competition is more fierce. The wines are still good, but perhaps they stand out less than they used to. Salwey is also renowned for his fruit schnapps, which, even in a region well known for this product, can be outstanding.

W.G. SASBACH AM KAISERSTUHL

Jechtinger Str 26, 79361 Sasbach. Tel: +49 (0) 7642 90310. Fax: 903150. www.sasbacher.de. 105 ha (260 acres). 60,000 cases.

This is the smallest cooperative in the Kaiserstuhl, but it vinifies almost the entire crop from Sasbach, which has no private estates. About half the production is of Pinot Noir. For many years, the cooperative has avoided heating the must and the reds are given a proper maceration. The regular cuvée is aged in large casks, but there are also barrique wines. Indeed, Sasbach has been a member of the German Barrique Forum since 1991. Overall, the reds are fairly simple but they are attractive and show abundant fruit. There are good sweet wines too, from Spätburgunder Weissherbst and Ruländer.

W.G. SASBACHWALDEN "ALDE GOTT"

Talstr 2, 77887 Sasbachwalden. Tel: +49 (0) 7841 20290. Fax: 202918. www.aldegott.de. 240 ha (593 acres). 180,000 cases.

This Ortenau village has a good deal of granitic soil, which makes it well suited to Pinot Noir, which dominates production here. The village is famous for its 180-ha (445-acre) Alde Gott vineyard, and many of the cooperative's best wines come from here. The range is wide indeed, with mineral Riesling on the one hand and some serious red wines aged in barriques.

REINHOLD UND CORNELIA SCHNEIDER

Königsschaffhauser Str 2, 79346 Endingen. Tel: +49 (0) 7642 5278. Fax: 2091. www.weingutschneider.com. 8 ha (19.8 acres). 5,000 cases.

This family estate, based just outside the gates of Endingen, has won much acclaim in recent years, so it is often thronged with visitors. This may explain why Reinhold Schneider looked decidedly grumpy when I called, even though I had an appointment. His taciturnity made it very difficult to extract information. He admits that his soils are not exceptional, so he dispenses with vineyard designations on the labels. He attains high quality by cropping low, and espousing viticultural practices that are close to organic. All the wines are vinified with their natural yeasts and go through malolactic fermentation.

Although there are no sites mentioned on the label, Schneider has evolved a rather complicated system of lettering to denote the different soil types in his Kaiserstuhl vineyards: volcanic, loess, and loam. This allows you to compare the same variety grown on different soils. There are also some wines designed as Trio, which means they are a blend of all three.

The Silvaner is fresh and creamy – and like Joachim Heger's, a vindication of this variety in the Kaiserstuhl. Unfortunately, Schneider plans to phase it out. Despite the use of malolactic fermentation, the Grauer Burgunder and Weisser Burgunder are tangy, racy, and show good length. The Spätlesen Trocken are, as one would expect, particularly good. Which of the three soil types one prefers is, of course, a matter of taste. I found the wines from volcanic soils lean and mineral, a style I happen to enjoy. The Spätburgunder Spätlesen Trocken are good (I have a marginal preference for loess over loam in this case), but are less exciting than the whites; the Auslese Trocken in 1999 was predictably powerful but a touch overextracted.

SEEGER
Rohrbacher Str 101, 69181 Leimen. Tel: +49 (0) 6224 72178. Fax: 78363. www.seegerweingut.de. 8 ha (19.8 acres). 3,000 cases.

Just south of Heidelberg in the Badische Bergstrasse, Thomas Seeger produces a large number of wines, all dry, but he is best known for his red wines. Cuvée Anna is one of his top wines: a barrique-aged blend of Pinot Noir, Lemberger, and Portugieser, but twenty months in oak is far too long and the wine is often lean and woody. The Pinot Noirs are extracted and very expensive.

STIGLER
Bachenstr 29, 79241 Ihringen. Tel: +49 (0) 7668 297. Fax: 94120. 8 ha (19.8 acres). 5,000 cases.

The estate, a neighbour of Joachim Heger's in Ihringen, was founded in 1881, and Andreas Stigler took over in 1991. The Ihringer Winkler-berg is the estate's principal vineyard, but Stigler also leases vines on Freiburger Schlossberg. The Rieslings have body, minerality, and persistence. The Weisser Burgunder can also be a fine zesty wine. I find a trace of bitterness in the 1999 Grauer Burgunder Spätlese Trocken. My experience of the Pinot Noir is too limited to attempt any judgment, though I have enjoyed the 1997 Spätburgunder Weissherbst Beerenauslese. The Stigler estate won its spurs as a sweet wine producer by making the first TBA in Baden, a Riesling from the Winklerberg in 1930.

GRAF WOLFF METTERNICH

Grohl 4, 77770 Durbach. Tel: +49 (0) 781 42779. Fax: 42553. www.weingut-metternich.de. 36 ha (89 acres). 16,000 cases.

This is one of the largest estates in Baden, and for forty decades the winemaker was Ottmar Schilli, now succeeded by Franz Schwörer. There are no fewer than three *Alleinbesitz* vineyards, with weathered granitic soils on the steepest slopes, and loess elsewhere. The Riesling here is renowned, but one unique feature of the estate is that Sauvignon Blanc was originally planted here in 1830, when cuttings were brought here from Château d'Yquem. 0.5 ha (1.2 acres) remains in production. All the wines are bottled early, which means they can be somewhat aggressive when young, so they benefit from some bottle age.

16

Württemberg

Visiting Württemberg was not a lengthy business in the mid-1980s. Renowned for red wines of unrivalled insipidity, there was little to detain the wine-seeking visitor. I found some good wines at the Adelmann estate, but that was about it. That has changed a great deal, although Württemberg overall still lags behind most other important wine regions of Germany. It remains a red-wine region, with sixty-two per cent of the vineyard, area planted with red varieties.

In the 1920s Morton Shand reported that "more than twice as much red wine as white is grown, but rather more Schillerwein is made than both put together."[1] Schillerwein, a kind of rosé, is still produced by pressing red and white grapes together. It has its origins in the years following the Thirty Years' War. With most vineyards wrecked, it was imperative to replant them as fast as possible, without paying too much attention to niceties such as grape variety. Consequently red and white varieties were planted, harvested, and vinified together.[2]

In 1917 there were 11,000 ha (27,181 acres) under vine. Production slumped after World War II, and by 1953 there were only 7,000 ha (17,297 acres) in cultivation. By the early 2000s this had risen again to 11,250 ha (27,799 acres), which sounds impressive until one realizes that in the early seventeenth century there were 40,000 ha (98,840 acres) under vine. However, the new vineyards were not always planted on good sites. With so much production in the hands of cooperatives, growers were keen to plant on sites easily adapted to mechanization. Nor were high yields discouraged. In 1989 the average yield for Trollinger, the region's most beloved red wine, was 189 hl/ha (76.5 hl/acre). This had

[1] Shand, p. 62.
[2] Hallgarten, p. 87.

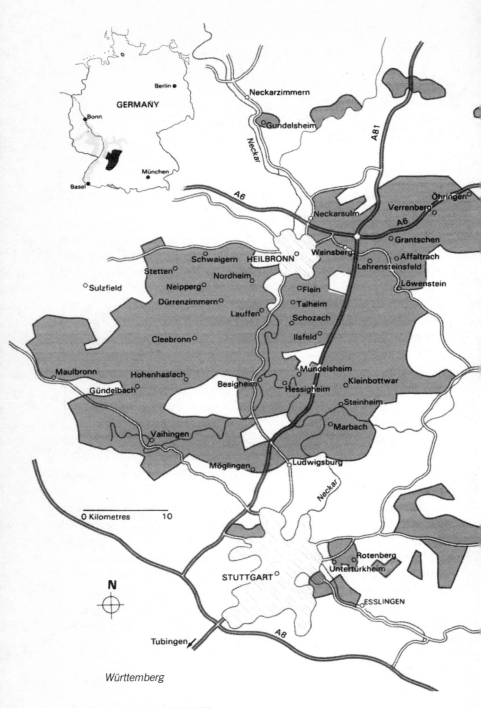

Württemberg

improved somewhat by 1998, when the average yield was 120 hl/ha even though the maximum production permitted for any producer each year since 1990 is supposed to be 110 hl/ha.

Cooperatives have diminished in importance, but only slightly. In the late 1980s they accounted for eighty-five per cent of production; today it is closer to seventy-five per cent. Their continuing dominance means not only that a good deal of mediocre wine comes on to the market, but that packaging and presentation often remain dismal, which doesn't help the image of Württemberg wines. Younger drinkers, I have been told, take one look at some of the bottles offered for sale and pass them over in favour of smartly packaged Italian Pinot Grigio and other imported wines.

Until *Flurbereinigung* in the 1970s, most vineyards planted on slopes were terraced. After the vineyard reorganization they were replanted vertically, but this caused problems of erosion. According to Graf Neipperg, the obvious solution to this new problem was to plant green cover to help keep the soil in place, but greenery in the vineyard was interpreted as a sign of laziness rather than thoughtfulness.

It is extremely difficult to generalize about Württemberg wines, because the variety of soil types and grape varieties means that there are many local traditions and styles. The most enduring of these is the production of Trollinger, which accounts for twenty-three per cent of all plantings. This is a red grape that produces a wine most people would identify as a rosé. It's light and quaffable, which is no bad thing, but many examples also seem to lack the slightest flavour. It goes down a treat in the bars and restaurants of industrial cities such as Stuttgart, where it is usually drunk in quarter-litre mugs. The average wine consumption for citizens of Württemberg is around 40 litres per year, which is about double the national average. Only ten per cent of production leaves the region.

It may come as a surprise that there is just as much Riesling planted as Trollinger, especially around Stuttgart and Weinsberg. Producers who specialize in Riesling tell me that Württemberg used to make rather broad Rieslings, and then switched to a leaner and more sour style. Today there is a move toward wines with better balance and a more pronounced minerality. Malolactic fermentation, which was tolerated for Riesling twenty years ago, is now discouraged. There are a handful of producers, such as Wöhrwag, who make Riesling of the highest quality.

Other important varieties are Schwarzriesling (Pinot Meunier), which accounts for seventeen per cent of plantings. There is roughly eight per cent each of Lemberger, Kerner, and Müller-Thurgau. Lemberger, which is the same as the Austrian Blaufränkisch, can be very good if picked ripe, when its naturally high acidity has lost its aggression. Samtrot is a mutation of Schwarzriesling and can deliver very good wine. Frühburgunder is present in Württemberg too, where it is known locally as Clevner.

The presence of an important wine college and research station at Weinsberg has led to the development of a large number of new crossings, especially red grapes that can give wines a depth of colour that Schwarzriesling and Trollinger can never attain. These new varieties include Acalon, Cabernet Dorio, Cabernet Dorsa, and Cabernet Cubin, and are discussed in chapter 5.

Nonetheless, a good deal of red wine is being made either from traditional varieties such as Samtrot or Lemberger, or from international varieties such as Merlot and Cabernet Sauvignon. Mediocre reds continue to be produced, especially by cooperatives that use short cuts such as heating the must to extract colour and fruit (and not much else) as rapidly as possible. But there is also a major move toward better use of barrique-ageing, and an exploration of modern techniques such as micro-oxygenation to diminish green flavours in a red wine. Some estates are using must concentration on an experimental basis as an alternative to chaptalization. Many red wines seem overextracted, because some soils and microclimates in Württemberg are never going to produce rich deep wines. Ernst Dautel points out that cool nights in his vineyards means that the wines have natural aroma, fruit, and elegance, and those are the features that he tries to accentuate with his winemaking. In 1986 a number of red-wine producers clubbed together to form an association called HADES, lending its logo to wines made from low-yielding vines and aged in barriques. The HADES group includes Hohenlohe-Öhringen, Adelmann, Drautz-Able, Ellwanger, Sonnenhof, and Staatsweingut Weinsberg.

Little sweet wine has been produced in Württemberg, at least not until recently. The long dry autumn weather usually deters botrytis from making an appearance, so such wines are infrequent. The difficulty with producing them, says Graf Adelmann, is not that growers can't attain high sugar levels, but that the acidity is often too low to result in a balanced wine. But there are some impressive exceptions, such as Haidle's Gewürztraminer Eiswein picked on December 29, 1995 with 236 Oechsle. And there are a growing number of excellent Riesling Eisweine.

There has been some preliminary talk about vineyard classification among the VDP members, only a handful of sites have been accepted as Grosses Gewächs.

Vineyards

There are three Bereiche and sixteen Grosslagen.

Bereich Kocher-Jagst-Tauber (named after three rivers). Grosslagen: Tauberberg, Kocherberg.

Bereich Württembergisch Unterland. Nine Grosslagen: Stromberg, Heuchelberg, Schalkstein, Kirchenweinberg, Staufenberg, Schozachtal, Wunnenstein, Salzberg, and Lindelberg.

Bereich Remstal-Stuttgart. Five Grosslagen: Weinsteige (Stuttgart), Kopf (Remstal), Wartbühl (Remstal), Sonnenbühl (Remstal), and Hohenneuffen (Neckartal).

Grosses Gewächs vineyards:
Fellbach: Lämmler
Kleinbottwar: Süssmund
Schwaigern: Ruthe
Stetten: Pulvermächer

BESIGHEIM

A charming little town on the spot where the Neckar and Enz rivers meet. Its sole vineyard is Besigheimer Wurmberg, terraced on limestone and clay soils. Planted by Dautel with Riesling and Muskateller. A very steep site, so there's a monorail to get materials up there

FELLBACH

Close to Stuttgart, there are two sites: Goldberg, 115 ha (284 acres) and Lämmler, 32 ha (79 acres), which is a major source of red and white wines from Aldinger. Stony clay and loam.

HOHENBEILSTEIN

Hohenbeilsteiner Schlosswengert. 10 ha (24.7 acres). *Alleinbesitz* of Schlossgut Hohenbeilstein.

KLEINBOTTWAR

Three sites: Götzenberg, 20 ha (49.4 acres), Oberer Berg, 8 ha (19.8 acres), and Süssmund, 6 ha (14.8 acres), the latter a Grosses Gewächs for Adelmann.

MAULBRONN

Maulbronner Eilfingerberg. 13.4 ha (33.1 acres). *Alleinbesitz* of Hauses Württemberg. Sandstone soil. Planted with Riesling and Lemberger.

MUNDELSHEIM

Wine village on the Neckar with limestone soils.

Mundelsheimer Käsberg. 20 ha (49.4 acres). Steep terraced limestone site on Neckar. Limestone. Planted with Trollinger, Lemberger, and Pinot Noir, and gives soft wines with fairly low acidity.

Mundelsheimer Mühlbächer. 50 ha (124 acres). Faces west and southwest.

Mundelsheimer Rozenberg. 110 ha (271 acres).

NEIPPERG

Neipperger Schlossberg. 24 ha (61.8 acres). *Alleinbesitz* of von Neipperg. The steepest slopes are planted with Lemberger, Riesling, Trollinger and Weissburgunder; on the plateau, Samtrot, Pinot Noir, and Schwarzriesling.

Neipperger Steingrube. 100 ha (247 acres).

OBERTÜRKHEIM

Now a suburb of Stuttgart. The vineyards are mostly planted with red varieties. Two sites: Allenberg, 12 ha (29.7 acres) and Kirchberg, 22 ha (54.4 acres).

SCHOZACH

This wine village has two sites: Schelmenklinge, 60 ha (148 acres) and Roter Berg, the 18-ha (44.5-acre) *Alleinbesitz* of Bentzel-Sturmfeder.

SCHWAIGERN
Schwaigerner Grafenberg.
> Schwaigerner Ruthe. 6.5 ha (16 acres). *Alleinbesitz* of Neipperg. The terraced south-facing site takes its name from the local word for land cleared of forest to make way for vines. Planted with Lemberger, Riesling, and Trollinger.

STETTEN
West of Heilbronn. Seventy per cent white grapes. Stony clay soils.
> Stettener Brotwasser. 3 ha (7.4 acres). Good Riesling vineyard. *Alleinbesitz* of Weingut des Hauses Württemberg.
> Stettener Lindhälder. 40 ha (99 acres). Planted with Kerner and Müller-Thurgau.
> Stettener Pulvermächer. 35 ha (86.5 acres). A fine site greatly expanded in 1971. Planted with ninety-five per cent Riesling and a little Gewürztraminer.

UNTERTÜRKHEIM
Like its neighbour Obertürkheim, this is in effect a suburb of Stuttgart.
> Untertürkheimer Altenberg. 23 ha (56.8 acres). A steep site.
> Untertürkheimer Gips. 9.5 ha (23.5 acres). *Alleinbesitz* of Aldinger.
> Untertürkheimer Herzogenberg. 15 ha (37 acres). Much Riesling. The source of many of Wöhrwag's best wines.
> Untertürkheimer Mönchberg. 50 ha (124 acres).

Producers

GRAF ADELMANN
Burg Schaubeck, 71711 Kleinbottwar. Tel: +49 (0) 7148 921220. Fax: 921 2225. www.graf-adelmann.com. 18 ha (44.5 acres). 10,000 cases.

About 20 kilometres (12.4 miles) north of Stuttgart, on the edge of the village of Kleinbottwar, is the exquisite tall Schaubeck castle which is home to the Adelmann family and headquarters of their wine estate. Portions of the castle date from the thirteenth century, although the courtyard was built a few centuries later. In the park there's a log house with verandahs that was once a playhouse for the son of Napoleon. From 1853 it belonged to the Von Brüssele family, and was inherited by Gräfin

Adelmann in 1914. Michael Adelmann has been running the estate for more than twenty years, and began using barriques in 1981, making him one of the pioneers of this style of wine.

Riesling is quite important here, with twenty-six per cent of the vineyards planted with the variety. The main vineyard is called Süssmund, and Riesling is planted at the top on poor soil. The property also has more Traminer than is customary in this part of Württemberg. But Adelmann is better known for its red-wine cuvées from Lemberger, Samtrot, and Pinot Noir. Cabernet Cubin has been planted recently with a view to beefing up some of the blends. The vineyards are steep here, and yields are fairly low, ranging from 50 to 63 hl/ha. Harvesting starts in early October and can continue into November.

For white wines, and especially Riesling, Adelmann prefers whole-cluster pressing; he admits that you obtain less extract, but on the other hand you end up with more fruitiness. The dry Rieslings can be good here, but the Auslesen are sometimes made in a style with relatively high alcohol and correspondingly little residual sugar (about 20 grams), which is not to everyone's taste. The Grauer Burgunder is rather oily and flat, but there is delicious dry Traminer, and flowery Muskateller Spätlese, with just a touch of sweetness.

In recent years Adelmann has created two white wine cuvées: Loewe and Die Mauern von Schaubeck. Loewe blends Grauer Burgunder, Silvaner, and Riesling, and spends some time in barrique; with about 5 grams of residual sugar, it's an easy drinking wine to be consumed fairly young. Die Mauern is mostly Riesling, with twenty-five per cent Silvaner, and is aged on the fine lees in small oak for a few months.

As well as Trollinger, Adelmann produces the exceedingly rare Trollinger mit Urban from what he believes are the last surviving vines of this variety. It can be dire or excellent, depending on vintage conditions. The 1999 had a nose of rose petals, and charm and tenacity on the palate, being both fresh and delicate. Another unusual wine is Muskat-Trollinger, which is lightly reminiscent of Moscato Rosa (Rosenmuskateller) from northern Italy. In 2001 he produced an intense and creamy Muskat-Trollinger Eiswein, probably the first example of such a wine.

The red wine range includes a pungent Clevner, smelling of raspberries, and a ripe, cherryish Lemberger. Adelmann has created a range of cuvées. Herbst im Park ("Autumn in the Park"), is from Dornfelder, Lemberger and Pinot Noir, aged for nine months in oak. A spicy yet supple wine, it's designed to be drunk with game. Carpe Diem is a Lemberger-dominated blend, only produced in very good years such as 1997. It is aged for two years in oak.

The top cuvée is Vignette, also made only in very good years, beginning in 1989. It's a blend of Lemberger, Samtrot, Dornfelder, and Cabernet Sauvignon, aged in one-third new French and German oak for eighteen to twenty-four months. Early vintages were overoaked, but 1997 and 1999 were excellent, with real weight of fruit and ample vigour.

GERHARD ALDINGER

Schmerstr 25, 70734 Fellbach. Tel: +49 (0) 711 581417. Fax: 581488.
www.weingut-aldinger.de. 20 ha (49.4 acres). 15,000 cases.

The Aldingers trace their ancestry back to 1492 in this area, and the present owner, Gert Aldinger, is best known for his red wines. The Trollinger is better than most. He offers more than one Pinot Noir, and an uncomplicated fresh red cuvée from Lemberger and Dornfelder. Cuvée C is a Bordeaux blend, aged for sixteen months in new barriques and bottled without filtration. This is an excellent wine, not unlike a Bordeaux but with more spice.

Among the white wines are Cuvée S, a barrique-fermented Sauvignon Blanc planted in Untertürkheimer Gips, an Aldinger *Alleinbesitz*. Cuvée A is an unusual blend of Riesling and Gewürztraminer, fermented and aged in new Allier barrels. (The blend can vary from year to year.) A more traditional wine is the Grosses Gewächs from Fellbacher Lämmler, which produced tight and concentrated Riesling in 2001. In 2000 the crop was severely reduced by hail damage.

GRAF VON BENTZEL-STURMFEDER

74360 Ilsfeld-Schozach. Tel: +49 (0) 7133 960894. Fax: 960895.
www.sturmfeder.de. 18 ha (44.5 acres). 12,000 cases.

Graf Kilian is the present owner of the property, which dates back to 1396. Because he lives elsewhere, the estate was managed for more than thirty years by Hermann Blankenhorn. Now Blankenhorn has retired, and the Graf has brought in a new cellarmaster to raise quality further. It's the tradition here to give the wines long ageing in casks, on the grounds that they are not intended to be drunk young. Two-thirds of the production is red wine, notably Pinot Noir and Samtrot. There's Riesling too, though I find it can be rather sweet and broad. The Lemberger is fresh, juicy, and straightforward, with a peppery finish. Older vintages of Samtrot have shown a surprising longevity. The Pinot Noir is fairly simple.

ERNST DAUTEL
Lauerweg 55, 74357 Bönnigheim. Tel: +49 (0) 7143 870326. Fax: 870327. www.weingut-dautel.de. 10 ha (24.7 acres). 5,500 cases.

Although the Dautels have been growing grapes since the sixteenth century, Ernst Dautel sold his grapes to the local cooperative until 1978. The main varieties planted here are Riesling and Lemberger, and he has reduced the proportion of Trollinger and Schwarzriesling in favour of Pinot Noir. Dautel has tried Merlot and it can ripen here, but he's not sure it's right for the region. Red grapes occupy sixty per cent of the vineyards.

Because most of the wines are dry, Dautel doesn't like to use the term Spätlese, so he has substituted a star system to denote quality levels. The Rieslings have remarkably vigorous acidity, especially the Trocken***. The Auslese is not very exciting, but he tries to make Eiswein every year, and usually succeeds. The 1998, from a great Eiswein year, was classic.

Other white wines include a rather neutral Weissburgunder***, and a toasty stylish barrique-aged version, with four stars. There's also a cuvée called Kreation, a blend of Kerner, Riesling, and Weissburgunder, with just a dash of barrique-ageing. Although Dautel makes both Chardonnay and Weissburgunder, he prefers the latter, which he believes has more potential in this region. It's certainly more harmonious than the rather raw oaky Chardonnay.

Dautel has been ageing his best red wines in barriques since 1986. He uses many different kinds of oak, mostly French, arguing that the fine grain of the oak is more important than the exact origin. The Samtrot seems more successful than the rather hollow Schwarzriesling. The oak-aged Lemberger is a powerful and dense expression of this variety, and needs bottle-ageing to tame its tannins.

There's a wide range of Spätburgunder, the simpler wines being aged in large casks and showing pleasant raspberry fruit, but otherwise lacking personality. The oak-aged wines are more concentrated and stylish. Easily the best of them is the parcel and barrel selection known as "S," made only in top years, a sumptuous fruity wine, with a firm tannic finish. The top-of-the-range red Kreation is an oaked blend of Merlot, Cabernet Sauvignon, and Lemberger, first made in 1995. The wine has a bright perfumed cherry nose, while on the palate it is rich, supple, and has good acidic backbone.

DRAUTZ-ABLE

Faiss-Str 23, 74076 Heilbronn. Tel: +49 (0) 7131 177908. Fax: 941239. 18 ha (44.5 acres). 13,000 cases.

Richard Drautz and his sister Christel Able run this estate, which came into being after Christel married Martin Able. Red grapes dominate the vineyards, the most important varieties being Trollinger, Lemberger, and Pinot Noir, plus Samtrot, Dornfelder, and Schwarzriesling. Riesling is the most significant white variety, plus Burgundian whites and Sauvignon Blanc. The range of wines is enormous, excessively so.

Drautz is keen on barriques, and there are cuvées of Sauvignon Blanc, Grauburgunder and Weissburgunder that spend twelve months in new oak. White wines that have stood out in tastings include a brash flavoury 1998 Riesling Kabinett Trocken and a silky if atypical 1997 Sauvignon. I positively dislike the 1999 Riesling aged in barriques, and showing more raw wood than fruit. The 1999 Weisswein Cuvée blends Grauburgunder and Weissburgunder but is a touch drab. So is the 1998 Rotwein Cuvée, blending Lemberger and Pinot Noir, a wine with a worrying acetone smell. The Lemberger Spätlese Trocken is a better bet.

Jodokus, named after a fifteenth-century ancestor and first made in 1988, is a barrique-aged blend of Cabernet Sauvignon, Cabernet Dorio, and Lemberger, aged for twenty-four months in new oak. The Cabernet dominates the nose, while the Lemberger gives an edgy acidity to the wine, which needs time in bottle to become harmonious.

Two curiosities: in 1989 Richard Dautz introduced a sparkling Pinot Noir aged in barriques, and a sparkling pink Trollinger.

JÜRGEN ELLWANGER

Bachstr 21, 73650 Winterbach. Tel: +49 (0) 7181 44525. Fax: 46128.
www.weingut-ellwanger.de. 20 ha (49.4 acres). 10,000 cases.

Winterbach is located just east of Stuttgart. The vineyards are planted
with a wide range of varieties: twenty per cent Trollinger, twenty per cent
Riesling, ten per cent Pinot Noir, as well as Kerner, Dornfelder,
Lemberger, Zweigelt, Pinot Blanc, and Pinot Gris. Ellwanger says he
makes wine to please his own tastes. It was in 1983 that he first started to
use small oak barrels. He admires German oak, which gives less pronounced oaky flavours, he says, than French. On the other hand, when
he does use small oak, he likes a high proportion of new barrels.

The whites are a mixed bag: a clean, bracing Riesling Kabinett
Trocken, a rather sappy Kerner Kabinett, and a severe Kerner Auslese
Trocken, with hints of mango on the nose. Nicodemus Candidus a is
barrique-aged Kerner, primarily a mouthful of oak. Barrique-aged
Grauburgunder is creamy but has slight bitterness on the finish. The
Riesling Eiswein is more interesting than the version from Kerner.

There's a range of wines in burgundy bottles, all with vineyard names.
These are simple wines with highish yields, soundly made if dilute, and
with no pretensions.

The barrique wines include a fruity if tannic Zweigelt; lush supple
Dornfelder; an oaky, dryish Merlot; Nicodemus, a juicy, oaky blend of
Lemberger, Merlot, Pinot Noir, and Portugieser; Lemberger with a nose
of cherry, pepper and cloves, and a lively palate with a lot of oak tannin;
and a ripe, oaky, modestly concentrated Spätburgunder with a spicy
finish.

Overall, his wines have too much oak, giving a marked dryness on the
palate. But the fruit quality is good.

WEINGÄRTNERGENOSSENSCHAFT GRANTSCHEN

Wimmentalerstr 36, 74189 Weinsberg-Grantschen. Tel: 7134 98020.
Fax: 980222. www.grantschen.de. 140 ha (346 acres). 130,000 cases.

Grantschen is just east of Heilbronn, in the north of the wine zone. This
enterprising cooperative has 200 members and offers a bewildering range
of wines. The dry Rieslings lack excitement, and there are some weird
oaked whites. The 1999 Chardonnay, aged mostly in new Swabian oak, is
sour and reminiscent of gherkins – not nice. Celine is an overoaked blend

of Riesling, Chardonnay, and Gewürztraminer, which lacks fruit and persistence.

The reds are considerably better. There's a soft plump Lemberger Spätlese Trocken, and a slightly jammy blend called SM, composed of Dornfelder and Lemberger. The barrique-aged Lemberger is powerful and well structured. Their flagship wine is Grandor, strictly selected Lemberger aged for eighteen months in small barrels of Swabian and French oak. It's a dense peppery wine with a fine core of fruit, and is easily the cooperative's best wine.

KARL HAIDLE

Hindenburgstr 21, 71394 Kernen-Stetten. Tel: +49 (0) 7151 949110. Fax: 46313. www.weingut-karl-haidle.de. 17 ha (42 acres). 11,000 cases.

The good-humoured Hans Haidle took over running the estate when he was twenty-three. Haidle also buys in fruit from some of his neighbours. Stetten is just west of Heilbronn and is dominated by white grapes. Riesling comes from Stettener Pulvermächer, reds from Stettener Mönchberg. Half the production is Riesling, which is of high quality. The white grapes are usually destemmed but there is whole-cluster pressing for Grauburgunder. Many of the wines are aged in large oval casks rather than steel tanks. The Weissburgunder here is excellent, and I prefer it to the barrique-aged Chardonnay.

Trollinger "S" is quite fruity for the variety but has a rather bitter finish. The unoaked 1998 Zweigelt has an attractive plummy nose; on the palate it's rich, soft, and reasonably concentrated. The barrique-aged Zweigelt has vanilla as well as plums on the nose; and the oak gives spice to the finish. The Dornfelder "Barrique" smells of rosemary, and is plump, rather bland and jammy. Barrique-ageing works much better with Lemberger, giving a slightly herbal nose, and ample concentration of flavour behind the plump texture. "Ypsilon" is a barrique wine from Lemberger and Acalon. The oak gives a rather jammy vanilla and plum nose; there's plenty of sweet almost overripe fruit, but the wood delivers a rather dry finish.

The simpler Pinot Noirs are made by heating the must; the more serious bottlings receive a proper maceration. The oaked cuvées are concentrated thanks to very low yields; the oak is present but not too dominant, and the wines have an elegant sheen and texture.

Overall, Haidle's reds have a strong family resemblance: dark, dense, very ripe, jammy.

SCHLOSSGUT HOHENBEILSTEIN

Im Schloss, 71717 Beilstein. Tel: +49 (0) 7062 937110. Fax: 9371122.
www.schlossgut-hohenbeilstein.de. 13 ha (32.1 acres). 8,500 cases.

The stocky, bearded Hartmann Dippon has spent some time in California, and adopted organic principles here in 1987. The most important varieties are Riesling and Trollinger, with smaller quantities of Samtrot, Schwarzriesling, and Kerner. There are some mediocre wines in the range: a confected Schwarzriesling Spätlese, and dilute Spätburgunder Spätlese. The Lembergers are considerably better, but the oaked version is coarse. The 1999 Spätburgunder Auslese Trocken lacked sufficient fruit to support the oak. Dippon is proud of his Spätburgunder Weissherbst Eiswein, which is aged for two years in barriques. I have not tasted it.

FÜRST ZU HOHENLOHE-ÖHRINGEN

Im Schloss, 74613 Öhringen. Tel: +49 (0) 7941 94910. Fax: 37349.
www.verrenberg.de. 20 ha (49.4 acres). 15,000 cases.

This princely family has owned vineyards here since 1360. Half are planted with Riesling. There is a fair amount of Lemberger and Pinot Noir, and the estate belongs to the HADES group. This was one of the first estates in Württemberg to use barriques, beginning in 1983. The red wines are undoubtedly serious. The 1997 Lemberger Auslese Trocken is tannic and rather overextracted but certainly doesn't lack body and richness. There is also an oaked cuvée called Ex Flammis Orior: sweet, ripe, and fleshy on the nose, and somehow both jammy and peppery on the palate, adding up to a slightly cloying wine. The estate has recently launched two other red cuvées: the simple Ego 1 and the very expensive In Senio, neither of which I have tasted.

BURG HORNBERG

74865 Neckarzimmern. Tel: +49 (0) 6261 5001. Fax: 2348. www.burg-hornberg.de. 10 ha (24.7 acres). 3,500 cases.

Baron Dajo von Gemmingen-Hornberg owns what may be the oldest estate in Württemberg, based in a castle with its vineyards high above the Neckar. One-third of the vineyards are planted with Riesling, twelve per cent with Weissburgunder, eleven per cent with Trollinger, and there are smaller areas of Spätburgunder and Schwarzriesling. There are two *Alleinbesitz* sites, with terraced vineyards over limestone soils: Burg Hornberger Götzhalde and Wallmauer.

WEINGUT DES GRAFEN NEIPPERG
Schlossstr 12, 74190 Schwaigern. Tel: +49 (0) 7138 941400. Fax: 4007. 31 ha (76.9 acres). 16,000 cases.

The Neippergs have been producing wine here since the thirteenth century. The present Graf zu Neipperg takes a back seat these days, and leaves the running of this important estate near Heilbronn to his son Karl Eugen, a forceful personality with a tendency to address visitors as if they constituted a public meeting. His brother Stephan von Neipperg is well known to lovers of St Émilion as the proprietor of Château Canon La Gaffelière and other properties.

Two sites belong exclusively to the Neippergs: Schwaigener Ruthe, which is terraced, unlike the adjoining Grafenberg vineyard which is vertically planted; and Neipperger Schlossberg, which is located around the ruinous castle. The soils are stony clay, and the most important varieties are Riesling, Lemberger, and Schwarzriesling. Neipperg is a strong believer in low yields, and the average for the whole estate is 50 hl/ha.

Karl Eugen von Neipperg is a traditonalist, preferring to stick to varietal wines, because with cuvées you have to enter the international scene, where, as a northerly wine region, it's hard to compete with red wines from balmier climates. However, he had a change of mind in 1999, producing an expensive blend called "S.E.", which I have not tasted.

He makes red QbA, no Kabinett, then vineyard-designated Spätlesen. All reds are fermented with maceration and go through malolactic fermentation. Wines that are oaked are aged in small barrels coopered from wood hewn in the family's own forests.

The Rieslings are marked by quite high acidity and lack complexity, but the Weissburgunder is attractive. The strength of the Neipperg estate is clearly the red wines. The 1998 Schwarzriesling had a light elegant nose, but it's a simple wine with little length of flavour. Much better is the new-oaked 1997 Schlossberg Samtrot, rounded and plump and not as oaky as one might expect. The Lembergers are first-rate. The simpler bottlings are lively and pretty; the single-vineyard bottlings from Ruthe and Schlossberg are rich, concentrated, oaky, and peppery.

One curiosity here is Gelber Muskateller. In certain years, such as 1993, Neipperg has made splendid TBA from this variety.

WEINGÄRTNERGENOSSENSCHSAFT ROTENBERG
Württembergerstr 230, 70327 Stuttgart. Tel: +49 (0) 711 337610. Fax: 331015. 48 ha (119 acres). Case figure not available.

This is the smallest cooperative in Württemberg. Its range of wines is unusually coherent, because most of the vineyards are on a single site, Rotenberger Schlossberg. A system of incentive payments to the seventy-five members has allowed the cooperative to make selections of the oldest and best parcels, where the yields are kept low. The first level of selection is bottled with a white label, while the top selections carry a blue label. This principle is even applied to Trollinger, but not even the Trollinger Selection can attain any complexity. The Dornfelder has much better fruit, if a slightly harsh aftertaste.

One house speciality is Heroldrebe, but I find the wine one-dimensional, with sharp acidity. There's initial lushness, but no depth. The Lemberger is much more interesting, especially the oak-aged Blue Label, which has just that lively peppery character one looks for in Lemberger. The oaked Spätburgunder lacks the weight for the amount of new oak employed. The top red wine is a blend called Cantus, from Lemberger, Spätburgunder, Heroldrebe, Dornfelder, and Trollinger, using the best casks of each. The 1997 had an attractive texture, but lacked fruit definition.

The oaked Riesling is forgettable, but the other dry Rieslings are appealing, especially a top bottling called Katharina, which has an earthy pungency that is arresting. The oaked Grauer Burgunder is disastrous. The white counterpart to Cantus is Cantica; first made in 1997, it blends Riesling, Müller-Thurgau, Kerner, and Grauer Burgunder, and is aged on the fine lees, with *bâtonnage*. It's carefully made and attractive, yet lacks personality.

1998 was a great year for Eiswein, but the Kerner Eiswein had clearly got out of control, and ended up with 16.5 per cent alcohol, which is far too high.

There's no doubting the cooperative's commitment to quality, and yet the wines don't quite match the ambition. In general, the simpler wines are more appealing than the more extracted, oaked bottlings.

ALBRECHT SCHWEGLER

Steinstr 35, 71404 Korb. Tel: +49 (0) 7151 34895. Fax: 34978. 1.5 ha (3.7 acres). 600 cases.

With such tiny production, you're unlikely to encounter bottles from this red wine specialist, but they have a high reputation. Schwegler makes only cuvées, such as Beryll from Lemberger and Zweigelt, Saphir from Merlot and Zweigelt and, in top years only, Granat from mostly Merlot. All wines are aged in barriques and bottled without filtration. There is also a minute amount of sweet wine, including one picked in 2000 at a mind-blowing 316 Oechsle, bottled, appropriately, under the name of Monster.

SONNENHOF

Bezner-Fischer, Sonnenhof 2, 71665 Vaihingen Gündelbach. Tel: +49 (0) 7042 818880. Fax: 818886. www.weingutsonnenhof.de. 30 ha (74.1 acres). 22,000 cases.

Most of the wines here are red, from steep sites north of Stuttgart. My experience of these wines is limited, but I have enjoyed the 1997 Lemberger "Hades" with its silky texture and dense fruit (Sonnenhof is a member of HADES, see p. 354); and the supple, elegant 1997 Spätburgunder QbA Trocken.

STAATSWEINGUT WEINSBERG

Traubenplatz 5, 74189 Weinsberg. Tel: +49 (0) 7134 504167. Fax: 504168. www.lvwo.de. 40 ha (99 acres). 25,000 cases.

This wine college and research institute, the oldest in Germany, having been founded in the 1860s, has three estates of its own, and its wine-making division fizzles with ideas and energy. Their micro-vinifications include experiments in micro-oxygenation, carbonic maceration, different yeast strains, malolactic fermentation, and other variables. The main focus is on red wines, but about one fifth of the vineyards is planted with Riesling. The college has been experimenting with barriques for fifteen years, and many of its red wines are oaked.

In 1999 Weinsberg officially launched six new crossings, which they had been working on for three decades. These include Cabernet Dorsa and Acalon, and other deep-coloured varieties that have been quite widely adopted in parts of Germany. The institute also reports strong demand from countries such as Thailand, which is not necessarily an encouraging sign.

The wines are bottled without vineyard designations. Among the whites I liked the fairly austere 1998 Riesling Spätlese Trocken, but found a Kerner aged in fifty per cent new oak unpalatable. Among the reds the most appealing wines are the Clevner (Frühburgunder) and the Lemberger. The best bottles carry the HADES association logo. As for the new crossings, the Acalon seemed jammy and short, but the Cabernet Dorio had a strong mulberry and coffee nose, and plenty of rounded fleshy fruit on the palate.

WÖHRWAG

Grunbacherstr 5, 70327 Untertürckheim. Tel: +49 (0) 711 331662.
Fax: 332431. 17 ha (42 acres).

Hans-Peter Wöhrwag married a daughter of the Johannishof estate in the Rheingau, so it's perhaps not surprising that he makes probably the best Riesling in Württemberg. Here on the edges of Stuttgart it's Riesling country, and almost half his vineyards are planted to the variety, mostly in Untertürkheimer Herzogenberg. Whether it's an accident of *terroir* or an exercise of winemaking will, the Rieslings are lean and elegant rather than broad and fruity. They manage to combine that elegance with power and intense flavour. The Goldkapsel wines come from vines more than forty years old; wines labelled "SC" come from Riesling cropped at no more than 50 hl/ha and are rich, powerful and dry. He tries to make Eiswein most years, and often succeeds brilliantly.

The oak-aged Grauer Burgunder, labelled "R," is too oaky for my taste. The best Trollinger is called Rädles, but even Wöhrwag admits it's still just a quaffing wine. There are two red cuvées. The simpler of the two is Moritz, which is mostly Dornfelder, aged in older barriques. The other is Philipp, which is Lemberger and Pinot Noir. Hans-Peter Wöhrwag is a claret lover, so he couldn't resist planting a little Cabernet Sauvignon, and ten per cent of Philipp is Cabernet, which only ripens here if yields are kept very low.

Wöhrwag is one of the few winemakers in Germany to admit to the use of must concentration – in his case, reverse osmosis – which may account for the consistency of his wines.

WEINGUT DES HAUSES WÜRTTEMBERG HOFKAMMERKELLEREI

Schloss Monrepos, 71634 Ludwigsburg. Tel: +49 (0) 7141 225525. Fax: 225530. www.hofkammer.de. 40 ha (99 acres). 30,000 cases.

Founded in 1677, and now owned by Carl, Herzog (Duke) of Württemberg and his son Friedrich, this large estate has vineyards in good sites such as Maulbronner Eilfingerberg, Gündelbacher Steinbachhof, Stettener Brot-wasser (fine Riesling) and Untertürkheimer Mönchberg. Riesling from the Mönchberg is full-bodied and assertive. The best Pinot Noir comes from the steep, terraced Mundelsheimer Käsberg.

17

Franken

Franconia is one of the most easterly wine regions in Germany, and this gives the wine a distinctive character, diametrically opposed to that of, say, the Mosel or Nahe. Summers here can be hot and prolonged, winters can be fiercely cold. Frost is common, and in 1985 more than two million vines were killed when temperatures plummeted. The wines produced by the vines that survive this kind of climatic endurance test are robust: quite powerful and rich in extract, often with a pronounced earthy taste that usually adds to the complexity. The best wines are much sought after in Germany and are rarely exported.

There have been vineyards here since at least the eighth century, when Charlemagne presented existing vineyards to local monasteries, foundations that gradually built up the region into one of the largest wine zones in Germany. The Thirty Years' War led to the destruction of many of the vineyards, which at that time occupied 40,000 ha (98,840 acres). Later, secularization broke up some of the large powerful estates, though others survive to this day. They include the vineyards and cellars established by the immensely powerful prince-bishops of Würzburg. They had secular counterparts in the charitable foundations such as the Bürgerspital and Juliusspital, which supported their good works with the profits from the vineyards they acquired, usually as legacies. These, too, have survived to this day.

As a wine region, Franken is very dispersed. The most important sector is focused on the city of Würzburg. This sector is the Maindreieck (Main Triangle), following the course of the river Main from Schweinfurt down to Escherndorf and Ochsenfurt, then northwest toward the city and continuing almost as far as Gemünden. Here the soils are fossil limestone mixed in some places with clay. Further east is the Bereich

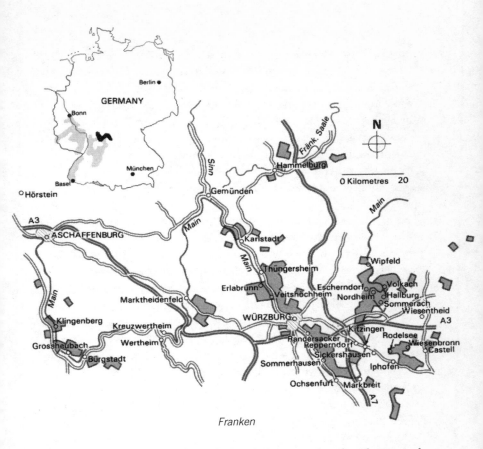

Franken

Steigerwald (not on map), which has heavier marl soils. The westerly sector around Kreuzwertheim and Bürgstadt has loam and sandstone soils, and many of Franken's best red wines come from here.

The area under vine has grown steadily during the twentieth century. In 1915 there were 3,500 ha (8,649 acres) under vine, and by 1923 that had risen to 4,300 ha (10,625 acres). The major period of expansion took place in the 1950s and 1960s, and today the area is 6,000 ha (14,826 acres). Before then Silvaner had been the dominant grape variety, with a good deal of Müller-Thurgau as well. The development of frost-resistant crossings such as Bacchus and Kerner meant that these varieties could be planted in lower flatter sites formerly considered too risky for viticulture. This may have been good news for grape farmers, but it led to an overall decline in quality. This seems to have gone largely unnoticed, because domestic sales remained strong, and there is still twelve per cent of Bacchus in the vineyards. By 2001, Müller-Thurgau accounted for forty per cent of the area under vine, Silvaner for twenty-one per cent. Cooperatives play an important role. There are only seven of them but they are responsible for more than half the region's production.

Franken is one of the few regions where even the intrinsically mediocre Müller-Thurgau can produce a sound and enjoyable wine, but its strengths certainly lie more with Silvaner and Riesling. Silvaner here can be pungent and bracing, and its occasional earthiness usually gives it character rather than coarseness. Riesling too has that character, and a good deal more breadth than Rieslings from the Rhein or Mosel. Riesling is fairly rare in Franken not because it is not prized, but because there are few sites available where it is likely to ripen properly, because it's a variety that likes a longer growing season than usually occurs in the region.

The warm summers usually mean that the grapes do ripen fully, so there is no problem fermenting the must to dryness. Even though the wine law allows up to 8 grams of residual sugar in a wine labelled Trocken, there is a widely observed convention in Franken to regard as Trocken wines with no more than 4 grams. Trocken, in Franken, means Trocken. In 1990, maximum yields were fixed at 90 hl/ha, but this is applied only to the amount of wine any producer may *sell* in any given year. The rule contains the absurd proviso that any excess production can be held over to top up a weaker future vintage; this provides little disincentive to overcropping. Although dry Spätlesen are very common, dry Auslesen tend to be rare, because the higher ripeness of Franken grapes would lead to wines with unpalatably aggressive alcohol levels if fermented to dryness.

Although Franken does not place much emphasis on sweet wine production, Silvaner and Riesling Eiswein and TBA can compare in quality to their counterparts from the Rhein or Mosel. The style, however, is very different, because the wines naturally attain higher alcohol levels, and thus the levels of residual sugar are lower than they would be, say, in the Mosel. This results in slightly broader but very powerful sweet wines, rich in extract.

The director of a major Franken estate once told me that the local people enjoy light fruity reds, so there was no point producing richer, more complex styles. That may explain why for many years Franken reds were mediocre. Today there are a few producers, notably Paul Fürst, who make reds, usually Pinot Noir, of very high quality. There is a good deal of Domina planted too.

Würzburg is home to three of the largest wine estates in Germany, and to the region's most celebrated vineyard: the Würzburger Stein, which is clearly visible on the slopes rising from the bank of the Main opposite the principal part of the town. Würzburg is one of the most handsome Baroque cities in Germany, and few visitors would be aware that it was nearly flattened by bombing in March 1945 and that the palaces and public buildings destroyed by that aerial pounding have since been rebuilt. The vineyards, however, survived unscathed.

So renowned was the wine from Würzburger Stein that in the past it was known simply as Steinwein. One of the most celebrated vintages was 1540 when, according to legend, part of the crop was left on the vine and yielded an exceptionally rich wine when it was eventually harvested for the cellars of the Prince-Bishop. The wine was kept in cask for decades, as was the custom, and hidden in the cellars of his palace, the Residenz, when Swedish forces invaded Würzburg in 1631. It was re-discovered in 1694 and transferred into a new cask known as the Schwedenfass. The Schwedenfass can still be seen in the cellars of the Staatliche Hofkeller in Würzburg. A few bottles of the 1540 survived, and one of them was tasted by Hugh Johnson, who pronounced it to be drinkable though with a distinct sherry-like flavour.

Steinwein was also known in England, and there is an entry in the cellar book of the Earl of Bristol recording a purchase in 1740. When older Steinweine were sold at auction in Würzburg in 1864, vintages on offer included many from the eighteenth century, such as the 1783 and 1789. Morton Shand has given a very flowery, and fairly incomprehensible, note on the Steinwein he was tasting in the early twentieth century. It had, he noted, "a bland elusive flavour like the smell of a dewy posy of wild flowers, fresh picked by fairy fingers from lush, early morning pastures. It is a wine of noble breed and an unsuspected strength of body, which imparts to it lasting qualities unsurpassed among unfortified wines: a wine of subtle delicacy of flavour and a rare, if almost evanescent, bouquet, best compared, if compared it must be, to one of the great Saar wines."[1]

[1] Shand, p. 59.

The Franconians are sticklers for tradition. This is positive in some respects, especially the lingering devotion to Silvaner, not a grape variety held in high regard elsewhere. However, they are equally devoted to the Bocksbeutel, the dumpy flagon in which almost all the region's wines, even its costliest TBAs, are bottled. It has certainly been around for a long time: a relief from 1576 in the cellars of the Juliusspital clearly depicts a Bocksbeutel, and by 1685 glass versions were being manufactured. Its use became ubiquitous after the Prince-Bishop of Würzburg decreed it should be thus in 1726. More recent regulations permit only wines of QbA or QmP status, with a minimum must weight of 70 Oechsle, to be sold in the Bocksbeutel. So a Landwein from Franken can be bottled in the shape of the producer's choice.

Unfortunately, it is not only aesthetically unappealing, it is severely impractical, its shape making it impossible to stack or bin. Although today they have the option of using other bottle shapes, the Franconians are unmoved. Dr Heinrich Wirsching once told me: "I'm not prepared to give up the Bocksbeutel just to increase exports by a few percentage points. We sell most of our wines within Germany, where there is no problem with the Bocksbeutel." Still, one does wonder what the fate of Chablis might have been if its growers had adopted a similar strategy for their wines.

Vineyards

Franken is divided into four Bereiche, twenty-four Grosslagen, and 218 Einzellagen. The vineyards are very dispersed, and many are small. Only vineyards of significance are listed below.

Bereich Mainviereck (from Aschaffenburg to Wertheim). Grosslagen are: Reuschberg and Heiligenthal.

Bereich Maindreieck. Grosslagen: Rosstal (Karlstadt), Ravensburg (Thüngersheim), Ewig Leben (Randersacker), Teufelstor (Eibelstadt), Ölspiel (Sommerhausen), Hofrat (Kitzingen), Honigberg (Dettelbach), Kirchberg (Volkach), Engelsberg (Sommerach), Markgraf Babenberg (Frickenhausen), Marienberg (Würzburg), and Burg (Hammelburg).

Bereich Steigerwald (east of Maindreieck). Grosslagen are: Frankenberger Schlossstück (Ippesheim), Burgweg (Iphofen), Schlossberg (Rödelsee), Herrenberg (Castell), Schild (Abtswind), Steige (Oberschwarzach), Zabelstein (Donnersdorf), Ipsheimer Burgberg (Ipsheim), and Kapellenberg (Zell am Main).

Bereich Bodensee. Only one Grosslage: Seegarten.

Grosses Gewächs vineyards:
Bürgstadt: Centgrafenberg.
Castell: Schlossberg.
Escherndorf: Lump.
Homburg: Kallmuth.
Iphofen: Julius-Echter-Berg.
Randersacker: Sonnenstuhl.
Volkach: Karthäuse.
Würzburg: Innere Leiste, Stein.

BÜRGSTADT
One of the most westerly areas within Franken.

Bürgstädter Centgrafenberg. 70 ha (173 acres). Red sandstone, as you can see from red cliffs along the Main, where there are abandoned terraces. A sheltered site in a kind of bowl. Many red vines are planted here, and it can produce very good Pinot Noir.

Bürgstädter Mainhölle. 7 ha (17.3 acres). Juliusspital is the owner here.

CASTELL
The entire Grosslage of the town, Casteller Herrenberg, consists of vineyards owned exclusively by the Castell family. The vineyards are at an elevation of 320–380 metres (1,050–1,246 feet). Soils with marl, loam, and clay.

Casteller Bausch. 15 ha (37 acres). North-facing and planted mostly with Müller-Thurgau.

Casteller Feuerbach. 4 ha (9.9 acres). Planted only with red grapes.

Casteller Hohnart. 5 ha (12.4 acres). Planted with Silvaner and Riesling.

Casteller Kirchberg. 1 ha (2.5 acres). A Silvaner site.

Casteller Kugelspiel. 17 ha (42 acres). North-facing and never suffers from drought stress.

Casteller Reitsteig. 1 ha (2.5 acres). South-facing.

Casteller Schlossberg. 4 ha (9.9 acres). A very steep site, with marl soils, widely regarded as Castell's best. Planted with Riesling, Silvaner and Rieslaner.

Casteller Trautberg. 2 ha (4.9 acres). South-facing and planted with Kerner and Silvaner.

DETTELBACH

A charming walled town due east of Würzburg on the Main.

Dettelbacher Berg-Rondell. 80 ha (198 acres). Limestone-loam.

Dettelbacher Sonnenleite. 75 ha (185 acres). South-facing site of fossil-limestone.

ESCHERNDORF

East of Würzburg on the Main.

Escherndorfer Berg. 45 ha (111 acres).

Escherndorfer Fürstenberg. 70 ha (173 acres).

Escherndorfer Lump. 30 ha (74.1 acres). A magnificent amphitheatre of vines, on clay and limestone soils. No Müller-Thurgau is planted here, because the site is given over to late-ripening varieties.

HOMBURG

Near Kreuzwertheim in western Franken.

Homburger Edelfrau. 60 ha (148 acres). A good Silvaner site.

Homburger Kallmuth. *Alleinbesitz* of Löwenstein. 8.5 ha (21 acres), but some parts are overgrown and have not been planted, so there is a potential of 12 ha (29.7 acres). The site was first documented in 1102. It shows its quality in average years, when its grapes nonetheless ripen well. Although the original historic site is *Alleinbesitz*, there are other neighbouring vineyards which have the right to use the name. Red sandstone soils. Very sheltered and dry, so in hot summers it can suffer from drought stress. Seventy per cent Silvaner, plus Riesling and Rieslaner.

IPHOFEN

Iphöfer Domherr. 21 ha (51.9 acres). *Alleinbesitz* of Juliusspital.

Iphöfer Julius-Echter-Berg. 40 ha (99 acres). Gypsum with red sandstone that gives the wine spiciness. The site is perfectly protected by woodland. The greenish sandstone in the vicinity is the same stone used for the Residenz. Major owners are Juliusspital and Wirsching, who have Silvaner below and Riesling higher up on more meagre soils. Powerful wines.

Iphöfer Kalb. 65 ha (161 acres). Lighter soils, giving precocious elegant wines.

Iphöfer Kronsberg. 130 ha (321 acres). The steep parts are very good and can resemble those from the Julius-Echter-Berg.

LENGFURT

Fossil limestone soils in two sites: Alter Berg, 2 ha (4.9 acres) and Oberrot, 2.3 ha (5.7 acres). Löwenstein has vineyards here.

RANDERSACKER

240 ha (593 acres), of which about one-third is owned by the big Würzburg estates, one-third by smaller growers, and the rest by the cooperative. The side valleys are less good because they are shaded from the setting sun later in the day. Ewig Leben, confusingly, is both the name given to parcels that did not belong to other named sites, and a Grosslage, and there's no way to tell from the label. Essentially limestone soils.

Randersackerer Dabug. 20 ha (49.4 acres). Planted with Silvaner and Müller-Thurgau.

Randersackerer Lämmerberg. 15 ha (37 acres). Mostly planted with Müller-Thurgau.

Randersackerer Marsberg. 42 ha (104 acres). Heavier soil than some other sites.

Randersackerer Pfülben. 15 ha (37 acres). The village's top site, facing south and southwest, the latter being the best section because of evening sunlight. Retains water well, so drought stress is almost unknown. Some Riesling is grown here.

Randersackerer Sonnenstuhl. 50 ha (124 acres).

Randersackerer Teufelskeller. 28 ha (69 acres). Bürgerspital owns much of the site.

RÖDELSEE

Village just north of Iphofen.

Rödelseer Küchenmeister. 55 ha (136 acres). Fine site that adjoins the even better known Iphöfer Julius-Echter-Berg.

SOMMERHAUSEN

Sommerhäuser Ölspiel. Steep. South-facing, limestone, prone to drought. Also used as Grosslage name.

Sommerhäuser Reifenstein. 50 ha (124 acres). Good for Silvaner.

Sommerhäuser Steinbach. 35 ha (86.5 acres). A steep fossil limestone site, well suited to Riesling.

SULZFELD

A village in the southern part of the Maindreieck.

Sulzfelder Cyriakusberg. 120 ha (297 acres). Planted with Riesling, Pinot Blanc, and Müller-Thurgau.

Sulzfelder Maustal. 60 ha (148 acres). Fossil limestone soil, quite steep. Planted with Silvaner, Riesling, and Pinot Noir.

THÜNGERSHEIM

Twelve kilometres (7.5 miles) northwest of Würzburg.

Thüngersheimer Johannisberg. 110 ha (271 acres). Red sandstone and limestone.

Thüngersheimer Scharlachberg. 130 ha (321 acres). Red sandstone and fossil limestone. The Bürgerspital and Staatliche Hofkeller have holdings here.

WÜRZBURG

The city is home to Franken's best-known vineyards, which grow on fossil limestone soils.

Würzburger Abtsleite. 45 ha (111 acres). South-facing, good for Riesling and Silvaner of exquisite elegance. South of the town along the river.

Würzburger Innere Leiste. 10 ha (24.7 acres). Immediately below the Marienburg castle.

Würzburger Pfaffenberg. 50 ha (124 acres).

Würzburger Schlossberg. 5 ha (12.4 acres).

Würzburger Stein. 85 ha (210 acres). Not only above the river; it also continues some way to the east. The wines often show mineral smoky tones. Juliusspital owns 26 ha (64.2 acres).

Producers

BICKEL-STUMPF
Kirchgasse 5, 97252 Frickenhausen. Tel: +49 (0) 9331 2847. Fax: 7176.
www.bickel-stumpf.de. 8 ha (19.8 acres). 6,000 cases.
Simple Kabinett wines from Müller-Thurgau and Silvaner can be delicious here. Reimund Stumpf has also signed up to the Wine Institute's "Classic" and "Selection" system. Indeed, they tend to be more successful than wines such as the Traminer Spätlese and Rieslaner Auslese, which can be cloying. In 1999 the estate was able to produce Riesling BA, Rieslaner and Scheurebe TBAs, and Silvaner and Riesling Eisweine, a rare occurrence in Franken. The top red wine here is a Domina, with backing from Cabernet Dorsa, aged fifteen months in barriques.

BÜRGERSPITAL ZUM HEILIGEN GEIST
Theaterstr 19, 97070 Würzburg. Tel: +49 (0) 931 350 3441. Fax: 350 3444.
www.buergerspital.de. 140 ha (346 acres). 75,000 cases.
Founded in 1319, the Bürgerspital plausibly claims to be the oldest wine estate in Germany, as well as one of the largest. Like the Juliusspital, this is an active charitable foundation, using the sales of its wines to support a convalescence home and other good works. The Bürgerspital probably has more Riesling (about thirty per cent) than any other Franken estate. Many of these vineyards are within Würzburg, so they are of excellent quality.

The winery is very well equipped. There are two centrifuges, but I was assured that they are rarely used. The winemakers like a clear must to ensure a long fermentation of up to four weeks. Selected yeasts are used to ferment the wines in steel tanks at cool temperatures, and almost all the wines spend some months in large casks.

Since the mid-1980s the simpler wines have been labelled only with the variety and vintage; higher-quality bottlings such as Spätlesen are also labelled simply, but more detailed information, such as vineyard origin, is provided on a back label. The Silvaner here is piquant and enjoyable, though I am less keen on the off-dry style, which is here labelled as Feinherb. The Riesling from Stein has aromas of pears and is certainly concentrated, if not notably complex. The Bürgerspital is also well known for its Weissburgunder, because it was one of the first estates to introduce this variety in Franken. However, its Weissburgunder usually goes through malolactic fermentation and can be rather broad.

There are a few exotic varieties on the menu, such as a delicate but simple Gewürztraminer and a Bacchus reeking of tropical fruit, but with little persistence on the palate. I have not tasted any Pinot Noir from the Bürgerspital that has been memorable. Occasionally, some splendid nobly sweet wines are made, though in small quantities. Most recently, a 1999 Grauer Burgunder TBA, toasty and powerful, has scaled great heights.

FÜRSTLICH CASTELL'SCHES DOMÄNENAMT

Schlossplatz 5, 97355 Castell. Tel: +49 (0) 9325 60170. Fax: 60185. 65 ha (161 acres). 40,000 cases.

Castell is one of those relics of a feudal past that one would imagine (incorrectly) had become extinct in the twenty-first century. The Castell family, now in the twenty-sixth generation, owns not only all the vineyards of the village, but the town itself and banking houses. Its private army was disbanded in 1806. The Schloss dominates the town, and its archives, dating from the thirteenth century, are the largest private collection of this kind in Germany. The village was first documented in 816 and vineyards mentioned in documents from 1258. The Castells became Grafs in the fourteenth century, but their elevation to princely status is much more recent, and dates from 1901. When I first visited Castell in the mid-1980s the wine estate was managed by Prinz Michael Salm. After he married one of his boss's daughters, the couple returned to the Nahe to occupy themselves with his own castle and estates in Wallhausen.

In 1997 the present Fürst's son took over the management. Ferdinand zu Castell-Castell is a model of quiet courtesy, yet clearly a man with a will of his own. Aware that the wines were not as good as they should have been, he made some radical changes. The cellarmaster, who had been here for more than twenty years, was eased into retirement and replaced by a team of two. "One of the first things I did," Graf Ferdinand told me, "was to focus on some of our top sites and round up the entire winery team to do everything, from pruning the vines to working on the bottling line. And of course I was working alongside them. The idea was to ensure that the sales team understood how we made our wines, and that the new cellarmasters understood what the sales and marketing people were up against. The exercise also meant that we understood our vineyards much better."

Under the previous cellarmaster, no risks were ever taken. I remember him telling me in 1986 that the must was centrifuged before and after fermentation, and cultivated yeasts were routinely used. Today the grapes are whole-cluster pressed, and fermented in stainless steel. The Riesling is aged in large casks. Some crossings such as Albalonga and Ortega have been grubbed up, but Bacchus remains.

In addition to the vineyards of Castell, the family owns about 20 ha (49.4 acres) in Neundorf, which enjoys a similar climate. Since 1973 grapes have also been purchased from sixty contract growers, and these are bottled as négociant wines. Almost all the Castell vineyards are on slopes, and one-third of them are steep, notably the Schlossberg. The cultivation is close to organic, and because erosion can be a problem, a good deal of green cover is planted. Yields from the steepest sites vary from 30 to 50 hl/ha, and the average for the entire estate is 50 hl/ha.

This is a large property and there are a number of different ranges. The most basic is the litre bottling. Then there is Casteller Art, simple wines, jazzily packaged. Then there is the Schloss Castell range, which specifies only variety and vintage. More serious are the vineyard-designated wines, but these are not necessarily made every year, because Castell feel it is important that such wines exhibit the typicity of those vineyards. The top wine is from Schlossberg.

The Silvaner is very good here, ripe and dense and with no harsh acidity. The Schlossberg is the finest, but the Kirchberg runs it a close second. The Schlossberg Riesling is delicious, a wine with lovely fruit and lemony zest. Castell Riesling ages well; a 1993 Kugelspiel Spätlese, tasted in 2000, was sumptuous and underpinned by firm acidity and showed exceptional length.

Occasionally fine sweet wines are made, but quantities are small. I recall Riesling Eisweine from Castell in the 1980s; more recently, in 1997 and 2000, there have been Silvaner Eisweine from Kugelspiel, succulent wines with a creamy texture and fine acidity and length. Indeed, the difficult 2000 vintage also yielded a Riesling TBA from the Schlossberg and a Rieslaner BA from Kugelspiel, though I have not tasted them.

Although the top wines from Castell are serious, the majority of them are attractive wines that can be enjoyed young.

RUDOLF FÜRST

Hohenlindenweg 46, 63927 Bürgstadt. Tel: +49 (0) 9371 8642. Fax: 69230.
www.weingut-rudolf-fuerst.de. 15 ha (37 acres). 8,000 cases.

Paul Fürst, a brisk and somewhat humourless man, is well aware that his red wines are probably the best Franken has to offer. Although half his production is of red wines, he also makes excellent whites. 11 of his 15 ha (27.2 of 37 acres) are in the Centgrafenberg, and the Silvaners from this site are delicious: fresh, sometimes smoky, often with a suggestion of white pepper on the palate. The Rieslings can be a touch austere and robust when young and benefit from some bottle-age. There is also Rieslaner, a wine heady with aromas of apple compote, but more spicy on the palate. I am less keen on the heavily oaked Weissburgunder.

The red wines are aged in a blend of large casks and barriques, which were introduced here in 1985, and bottled without filtration. The Centgrafenberg Spätburgunders are the most serious of the reds. Both the Spätlese Trocken and the reserve parcel selections (Spätlese and sometimes Auslese Trocken) known as "R" are full of rich cherry and damson fruit, and there is ample tannin behind them. Fürst has recently introduced a bottling from a single French clone that he labels "PN 555." The Frühburgunder "R" can also be exceptional, but is produced in very small quantities. There is also a blend of Pinot Noir and Domina called Parzifal, which also comes in an "R" version in top years such as 1999. Unlike many Franken red-wine producers, Fürst has mastered the use of oak, which is never too overt in his wines. His red wines may be the best Franken has to offer, and among the best from Germany, but prices are very high.

GLASER-HIMMELSTOSS

Langgasse 7, 97334 Nordheim. Tel: +49 (0) 9381 4602. Fax: 6402.
www.weingut-glaser-himmelstoss.de. 11 ha (27.2 acres). 8,000 cases.

Wolfgang Glaser's wife Monika is née Himmelstoss, thus giving rise to this estate's name. Glaser practises the odd technique of prolonging fermentation for as long as possible, but then bottling relatively soon after fermentation is complete. The wines have been acquiring a good reputation but I found many of them surprisingly soft and even coarse, including a 2001 Rieslaner Spätlese Trocken. The 1999 Grauer Burgunder Kabinett was lame, and the 1998 Spätburgunder, after six months in barrique, emerged with an unwelcome touch of acetone on both nose and palate.

HÖFLER

Albstädter Str 1, 63755 Alzenau-Michelbach. Tel: +49 (0) 6023 5495. Fax: 31417. 8.5 ha (21 acres).

Michelbach is located in the most westerly region of Franken, and almost half of Höfler's vineyards are planted with Riesling, which is well suited to the gneiss and slate soils. Both the Riesling and the Weissburgunder are spicy and quite broad, but the Pinot Noir lacks interest.

JULIUSSPITAL

Klinikstr 1, 97070 Würzburg. Tel: +49 (0) 931 393 1400. Fax: 393 1414. www.juliusspital.de. 160 ha (395 acres). 80,000 cases.

The winery is attached to the magnificent hospital buildings of this charitable foundation, although they are a reconstruction following the bombing of 1945. The hospital, named after Bishop Julius Echter, who founded the institution in 1576, owns one of the largest wine estates in Germany, and its profits help to fund its hospice, old people's home, and other good works. The cellars themselves are palatial, some 250 metres (820 feet) long and containing 280 casks, many still in use.

The hospital is a major owner of vineyards within Würzburg, including 26 ha (64.2 acres) of Stein. There are also significant holdings in important villages such as Randersacker, Iphofen, and Escherndorf. Silvaner remains a very important variety, accounting for forty per cent of plantings.

For some years the manager has been Horst Kolesch, a strong believer in local traditions. He insists that only by remaining true to vintage, grape variety, and vineyard can Franken producers hope to compete with international styles pursued by the New World wine industry.

There is a very strong range of Silvaners from various vineyards; among the best are the dry Spätlesen from the Innere Leiste and Abtsleite, which are citric, spicy, and concentrated. Riesling is delicious too, the

Iphofer Julius-Echter-Berg broader than the racy, more vigorous wine from Stein. Weissburgunders from Volkach are unusually muscular and powerful, without being blowsy.

Although Rieslaner is usually vinified as a lightly sweet wine, Juliusspital produces a splendid Spätlese Trocken, with high alcohol, which is not discernible beneath the zesty mandarin and grapefruit flavours. There are sweet Auslesen too, the Stein superior to the Randersackerer Pfülben. It's a wine of tremendous fruit and extract. The lightly sweet Abtsleite Traminer Spätlese is delicate and charming, and at the top of the range are superb nobly sweet wines, such as the 1997 Stein Riesling Beerenauslese, with its lean racy structure, and a rare, peachy Weissburgunder TBA.

WEINGUT FÜRST LÖWENSTEIN

Rathausgasse 5, 97892 Kreuzwertheim. Tel: +49 (0) 9342 92350. Fax: 923550. www.loewenstein.de. 30 ha (74.1 acres). 15,000 cases.

The princely Löwenstein family owns two estates, one in Hallgarten in the Rheingau (q.v.), and the other in western Franken. The best vineyards are Homburger Kallmuth and Bronnbacher Kemelrain. The Kallmuth is a splendid terraced site that dates back to early medieval times. The estate also owns vineyards in Bürgstadt, and others just across the border in Baden. Robert Haller has been the energetic manager of both estates since 1995.

Grapes are harvested selectively, and Haller has put the centrifuge into retirement. The whites are fermented in steel tanks at up to 18°C, usually with natural yeasts. The wines are fermented to dryness and the better wines are aged in casks. The top range is the Asphodill label, referring to the rare flower found in the Kallmuth.

Silvaner from the Kallmuth is low-yielding and highly distinctive, and not everyone warms to it. It has a strong, assertive, earthy flavour, sometimes smoky too, that is austere and pungent when the wine is young. There is also some Rieslaner planted in the Kallmuth, but the wine can be marked by quite high acidity that gives it some severity.

Among Löwenstein's other wines are Weissburgunder, aged, excessively, in fifty per cent new barriques, and some Spätburgunder, which accounts for twenty per cent of production. These Pinots, mostly from Bürgstadter Centgrafenberg, have spicy cherry fruit and are often quite marked by new oak. I have also enjoyed an impeccable, strawberry-scented 1998 Silvaner Eiswein from Kemelrain.

WINZERGENOSSENSCHAFT NORDHEIM
Langgasse 33, 97334 Nordheim. Tel: +49 (0) 9381 809918. Fax: 809932. 269 ha (665 acres). 180,000 cases.

Nordheim is in a good sector of the Maindreieck, close to Escherndorf, and this cooperative, the second largest in Franken, has been given impetus under the dynamic direction of Paul Glaser, who has been here since 1993. The 240 members cultivate a wide range of grape varieties, and the cooperative has a good reputation for sparkling wine. The top range is called Franken Fascination: made from low-yielding vines, their crop reduced by green harvesting in summer, it is bottled in an unusual black Bocksbeutel. The range includes a rather neutral Chardonnay, a spicy Silvaner Kabinett Trocken, an overalcoholic Silvaner Spätlese Trocken, and a creamy Traminer Spätlese. Spätburgunder is made in a simple commercial style that Glaser admits is the kind of red wine that sells well locally. The sweet wines I tasted were mediocre, with the exception of a 1998 Silvaner Eiswein.

JOHANN RUCK
Marktplatz 19, 97346 Iphofen. Tel: +49 (0) 9323 800880. Fax: 800888. www.ruckwein.de. 14 ha (34.6 acres). 7,000 cases.

The Rucks trace their ancestry back to the tenth century, and Hans Ruck claims one of his ancestors was rewarded for his participation in the Crusades with land and a house near Stuttgart, and thus became a wine-grower. Ruck takes pains in his vineyards: he plants green cover to prevent erosion, and uses compost of his own making. Silvaner accounts for one-third of the plantings; for the Pinot Noir he has selected low-yielding French clones. His oldest vines are forty year old Grauer Burgunder, which only produce around 20 hl/ha; this wine is fermented in barrels from various sources, including local oak. Ruck likes to bottle the simpler wines early to preserve the primary fruit, but more and more of the white wines are being fermented and aged in barriques.

Of the three single-vineyard Silvaners, I easily prefer the Spätlese Trocken from the Julius-Echter-Berg, with its honeysuckle nose, and fine attack and concentration. Equally fine is the Riesling from the same site, a fresh, vigorous wine with good extract. The Grauer Burgunder from Rödelseer Schwanleite is a hefty wine, stylistically the complete opposite of the Silvaner and Riesling, but impressive in its own powerful terms. There's also a Spätlese Trocken from Rieslaner, which has a cocktail of flavours of apricot, mango, and quince.

All in all, this is one of the most meticulous and reliable sources of typically Franken wine.

HORST SAUER

Bocksbeutelstr 14, 97332 Escherndorf. Tel: +49 (0) 9381 4364. Fax: 6843. 10 ha (24.7 acres). 6,000 cases.

Horst Sauer is the fourth generation of his family to cultivate vineyards, but he only started bottling in 1977. About one-third of his plantings are of Müller-Thurgau, and there is a similar proportion of Silvaner. All grapes are hand-picked with selective harvesting. The wines are fermented in steel tanks, and spend a long time on the fine lees in Sauer's impeccably clean cellars. Although most of the wines are dry, about one-quarter of production is in a Halbtrocken style. There is a tendency in Franken to bottle quite early, but Sauer likes to leave his wines in tanks until the late summer.

The Silvaners come from Escherndorf's best site, the Lump, and they are bright, crisp, and mineral, sometimes with a nutty finish. The Lump Rieslings are very fine too: melony, pungent and racy, but with a distinctly Franconian breadth of flavour. The 2001 Rieslings have an unusual power and depth of fruit as well.

In certain vintages, such as 1994, 1997, 1998, 2000 and 2001, Sauer makes lush creamy Silvaner and Riesling TBAs from the Lump. The Silvaner Eiswein can be a touch too broad, but its Riesling counterpart, at least in 1997, had a rich mango nose, racy green-apple flavours, and tremendous concentration and length. These are surely among the best sweet wines of Franken, and the dry wines too are of exemplary quality.

SCHMITT'S KINDER

Am Sonnenstuhl, 97236 Randersacker. Tel: +49 (0) 931 705 9197. Fax: 705 9198. www.schmitts-kinder.de. 14 ha (34.6 acres). 9,000 cases.

When, in 1917, this estate was to be passed on to the next generation, it was deemed sensible for the six sisters and one son to join forces rather than divide the spoils between them: hence the unusual name of this property. Today it is run by Karl-Martin Schmitt, one of seven Schmitts tending vineyards in Randersacker. The soils here are limestone, making them well suited to Silvaner and Müller-Thurgau, less well suited to red grapes.

Schmitt likes to work with clean must, which he clarifies by filtration or centrifuging. The wines are aged in large casks, but he also uses barriques, including new Allier barrels. Karl Schmitt is always experimenting and finds top wines benefit from oak. However, I can't say I find his Müller-Thurgau aged twelve months in barriques to be a rewarding wine. The Silvaners, on the other hand, are aromatic and grapefruity, and have rather more character than the Rieslings. Auslese from Bacchus has a rather overwhelming bouquet of banana and mango, but is more elegant and spicy on the palate. His Rieslaner Beerenauslese also has exotic fruits on the nose, but is tight, concentrated and persistent.

WEINGUT GRAF VON SCHÖNBORN
Schloss Hallburg, 97332 Volkach. Tel: +49 (0) 9381 2415. Fax: 3780. 30 ha (74.1 acres).

The Schönborns own not only their well-known estate in the Rheingau, but have been proprietors of this Franken property since 1806. The wines are disappointing, lacking concentration and refinement. A touch of earthiness gives personality to Franken wines, but the simpler Müller-Thurgaus and Silvaners from here have rather too much of it. And sweeter wines from Riesling and Rieslaner are sound but bland.

SCHWAB
Bühlstr 17, 97291 Thüngersheim. Tel: +49 (0) 9364 89183. Fax: 89184.
www.weingut-schwab-franken.de. 10 ha (24.7 acres).

Thomas Schwab specializes in Riesling, but also has many other varieties planted in Thüngersheimer Johannisberg and Scharlachberg, which lie northwest of Würzburg. I have tried Silvaner, Müller-Thurgau, Kerner, and Riesling from this estate, and in general find them rather ungainly.

WEINGUT "ZUR SCHWANE"
Hauptstr 12, 97332 Volkach. Tel: +49 (0) 9381 847373. Fax: 847374.
www.schwane.de. 15 ha (37 acres). 6,500 cases.

This property takes its name from the old inn run for generations by the Düker family. The wines, half of which are Silvaner, are often somewhat nondescript and rather plump.

SCHLOSS SOMMERHAUSEN

Ochsenfurter Str 17–19, 97286 Sommerhausen. Tel: +49 (0) 9333 260. Fax: 1488. www.weingut-schloss-sommerhausen.de. 20 ha (49.4 acres). 12,000 cases.

The youthful Martin Steinmann, who now runs this estate, studied at Weinsberg and worked at Müller-Catoir, where he was greatly influenced by Hans-Günther Schwarz. Sommerhausen was a small Protestant enclave that in 1135 was divided between the noble Limburger and Castell families. The Limburgers bought out the Castells. The present Schloss dates from the sixteenth century and has magnificent cellars that pre-date the structure above. The Steinmann family were hereditary stewards of the Graf's wine estate for five generations, and when in 1968 the last countess died, the Steinmanns bought the estate.

About one-quarter of the vineyards is given over to Silvaner, and slightly less to Riesling. But almost one-third consists of Burgundian varieties, in which they strongly believe because they have more intrinsic elegance than Silvaner. Steinmann also buys in grapes. His own vineyards are in Randersackerer Sonnenstuhl (mostly Silvaner), Iphofer Burgweg, and in Sommerhausen itself. The Burgundian varieties come mainly from Eibelstadt.

Schloss Sommerhausen is well known for its sparkling wines. Steinmann finds Auxerrois exceptional for sparkling wine, because it needs no dosage. The non-vintage is made from Riesling, Silvaner, and Scheurebe, and for my taste is a touch sweet and broad. The vintage Riesling Sekt is aged three years on the yeast and then, unusually, finished with Scheurebe Eiswein: an assertive style with character and concentration. I prefer the vintage Auxerrois, which is more biscuity and persistent.

As for the dry white wines, the Silvaner works best in a fresh clean Kabinett style. The grander expressions of Silvaner strike me as too broad and lacking in zest. The Rieslings from Sommerhäuser Ölspiel can be very good, with a bracing austerity that promises an interesting evolution in bottle. Weissburgunder and Chardonnay are a touch neutral, but the barrique-aged Auxerrois was a surprise, with ample fruit and body to support the oak.

Schloss Sommerhausen also produces some outstanding sweet wines, such as the intensely peachy 1997 Sommerhäuser Steinbach Rieslaner TBA, the sumptuous, succulent 1998 Scheurebe Eiswein, and the rich, broad 1994 Chardonnay TBA, picked at 210 Oechsle.

STAATLICHE HOFKELLER WÜRZBURG

Residenzplatz 3, 97070 Würzburg. Tel: +49 (0) 931 305 0931. Fax: 305 0967. www.hofkeller.de. 120 ha (297 acres). 80,000 cases.

This estate was once the personal property of the prince-bishops of Würzburg, and it was during the reign of Johann Philipp in the second quarter of the eighteenth century that the magnificent cellars by Balthasar Neumann were constructed. In 1803 the estate passed to the duchy of Würzburg, before being taken over in 1816 as the state property of the Bavarian royal house of Wittelsbach. Although the Residenz was very badly bombed during World War II, the cellars remained intact. They are surprisingly lofty as well as being 180 metres long. When visitors are shown round, candles are lit above each oval cask, giving the cellars a richly romantic aura. The oldest casks date from 1784.

In addition to the vineyards throughout Franken owned by the Hofkeller, an additional fifty are managed by them. This has always been a traditional estate, and when I first visited in the 1980s the range of wines was immense, because cellarmaster Helmut Brünner (who retired in 2000 after forty years of service) was reluctant to blend wines, so a large number were bottled individually. In 2000 a centrifuge was still being used to clean the must, which was then fermented in steel tanks, but at fairly high temperatures to ensure the wines attained complete dryness.

In 2000 a new director took charge, Dr Jürgen Dietrich, but two years later he was replaced by Dr Becker. It is rather unfair to assess the wines during a transitional stage in the management of the property, but bread-and-butter wines such as Müller-Thurgau and Silvaner have not been very exciting, suggesting rather high yields. These wines are correct rather than inspired. But there is impressive Riesling Spätlese Trocken from the Stein, and succulent apricoty Rieslaner from Randersackerer Marsberg. The Hofkeller is proud of its red wines, such as the barrique-aged Domina, which I find thick and plummy. The barrique-aged Frühburgunder is soft and slightly stewed. Red wines account for one-fifth of production.

In 2001 the Hofkeller launched a new cuvée called Franconia, a blend of Kerner, Müller-Thurgau, and Scheurebe. It is made in an off-dry style with 12 grams of residual sugar. It is aimed at the export market, and at last the Bocksbeutel has been abandoned in favour of a more Burgundian-style bottle reminiscent of that in which the legendary 1540 Steinwein was bottled.

JOSEF STÖRRLEIN

Schulstr 14, 97236 Randersacker. Tel: +49 (0) 931 708281. Fax: 701155.
www.stoerrlein.de. 8 ha (19.8 acres). 5,500 cases.

Armin Störrlein has defined the style of wine he likes to make. He doesn't want aggressive acidity, so his wines have no more than 6 grams; but on the other hand they are entirely dry. All the grapes are picked by hand, fermented in steel, and aged mostly in large casks. The top range is called "SE" and the fruit is always of Spätlese or Auslese quality, but vinified dry.

I find the Silvaner without interest, but the Weissburgunder, aged for four months in new oak, is an attractive mouthful, rich but not heavy, and not especially oaky. The top Spätburgunder is aged for fifteen months in new oak, and almost collapses under the strain, which is a shame because the fruit quality is basically good. Casparus is a cuvée of mostly Domina, with a backing group composed of Pinot Noir and Schwarz-riesling. This is aged six months in new oak to give a soft accessible fruity wine with a touch of dryness on the finish.

HANS WIRSCHING

Ludwigstr 16, 97343 Iphofen. Tel: +49 (0) 9323 87330. Fax: 873390.
www.wirsching.de. 70 ha (173 acres). 42,000 cases.

This estate was founded in 1630, making Dr Heinrich Wirsching the fourteenth generation. The daily management of the property has since 1993 been in the hands of the meticulous, studious Dr Uwe Matheus. This is the largest private estate in Iphofen, and Wirsching owns 11 ha (27.2 acres) in the Julius-Echter-Berg. About forty per cent of the vine-yards are planted with Silvaner, and some fifteen per cent of production is of red wine. When in 1985 the red vines were devastated by frost, Hans

Wirsching (who ran the estate until his death in 1990, when his brother Heinrich took over) took the bizarre decision to replant with Portugieser. He did so on the grounds that he would rather make a really good Portugieser than an indifferent Pinot Noir.

Standards are high here. Viticulture is close to organic, and there is a good deal of green harvesting during the summer. All the grapes are hand-picked, though Wirsching experimented with machine-picking in 1988 for some Müller-Thurgau and found no problem with the quality. Pneumatic presses are used, and some whole-cluster pressing. Fermentation takes place in steel tanks, with minimal use of cultivated yeasts. There is little use of barriques, except for a barrel-fermented Grauer Burgunder, first made in 1986.

The Silvaner here is excellent, especially the high-priced reserve called "S," a wine of vigour and depth of flavour. The simpler Rieslings are zesty, even racy, and the "S" has a spicy nose of dried fruits, while on the palate it has fine attack and a strong mineral tone. Among other varieties, the Scheurebe Spätlese Trocken is exotic and broad, the Traminer Spätlese delicate and discreet, and the Rieslaner "S" Spätlese again has a dried-fruits character and a tight mineral finish. As for the Grauer Burgunder aged in thirty-five per cent new Allier for fifteen months, it works surprisingly well, in large part because the yields are low and the wine is powerful and piquant rather than overtly oaky. The 1997 Spätburgunder was lean but tannic, with a dry finish. Sinfonia is a blend of Dornfelder and Pinot Noir; it has a juicy plummy nose, with a rather lean woody aftertaste.

Wirsching's strength lies with dry wines. The only nobly sweet wine I have encountered was a 1990 Silvaner TBA, which had far too much alcohol and a coarse finish, despite oodles of ripe mango and pineapple fruit.

ZEHNTHOF

Kettengasse 3–5, 97320 Sulzfeld. Tel: +49 (0) 9321 23778. Fax: 5077.
www.weingut-zehnthof.de. 12 ha (29.7 acres). 7,500 cases.

This property was acquired by the Luckert family in 1970. The Silvaner and Riesling have supple textures, but lack some zest and concentration. The Rieslaner Auslese Trocken is powerful and undeniably concentrated. A 1997 Domina, aged fifteen months in new barriques, turned out to be rather confected and chocolatey. Cuvée TL is a blend of Pinot Noir, Dornfelder, and Domina, aged in thirty per cent new oak, but the oak overwhelms the structure of the wine. There are also occasional sweet wines, such as BAs from Weisser Burgunder and Silvaner in 2000.

18

Sachsen and Saale-Unstrut

The vineyards of Saxony and Saale-Unstrut suffer from a double misfortune: they are not only by far the most easterly and thus continental of Germany's wine regions, but they are also the most northerly, lying on roughly the same latitude as Cologne. Their wines were, and indeed still are, consumed locally for the most part. Before the 1990s opportunities to taste them were rare, and on the few occasions when they passed my lips, the experience was not memorable. Most of the wines were Müller-Thurgau at its most tart.

Viticulture seems to have developed in Saxony during the ninth century, with the direct participation of the church and its institutions. Rather surprisingly, there were pockets of viticulture in present-day Silesia and close to Berlin, neither of which regions strike one as ideally suited for grape-farming. But it seems that they did not survive long past the sixteenth century.

Both Sachsen and Saale-Unstrut lie within the former East Germany, which meant that for four decades they were isolated from viticultural and marketing developments taking place in the rest of Germany. Wine production was poorly coordinated, and winemakers found themselves ordering yeasts from one country within the Eastern bloc, and corks from another. Many of the vines were high-trained and widely spaced to facilitate mechanization, which did not ensure a high quality of grapes.

The history of Schloss Wackerbarth, one of the best known estates in Sachsen, illustrates the chaotic conditions in which the East German winemaker was obliged to work. After the Russians arrived in 1945, the Schloss was used as a prison, and then converted into a *Staatsweingut*. The vineyards occupied 130 ha (321 acres) but no winemaking, other

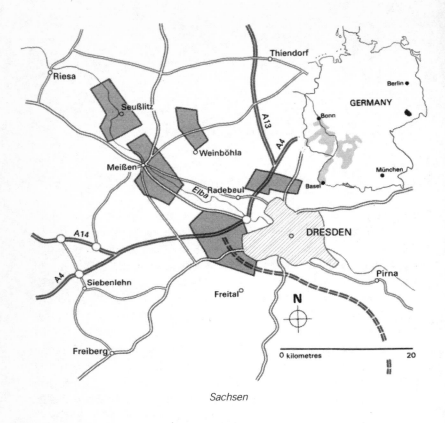

Sachsen

than for sparkling wine, was undertaken here. The property was run by an army of 300 employees that included a permanent dentist (it's tempting to speculate that his services were required to repair the damage inflicted on the staff by overacidic wines). After the collapse of the regime in 1989, the Schloss resumed wine production, but the state was keen to find a private buyer, which it did in the late 1990s.

A new team arrived at the estate two weeks before the 1999 harvest. The winemaker Jan Kux recalls: "We tried to make the existing estate workers understand the need for radical change, but they were reluctant. We encountered workers who had their own keys to tanks, so that they could indulge in private tasting parties! So we fired the entire cellar staff, and essentially made the 1999 wines with the help of students. A lignite-burning central heating plant provided energy to the entire property, and I was appalled to see that the lower vineyards close to the Schloss were

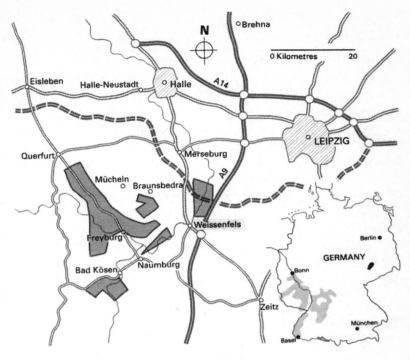

Saale-Unstrut

covered with a film of soot. This of course blocked photosynthesis, and thus ripening. The whole place was a disaster area."

Once collectivized vineyards had been returned to their former owners or sold off, it took a few years for wineries to be established, and commercial systems for distributing the wines had to be built up from scratch. The Sachsen growers in particular were aided by the proximity to Meissen and Dresden, which guarantees a strong local following for the wines. But in terms of quality there is a long way to go. Both regions must struggle against an inclement climate, even though scrupulous viticulture can ensure surprisingly high ripeness levels in most years. At present, prices can be unrealistically high. The least expensive and thus simplest wines are rarely worth bothering with, and the more concentrated and expensive bottlings do not easily withstand comparison with equivalent dry wines from, say, Franken or Baden.

SACHSEN

The more easterly of the two regions is Sachsen, with vineyards gravitating toward the River Elbe around Meissen and Dresden. The soils are mostly loess, loam, and sandstone over a granitic subsoil. Viticulture was first documented here in 1161, so it is no newcomer. At one time there were 6,000 ha (14,826 acres) under vine, but by the nineteenth century this had dwindled to 1,700 ha (4,201 acres), and declined further because disease struck the vineyards. At one point in the twentieth century the area shrank to a mere seventy ha (173 acres), but has since grown to around 440 ha (1,087 acres). Not surprisingly, most of them – eighty-eight per cent – are given over to growing white grapes, and the major varieties are Müller-Thurgau, Riesling, and Pinot Blanc. The average temperature, I have been informed by Schloss Proschwitz, is slightly higher than that at Trier or Würzburg, but the winters are more severe and there is a constant risk of frost. Indeed, the frost of 1997 reduced the crop at Schloss Proschwitz to a trifling 6 hl/ha.

Vineyards
There are two Bereiche: Elbtal and Elstertal.

Producers

SCHLOSS PROSCHWITZ
Dorfanger 19, 01665 Zadel über Meissen. Tel: +49 (0) 3521 76760.
Fax: 767676. www.schloss-proschwitz.de. 54 ha (133 acres). 25,000 cases.
The princely Lippe family can trace its ancestry back to the twelfth century, although it acquired the property here more recently. In medieval times the Proschwitz vineyards belonged to the bishops of Meissen, and from the sixteenth century to various aristocratic families, including, at the end of the line, the Lippes. The estate was confiscated by the Russians in 1945, and the Lippes found they were not eligible for compensation after 1989. Nonetheless, in 1990 Dr Georg Prinz zur Lippe decided he would, at considerable cost, buy back his own property, which he was able to do thanks to his successful computer business. In 1997 he bought a 300 year old mansion at Zadel to function as both cellar and office; the house and outbuildings have been almost entirely

rebuilt. Only in 1998 was the estate able to vinify its wines on its own property. In 1998 Prinz zur Lippe also bought back the actual Schloss, which is set in a fine park just across the river from Meissen.

The vineyards are divided into four large parcels, and form an Einzellage, because there are no other proprietors. The soils are loess-loam over granitic cliffs, and average yields are low at 36 hl/ha (14.6 hl/acre). The grapes are the usual ones found in Sachsen, although Pinot Gris is even more widely planted than Müller-Thurgau and accounts for almost one fifth of the surface. There is also some Dornfelder and Pinot Noir for red wines, and small quantities of Scheurebe and Früh-burgunder. The white grapes go through whole-cluster pressing; the must is filtered and then fermented using cultivated yeasts in steel tanks at around 18°C; no *Süssreserve* is used.

The wines are assertive, and reductive in style, being tight and racy in structure. The simpler wines such as Müller-Thurgau and Elbling fail to excite; the Dornfelder can be both jammy and acidic, while the Pinot Noir is often dry and extracted, though the best examples have a bracing bitter-cherry quality. It seems to me that, despite low yields, these red wines do not have sufficient structure to justify their being aged in barriques for any length of time.

The most successful wines are the dry Kabinetts and Spätlesen from Scheurebe, Riesling, and Weissburgunder. One curiosity here is a lush but vigorous Traminer Eiswein made in November 1998.

The second wines are released under the Meissener Weinhaus label.

VINCENZ RICHTER

Dresdener Str 147, 01662 Meissen. Tel: +49 (0) 3521 731606. Fax: 731923. Vincenz-richter.de. 8 ha (22.2 acres). 8,000 cases.

Thomas Herrlich's winery and sales room lie along the main road between Meissen and Dresden. The Richter wines are also available at the popular inn he runs next to the Frauenkirche in Meissen. Herrlich buys in grapes from other vineyards, and about half his production is of Riesling. I have not tasted the wines.

SCHLOSS WACKERBARTH

Mittlere Bergstr, 01445 Radebeul. Tel: +49 (0) 351 895 5112. Fax: 838 7073. Schloss-wackerbarth.de. 90 ha (222 acres). 40,000 cases.

The baroque Schloss on the outskirts of Dresden takes its name from a former owner, Marshal Wackerbarth. Most of the vineyards lie on the slopes behind the Schloss. The best are Radebeuler Steinrücken and Radebeuler Goldener Wagen, which are terraced. Here the yields are low, at around 40 hl/ha, though they are considerably higher in other sites. As has already been explained, the vineyards were in poor shape after four decades of neglect, but winemaker Jan Kux and his team have been repairing the damage and have instituted a kind of hoeing to dissuade the roots from remaining close to the surface.

The property was acquired in the late 1990s by the Sachsische Aufbau Bank, which is also restoring the Schloss and its grounds as an additional tourist attraction for the splendid city of Dresden. The winery is well equipped and operates by gravity. Whites are whole-cluster pressed and, when the harvest is healthy, receive some skin contact to help reduce acidity. The new winemaking team eliminated the use of *Süssreserve* in 2000, and there is no deacidification.

In 2001 one-third of production was of sparkling wine, but most of it was a kind of Euro-blend from grapes bought in from other countries in Europe. However, Wackerbarth plans to produce higher quality sparkling wines in the future, including wines fermented in large casks. Sparkling wines tasted in 2001 all suffered from high dosage, which is likely to be lowered in the future. The best cuvée is the 1999 Hommage, from Riesling and Elbling.

Only four per cent of production is of red wine. The best grapes are used for Cuvée Wackerbarth, a blend of Dornfelder, Lemberger, and Zweigelt, aged in older barriques. There is also some Pinot Noir. None of these wines suggest that Sachsen is likely to become a mecca for red wines.

There is a stark contrast between the dilute, flabby, and tired wines from the 1998 vintage, and those made in 1999 by the new team. The 2000s are even better, and there are good assertive wines from Riesling and Weissburgunder. The Traminers are rather dull. In 2000 Kux was able to make a Riesling TBA, apparently the first ever made in Sachsen. Tasted from tank, it was too lees-saturated to be judged, but had strong aromas of overripe pears and marzipan.

Schloss Wackerbath has the resources and the winemakers to produce wines of character and quality, as the 2000 vintage showed.

KLAUS ZIMMERLING

Bergweg 27, Pillnitz, 01326 Dresden. Tel/fax: +49 (0) 351 261 8752. 4 ha (9.9 acres). 1,500 cases.

Klaus Zimmerling has had the courage to convert his vineyards, in this unpropitious climate, to organic viticulture. Yields are astonishingly low, often around 20 hl/ha. All the wines are dry. His Polish wife is a sculptress, and her work provides arresting images for the labels. The wines suffer, rather oddly, from a lack of length, but they are concentrated and fairly stylish. The range consists of two Rieslings, Gewürztraminer, Grauer Burgunder, and Traminer, all very much in the same style.

SAALE-UNSTRUT

With 640 ha (1,581 acres) under vine, Saale-Unstrut is somewhat larger than its eastern neighbour and even further north. The soils are quite varied predominantly weathered fossil limestone, with some sandstone, gypsum, and clay. The climate resembles that of Sachsen, with extremely cold spells in winter the main hazard. In 1991 about one-quarter of the vines were destroyed by a severe winter frost, and another frost, though less damaging, occurred in 1996. Summers can be very dry, and in some vintages, such as 1999, the vines can suffer from a lack of water. The growing season is relatively short, because of late budbreak. Although most other regions would rather not relive the conditions of the 2000 harvest, the weather here was much better, resulting in one of the best vintages of the decade.

It is known for sure that vines were being cultivated at the Cistercian monastery of Kloster Pforta by 1137, and some evidence of viticulture being pursued in 998. Once this part of Germany came under Russian control in 1945, all estates larger than one hundred ha (247 acres) were confiscated. A number of smaller properties continued under private ownership, but their survival was brief, and by 1960 all farms, whatever their size, were confiscated and nationalized. In those days there were hardly any estates solely devoted to wine production. Polyculture was the order of the day, with vines representing a fairly small sector within each farm. So from 1960 to 1989 all Saale-Unstrut wines were produced by cooperatives. Today the Freyburg cooperative controls the production of some 260 ha (642 acres).

As in Sachsen, the Communist regime did little to encourage the production of good-quality wines, even though the East German wine laws were not dissimilar to those applied in the rest of the Germany. The East Germans, however, did not produce wines labelled Kabinett or Auslese, and wines labelled Spätlese could not be chaptalized. Sulphur dioxide was used with a heavy hand, according to present-day winemakers who were plying their trade before 1989, and plant material had to be imported from Yugoslavia or the USSR. This did, however, have the benefit of excluding the crossings that disfigured the West German vineyards during the same period. As in Sachsen, high-trained vines – the Lenz Moser system – were standard here before 1989.

Müller-Thurgau accounts for twenty-three per cent of the surface area under vine. It has been declining in the course of the 1990s, and the main beneficiaries have been red varieties, such as Dornfelder, Portugieser, and Pinot Noir. In the 1980s a little Zweigelt was also planted. However, it is hard to avoid excessively high acidity levels in Pinot Noir, even after allowing the wine to complete malolactic fermentation. There is evidence that Pinot Noir was quite widely planted here about a century ago, but difficulties in cultivating and vinifying the variety led to its decline in the 1960s and 1970s, when its place in the red-wine repertoire was taken by Portugieser.

Riesling is on the increase, and there are signs of a slight revival in Silvaner, which used to be quite widely planted in Saale-Unstrut. Wines for everyday drinking still tend to be produced from Müller-Thurgau or Gutedel. Traminer is another traditional wine of the region, but it can experience difficulties at flowering, can have low yields, and is scorned by most modern consumers.

Most estates are happy to receive visitors and offer tastings; there is also a communal tasting room at Marienstrasse 16 in Naumburg, where five wineries are represented.

Vineyards

There are three Bereiche: Neuenburg, Thüringen, and Naumburg. Neuenburg has two Grosslagen (Freyburger Schweigenberg, Grossjenaer Blütengrund), Naumburg has one (Göttersitz), but Thüringen has none.

Grosses Gewächs.
Freyburg: Edelacker.

FREYBURG

Freyburger Edelacker. Terraced and south-facing. Fossil-limestone with loess.

Freyburger Schweigenberger. A Grosslage that includes the terraced vineyards on weathered fossil limestone soils behind the town. It also includes the 40-ha (99-acre) site of Dorndorfer Rappental.

GOSECK

Gosecker Dechantenberg. 3.5 ha (8.6 acres). Pure red sandstone and walled terrraces. *Alleinbesitz* of Kloster Pforta.

KAATSCHEN

Kaatschener Dachsberg. *Alleinbesitz* of Gussek. A 2-ha (4.9-acre) limestone site, the last surviving steep terraced vineyard in the Thüringen sector.

KARSDORF

Karsdorfer Hohe Gräte. 3.6 ha (8.9 acres), mostly owned by Lützkendorf. The vineyard is planted within a quarry and is surrounded by high walls above and below. An unusually warm site that enjoys excellent drainage.

NAUMBURG

Naumburger Paradies. *Alleinbesitz* of Kloster Pforta. Deep loess-loam soils.

Naumburger Steinmeister. This 1.8-ha (4.4-acre) sloping vineyard lies within the town and is now surrounded by buildings. Leased by Gussek.

Saalhäuser. A 10-ha site of weathered limestone. It is an *Alleinbesitz* of Kloster Pforta and, like Steinberger in the Rheingau, is entitled to drop the commune prefix, in this case Naumburg.

Producers

KLAUS BÖHME

Lindenstr 42, 06636 Kirchscheidungen. Tel: +49 (0) 34462 20395. Fax: 22794.
8 ha (22.2 acres). 4,500 cases.
Böhme's grandfather had produced wine before the nationalization of

1960, and Klaus Böhme was among the first growers to resume production after the fall of the East German regime. He bought and exchanged land in order to build up the estate, which was formally established in 1994. The winery is well equipped, and Böhme favours a reductive style of winemaking: the whites are whole-cluster pressed, fermented in temperature-controlled steel tanks, and do not go through malolactic fermentation. The reds are usually a blend of wine aged in tanks with parcels aged briefly in barriques.

Böhme's Pinot Noir is pretty but lightweight, and there is also a Weissherbst made from surviving clones that do not resist frost and need to be picked earlier than clones intended for the red wine. As for the white wines, the Gutedel is dull, but the Silvaner is clean and fresh. The best wines are the Spätlesen Trocken from Riesling and Weisser Burgunder, which retain just a hint of sweetness to balance the acidity. Overall, these are fresh, well-made wines with considerable charm but little depth of flavour.

GUSSEK

Kösener Str 66, 06618 Naumburg. Tel/fax: +49 (0) 3445 365133. 4.5 ha (11 acres). 2,000 cases.

André Gussek was the cellarmaster at Kloster Pforta, and in 1991 managed to buy some land and buildings; he expanded his holdings by leasing other vineyards, notably in Kaatschen. At first he sold his grapes to the cooperatives, but in the mid-1990s began making his own wine.

Gussek is keen on red wines, which account for just more than one-quarter of his production. He bleeds the tanks during fermentation to give the remaining must greater concentration. Some wines, including the Portugieser, are aged in German and Hungarian oak. The Zweigelt seems to be the most successful of the reds. As for the white wines, the Silvaners are quite good, but the Weisser Burgunders – one unoaked, the other barrique-fermented – can be rather alcoholic, though they are undoubtedly rich. Occasionally, Gussek is able to make sweet wines, such as the spicy, almost oily TBA he produced from Müller-Thurgau in 2000.

LANDESWEINGUT KLOSTER PFORTA

Saalhäuser 73, 06628 Bad Kösen. Tel: +49 (0) 34463 3000. Fax: 30025. 55 ha (136 acres). 25,000 cases.

This celebrated estate was founded in 1899 by the Prussian state, which endowed it with some outstanding terraced vineyards lining the slopes above the River Saale, after which the region is named. Although the estate was re-established in 1993, it had to go through many years of uncertainty, because a procession of directors arrived and departed. By 2000 the situation seemed to have stabilized.

Its best-known site is the *Alleinbesitz* Saalhäuser, which lies beneath cliffs towering over the river shore. About three quarters of production is of white wine, and the estate has the highest proportion of Riesling of any property in the region. Among the specialities are Irsay Olivér, from the Hungarian grape of that name, and André, a Czech crossing which ripens late. The white wines are fermented and aged in steel tanks, but some large casks are used to age the reds.

The wines are a mixed bunch. They do have an unusual racy mineral quality, especially the Riesling and Weisser Burgunder, but they are not exactly bursting with fruit. Nor do they have much finesse. However, they do have ripeness and a certain spiciness. The sweet wines, such as the 2000 Traminer Beerenauslese, can lack concentration. Given the fine array of vineyards at the estate's disposal, it seems certain that quality should and will improve further.

LÜTZKENDORF

Saalberge 31, 06628 Bad Kösen. Tel: +49 (0) 34463 61000. Fax: 61001. www.weingut-luetzkendorf.de. 10.5 ha (26 acres). 5,000 cases.

Udo Lützkendorf used to be the director of the Landesweingut Kloster Pforta. He established his own estate in 1991, basing it on the 2 ha (4.9 acres) of vineyards his father had cultivated until the national-ization of 1960. Today the property is run by his ambitious son Uwe. Uwe is convinced that the vineyards of Saale-Unstrut are capable of making excellent wines, and he employs techniques such as severe pruning and bunch-thinning, resulting in yields that average only 40 hl/ha.

Silvaner is important here, and is released in versions from different vineyards. They are exceptional examples of this grape, especially those made from Karsdorfer Hohe Gräte. Lützkendorf himself describes these Silvaners as "wines with muscle." The dry Rieslings and Weisser Burgunders are excellent too, but occasionally the wines can show too much alcohol. The Spätburgunder is surely one of the best from the region, lean but concentrated and elegant.

Lützkendorf has set his sights high and is enjoying considerable success. Some years ago the estate was accepted into the strict ranks of the VDP, and prices are quite high.

PAWIS

Ehrauberge 12, 06632 Freyburg. Tel: +49 (0) 34464 27433. Fax: 27385. www.weingut-pawis.de. 8 ha (22.2 acres). 4,000 cases.

Bernhard Pawis has invested bravely in a new winery, and has also demonstrated the potential for Riesling here, with a fine 2001 Grosses Gewächs from Freyburger Edelacker. One-third of the vineyards are planted with Riesling, and Müller-Thurgau, Grauer Burgunder, and Silvaner are also important varieties. A 2001 Grauer Burgunder Spätlese Trocken was ripe yet peppery.

19

Négociant Wineries

Most large *négociant* wineries focus on the lower end of the market, so the quality of their products tends not to be high. This book has tried not to neglect some of the large-volume producers such as cooperatives, and many are listed in the regional chapters. There are also a few companies that are of great commercial importance. The handful of German wines found on the shelves of national chains and supermarkets almost all come from these large-scale producers. Some of them remain of dismal quality, others are making a determined effort to produce and market fresher, more attractive wines.

DEINHARD
Biebricher Allee 142, 65187 Wiesbaden. Tel: +49 (0) 611 63231. Fax: 63224.
www.deinhard.com.

Founded in 1794. Bought by Henkell & Söhnlein in 1997. The change in ownership spelt the end for the innovative range of wines pioneered by winemaker Manfred Völpel, who retired in 2001. These were dry wines from the major villages, aimed at reflecting the differences in terroir and style between, say, Piesport and Nierstein. Most of the excellent Deinhard vineyards in the Mosel, Rheingau, and Pfalz are leased to the Wegeler family, and are discussed in the regional chapters. One Deinhard classic remains in the portfolio – the Lila Rieslingsekt – which is lean, racy, and has plenty of fruit and good length. Most of the wines now bearing the Deinhard label are of modest quality.

HENKELL & SÖHNLEIN
Biebricher Allee 142, 65187 Wiesbaden. Tel: +49 (0) 611 63231. Fax: 63224.
Henkell was founded in 1865 with the aim of producing sparkling wine,

which it still does, in volumes of millions of cases. In 1934 the Metternich winery signed a forty year contract with them for sparkling wine, and this evolved into the higher quality Fürst von Metternich brand. In 1986 Henkell merged with Söhnlein. The new company owns thousands of hectares of vineyards in Germany, Hungary, and the Czech Republic.

LANGENBACH & CO
Trier.
This sparkling wine producer was founded in 1852 in Worms, but only began Sekt production in 1911. In 1995 it was bought by the Bernard-Massard group, but continues to produce a wide range of sparkling wines

F.W. LANGGUTH ERBEN
Dr Ernst Spies Allee 2, 56841 Traben-Trarbach. Tel: +49 (0) 6541 17275.
Fax: 810393.
In 1921 the firm of H. Sichel created the Blue Nun brand. In 1995 Sichel merged with Langguth.

The original Blue Nun enjoyed steady popularity from the 1930s onward, and by the 1970s was selling one million cases in Britain alone. But quality plummeted, and so did sales, which by 1994 were down to 50,000 cases. The brand was relaunched in 1996. In 2001 the range was expanded to include Cabernet Sauvignon and Merlot (both from the Languedoc!), a dry Riesling, and two sparkling wines.

FERDINAND PIEROTH
55452 Burg Layen. www.pieroth.de. Tel: +49 (0) 6721 965609. Fax: 650.
This merchant house now belongs to a company called WIV Wein International, and owns some vineyards between its winery in Burg Layen and Bingen in the Nahe. It specializes in selling wines directly to consumers throughout the world by means of "wine consultants" who offer tastings in potential customers' homes and then hope for an order. We need not concern ourselves with the wines they offer.

REH KENDERMANN
Am Ockenheim Graben 35, 55411 Bingen. Tel: +49 (0) 6721 9010.
Fax: 901240.

This well-known company, whose best known brand is surely Black Tower, was acquired in 2000 by Carl and Andrea Reh, already major players in large-volume wine production, especially in the Mosel. As part of their attempt to gauge more closely the needs of international markets, they hired a young winemaker, Jürgen Hofmann. Reh Kendermann continues to produce successful brands such as Bend in the River, and has also introduced better quality wines such as its Vineyard Selection Dry Riesling. The Black Tower range has been re-packaged and indeed expanded by the addition of a red made from Dornfelder and Spät-burgunder. Another innovation has been the launch in 2002 of a Weight Watchers Riesling containing Mosel fruit. As well as two wineries in Germany, there are large-scale facilities in Romania. Reh Kendermann's annual production is around fifty million litres.

ST URSULA

Mainzer Str 186, 55411 Bingen. Tel: +49 (0) 7217 0226. Fax: 0266.
www.st.ursula.de.

This is the company behind Devil's Rock Riesling, a brand sourced from five cooperatives. The company's chief oenologist is Wolfgang Hess, who keeps a close eye on the growers from whom St Ursula regularly buys grapes, which are vinified at the company's modern winery in Bingen.

SCHLOSS WACHENHEIM

Niederkircherstr 27, 54294 Trier. Tel: +49 (0) 651 8140. Fax: 4104.
www.schloss-wachenheim.de.

This long-established sparkling-wine house is now owned by the Reh company, which also owns Reh Kendermann. In 1997 Schloss Wachenheim merged with the equally well-known Sektkellerei Faber, a label retained for the cheaper ranges. The top wines are bottled-fermented and sold under the Schloss Wachenheim Senator label. The company also has extensive joint ventures and investments in Poland, the Czech Republic, and Romania.

SCHMITT SÖHNE

Weinstr 8. 54340 Longuich. Tel: +49 (0) 6502 4090. Fax: 024093.
www.schmittsohne.com.

This company created the Deer Mountain brand of dry Riesling. They also devised a sweet and medium-dry style called Relax Riesling, and a range called Blue Riesling. The Flying Goose Riesling is an overtly fruity style of Rhein Riesling. There are also wines from Einzellagen and Grosslagen in the Mosel and Rheinhessen.

H. SICHEL SÖHNE

Draiser Str 132, 55128 Mainz. Tel: +49 (0) 6541 7259. Fax: 810393.

Founded in the nineteenth century, Sichel is now best known as the producer of the Blue Nun brand. It has merged with Lanzguth (q.v.).

ZIMMERMANN-GRAEFF & MÜLLER (ZGM)

Marientaler au 23, 56856 Zell. Tel: +49 (0) 6542 4190. Fax: 419150.

The Swiss winemaker Thierry Fontannaz created the Fire Mountain brand of Riesling, as well as Private Reserve Riesling, Fire Mountain Chardonnay, and Pinot Noir from the Pfalz packaged in Bordeaux bottles. Regrettably, this company's focus, which may be commercially shrewd, is to persuade consumers that German wines have no German character other than an underlying tartness.

20

Vintages

Because viticulture was an important part of the German economy, and because for many centuries it was largely under the control of ecclesiastical foundations, there are records about vintages of the distant past. These were maintained by institutions in the Rheingau. The outstanding vintages of the eighteenth and nineteenth centuries in the Rheingau were, according to the historians of Schloss Johannisberg: 1700, 1704, 1718, 1719, 1723, 1748, 1749, 1779, 1781, 1783, 1806, 1807, 1811, 1822, 1825–7, 1831, 1834, 1842, 1846, 1857, 1858, 1861, 1862, 1865, 1868, 1880, 1886. In 1893 very high daytime temperatures were balanced by rainy nights, providing sufficient moisture for the grapes to ripen superbly. 1900 was a good vintage in the Rheingau and an outstanding one in the Pfalz. In the Rheingau the next excellent vintages were 1904 and 1911, which was a hot and very dry year. 1915 was another very good year.

In the Mosel, acclaimed vintages included 1837, 1846, 1857, 1865, 1874, 1893, 1895, 1897, 1904, 1911, 1915, and 1917.

More recently, German wine producers have been spoiled by a run of fine vintages in the 1990s. Perhaps some wine drinkers, and indeed producers, may have been lulled into a misconception that most vintages turn out well. In the past that was emphatically not so. The good, and even rarer great years, were celebrated and remembered. All too many vintages were either a wash-out or marred by climatic conditions that resulted in unbalanced wines. Although freaks of nature, such as devastating hailstorms, are as likely to occur today as in the past, today it is possible to anticipate and treat vine diseases. Harvesting has become more selective. Technological advances make it possible to minimize problems arising from disease and rot. The last dreadful vintage, at least in northern Germany, was probably 1972. For thirty years the wines, from good estates, have been drinkable, if not always brilliant. A look at the vintages of the 1990s prompts a discussion about style and balance, and regional variation. It remains possible that another frightful vintage will occur and remind us all that Nature should never be taken for granted. 2000 was a year of very bad weather at the end of the ripening season. Thirty years ago it would have been a complete disaster; today, thanks to more sophisticated methods and the expenditure of a great deal of time and money, it was possible for many estates, even in hard-hit regions such as the Pfalz, to make excellent wines. Long may it continue.

1920
A very good year in the Rheingau, with excellent nobly sweet wines from the Rheingau and Pfalz. Good Mosel wines from top sites.

1921
A great year in the Rheingau, with very rich wines. Many are still drinking very well. Superb in the Mosel, with many TBAs made for first time.

1922
Poor in the Rheingau and Mosel.

1923–5
Average in the Rheingau and Mosel.

1926
Quite good in the Rheingau and Mosel.

1927
Average in the Rheingau and poor in the Mosel.

1928
Poor in the Rheingau and Mosel.

1929
A very dry hot year in the Rheingau, with many excellent long-lived wines. Quite good in the Mosel.

1930
Poor in the Rheingau and Mosel.

1931–2
Average in the Rheingau, but 1932 was quite good in the Mosel.

1933
Excellent in the Rheingau but a very small crop. Very good in the Mosel.

1934
Exceedingly hot early summer in the Rheingau, and a hot August. The crop was enormous but the quality was high. Excellent in Mosel.

1935
Quite good in the Rheingau and Mosel, with aromatic wines.

1936
Average in the Rheingau. Autumn frosts marred the Mosel crop.

1937
Outstanding in the Rheingau, and exceptional in the Mosel with some TBAs.

1938–40
Modest to good quality in the Rheingau and Mosel.

1941
Poor in the Rheingau and Mosel.

1942
Good in the Rheingau, mediocre in the Mosel.

1943

Good in the Rheingau and Mosel.

1944

Average in the Rheingau and Mosel.

1945

Excellent in the Rheingau, despite late frosts which diminished the crop. Weather and war reduced the crop to almost nothing in the Mosel, though what was produced was excellent.

1946

Fruity wines in the Rheingau, with higher acidity than usual. In the Mosel a lack of sugar for chaptalization meant that most wines were tart.

1947

Very hot weather in the Rheingau led to wines that were low in acidity but nonetheless aged well. Often compared to 1921. According to Wolfgang Schleicher of Schloss Johannisberg, it was so hot that apples baked on the trees. Drought led to a failure of the potato crop, so that growers swopped wine for potatoes. Very good wines in the Mosel, with relatively low acidity, but exceptional in the Saar.

1948

A large crop in the Rheingau and Mosel. Warm conditions resulted in very good wines, especially at higher quality levels. High acidity in Mosel.

1949

Very warm in the Rheingau, but there was enough rain to ensure full ripening and ample botrytis. A great year in the Mosel though frost kept the crop low.

1950

Average in the Rheingau, with some rot. Quite good quality in the Mosel.

1951
Mediocre in the Rheingau and Mosel.

1952
Average in the Rheingau, but good in the Mosel.

1953
A great year in the Rheingau, with rich perfumed wines. Outstanding if less consistent in the Mosel, with excellent botrytized wines.

1954
Modest in the Rheingau, poor in the Mosel.

1955
Drinkable but unexceptional wines in Mosel and Rheingau.

1956
Poor.

1957
Poor in the Rheingau but better in the Mosel, though a small crop.

1958
Average in the Rheingau. Good in the Saar and better than in the Mosel.

1959
A brilliantly sunny summer gave Rheingau and Mosel wines of enormous ripeness, but conditions were too dry to give much botrytis. Very low acidity has meant that some wines are in decline, except at the top levels.

1960
Mediocre. A record crop in quantity, but not in quality.

1961
Average in the Rheingau, but good Eiswein from the Saar and average wines from the Middle Mosel.

1962

Mediocre in the Rheingau and Mosel.

1963

Quite good in the Rheingau, poor in the Mosel.

1964

A fine if not outstanding year in the Rheingau, and excellent in the Saar and Ruwer. Very good wines but lowish acidity meant they aged rapidly.

1965
Awful.

1966

Quite good in the Rheingau, but some Mosel wines lacked acidity. Nonetheless a good year in the Mosel, better balanced than 1964.

1967

Good though not exceptional in the Rheingau with a good deal of botrytis. Hail damaged the crop in parts of the Mosel, but the wines at the top quality levels are very good.

1968

Mediocre. In the Mosel the least sunny year since 1912.

1969

Quite good in the Rheingau, and very good sweet wines in the Mosel.

1970

Good in the Rheingau. A large crop in the Mosel; better quality in the Mosel than in Saar and Ruwer.

1971

Exceptional year throughout, with long-lived wines. The best are still very much alive.

1972
Awful.

1973
Average in the Rheingau and better in the Mosel with some excellent Eiswein.

1974
Poor.

1975
Good in the Rheingau and outstanding in the Mosel, with sweet wines of exceptional elegance.

1976
Very good in the Rheingau, but many wines are now fading, because acidity levels were low. Ripe golden wines, exceptionally lush. Brilliant botrytized wines in the Mosel and Saar, and outstanding in Franken.

1977
Light wines in the Rheingau and Mosel with sharp acidity.

1978
Mediocre in the Rheingau but better in the Mosel.

1979
Good in the Rheingau and excellent in the Mosel.

1980
Many unripe wines in the Rheingau, but better in Baden and the Pfalz. Mediocre in the Mosel.

1981
Mediocre in the Rheingau, with austere wines, though some of them aged reasonably well. A good if not exceptionally ripe year in the Mosel. Very good in the Pfalz.

1982

A very large crop in the Rhein and Mosel regions, boosted further by rain during harvest. The average yield in the Rheingau was an astonishing 148 hl/ha, rather than the 70 or 80 hl/ha obtained in most years. Many growers rushed to pick when rain fell, resulting in unripe wines. Those who delayed were rewarded in many cases with rot. Good wines from the Saar and Saale-Unstrut.

1983

Overall, a dry year, with some problems arising from drought. Good in the Rheingau, with some outstanding wines.

Splendid wines, notably Eiswein, from the Mosel, Saar and Ruwer. But yields were very high and some wines suffered from dilution.

Excellent in the Nahe, but low acidity led to short-lived wines from the Pfalz. Sound wines from southern Germany.

1984

An unripe year in the north, with a few fairly good wines from the Mosel and Pfalz. Good wines from Baden and Württemberg.

1985

Good if not exceptional in the Rheingau.

Very good in the Mosel, where the wines had firm acidity and are proving long lived. Not quite as good in the Saar and Ruwer.

Excellent in the Pfalz and Franken, although frost damage reduced the crop in Franken.

1986

A rainy year led to considerable variations in quality; precocious sites tended to fare better. Good rounded wines from the Rheingau that evolved quite rapidly. Very good wines from the Pfalz, and some good wines from the Nahe and Franken.

Rain also marred the harvest in the Mosel, but many Saar wines have proved better structured than the 1985s.

1987

After a cool damp summer, fine weather returned in the autumn. In the Rhein regions this was a fine year for QbA and Kabinett wines, which had strong flavours and were high in extract. Much the same was true in Franken and Württemberg, where the wines were marked by high acidity.

In the Mosel, acidity levels were high and the wines did not prove popular, although estates that were highly selective during harvest produced some very good ones.

1988

A good, stylish year in the Rheingau, with most wines at Kabinett level. The same was true in the Pfalz, because growers tended to pick early before rot set in.

The summer in the Mosel was warm and dry, and in the best sites the grapes withstood the autumn rain without too much damage. Yields, however, were low. For many estates this was the best vintage since 1983.

Very good in the Rheinhessen, and above average in Franken and Baden.

1989

Excellent in the Rheingau and Pfalz, with a sizeable proportion of botrytized wines that had the highest sugar levels since 1959. Excellent reds from Assmannshausen too. Many growers believe that 1989 overall was the best vintage since 1971. Yields were very high in the Rheingau, at an average of 115 hl/ha.

In the Mosel too a great vintage, though less botrytis-affected than the Rhein, because the Indian summer kept the grapes ripe and healthy. The majority of the crop was of Spätlese quality. Nonetheless, many top estates produced BA and TBA, often from grapes that attracted botrytis relatively early.

In the Nahe, arguably better than 1990. Excellent too in Rheinhessen. A large crop of very good wines in Württemberg.

The only question mark over the vintage concerns its longevity. Many wines, including sweet ones, have very low acidity and are evolving fast. But that is by no means true across the board.

1990

A hot dry summer followed by a cool September and a fine October led to a remarkable vintage in the Rhein regions and Mosel, combining high must weights (in some cases exceeding those of 1989) with high acidity levels. On the other hand, botrytis was limited, and drought conditions kept the size of Riesling berries small, resulting in low yields and wines of exceptional concentration. BA and TBA wines were rare, but those that were made are of brilliant quality.

Excellent in Baden, especially for red wines, and in Franken. Outstanding in Württemberg too, though some producers preferred 1989.

Overall, these wines have held the course and fulfilled their promise. Many of them still have a long life ahead of them.

1991

Spring was cool and wet, leading to a late flowering. Better temperatures in the summer helped the grapes to ripen, although not all regions had sufficient rainfall. A fairly large crop in the Rhein regions. In the Pfalz a lack of water also interfered with ripening.

In the Mosel the harvest was marred by rain: quality was mixed and quantities were low. It was widely regarded as better than either 1986 or 1987. There were a few botrytized wines and some very good Eiswein.

In Rheinhessen the wines were relatively light, with less body and extract than usual. Poor in Württemberg, but good in Baden.

1992

A better year than 1991, and a larger crop. In the Rheingau some of the flatter sites overproduced. There was some rot, so careful selection of the grapes was essential. Acidity levels were roughly the same as in 1989. Some exceptional TBA was produced.

In the Mosel the flowering was swift and early, and the summer was hot. Cool wet weather set in during October, and many vineyards were picked before the rain; growers who waited were able to make some sweeter wines that emerged in a rather broad style that lacked some elegance. There was more botrytis than in 1990, and the vintage overall was better than in 1991. The crop was enormous, averaging 175 hl/ha, though of course the best growers produced far less.

Very high quality in the Pfalz, despite some problems with drought.

Low yields ensured high quality in the best parts of Rheinhessen, in some ways comparable to 1990, but the Nahe fared less well.

This was a very fine year in Baden, in many ways comparable to 1990, though extracts and acidity were lower, so that red wines evolved fairly fast. An average year in Württemberg.

1993

Flowering was early in most regions, and exceptionally early in the Rheingau; the summer that followed was warm and sunny. Unfortunately, the vintage was marred by rain, which began falling in mid-September, and continued into October, provoking considerable rot and botrytis. It was not a good year for dry Rieslings here.

In the Mosel the cool wet September caused problems, yet the vintage was above average in quality, with aromatic wines and good acidity levels. The soils of the Mosel absorbed the water rather better than the heavier soils of the Rheingau. Many producers rated it as slightly better than 1992, and overall the Mosel performed better than the Rheingau. There were plenty of opulent Auslesen, but little botrytis. Botrytis was more common in the Saar.

Drought problems affected some sites in the Pfalz and Rheinhessen, but it was still a good vintage overall, just as it was in the Nahe.

This was an excellent vintage in Franken, giving a vintage comparable to 1971 or 1976. The crop was low, and many growers reported better quality than 1990 or 1992. In Baden this was superlative vintage for red wines as well as white, because rainfall kept water stress at bay. The vintage was equally fine in Württemberg.

1994

The year began badly in the Mosel, with severe flooding in January and a wet winter. But the summer was hot, until mid-August, when cooler, wetter weather set in, followed by rot. The weather improved in late September, leading to many superb sweet botrytized wines, including great TBAs. The yield was relatively low. This has proved a classic vintage in the Mosel, leaner than 1993, but with fine acidity and minerality.

In the Pfalz, Rheinhessen, and Franken it was essential to wait for good weather to return in October. Those who picked too soon had grapes of poor quality; those who waited had excellent fruit, with good acidity, and considerable botrytis for those seeking to make sweet styles. This was probably the best vintage for botrytized wines in the Pfalz since 1976, with generous crops of BA and TBA. In the Nahe, 1994 was a great year, with excellent sweet wines. In Franken the overall verdict was that the year was very good but not as fine as 1993.

The summer in Baden was exceptionally hot, but heavy rain fell in September, leading to rot. Producers who harvested selectively and culled rotten grapes had surprisingly good wines, whites more so than reds, but overall it was not a great year. In Württemberg too, this was no more than an average year.

1995

After a mild winter, spring was cool, which delayed and complicated flowering. As a consequence, yields were lower overall. After a good summer, September was cool, but fine weather returned to the Rhein regions in early October, and to the Mosel later in the month. This was a lovely vintage in the Mosel, with ample Spätlese and Auslese that showed good acidity and extract, but the Saar fared less well. There was some rot in the Mosel, but only on the flatter sites.

Many Rheingau growers panicked and picked too early, and only those who waited for the fine weather to return in October made really exceptional wines. In the Pfalz too, September rain provoked rot, so most growers picked as fast as they could. Results were not optimal. Much the same is true of Rheinhessen and the Nahe.

In Baden this was a good but not exceptional year, though there were some good sweet wines. Considerable rot in Franken meant this was a mediocre year, and it was scarcely much better in Württemberg.

1996

From the outset it seemed likely that this would be a problematic year. Flowering was late, and the fruit set irregular. The summer was fairly cool and variable, with some cold spells in August that delayed ripening. Fortunately, by late September fine weather returned and continued well into October, bringing grapes to greater maturity. Growers could afford to wait, and the harvest in the Mosel was exceptionally late, with many growers still picking in mid-November, when rain returned and put an end to the vintage. Those who picked too soon had wines with uncomfortably high acidity levels, but those who waited had considerable ripeness, although the malic acidity remained unusually high. The Saar was less good than the Mosel, but acidity levels were not that high. There was very little botrytis.

In the Rheingau too the harvest began late, in mid-October for many top estates. The fruit had remained healthy. In Rheinhessen the wines showed great concentration, but high acidity. Pinot Noir from Assmannshausen was of fine quality.

Outstanding in the Pfalz, and better than 1995.

In Baden the crop was small, but Pinot Noir was of very good quality. Red wines from Württemberg and whites from Franken had good extract, but this was not an exceptional year in those regions.

There is still a question mark over this vintage. The racy acidity of the Mosel wines seemed reminiscent of the great 1990s, but over the years it has become clear that the acidity is not always as ripe as it should been, and some wines, though by no means all, are showing vegetal aromas and flavours.

1997

In the Mosel the flowering was early and problematic in cooler sites, followed by a wet June that did little damage, although the Saar experienced some rot. The summer was hot, lasting well into September, and the rain that started to fall in October was welcome. This was another late harvest, beginning toward the end of October and continuing until around November 20. There were considerable quantities of Spätlese and Auslese, and acidities were more mellow than usual. There was little botrytis. In general, and despite some frost damage, the Saar and Ruwer produced superior wines to the Middle Mosel. In the Saar ripeness levels were comparable to 1999, but the acidity was higher.

The Rheingau enjoyed a warm spring and fine summer and the harvest took place in perfect conditions. The grapes were ripe and healthy but acidities were lower than usual.

In the Nahe there was some frost damage, which greatly reduced yields. The weather was comparable to that of the Mosel, although the harvest was interrupted briefly by a cold wet spell. The fruit was very ripe but there was no botrytis. The harvest went well in the Rheinhessen, with no botrytis and high must weights, resulting in clean ripe wines.

Flowering was later in the Pfalz, but followed by a very hot summer. The harvest was late, many growers waiting until October 18 or 20 before picking. These are very ripe wines for short to medium-term drinking, because the acidity levels are low.

In Württemberg the crop was small, but quality overall was good. The low acidity that marked the vintage across Germany benefited the red vineyards of southern Germany, and both Baden and Franken produced excellent red wines, as did the Ahr. The whites too are quite opulent.

The high ripeness levels and relative lushness of the fruit led some producers and commentators to acclaim 1997 as a truly great vintage. Such enthusiasm seems misplaced, because the wines, while undoubtedly delicious and attractive, lack structure, and few will still be improving after ten or twenty years.

1998

In the Rheingau flowering was early, and although there was wet weather in September, the grapes were very ripe by harvest time, and quality was good. But the crop was small, and some wines were marked by high acidity.

In the Mosel spring came early, and a hot May led to early flowering. July was cool but dry, and temperatures rose in August, with some days at more than 40°C in the Middle Mosel. September was drizzly and there was rain in October, but the long ripening season ensured that the grapes were ripe, though yields are lower than in 1997. The harvest began in the last week in October. The very hot dry weather had kept the size of berries small, which aided concentration and helped the Riesling grapes to resist the downpours, although other varieties suffered dilution. Despite a wet harvest, quality is surprisingly high, at least from the top estates, which took care not to pick during the wettest days and to eliminate rotten grapes. The Middle Mosel is overall better than the Saar and Ruwer. Quality varies from good to excellent, largely depending on the care growers and estates took in the vineyard and their degree of selection. There was little botrytis, but this was a very great Eiswein year (in the Nahe and Rheingau as well), with grapes picked in November, and the early harvest ensured that the grapes were very healthy and clean. There were only a few nobly sweet wines.

The Nahe experienced similar harvest conditions to the Mosel, but the grapes mostly remained healthy and quality was excellent, especially in the northern part of the region, where most growers prefer 1998 to the two succeeding vintages.

Rieslings in the Pfalz were of very good quality, thanks to an Indian summer that followed a period of rain and rot. A few growers, who did not rush to pick during the rain and waited for fine weather to return, thought this the best Pfalz vintage since 1990; others were troubled by some dilution in the wines. In Rheinhessen, growers had to be selective because the wet weather provoked some rot, but top estates were very satisfied with the quality.

In Baden grapes remained healthy and quality was high. In Franken there were drought conditions, but the weather deteriorated shortly before the harvest and it rained from mid-September to mid-October; nonetheless, the vintage for late-ripening varieties was a success, especially for estates that were able to wait until November to start picking, though acidities were relatively low.

In Württemberg, the summer was dry and hot, but the vineyards were refreshed by showers. The crop was very large, and the best growers green-harvested. The reds are somewhat light, while the whites have an overt fruitiness, as well as good acidity.

1999

Across Germany this was the warmest growing season in half a century, with the northern regions drier than the southern. The crop was considerably higher than in 1998, but quality was undoubtedly very fine throughout the country. There was rain in late September and early October, which affected thin-skinned varieties adversely, but Riesling withstood the wet weather without difficulty.

In the Rheingau the winter and spring were mild, and May was sunny. The hot summer weather caused some vines to shut down, and overall acidities were low. The crop was large and the best estates green-harvested. There was some botrytis. For Spätburgunder too, this was an excellent year for those who reduced the crop.

In the Mosel spring was early and warm, and flowering took place in perfect conditions. The summer was very warm and dry, to the extent that the heat slowed maturation. So wet weather in late September proved beneficial, although in some vineyards grapes were swollen by the rain. There was some rot in the Saar and Middle Mosel. The rain ended on October 10, and the harvest took place over the following four to six weeks. Sugar levels were high, except in a few sites affected by drought. In general, sugar levels were higher in the Saar and Ruwer than in the Middle Mosel. The vintage was acclaimed as great, and the wines showed beautifully from the outset; but it has to be noted that acidities were low (comparable to 1964, 1976, 1982), and some of the wines are soft, dilute, and will develop fast. Moreover, green harvesting was essential, because the crop was enormous.

In the Nahe too, the grapes were very ripe but acidity was low.

In the Pfalz harvest conditions were excellent, allowing very healthy grapes to be picked through October. The weather was cooler overall than in 1998, so the wines have better structure, but opinions among growers are divided, some acclaiming the vintage as great, others finding the wines lacking in concentration, largely because of uneven ripening. A fine year in the Pfalz for red wines.

In Württemberg the dry summer ended with heavy rain in late September, which inflated some grapes, but there was little rot. The crop was large and needed to be reduced. Ripeness levels were high (especially for reds), but acidities levels were only fair. In Baden too, yields were high so green harvesting was essential. But many excellent red wines were produced. A very good year in Franken, but, again, green harvesting was necessary in many sites. Finally, in the Ahr this was probably the vintage of the decade.

2000

A difficult year across Germany. The winter was wet, the spring warm and dry, leading to early flowering. June was perfect, but July proved the coolest and wettest on record. Temperatures warmed up in August, but wet weather continued. By September mildew and black rot had set in, and only in mid-October did fine weather return. One benefit of the miserable autumn was that many regions were able to produce good botrytized wines.

In the Rheingau the summer began well, with maturation two weeks ahead of normal. But a combination of high temperatures and rain from August led to rot in most vineyards. Repeated forays into the vineyards to remove rotten bunches were essential. The autumn remained warm, compounding the problems of rot. Growers who panicked and picked too early had poor quality grapes; those who waited, and selected, had good if not exceptional wines. Yields were in places as low as 20 hl/ha (8hl/acre), thanks to heavy selection.

In the Mosel, vineyards in steep slate slopes were able to resist damage from the heavy rain in September, especially if the crop had been thinned during the summer. Strict selection during the harvest was essential. There was only minor variation within the Mosel-Saar-Ruwer, though Piesport seems to have been spared some of the worst damage. Harvesting took place roughly from mid-October to mid-November. The best wines have high extracts and ripe acidity, giving them body and substance. The crop was small.

The Nahe also suffered from rot, but to a lesser extent than the Mosel, and some good wines were made. Vineyards on steep slopes fared best, and produced good wines as long as rotten fruit was eliminated.

Conditions in the Pfalz were similar to those in the Rheingau. Rot was especially severe in the most sheltered sites, such as Forst and Wachenheim, whereas vineyards such as those at Bad Dürkheim ventilated by side valleys were somewhat less tainted. The crop that survived the rot and selection was nonetheless of quite good quality, at least from good estates, and some producers preferred the more acidic 2000s to the softer 1999s. However, there were also some stuck fermentations exacerbated by rotten must and some wines are poor. Conditions were equally dreadful in the southern Rheinhessen, and in Baden too, strict selection was necessary, especially among the coveted Burgundian varieties. In Württemberg Riesling and Lemberger fared well, the Burgundian varieties less so.

Franken was less affected by bad weather than more westerly regions and many wines are of excellent quality. Another region that escaped the wretched conditions was Saale-Unstrut, which had a very good vintage.

2001

After a wet winter, climatic conditions were normal until late June in most parts of Germany. July was mixed, with some rainy days, but August was hot and dry. September was cool and wet, but just as growers began to fear for the health of their grapes, fine weather returned in early October and stayed fine into early November. This allowed the harvest to take place in perfect conditions. The Rheingau had an excellent vintage, although localized hail damage and other factors reduced the crop by eighteen per cent.

In the Mosel the grapes were perfectly ripe by mid-October, but acidity levels remained rather too high. Top estates waited a week or so, and began harvesting very well balanced fruit. The harvest was completed by mid-November. The grapes were small and thick-skinned and yields were significantly lower than usual. Botrytis was not uniform but many growers were able to produce BA, TBA, and, later, Eiswein. Many estates found that most of their crop came in at Auslese levels, but the ripeness was balanced by fine acidity and ideal pH, all of which promises a superb year.

Conditions were similar in the Nahe, but overall growers were less excited by the quality of the vintage than their counterparts in the Mosel.

In the Pfalz the summer was very dry, and some grapes were showing signs of sunburn, so some rain in September proved welcome. The grapes, both here and in the Rheinhessen, were healthy and ripe.

Baden growers experienced the same small berry size and thick skins as Riesling growers further north. Both reds and whites turned out extremely well.

Initial tastings suggest that the excitement of growers throughout Germany is justified and that 2001 could be a classic vintage, comparable, as some have indicated, with 1971.

2002

After a warm spring, which culminated in an early and successful flowering, the summer throughout Germany was generally warm, with some stormy patches and limited hail damage. By the end of September a classic vintage seemed probable, but then the weather deteriorated. Growers who had kept yields to reasonable levels, and who took care to remove rotten bunches where they occurred, found that quality was nonetheless high, with excellent ripeness levels in most regions. The Saar and Ruwer fared particularly well.

There was little botrytis in the Mosel, but in the Pfalz noble rot was abundant, and many TBAs were produced.

Throughout Germany this was a fine Eiswein vintage, thanks to a very cold snap in the second week of December.

Glossary

Abfüllung bottling
Alleinbesitz vineyard with a single owner
Amtliche Prüfung quality certification resulting in an AP number
Anbaugebiet wine region
Apfelsäure malic acidity
Auslese selectively harvested
Bereich subregions within a Gebiet
Beerenauslese sweet wine selectively harvested at high ripeness levels, usually of botrytis-affected grapes; distinguished from Auslese by higher must weight
Biologische Säureabbau malolactic fermentation
Bocksbeutel dumpy flagon in which most Franken wines are bottled
Bodengeschmack a taste of the soil – not pejorative
Botrytis noble rot
Breit broad
Brut sparkling wine with under 15 grams of residual sugar
Bukett bouquet
Buntsandstein red sandstone
Bunte Mergel heavy clay loam
Duftig fragrant
Durchgegoren fully fermented to dryness
Edelfäule botrytis (noble rot)

Einzellage individual vineyard site
Eiswein icewine
Erben heirs
Erzeugergemeinschaft producers' association
Erzeugerabfüllung estate bottling
Etikett wine label
Fass a cask, sometimes bottled individually under its number
Feinherb synonym for Halbtrocken
Flaschenweinverkauf sales of wine in bottle
Flurbereinigung vineyard remodelling to improve access
Freiherr baron
Fuder 1,000-litre oval cask used in Mosel
Fürst prince
Gebiet major wine region
Gemeinde village
Gerbstoff tannin
Gewächs growth
Gipskeuper gypsum with stony clay
Glimmerschiefer mica slate
Glühwein mulled wine
Graf count
Grauwacker grey slate
Grosser Ring Mosel/Saar/Ruwer growers' association
Grosslage a collective vineyard, embracing a number of Einzellagen

Halbfuder Mosel cask of 500 litres
Halbstück Rhein cask of around 610 litres
Halbtrocken off-dry, usually with 8–15 grams per litre of residual sugar
Herzog duke
Hochgewächs a wine that exceeds minimal Oechsle requirements and scores well at AP tastings
Jahrgang vintage year
Kabinett lowest level of QmP wines
Kalk limestone
Kellerei wine wholesaler
Kellermeister cellar master (usually the winemaker)
Kelter wine-press
Keuper clay with stone and slate
Kies gravel
Lage vineyard site
Lehm loam
Lese harvest
Lieblich sweet wine style such as Spätlese
Mergel heavy loam
Mostgewicht must weight, or sugar content of grapes at harvest
Naturrein unchaptalized wine (before 1971)
Neuzuchtungen new grape crossings
Oechsle system based on specific gravity for measuring a grape's sugar content
Offene Weine carafe wine served in pubs and restaurants
Perlwein a semi-sparkling wine perked up with carbon dioxide before bottling
Prüfungsnummer AP number (see Amtliche Prüfung)
Rebsorte grape variety

Restsüsse/Restzucker residual sugar
Rotliegendes reddish slate
Schatzkammer literally: treasure chamber; the grower's personal cellar of old vintages
Schaumwein basic sparkling wine
Schloss castle or château
Schotter Gravel
Schwefel sulphur
Sekt sparkling wine, usually of better quality than Schaumwein
Spätlese late-harvest grapes, and a category within the QmP system introduced in 1971
Spritzig lightly sparkling, petillant
Stiftung charitable trust
Stück 1,200-litre round cask traditional in the Rhein lands
Süssreserve unfermented grape juice added to wine
Ton clay
Trocken dry, i.e., up to 9 grams per litre of residual sugar
Verband association
VDP Verband Deutscher Prädikatsweingüter
Versteigerung auction
Verwitterungsboden weathered soils
Vorlese harvest in advance of main harvest to eliminate rotten or defective bunches
Weingärtnergenossenschaft cooperative (in Württemberg)
Weingut wine estate
Weinsäure tartaric acid
Weissherbst rosé
Winzer wine grower
Winzergenossenschaft cooperative
Wwe abbreviation for Witwe (widow) on wine label

Bibliography

Ambrosi, Hans, and Bernhard Breuer. *Ahr.* Herford: Busse Sewald, 1992.
Ibid. *Franken.* Herford: Busse Sewald, 1993.
Ibid. *Hessische Bergstrasse.* Herford: Busse Sewald, 1991.
Ibid. *Rheingau.* Herford: Busse Sewald, 1991.
Ambrosi, Hans, Bernhard Breuer, and Manfred Birmele. *Württemberg.* Herford: Busse Sewald, 1996.
Clarke, Oz. *Oz Clarke's Wine Atlas.* London and New York: Little Brown, 1995.
Clarke, Oz, and Margaret Rand. *Grapes and Wines.* London: Websters, 2001.
Diel, Armin, and Joel Payne. *Weinguide Deutschland 2002.* Munich: Heyne, 2001.
Eichelmann, Gerhard. *Deutschlands Weine 2002.* Munich: Hallwag, 2001.
Dr Entholt. *The Bremer Ratskeller.* English ed: 1930s.
Hallgarten, S.F. *Rhineland Wineland.* London: Elek, 1951.
Henderson, A. *The History of Ancient and Modern Wines.* London: 1824.
Jamieson, Ian. *German Wines.* London: Faber, 1991.
Jamieson, Ian. *Guide to the Wines of Germany.* London: Mitchell Beazley, 1992.
Jefford, Andrew. *The Wines of Germany.* Mainz: German Wine Institute, 1994.
Jeffs, Julian. *The Wines of Europe.* London: Faber, 1971.
Johnson, Hugh. *Atlas of German Wines.* London: Mitchell Beazley, 1986.
Ibid. *Wine Companion.* 4th edition. London: Mitchell Beazley, 1997.
Johnson, Hugh, and Jancis Robinson. *The World Atlas of Wine.* 5th edition. London: Mitchell Beazley, 2001.
Knoll, Rudolf. *Edelsüsse Weine.* Munich: Heyne, 2000.
Koeppen, Ulrich. *Baden: Wein – Und Spezialitätenführer.* Mainz: Woschek Verlag, 1994.
Langenbach, Alfred. *German Wines and Vines.* London: Vista Books, 1962.
Loeb, O.W., and Terence Prittie. *Moselle.* London: Faber, 1972.
Mildenberger, Gisela. *Saale-Unstrut.* Herford: Busse Sewald, 1995.
Pigott, Stuart. *Great Wines of the Rhine and Mosel 1988/1989.* London: Pigott Books, 1990.
Ibid. *Great Wines of the Rhine and Mosel 1990.* London: Pigott Books, 1991.
Ibid. *Die Grossen Deutschen Rieslingweine.* Munich: Econ, 1995.

Ibid. *Die Grossen Weissweins Deutschland.* Munich: Hallwag, 2001.

Ibid. *Riesling.* London: Viking, 1991.

Pigott, Stuart, and Ursula Heinzelmann. *Die Fuehrenden Winzer und Spitzenweine Deutschlands.* Munich: Econ, 1998.

Ray, Cyril. *The Wines Of Germany.* London: Allen Lane, 1977.

Redding, Cyrus. *A History and Description of Modern Wines.* London 1851.

Robinson, Jancis. *The Oxford Companion to Wine.* 2nd edition. Oxford: OUP, 1999.

Robinson, Jancis. *Vines, Grapes and Wines.* London: Mitchell Beazley, 1986.

Scharfenberg, Horst. *Deutschlands Weine 2001/2002.* Munich: Hallwag, 2001.

Shand, Morton. *A Book Of Other Wines – Than French.* London 1929.

Staab, Josef, Hans Reinhard Seeliger and Wolfgang Schleicher. *Schloss Johannisberg.* Mainz: Woschek, 2000.

Stevenson, Tom. *Champagne and Sparkling Wine Guide 2001.* London: Dorling Kindersley, 2000.

Wolfram, Helmut. *Sachsische Wein, Winzer In Sachsen.* Radebeul: Wolfram, 2000.

Index

Note: Vineyards and wineries are indexed under their regional headings. These headings are themselves listed under "Wine regions".

Zur Schwane, 387–8
Staatliche Hofkeller, 45–6, 75, 373, 378, 389–90
Störrlein, 390
Wirsching, 38, 72, 376–7, 390–1
Zehnthof, 391–2

G

Geilweilerhof college, 33, 61, 67, 75
Geisenheim college, 23, 24, 33, 37, 60, 61, 62, 66, 69, 72, 80, 83, 133, 197, 198, 298
German Wine Institute, 24, 29, 52, 55, 56, 89, 124, 231, 255
"Classic" wines, 29, 52–3, 196, 241, 243
"Selection" wines, 29, 52–3, 196, 231, 241, 255
Grans, Gerhard, 40–1, 182
Grape varieties:
Acalon, 74
Albalonga, 48, 60
André, 74
Auxerrois, 60–1
Bacchus, 61, 371
Blauer Silvaner, 61
Cabernet Cubin, 74
Cabernet Dorio, 74
Cabernet Dorsa, 74
Cabernet Franc, 75
Cabernet Mitos, 75
Cabernet Sauvignon, 74, 75, 76, 276, 316, 346
Chardonnay, xi, 40, 61, 83, 94, 120, 142, 313, 325, 341–2
Domina, 75, 373, 391–2
Dornfelder, 60, 75–6, 142, 253, 278, 281, 306
Dunkelfelder, 76
Ehrenfelser, 62
Elbling, 62, 152
Faberrebe, 62
Findling, 62
Freisamer, 63
Frühburgunder, 76, 142, 143, 181, 354
Gelber Orleans, 63, 252, 303
Gewürztraminer, 63–4
Goldriesling, 64
Grauburgunder. See Pinot Gris
Gutedel, xii, 59, 64, 67, 319, 323–4, 327, 333, 336, 337, 344–5
Helfensteiner, 77
Heroldrebe, 77, 366
Huxelrebe, 64
Irsay Oliver, 65
Kanzler, 65

Kerner, 4, 65, 371, 372
Klingelberger. See Riesling
Lemberger, 42, 77, 347
Mariensteiner, 65
Merlot, 77–8, 238
Morio-Muskat, 65–6
Müller-Thurgau, xv, 4, 6, 60, 62, 66, 67, 69, 83, 88, 95, 173, 231, 247, 253, 278, 324, 371, 372, 393
Muskat-Trollinger, 78, 358–9
Muskateller, 66–7
Muskateller, Gelber, 66–7, 340, 366
Muskateller, Roter, 67
Noblessa, 67
Nobling, 67, 324
Optima, 10, 67, 68, 218
Ortega, 10, 48, 68, 218
Palas, 78
Perle, 68
Pinot Blanc, xv, 28, 30, 40, 60, 61, 68, 105, 241, 295
Pinot Gris, xv, 30, 45, 68–9, 325, 335
Pinot Meunier. See Schwarzriesling.
Pinot Noir, xii, xv, 11, 28, 29, 30, 43, 46, 54, 60, 76, 78–9, 80, 81, 83, 89, 91, 93, 94, 102, 103, 107–8, 137–9, 198, 294, 306, 314, 319, 324–5, 338, 341–2, 373, 382
Portugieser, 60, 75, 79, 80, 95, 137, 139, 142, 253, 278, 316
Regent, 60, 79–80
Regner, 80
Reichensteiner, 69
Rieslaner, 11, 45, 59, 69–70, 301, 309, 310, 384
Riesling, xi, xiv, 4, 5, 6, 10, 11, 17, 20, 28, 29, 30, 35, 39, 40, 42, 48, 49, 51, 59, 60, 62, 65, 66, 68, 70–1, 72, 83, 87, 94, 95, 99, 101, 110, 137, 146–7, 158–9, 230, 270–1, 273, 278, 283, 323, 346–7, 353–4
Rivaner. See Müller-Thurgau
Rotberger, 80, 273
Roter Gutedel, 80
Rotling, xii
Ruländer. See Pinot Gris
St Laurent, 80, 102, 274, 317
Samtrot, 81, 354
Sauvignon Blanc, 60, 71
Scheurebe, 11, 40, 71–2
Schönburger, 72
Schwarzriesling, 81, 354
Septimer, 72
Siegerrebe, 72